HISTORY OF THE GREAT WAR
SEABORNE TRADE
VOL. II

HISTORY OF THE GREAT WAR

BASED ON OFFICIAL DOCUMENTS

BY DIRECTION OF THE HISTORICAL SECTION OF THE
COMMITTEE OF IMPERIAL DEFENCE

SEABORNE TRADE

Vol. II
FROM THE OPENING OF THE SUBMARINE CAMPAIGN TO
THE APPOINTMENT OF THE SHIPPING CONTROLLER
WITH MAPS
IN SEPARATE VOLUME

BY
C. ERNEST FAYLE

The Naval & Military Press Ltd

Published by

The Naval & Military Press Ltd
Unit 10 Ridgewood Industrial Park,
Uckfield, East Sussex,
TN22 5QE England

Tel: +44 (0) 1825 749494
Fax: +44 (0) 1825 765701

www.naval-military-press.com
www.military-genealogy.com

In reprinting in facsimile from the original, any imperfections are inevitably reproduced and the quality may fall short of modern type and cartographic standards.

PREFACE

THE present volume covers the history of seaborne trade from the outbreak of the submarine campaign against merchant shipping, in February 1915, to the appointment of the Shipping Controller in December 1916.

The choice of these two incidents as starting point and terminal of the volume will indicate its dual character. It is a record both of the effect of the submarine campaign on seaborne trade, and of the measures taken to maintain the flow of essential supplies.

In considering the results of the submarine campaign it is no longer necessary, as with the surface raiders, to examine the effect of individual casualties, on particular routes. The submarines threatened all routes simultaneously, and their individual successes shrink into insignificance in comparison with the broad problem presented by the destruction of tonnage at a rate largely in excess of the rate of replacement.

It was not, however, the submarines alone that were responsible for the tonnage shortage. From the beginning of 1915 the demands of the Admiralty and War Office on British shipping continually increased. The operations for which the ships were required are described elsewhere; but it is the province of this volume to show how, and at what cost to British commerce, the ships were provided.

Nor was this all. Neither France, nor Russia, nor Italy could have continued the struggle for more than a few months, without imports of munitions, material, food, and fuel, on a scale far beyond the capacity of their own shipping. No part of the British contribution to the war-effort was of more vital importance than the provision of carrying-power; but the demands of the Allies could be fulfilled, whether by British or by neutral shipping, only at the expense of British commerce. The tonnage employed in the import service of the Allies, like that in naval and military employment, was drawn from the same pool of shipping as supplied the needs of the United Kingdom, and any increase in the proportion devoted to one service, involved a corresponding reduction in that available for the others.

Further, importing power is not solely a question of the tonnage available, but of the economy and efficiency with which it is employed. The annual carrying-power of the ships depends on the size and character of their cargoes, their employment in trades for which they are suited by their construction, the proportion of laden to ballast voyages, and the number of voyages made. The number of voyages made depends on the length of the routes, and the speed with which the ships can be loaded and discharged. Turn-round in port depends, in its turn, on readiness of cargo at the ports of shipment and on the facilities for distribution to inland centres from the ports of discharge.

From the first, the war interfered, at every turn, with the smooth working of the whole complex machinery of purchase, transport, and distribution, and early in the period covered by this volume, the loss of carrying-power arising from redistribution of trade, deviations, port delays, and the general dislocation of economic effort, became almost, if not quite as serious as the shrinkage in tonnage due to war casualties. These indirect effects of the war are less obvious and perhaps less generally appreciated than the destruction of shipping. It is the object of this volume to show how vitally they affected the maintenance of supplies essential to the conduct of the war.

For a detailed account of the defensive measures employed to meet the submarine attack, and of the sufferings and exploits of British seamen, the reader is referred to *Naval Operations*, by Sir Julian Corbett, and *The Merchant Navy*, by Mr. Archibald Hurd, both in this series. It is the task of the present writer to show how, and with what success, British shipping and British commerce adapted themselves to the requirements of a situation which imposed grave new demands upon them, simultaneously with the appearance of new difficulties and new dangers. It is his task also to trace the gradual growth and effects of State intervention, from the first tentative experiments in freight and price restriction, to the later efforts to grapple with the root problem, by acceleration of construction, acceleration of turn-round, co-ordination of British and Allied demands, control of neutral shipping, and adjustment of demand to supply by the exclusion of unessential imports. The culmination of these efforts, as of the tonnage crisis, will not be reached until the third and concluding volume, but neither the menace of the " unrestricted " submarine campaign nor the work of the Ministry of Shipping and the Allied Maritime Transport Council can be properly appreciated except in the light of the situation existing at the end of 1916, and the events by which that situation was produced.

In order to ensure an authoritative account of the steps by which the Transport Department of the Admiralty, and other bodies concerned with tonnage, grew into the Ministry of Shipping, as well as the work of the Ministry of Shipping itself (to be dealt with in the third volume), Miss L. K. Edmonds, B.A. Oxon. (now Mrs. W. F. B. Scott) was transferred from the Staff of the Ministry to that of the Historical Section. Her intimate knowledge of the records of the Transport Department and Ministry of Shipping has been invaluable, and she has been responsible for a large part of the necessary research work on the administrative side of the history.

The official material supplied by the Admiralty, Board of Trade, Ministry of Shipping, and other Government Departments has been very voluminous, comprising the minutes, memoranda, correspondence, and other records of a great number of Departments and Committees concerned with shipping and supplies. Very little of this material is at present generally accessible, and it has, therefore, been impossible to give references.

Statistical detail has been cut down to the minimum necessary to justify the statements in the narrative. Figures are always dry reading, and for that reason, have been relegated, where possible, to footnotes; but figures which measure the progress and failure of an attempt to starve Great Britain into submission will not lack interest. It will be seen, however, that there is no statistical appendix. Whereas the first volume was in large measure self-contained, there is no clear gap between this and the concluding volume, which is already practically complete. It seemed better, therefore, to avoid duplication and facilitate comparison by reserving for that volume the preparation of tables and statistical charts covering the whole period of the war.

To all those who have assisted him by reading the proofs or supplying material, the author is deeply indebted. He is under special obligations to Sir Norman Hill, Bart. (Secretary of the Liverpool Steam Ship Owners' Association), Sir Kenneth S. Anderson, K.C.M.G. (late Chairman of the Chamber of Shipping), Sir Lionel Fletcher (formerly Chairman of the Liverpool Steam Ship Owners' Association), and Captain Clement Jones, C.B. (late Secretary of the Shipping Control Committee); to the late Sir Frederic Bolton and Lieutenant-Colonel T. H. Hawkins, C.M.G., R.M.L.I., for invaluable assistance in all questions relating to ports and distribution; to the Hon. Mr. Justice Hill (late Chairman of the Ship Licensing Committee) for material relating to the licensing of voyages; to Mr. H. W. Macrosty, C.B.E., of the Board of Trade, for information with regard to meat supplies and insulated tonnage; to Mr. A. F. Fawcus for information relating to coal shipments and bunker supply; and for information on various points arising in this volume to Sir Thomas Royden, Bart. (Chairman of the Cunard Steamship Co.), Sir Ernest Glover (late Member of the Transport Department Advisory Committee), Mr. L. F. Goldsmid, O.B.E., of the Transport Department and Ministry of Shipping; and Lieutenant-Colonel V. M. Barrington-Ward.

C. ERNEST FAYLE.

CONTENTS

CHAPTER I

THE NEW PHASE IN THE WAR AT SEA

The submarine as a commerce raider—New character given to the war at sea—Effect on neutrals—The submarine "Blockade" announced —American protest—The Allies retaliate—Order in Council of March 11th, 1915 . . . . pp. 1-17

CHAPTER II

OPENING OF THE SUBMARINE CAMPAIGN FEBRUARY—APRIL 1915

New instructions to shipping—Defensive measures—Early losses— Traffic maintained—The submarines fail to frighten away neutral shipping —Economic importance of the Dardanelles Campaign—Safety of the Suez Canal—The submarine checked in the English Channel and Irish Sea—Summary of losses . . . . . . pp. 18-36

CHAPTER III

TONNAGE AND TRANSPORT AT THE BEGINNING OF 1915

Summary of tonnage position—Use of prizes and interned ships—New demands on requisitioned tonnage—Growth and organisation of Transport Department—Fourth Sea Lord's Conference—Appointment of Advisory Committee—Proportionate Requisitioning—Provision of collier tonnage for French State Railways—Tonnage for sugar—"Temporary Release" pp. 37-54

CHAPTER IV

THE PROBLEM OF IMPORT DISTRIBUTION TO MAY 1915

Study of the question before the war—Effect of war conditions on the ports—Shipowners' proposals for relieving congestion—Work of the Committee for the Diversion of Shipping—Board of Trade Committee on Port Congestion—Treatment of prize and diverted cargoes—Anxiety of Diversion Committee as to congestion . . . . pp. 55-73

CONTENTS

CHAPTER V

IMPORTS AND FREIGHTS IN THE SPRING OF 1915

General rise in freights, its causes and effects—Revision of Blue Book Rates—Rise in food prices—Indian Government control wheat—Problems of the meat supply—Action of the Board of Trade—Requisitioning of Insulated Space—Recovery of exports—Large excess of imports—Regulation of export trade—The War Trade Department . pp. 74–89

CHAPTER VI

EXTENSION OF THE SUBMARINE CAMPAIGN MAY—SEPTEMBER 1915

Submarine activity in the South-Western Approach—The *Lusitania*—Friction between Germany and the United States—New defensive measures and instructions to shipping—Heavy losses—Mine-laying submarines—The problem of the sailing trade—Record losses in August—The position in the Mediterranean—Italy enters the war—The submarine attack shifts to the Mediterranean . . . . . . pp. 90–109

CHAPTER VII

THE NORTH SEA AND RUSSIA DURING THE SPRING AND SUMMER OF 1915

Considerations limiting submarine activity in the North Sea—Effect of submarine campaign on trade with Holland—Germany competing for Dutch products—Trade with Scandinavia little affected by submarine campaign—Wood as contraband—The transit route to Russia—Increase in the trade of Vladivostok—White Sea trade carried on by requisitioned ships—Conditions at Archangel—The White Sea mine-field—Restricted limits of Russian trade—Pit-props . . . . pp. 110–126

CHAPTER VIII

THE COURSE OF TRADE TO THE AUTUMN OF 1915

Percentage losses—Developments of the State Insurance Scheme—Decrease in British entrances—Activity of neutrals—Great volume of imports—Expansion of export trade not maintained—Restrictions on exports, their necessity and effect—The Coal Exports Committee—Growth of the adverse trade balance . . . . . . pp. 127–143

CHAPTER IX

THE PROGRESS OF ECONOMIC PRESSURE DURING 1915

Early measures to restrict enemy supplies; copper, oil, and rubber—Revival of German trade—Effect of the Retaliation Order—The examina-

CONTENTS xi

tion service—The Contraband Committee—Stoppage of German and Austrian exports—Fall of the German exchanges—Enemy supplies—Methods of evading capture—Agreements with neutral merchants and shipowners—Coal and bunker pressure—German trade with contiguous neutrals—Shortage of metals and textile materials in Germany—The enemy's food supply—Effect of cutting off supplies of fodder and fertilisers—Rationing agreements with neutrals . . . . pp. 144–166

CHAPTER X

THE INCREASE OF REQUISITIONING IN THE SUMMER AND AUTUMN OF 1915

Decline in shipbuilding—Increased demands of Transport Department—Strain of Mediterranean transport—Cross-Channel transport, congestion of French ports—Increased demands on collier tonnage—The tonnage situation becomes serious—Appointment of the Mediterranean Transport Commission . . . . pp. 167–179

CHAPTER XI

THE STATE INTERVENES
NOVEMBER 1915

The Board of Trade become alarmed as to decline in wheat imports—The shipowners consulted—Causes of the decline—Freights and prices—Conference with the shipowners—Restriction of imports discussed—Appointment of the Requisitioning (Carriage of Foodstuffs) Committee—Appointment of the Ship Licensing Committee . . pp. 180–192

CHAPTER XII

THE PORT AND TRANSIT COMMITTEE
OCTOBER—DECEMBER 1915

Acute congestion at Liverpool—The Liverpool Co-ordination Committee and its work—The Committee for the Diversion of Shipping call attention to urgency of the port question—Appointment of the Port and Transit Executive Committee—Work of the Committee to December 1915
pp. 193–204

CHAPTER XIII

THE ALLIES DEMAND FURTHER ASSISTANCE FOR 1916

Submarines in the Mediterranean—Defensive arming of merchantmen—Losses of British, Allied, and neutral shipping—Report of Mediterranean Transport Commission—Allied services during 1915—Ships frozen up in White Sea—Meat supply of Great Britain and Allies—Allies' demands for further assistance . . . . pp. 205–216

CONTENTS

CHAPTER XIV

LICENSING AND DIRECTION OF SHIPPING, NOVEMBER 1915 TO FEBRUARY 1916—APPOINTMENT OF THE SHIPPING CONTROL COMMITTEE

Work of Ship Licensing Committee—Analysis of tonnage position in light of Allies' demands—Work of Carriage of Foodstuffs Committee—Carriage of grain for France and Italy—Wheat freights continue to rise—Change in policy of Carriage of Foodstuffs Committee—Port and Transit Committee urge restriction of imports—First import restrictions announced—Appointment of Shipping Control Committee . . pp. 217-230

CHAPTER XV

THE TONNAGE DEFICIT AT THE BEGINNING OF 1916—ASSISTANCE GIVEN TO THE ALLIES

Shipping and import figures—Shipping Control Committee's estimate of tonnage deficit—Work of Carriage of Foodstuffs Committee—Fall in North Atlantic grain freights—Efforts to increase shipbuilding output—Work of Shipping Control Committee—Developments in the organisation of the Transport Department—Formation of Requisitioning Branch—The Card Index of Shipping—Increase in commercial cargoes brought by requisitioned or temporarily released ships—Formation of Commercial Branch—Powers of Ship Licensing Committee extended—New services undertaken for Allies . . . . pp. 231-250

CHAPTER XVI

SUBMARINES, MINES, AND RAIDERS JANUARY AND FEBRUARY 1916

Submarines, mines, and aircraft—Reappearance of the surface raider—Cruise of the MOEWE—Destruction of the GREIF—The Germans concentrate on the submarine campaign—Heavy losses in the Mediterranean—Australian and Far Eastern shipping diverted from the Suez to the Cape route . . . . pp. 251-259

CHAPTER XVII

EFFORTS TO ADJUST THE BALANCE, APRIL—MAY 1916—RESTRICTION OF SUBMARINE WARFARE

Heavy decrease in British entrances—Increased requirements of Ministry of Munitions—The White Sea programme—Decision to limit allocation of tonnage to Allies—Employment of British shipping analysed—Submarines again active in home waters—The *Sussex*—Strong American protest—German submarines instructed to conform to Prize Court rules—Effect of this decision . . . . . pp. 260-271

CONTENTS xiii

CHAPTER XVIII

NEUTRAL SHIPPING IN BRITISH TRADE TO THE SUMMER OF 1916

Importance of neutral shipping to British and Allied trade—The Bunker Regulations—Difficulties of the ore trade—Appointment of the Official Ore Broker—Return Cargo Regulations in the Bay trade—The North Sea Return Cargo Regulations—" Alternative voyages " and the French coal trade—Extension of Bunker Regulations . . . pp. 272-282

CHAPTER XIX

CLEARING THE PORTS, JANUARY—JULY 1916

Shortage of labour at the ports—Exemption of dock-workers from military service—Formation of Transport Workers' Battalion—Pooling of railway wagons—Penalty rents—Development and work of Transport Workers' Battalion—Improvement in port conditions—Increased wheat imports—Strain on the West Coast ports—Wheat imports reduced—Investigation of conditions at French ports . . . pp. 283-294

CHAPTER XX

BRITISH AND GERMAN TRADE IN THE SUMMER OF 1916

Further decrease in entrances—Withdrawal of neutrals—Large imports, especially of wheat and ore—Increase in adverse trade balance—Measures to maintain American exchange—Causes restricting export trade—Improvement in woollen exports—Improvement in tonnage position—Economic position of Central Powers—Ministry of Blockade—Rationing Agreements—Embargoes—The " Navicert " system—The Statutory Black List—Modifications and final repeal of the Declaration of London Order in Council—Entry of Roumania into the war and its effects—Restriction of enemy's supplies of fish and agricultural produce—Increased shortage of metals and foodstuffs in Germany and Austria . . pp. 295-313

CHAPTER XXI

ALLIED SERVICES DURING THE SUMMER OF 1916—THE RUSSIAN SUMMER PROGRAMME—THE ITALIAN COAL CRISIS

The White Sea programme—Difficulties and delays at Archangel—Acute coal shortage in Italy—Shortage of collier tonnage—Further assistance promised—French Coal Freights Limitation Scheme—Discussion of Inter-Allied chartering—Conference with Italian Government—Allocation of neutral tonnage to Italy—Effect of Coal Freight Limitation Scheme on supply of tonnage . . . . pp. 314-328

CHAPTER XXII

THE WHEAT SITUATION IN THE AUTUMN OF 1916

Further submarine activity in the Mediterranean—Heavy losses of Allied and neutral shipping—Submarines in the Channel—Hull premiums raised under State Insurance Scheme—Good effects of defensive armament—Further efforts to facilitate shipbuilding—Escape of British vessels from the Baltic—Tonnage economies and employment of shipping—Wheat imports—Australian Government propose purchase of whole Australian surplus—Reported failure of North American wheat crops—Negotiations for purchase of Australian wheat—Appointment of Royal Commission on Wheat Supplies and Wheat Executive—Effect on the tonnage position of replacing North American by Australian wheat . . pp. 329–348

CHAPTER XXIII

INCREASED LOSSES AND A NEW TONNAGE CRISIS
OCTOBER—DECEMBER 1916

White Sea Programme fulfilled—Congestion at Vladivostok—Completion of Murman Railway—Russian winter programme—Other Allied services—Congestion of French coal ports—Coal-ore Agreement with Italy—Extension of Coal Freights Limitation Scheme to Italy—Great extension of submarine activity—Threatened withdrawal of neutral shipping from Allied trade—Insurance of neutrals against war risks pp. 349–362

CHAPTER XXIV

THE APPOINTMENT OF THE SHIPPING CONTROLLER
DECEMBER 1916

The Allied Wheat Programme—Tonnage agreement with France—Effect of partial abandonment of the Mediterranean—Difficulties of the meat supply—Army supplies maintained—Reduction of civilian supplies—Shortage and high prices of sugar—Discontent caused by high prices of foodstuffs and inequalities of distribution—Rationing discussed—Measures taken to alleviate tonnage position—Changed conditions of the problem—Appointment of the Shipping Controller and Food Controller—State building and purchase of shipping decided on—Appointment of Committee on restriction of imports—Continued increase of submarine activity and its effects . . . . pp. 363–383

CHAPTER XXV

THE ECONOMIC SITUATION OF THE BELLIGERENTS
AT THE END OF 1916

Summary of losses, British, Allied, and Neutral—Employment of British shipping—Imports maintained at a high level—Food supplies—Fisheries—Materials and manufactures—Freights and prices—Coal exports—Other exports—Increased volume of exports and re-exports—Trade balance—Redirection of trade—Exchanges—Position of France, Italy, and Russia—Increased stringency of blockade of Central Powers—Restriction of supplies from contiguous neutral countries—Food conditions in Germany become really serious—The "Turnip Winter"—Expectations of immediate relief through occupation of Roumania disappointed—Deterioration of internal transport—Anxiety as to metals and lubricants—Destruction of the Roumanian oil-wells—Continued fall in the foreign exchanges—Both groups of belligerents show symptoms of exhaustion . . . . pp. 384–409

INDEX . . . . pp. 411–424

MAPS

IN SEPARATE VOLUME

1. HOME WATERS.
2. CHANNELS OF RUSSIAN TRADE.

Note.—The first of these maps has been prepared to illustrate the chapters dealing with the submarine attack against merchant shipping. No attempt has been made, as in Volume I, to show the locality of individual losses, as this would have required a large number of maps to prevent confusion and, for the reasons indicated in the Preface, is unnecessary.

The second map may be referred to in connection with all passages relating to the trade of the United Kingdom or Germany with Scandinavia, as well as with reference to Russia.

Maps showing the principal trade routes of the world were included in Volume I.

Typographical Note.—As in Volume I, the names of warships and merchantmen commissioned as warships are printed in small capitals, those of all other ships in italics.

SEABORNE TRADE

CHAPTER I

THE NEW PHASE IN THE WAR AT SEA

THE sinking of half a dozen British merchantmen by German submarines on January 30th, 1915,[1] small as was the immediate effect on commerce, marked the opening of a new stage in the attack on seaborne trade. From that date onward the submarine was to take the place of the surface raider as the main instrument of the attack.

By the beginning of 1915 the majority of the German cruisers and armed liners which had harried British shipping during the first few months of the war had been sunk, captured, or driven into internment. They had inflicted appreciable losses and had caused considerable dislocation to trade, but the net effect of their operations had been to emphasise the limitations rather than the possibilities of commerce-destruction under steam.

At the height of their success, when the requirements of military convoy drew off British cruisers from the trade routes and German supply ships were still able to move with some freedom, the raiders had failed to produce more than a local and temporary effect on the flow of trade. Now that the flow of trade itself had been fully re-established, the protection of the routes improved, and the stringency of supervision over enemy shipping in neutral ports increased, there was very little prospect that, in the event of additional raiders reaching the Atlantic, they would be able to exert a decisive influence on the course of the war.

The German attack on commerce had thus hopelessly broken down; yet the importance of economic pressure as a factor in the war was coming into greater and greater prominence. The hope of a speedy German victory based on the superiority of their military preparation had been

[1] Vol. I, pp. 366–8.

definitely foiled. It was evident that, at the best, the struggle would be long and exhausting. It had already assumed the character of a war of attrition, and it was of vital importance to the Central Powers that they should, if possible, interpose some check to the stream of traffic by which Great Britain was able to place the resources of the whole world at the disposal of herself and her Allies. Experience had shown that the methods hitherto adopted were inadequate. A new weapon was required, and it was widely believed in Germany that that weapon had been found in the submarine.

Already the war had proved that the submarine was capable of more extended cruises than the German Naval Staff had hitherto believed. On the other hand, it had done little—despite isolated successes—to reduce the margin of superiority enjoyed by the British Fleet, or to affect in any decisive manner the naval situation. Thus the growing belief in the power of the new weapon and the experience gained as to its limitations combined to suggest the desirability of finding a new field for its activities. It was accordingly decided to entrust to the submarine the task which the surface raiders had hitherto carried on with such limited success.[1]

As compared with the surface cruiser, the submarine enjoyed one very important advantage for the attack on commerce: she could attack shipping at its point of greatest concentration. With the substitution of the submarine for the cruiser or armed liner, the point of impact of the attack shifted from the outlying trade routes, where no success could produce more than a temporary, local effect, to the main arteries of British commerce at their most vulnerable point. A surface raider operating anywhere within the cordon stretching from the Shetlands to the Cape Verdes could hope at most to carry on operations for a few days before she was run down or driven off. Even in more distant seas the focal points were effectively covered within the first few months of war, and on the main stretches of the trade routes themselves the chances of encountering a British cruiser were too great to permit a raider to make any prolonged stay. Moreover, when once the focal points were effectively guarded, the limitless possibilities of deviation in the open

---

[1] For the inception of the submarine campaign, see Grand Admiral von Tirpitz, *My Memoirs*, and General von Falkenhayn, *General Headquarters*.

sea rendered the hunt for British shipping extremely speculative. The submarine was in a very different position. Even when cruising on the surface she was by no means easy to see, and might well hope to approach her point of attack without being detected. If she was sighted while on the surface by a unit of the British patrols she could at once submerge, with something more than an even chance of making her escape without exhausting her motive power in a long chase, or giving any indication of her subsequent movements.

Thus, while the German cruisers operated at points far removed from any German base, and were driven more and more to rely on chance encounters with ships scattered on either side of the ocean tracks, the submarine was able to operate in the waters immediately surrounding the British Isles, where shipping was thickly crowded with little possibility of effective dispersal, and within easy reach of the German home ports. Her task was thus immensely simplified, for not only was her field of operations far more productive, but she was spared the necessity of adjusting her movements to those of supply ships, or of interrupting her operations for days at a time in order to take in fuel. The supply of oil in her tanks was sufficient for some three weeks' leisurely operations in British home waters, and when it approached exhaustion she could return to a German port to prepare for a new cruise.

The vulnerability of the submarine to the attack of even light guns was, of course, a point against her, and in the waters to which the operations of the existing types must necessarily be confined by their radius of action, she would be exposed to continual danger from destroyers and vessels of the Auxiliary Patrol, as well as to the risk of being run down if caught on the surface by a liner faster than herself. As against this, submarines could be built more quickly than cruisers, and at less cost; they could be produced in greater numbers, and more easily risked. There was thus some prospect that a campaign energetically and relentlessly waged in British home waters might produce that effective impression on the flow of trade which sporadic raiding on the ocean trade routes had failed to achieve.

On the other hand the use of the submarine as a commerce destroyer involved a disregard of the accepted canons of naval warfare which it was no light matter to accept. She could spare few men for prize crews, and operating so near to the British bases it was seldom that she could either send or take a prize into port with a reasonable chance of safety. Thus, like the German cruisers during the earlier phase of the war, she must necessarily destroy the majority of her prizes; but, unlike those cruisers, she had no means of providing for the safety of the crews. She had no accommodation for prisoners, she could not encumber herself in waters where an enemy might be encountered, with a surface consort to whom they might be transferred. Thus, at the best, she could only turn them adrift in their own boats, a course which, at any distance from land or in bad weather, was repugnant alike to the spirit of humanity and to international law. This, however, was not the worst. In order to effect a capture she must come to the surface and remain there until the crew of the prize had taken to their boats. This course involved considerable risk if British patrols were known to be in the vicinity, or if the ship attacked was fast and handy. The only alternative was to dispense with the process of capture altogether, and to discharge a torpedo without warning, subsequently diving and leaving the sinking merchantman to her fate. By no possible stretch of international law could such an attack be justified. Apart from its inhumanity, it precluded all possibility of visit and search, and of obtaining the ship's papers on which subsequent Prize Court proceedings could be founded. Nevertheless, it was evident that if the torpedoing of the ships at sight were ruled out, the utility of the submarine as a commerce destroyer would be subject to serious limitations, and the experiences of January 30th had already proved that the Germans were willing to accept the odium attaching to such methods of warfare sooner than circumscribe their activities. From their point of view, the one objection to the practice was that the torpedo was a costly weapon, and that the number which could be carried was limited. So long as no particular risk was incurred by a short stay on the surface, it was an economy both of money and of power to capture ships and subsequently to sink them by gunfire or bombs; but where danger was anticipated from this course, they were quite prepared to sink at sight.

Thus, with the opening of the submarine campaign, the war at sea took on a new character. The threat to British commerce was intensified, inasmuch as sporadic raiding was replaced by a sustained attack aimed at the very heart of the British commercial organism. The struggle was embittered by the indifference alike to law and to humanity involved in the nature of the attack.

Nor was it only in respect of the belligerents that the opening of the submarine campaign introduced a new element into the war. The interests of neutral States were seriously affected. Although it was not as yet anticipated that the Germans would go to the length of sinking neutral ships without warning, it was evident that, if the practice of torpedoing at sight became prevalent, there would be grave risks of accident or error which might have serious consequences to neutral shipping; nor could the Governments of neutral States be indifferent to the risk run by their nationals travelling in British ships.

It was not, however, only by accident or error that neutral ships were liable to be sunk. The right asserted in the case of the *Maria* to sink a neutral carrying conditional contraband,[1] would undoubtedly be claimed by the submarines, and operating, as they would, in British home waters, such occurrences were likely to be much more frequent than on the more distant trade routes. This was a serious matter, and yet another complication was introduced by the large number of neutral cargoes carried in British ships. It was not possible for the submarine, as it was for the cruiser, to select such ships to carry in the accumulated prisoners taken from other prizes. Either the ship must be released or the cargo must be sunk with it. So early as October 1914, the neutral cargo in the *Glitra* had been sent to the bottom in this way.[2] The Norwegian cargo-owners sued for compensation, and the case came on before the Hamburg Prize Court on January 29th, 1915. The Court dismissed the claim, and the cargo-owners appealed. In commenting on the judgment the *Neue Hamburgische Börsen-Halle* pointed out that if compensation had to be paid for neutral cargo carried in enemy ships, German commanders would often have to release their prizes, as Germany could not afford to meet the claims which would be made. Whether the claim was or was not good under the German Prize Court Regulations they regarded as very doubtful, and quoted a high German authority to the effect that " If

[1] See Vol. I, p. 256.   [2] *Ibid.*, p. 285.

the goods were not subject to seizure, an indemnity must be paid for them." Nevertheless, they concluded that, if the decision in the *Glitra* should be reversed on appeal, it would be necessary to alter the Regulations in such a way as to remove this restriction on submarine warfare.[1] There was thus little room for doubt that neutral cargo in British ships would be sunk with as little scruple as belligerent property, and in view of the extravagant hopes openly expressed in Germany as to the efficiency of the submarine campaign, the threat to neutral interests was very grave.

All these considerations were not without effect upon the relations of the respective belligerents with neutral Powers. In spite of the resentment aroused abroad by the methods of the German mine-layers and by the occasional misconduct of German cruisers and supply ships, it was Great Britain—the belligerent actually exercising the command of the sea—who had most frequently come into conflict with neutral, especially American, opinion. Indeed, the one factor which had restricted the application of economic pressure by the Allies was the deference due to neutral susceptibilities and the provisions of international law. The situation was now changed. The flagrant illegality of the German methods and the contempt shown by the German Government and commanders for legitimate neutral interests rendered it difficult for neutrals to protest against the adoption by the Allies, as measures of reprisal, of steps which, if taken earlier in the war, would undoubtedly have been met by the strongest opposition on the part of interested third parties. To these measures Germany replied by extensions of the submarine campaign involving her in continually accentuated friction with neutral States. The new weapon which Germany had forged was to yield striking results as the course of the war developed, but the price which she had to pay for it was heavy. When the German Government, at the beginning of 1915, committed themselves to the submarine campaign they did more than anything else could have done to strengthen their enemies' hands in the exercise of their control of the seas, and at the same time they embarked on a course of wilful defiance of the comity of nations which was eventually, in a very real sense, to

---

[1] Translation in *Lloyd's List*, 8 April, 1915. The appeal was finally dismissed in July 1915.

"call in the New World to redress the balance of the Old."

It would be absurd to suppose that these possibilities were not present to the minds of the German High Command when they decided on this new departure in their naval policy. There were, indeed, those in Germany who, from the first, protested against the adoption of a course which must inevitably tend to range neutral opinion on the side of the Allies, and there were others who wished, at any rate, to postpone its adoption until a large increase in Germany's submarine strength gave promise of greater tangible results to off-set the political disadvantages incurred. It is probable, however, that the German Government exaggerated the immediate possibilities of the campaign. From their point of view, almost any risk was worth the running which gave a prospect of shortening the war, for great as had been Germany's military preparation, neither her economic and financial resources nor her internal organisation were calculated to stand the strain of a long-drawn-out struggle. To the German Government, a long war, especially if it were not completely successful, meant the possibility of economic collapse and a rising against the governing class of the people whom they had so long deluded. The spectre of bankruptcy and revolution was constantly before their eyes, and to this must be attributed the apparent levity with which they accepted the most terrible risks for the sake of immediate military advantage.

It was not clear, moreover, that the risks were prohibitively great. Of the States most likely to be affected by the new departure, Denmark and Holland were contiguous to Germany, and were unlikely to risk suffering the fate of Belgium. Sweden was strongly anti-Russian, and at least partially pro-German. The United States had already been involved in a controversy with the Allies which threatened to become acrimonious. Norway, the most likely of all to suffer heavy losses, could do little without Swedish and Danish support. All were, to a greater or less degree, interested as customers or as sellers and carriers, in the maintenance of trade relations with Germany. It might very well be, therefore, that no degree of loss or suffering inflicted on neutral Powers would call forth anything more than a formal and ineffective protest.

8 THE NEW PHASE IN THE WAR AT SEA

The first official intimation that the German plan of campaign contemplated the deliberate terrorising of neutral traffic took the form of a notice which appeared in the *Reichsanzeiger*, the official organ of the German Government, on February 2nd. In this notice all peaceful shipping was urgently warned against approaching the coasts of Great Britain, on the ground of the serious danger which it would incur. Two days later, on February 4th, a further notice was issued, which, for the first time, laid down clearly and fully the lines of the new campaign to which the German Government had committed themselves.

This remarkable document began by setting out a long list of alleged grievances arising from the exercise of British sea-power. In particular the British Government were charged with abolishing the distinction between absolute and conditional contraband, and with aiming " not only to strike at German military strength, but also at the economic life of Germany; and finally, through starvation, doom the entire population of Germany to destruction." It went on to complain that neutral Powers had made no effective protest against these illegal measures, and had, in fact, " aided British measures which are irreconcilable with the freedom of the sea, in that they have, obviously under the pressure of England, hindered, by export and transit embargoes, the transit of wares for peaceful purposes in Germany."

In consequence of these alleged violations of international law by Great Britain, and this dereliction of duty on the part of neutral Powers, the German Government stated that it had become necessary to adopt measures of reprisal, and that these measures would assume the following form :

" Germany hereby declares all the waters surrounding Great Britain and Ireland, including the entire English Channel, an area of war, and will therein act against the shipping of the enemy. For this purpose, beginning February 18, 1915, she will endeavour to destroy every enemy merchant-ship that is found in this area of war, even if it be not always possible to avert the peril which threatens persons and cargoes. Neutrals are, therefore, warned against further entrusting crews and passengers and wares to such ships. Their attention is also called to the fact that it is advisable for their ships to avoid entering this area, for, though the German naval forces have instructions to avoid violence to neutral ships, in so far as they are recognisable, in view of the misuse of neutral flags ordered by the British Government, and the contingencies of naval warfare, their becoming victims of attack directed against enemy ships cannot always be avoided. At the same time it is especially noted that shipping north of the Shetland Islands, in the eastern area of the North Sea, and in a strip of at least thirty sea miles in width along the Netherlands coasts, is not in peril."

Disingenuous as it was, the preamble to the German Memorandum was of some interest as showing the irritation and anxiety produced in Germany by the economic pressure of British sea-power even under all the restrictions by which it had hitherto been shackled. The assertion that Great Britain had been guilty of abolishing the distinction between absolute and conditional contraband with the object of starving the civil population of Germany must be read in conjunction with an Order issued by the German Government which came into operation on January 25th. The hasty and ill-considered food legislation embarked on at the outset of the war had failed either to allay popular discontent or to remedy inequalities of distribution. Comparatively small as was the margin of imported foodstuffs now cut off, its loss had produced a serious dislocation of supplies, which the efforts of the Government tended rather to aggravate than to relieve, inasmuch as they were devoted rather to the regulation of prices than to the encouragement of production or of economy in consumption. The harvest of 1914 was a poor one, and the position with regard to cereals, though it was far from approaching famine, was becoming serious. In these circumstances the Government determined to take the distribution of grain and flour entirely into their own hands, and a special department was created to supervise the distribution of both home-grown and imported stocks, with the object of assuring undiminished bread rations for the troops, and enabling the Government to control civil consumption. By rendering the Government the sole purchaser, this step undoubtedly gave to all imported grain cargoes the character of contraband, whether consigned to a " base of operations " or not, since it was no longer possible to discriminate between cargoes intended for military use and cargoes destined to feed the civil population. It was no doubt anticipated, therefore, that it would lead to an increase in the stringency of the measures taken by the Allies to restrict German supplies, and the plea of threatened starvation was accordingly raised, in complete disregard of the fact that German jurists and statesmen had in the past insisted on the right to regard foodstuffs as contraband, whatever their destination.

Equally striking was the complaint as to export and transit embargoes in neutral countries. These restrictions had been placed by neutral Governments on trade with Germany either for the purpose of ensuring their own supplies, endangered by the cessation of imports from Germany and the laying up of German shipping, or for the purpose of securing for neutral ships exemption from detention by the British patrols and boarding steamers. There was only too much evidence that, despite these restrictions, Germany was still able to carry on a large indirect trade; but it was evident that the German Government viewed with grave concern the possibility of an extension of the system.

It was thus in reprisal for measures adopted by the British Government in the exercise of their undoubted belligerent rights, and by neutral Governments in defence of their own legitimate interests, that Germany claimed the right to dispense with the doctrine of visit and search and to sink at sight all ships even suspected of being British, for no other interpretation could be placed on the warning to neutrals against entering the war zone. It is true that this warning was based on an alleged order of the British Admiralty for merchant vessels to sail under neutral flags, and that this allegation, though incorrect in form, had some substratum of truth. No order for the use of false colours had been given, but after the events of January 30th the Admiralty informed shipowners that the use of neutral flags to avoid attack was a legitimate *ruse de guerre*. Such a method of disguise, not only by merchantmen but by warships was, in fact, a well-known and recognised stratagem, which violated no canon of international law so long as no actual hostile operation was carried on under its cover. The proper course for a belligerent warship suspecting that a neutral flag was being used for the purpose of disguising an enemy merchant-vessel was to visit and examine the suspicious craft. It was the right claimed by the Germans to torpedo suspected ships at sight, without verification of their nationality by visit and search, which created the danger to neutral shipping.

Taken in conjunction with the warning issued to neutrals on February 2nd, the German Memorandum could only be interpreted as an attempt to prohibit all intercourse with Great Britain, or in other words to obtain all the advantages of a commercial blockade of the British Isles without any of the conditions requisite for rendering such a blockade " effective " according to international law. The position thus taken up was at once challenged by the American Government, who pointed out that " the sole right of a belligerent dealing with neutral vessels on the high seas is limited to visit and search, unless a blockade is proclaimed and effectively maintained, which this Government does not understand to be proposed in this case." The Note ended by an intimation that the destruction of American ships or American lives on the high seas might be attended by very serious consequences. At the same time the American Government presented a note to Great Britain protesting against any such general use of neutral flags by British merchantmen as might constitute a danger to neutral shipping.

To the American protest the German Government replied by a note reiterating their allegations against Great Britain and against neutral Governments, and complaining of the export of munitions from the United States to Great Britain, although they admitted that this trade was perfectly legal. With regard to the operative part of their former notice they refused to give any satisfactory assurances, stating that neutral vessels passing through the war zone must do so at their own peril, and suggesting that if the American Government desired to ensure the safety of their merchantmen engaged in peaceful traffic they should do so by providing a naval escort.

Meanwhile the German submarines had been busy. Even before February 18th, the date named for the commencement of the " blockade," they had attacked several British merchantmen in the Channel and North Sea. Among these was the hospital ship *Asturias*, at which a torpedo was fired without warning on February 1st. Fortunately the torpedo missed. On February 15th the *Dulwich* was torpedoed off Havre, and went to the bottom with the loss of two lives. Next day the French steamer *Ville de Lille* was sunk off Barfleur. The other ships attacked succeeded in escaping, notably the *Laertes*, which was attacked with gunfire and torpedo off the Dutch coast, but put on full steam and showed a clean pair of heels to her assailant. From February 18th onwards the attacks became more frequent, and it was soon apparent that the risks run by neutral vessels traversing the war zone were by no means imaginary. On February 19th the Norwegian steamer *Belridge*, bound from New Orleans to Amsterdam, with a cargo of oil consigned to the Dutch Government, was torpedoed without warning off the Varne. Although seriously damaged, she was kept afloat and arrived at Thames Haven next day to effect repairs; but the Norwegian Government at once protested against the attack, and, under pressure, the Germans subsequently declared that the *Belridge* had been torpedoed in mistake, and that they were willing to pay compensation for the damage done.[1] Nevertheless, the incident created a profound sensation as showing how great were the dangers to neutral shipping even when taking no part in British trade.

There was thus no longer any doubt that the Germans were fully prepared to carry out their threats, and the way was open for the British Government to adopt such measures of retaliation as they might think proper. So far as Germany was concerned, it was clear that her repudiation of the restraints imposed by international law exposed her to reprisals; but it was not in accordance with the policy of the Allies that such reprisals should assume a form affording legitimate ground of complaint to innocent neutrals. On the other hand, it was evident that the whole situation with regard to the restriction of enemy trade had undergone a radical change. In face of the disregard shown by the enemy for neutral rights and for the dictates of international comity, it was no longer possible for neutrals to object with any show of reason to such modifications in existing practice as were necessary to bring the recognised laws of naval warfare into substantial accord with the conditions of modern commerce. Direct interference with German trade had hitherto been confined to articles coming within the contraband categories; exports from Germany in neutral bottoms, and

[1] *Times*, 4 June, 1915.

imports of non-contraband goods had been allowed to pass unchecked. It was true that difficulties of tonnage, finance, and insurance, the navigational dangers of the North Sea, and the dislocation of the German industries had greatly restricted the import, and still more the export, trade; but in both directions signs of greater activity were now visible, German finance and industry were recovering from the first shock of the war; new channels of trade had been discovered, and German exports, especially to the United States, were monthly increasing in volume. The import trade carried on through neutral ports in contiguous countries had also been developed on a large scale. By the Order in Council of October 29th, 1914, conditional contraband in a ship bound for a neutral port was declared liable to capture if consigned " to order," but the Germans had found no difficulty in making arrangements with persons in neutral countries who were willing to lend the use of their names as consignees. It was subsequently decided in the Courts that the provisions of the Order could not be considered as fulfilled by inserting the name of a dummy consignee [1]; but at this period the strict interpretation of the Order was by no means clear, and the British Government felt it difficult to interfere with shipments to named consignees. Under the most favourable interpretation the Order gave no power to stop cargoes consigned to a *bona fide* neutral purchaser,[2] even though his intention might be to resell to the enemy. The exports from America to Scandinavia, Holland, and Italy of goods in the " conditional " category steadily increased, and it seemed impossible to stop the traffic.

Nor was this all. Shipments were now going forward from the United States to Germany direct. Towards the end of January the *Wilhelmina*, with foodstuffs for Hamburg for the use of the civil population, was intercepted by the patrols and her cargo placed in prize. As if to confuse the issues, the German Government, on February 6th, repealed the decree of January 25th so far as concerned imports arriving after January 31st. There could be no doubt that, following the precedents set by the German Courts themselves, Hamburg might legitimately be pro-

[1] *British and Colonial Prize Cases.* Judgment of the Prize Court in the *Rijn*, 6 June, 1917, *Sydland* and *Indianic*, 31 July, 1916; of the Privy Council in the *Louisiania*, 1 February, 1918.

[2] *Ibid.* Judgment of the Privy Council in the *Kronprinsessan Victoria*, vol. iii, at p. 247.

claimed a " base of supplies," thus rendering the cargo liable to condemnation, whoever were the consignees; but, rather than risk friction with the United States, the British Government preferred to release it by agreement for sale to the Belgian Relief Commission, leaving the legal question undecided. In the absence of a decided test case no further attempt at direct importation of foodstuffs was made for the time being; but it was evident that the attempt might be renewed. Meanwhile the American cotton crop was about to come forward, and cotton was not even conditional contraband.

There were thus two separate problems to be considered : the direct trade with German ports, and the transit trade through contiguous neutral countries. The direct trade in non-contraband goods could only be stopped by the imposition of a blockade, but the development of the submarine rendered an effective close blockade of the German coast impossible, and, though the British command of the approaches to the North Sea amounted in effect to an effective long-range blockade, it might be doubted how far it fell within the definitions evolved under the widely different conditions of previous wars. Moreover, a blockade of the German coast itself would have little value so long as free goods and conditional contraband destined for the enemy could be poured into the ports of Scandinavia, Holland, and Italy. It was evident, in fact, that the exercise by the Allies of their belligerent rights was being stultified by the effect of economic conditions, and by a development of communications which rendered the precedents of previous wars inapplicable to the present struggle.

From a very early period of the war a small but vigorous and insistent group of critics had urged upon the British Government the necessity of such modifications in practice as would enable the economic pressure on the Central Powers to be intensified, and, in particular, the desirability of repudiating the provisions of the Declaration of Paris, which exempted from capture enemy goods, other than contraband, carried in neutral bottoms. To this course, however, there were grave objections. In the first place, it was incumbent upon the Allied Governments, representing as they did the cause of international law and international morality, to avoid any appearance of wresting the established laws of war to their own advantage. In the second place, common prudence dictated a careful regard for neutral susceptibilities even where there was room for doubt as to the legal merits of the case. Not only was there the danger that an unsympathetic attitude towards neutral claims might convert friendly States into enemies, but the importance of neutral countries as sources of supply, and the large part played by neutral tonnage in the carriage of Allied trade, emphasised the desirability of avoiding, so far as possible, even temporary friction.

The case, however, was now altered. The experience of the first six months of hostilities had shown clearly that the difficulties with which the Allies had to contend hampered them seriously in the exercise of their admitted belligerent rights. The conduct of the German Government greatly strengthened the Allies in their relations with neutral States. They were now able to free themselves at a stroke from many of the shackles by which they had hitherto been restrained, and to tighten their hold upon the enemy's maritime communications.

The measures finally adopted were foreshadowed by Mr. Asquith in a speech delivered in the House of Commons on March 1st, 1915, and were officially embodied in an Order in Council dated March 11th. The general effect of these measures was not, as in the case of the German war zone declaration, to introduce any new principle into naval practice, or to repudiate any of the recognised principles of naval law. They were inspired rather by the idea of adapting those principles to existing circumstances, and amounted in effect to the establishment of a blockade which should be effective under the conditions of modern warfare and modern commerce. It was not, however, considered desirable formally to announce a blockade; first, because the unprecedented conditions of the war would, in that event, inevitably give rise to endless controversies as to the interpretation of the rules laid down under altogether different conditions; secondly, because the Allies were anxious to cause as little loss as possible to neutral traders and shipowners, and had no wish to enforce generally the penalty—confiscation of ship and cargo—attaching to attempted breaches of a blockade.

For these reasons the Order in Council of March 11th was based upon the admitted right of retaliation, instead of upon the announcement of a formal blockade. Its principal provisions were as follows :

(I) " No merchant vessel which sailed from her port of departure after March 1, 1915, shall be allowed to proceed on her voyage to any German port. . . .

(II) " No merchant vessel which sailed from any German port after March 1, 1915, shall be allowed to proceed on her voyage with any goods on board laden at such port. . . .

(III) " Every merchant ship which sailed from her port of departure after March 1, 1915, on her way to a port other than a German port, carrying goods with an enemy destination, or which are enemy property, may be required to discharge such goods in a British or Allied port. . . .

(IV) " Every merchant vessel which sailed from a port other than a German port after March 1, 1915, having on board goods which are of enemy origin or are enemy property, may be required to discharge such goods in a British or Allied port."

In order to safeguard legitimate neutral interests, it was provided that goods in any ship so diverted which were neutral property at the time of seizure, if not requisitioned for the use of the Crown, should be restored by order of the Prize Court to the neutral owners. Goods which were enemy property at the time of seizure were to be detained or sold under the direction of the Prize Court. No provision was made for the confiscation of neutral vessels, except ships which had cleared for a neutral country from a British or Allied port, or which had been allowed to pass having an ostensible neutral destination, and then proceeded to an enemy port. Such vessels, if captured on any subsequent voyage, were to be liable to condemnation. Finally, it was provided that nothing in the Order should be deemed to affect the liability of any vessel or goods to capture or condemnation independently of the Order, or, on the other hand, should prevent the relaxation of the provisions of the Order itself in respect of merchantmen belonging to a country which excluded German commerce from the protection of its flag.[1]

Thus the immediate result of the new departure in

---

[1] *Manual of Emergency Legislation*, Supplement No. 3, pp. 513–15. As to the validity of the Order as binding on the Prize Court see *British and Colonial Prize Cases*, the *Zamora*, vol. i, p. 309, vol. ii, p. 169; the *Stigstad*, vol. iii, p. 347.

ECONOMIC PRESSURE INTENSIFIED

German policy was to provide the Allies with an opportunity of closing those indirect channels of German trade which had hitherto escaped their control. Great as was the difference between the methods pursued by the two belligerent groups, both were now attempting to paralyse all commerce, direct or indirect, with the enemy countries. Overshadowed by the clash of arms, and brought into public notice only by a few exceptional incidents, the silent process of economic pressure assumed for both sides an ever-increasing importance in the conduct of the war. More and more, neutral interests became subservient to the development of the conflict.

CHAPTER II

OPENING OF THE SUBMARINE CAMPAIGN

February—April 1915

WHATEVER success the new form of attack adopted by Germany might attain in the destruction of ships and cargoes, it was soon evident that it was not likely to have much effect in reducing the flow of trade, either by intimidating British shipping, or by inducing the Admiralty to depart from their policy of encouraging the free movement of commerce. The State Insurance scheme proved as effective in averting a panic arising from the events of January 30th and the subsequent announcement of the submarine " blockade " as it had been in the restoration of confidence at the outbreak of war. No sign of panic was visible among the officers and men of the Mercantile Marine. The Admiralty, steadfastly adhering to their settled practice, sent out at once orders that on no account were ships to be detained in port except in cases of special emergency, and that, while homeward bound vessels were to be warned of the dangers into which they were steaming, they were not to be turned back. Special care was taken that outward-bound shipping should not be delayed by unauthorised interference on the part of the military authorities at the ports.

It was necessary, however, that the general instructions issued to merchantmen with a view to minimising the risk of capture should be thoroughly overhauled. From the first definite appearance of the submarine as a commerce-destroyer, the Admiralty had been at work on the problem, and before the date fixed by the Germans for the opening of the new campaign a complete new set of instructions had been prepared and issued. These instructions, as finally settled, were dated February 10th, 1915, and during the next few days they were distributed to the Fleet, and through the usual channels, such as Lloyd's, the War

NEW INSTRUCTIONS TO SHIPPING

Risk Clubs, and the Customs Officials, to the masters and owners of British shipping. They were also cabled in an abbreviated form to the Naval Intelligence Officers abroad, and to the Governments of all Crown Colonies in the Atlantic and in Europe, in order that they might be communicated to homeward-bound vessels at their last port of call.

The gist of the instructions was as follows:

Merchantmen were warned that German submarines were likely to be met in the waters round the British Isles. British and French submarines had been ordered not to approach merchantmen in the area between 43° and 68° N., 4° E. and 13° W.; any submarine which closed a vessel within those limits was therefore to be considered as German. As an additional precaution, silhouettes of British, French, and German submarines were confidentially issued to shipping through the Board of Trade, and the localities in which French or British craft of this description were likely to be met were indicated.

The general sailing instructions were for outward-bound vessels to leave British ports at dusk, and for homeward-bound ships to make port, so far as possible, at dawn. Both outward-bound and homeward-bound vessels were advised to make landfalls only after dark, and ships obliged to wait outside ports before entering were to keep on the move and not to anchor. Lights were not to be completely darkened, but no bright lights were to be shown. Disguise and the use of false colours were recommended as a legitimate *ruse de guerre*. Wireless messages were not to be sent when within 100 miles of the British coast, except in a grave emergency.

Should an enemy submarine be encountered, masters were to remember that they had an excellent chance of escape, as a torpedo fired from astern could easily be avoided by the use of the helm, and the fire of guns carried by German submarines at this period was not very dangerous so long as the crew were kept below. The master of a vessel attacked should therefore endeavour to bring the submarine astern and proceed at full speed, keeping the enemy in his wake. If followed, he should make for the land or for shoal water. Should a submarine come up ahead of his ship he should steam straight at her, thus compelling her to dive and come up astern. While within the danger area, an extra turn of speed should always be ready, an extra sharp look-out kept, and boats kept ready and provisioned.

Masters were further warned that, with a view to minimising losses, ocean-going merchantmen were forbidden to go to the assistance of a torpedoed ship lest they too should fall a victim, this duty being left to small coasters, trawlers, and other vessels of light draught, who were comparatively immune from torpedo attack.

A ship attacked by a submarine was to fly the largest ensign available half-mast at the foremast head or on the triatic stay, as a call for assistance and a warning to other merchantmen. The emergency wireless signal was to be the S.O.S. call, followed by the S. alone, continually repeated. A list of British and French ports from which armed assistance might be expected was appended to the instructions.

For this assistance the Admiralty relied in the first place on the coastal Destroyer Flotillas, and in the second place on the Auxiliary Patrol, to the development of which the announcement of the submarine campaign against merchant shipping gave a new impetus. By April 30th there were, on their stations or fitting out, some 60 yachts and over 500 trawlers and drifters, in addition to 400 trawlers and drifters of the mine-sweeping service.[1]

To submarines on the surface, vulnerable as they were to the fire of light guns, the armed yacht, trawler, or drifter was a formidable opponent. The trawlers, handy little craft with strongly constructed stems, could do much even when unarmed, for submarines dreaded ramming even more than gunfire. The problem was to bring them to the surface, and here the drifters came into play. By January 1915 special nets were in use fitted with indicator buoys ingeniously devised so as to be automatically ignited on the net being carried away, thus revealing the presence of the submarine, and enabling her to be attacked by the nearest armed craft on coming to the surface to clear. Should she elect to remain on the bottom a unit of the flotilla would proceed to drag for her with a "modified sweep," a cable to which charges of guncotton were attached.

In the protection of trade the indicator-nets played a very important part. Nowhere was shipping so vulnerable as in the English Channel, and in the Irish Sea, with

[1] About 50 of the mine-sweepers were in the Mediterranean.

its extensions the North and St. George's Channels, for nowhere else was it so thickly concentrated. In the English Channel especially, the stream of traffic bound from every quarter of the world to London and the East Coast ports had to pass, at the point nearest to the German bases, through the narrow gut of the Straits of Dover, where it was confined to still narrower limits by the requirements of the examination service in the Downs. It was of the first importance to exclude the submarines, if possible, from the English Channel, and to prevent them from passing through the North Channel to operate in the approaches to the Clyde and Mersey.

An outer defence to the Dover Straits, against submarines travelling on the surface, was provided by the British minefield in the North Sea, which now extended very nearly to the Flanders coast.[1] As the presence of a new German minefield off Nieueport had been detected in January, navigation between the North Sea and the Channel was now exceedingly restricted; but the safe tracks were regularly communicated to the War Risks Clubs, and both the patrols and the Trinity House Pilots were available to indicate the courses to be followed either by British or by neutral shipping.

Behind this minefield Admiral Hood, who commanded in the Straits, was ordered to maintain a continuous line of drift-nets right across the Straits, except in impossibly bad weather, for which purpose he was provided with a strong force of drifters and many miles of indicator-nets. Great difficulty was at first found in maintaining the line at night owing to the insufficient number and unsatisfactory quality of the buoys available; but by the middle of February the net barrier was already in use, and with every week that went by it improved in efficiency. In support were the destroyers and armed trawlers and drifters of the Dover Patrol, to chase and destroy any hostile craft detected by means of the indicator-nets, to escort vessels of special importance, and to sink any floating mines discovered.

As an inner defence it was decided, towards the end of February, to construct a permanent boom of heavy netting from Folkestone to Cape Gris-nez, and by March 26th this work had proceeded so far that two light-vessels, marking the gate left for the passage of shipping, were in

[1] Notice to Mariners, No. 149 of 1915, dated 3 March.

22 OPENING OF THE SUBMARINE CAMPAIGN

position off Folkestone pier.[1] Progress, however, was slow, owing to the stupendous nature of the work and the great strength of the tides in the Straits, and the work was ultimately abandoned; but by the end of March a smaller boom had been placed in position across the Gull Stream, the northern entrance to the Downs, and through the gate in this boom some 800 vessels passed every week. On the opposite side of the Channel the French destroyers and armed trawlers kept watch on the ship channel left along the French coast, and at the principal ports on both coasts were local flotillas of destroyers, armed patrol-boats, and drifters, ready to deal with submarines which might pass the barrier in the Straits.

For the protection of traffic in the Irish Sea against submarines coming through the North Channel a somewhat different method was adopted. As the Straits of Dover have a depth of only about twenty fathoms and the bottom is piled high with the accumulated wreckage of centuries, the line of indicator-nets, with its attendant force of destroyers and armed patrol-boats, might reasonably be expected to form an efficient barrier to the undetected passage of an enemy. In the North Channel, on the other hand, the depth is between sixty and seventy fathoms, and a submarine could easily dive under a single line of nets. In this case, therefore, reliance was placed not on a single barrier but on an extensive netted and defended area through which a hostile submarine would be obliged to pass. For this purpose it was necessary to impose drastic restrictions on the course of shipping. A rectangular area, thirty miles long and twelve miles wide, extending from the Mull of Kintyre, on the north-eastern side of the Channel, to Rathlin Island on the south-western side, was absolutely closed to navigation by ships of every size and every nationality as from February 23rd, 1915, all traffic being confined to the passage, three miles wide, between Rathlin Island and the mainland of Ireland. Even this passage could be used only between sunrise and sunset, no vessel being allowed within four miles of Rathlin Island during the hours of darkness.[2] These restrictions constituted a very serious inconvenience to shipping passing round the north of Ireland to or from Liverpool and the Clyde, and led to a considerable diversion of traffic to

[1] Notice to Mariners, No. 228 of 1915, dated 26 March.
[2] *Ibid.*, No 137 of 1915, dated 22 February.

the southern route; but the importance of keeping submarines away from such great terminal points as the entrances to the Clyde and Mersey outweighed the disadvantages entailed.

For the protection of the southern entrance to the Irish Sea, another Auxiliary Patrol flotilla, based on Milford, kept watch on the St. George's Channel. Here the width of the passage forbade the employment of the methods adopted at the northern entrance, but as soon as sufficient indicator-nets were available they were shot by the drifters in the neighbourhoods most likely to attract the enemy's attention. An inner defence was provided by yet another flotilla which maintained a line of patrols between Kingstown and Holyhead.

While these were the areas at first most directly affected by the submarine attack on merchant shipping, the barriers in the Dover Straits and the entrances to the Irish Sea were only single items, though most important ones, in the work of anti-submarine defence. Harbour defence booms, with gates for the entrance and exit of shipping, were put in hand at a large number of ports and estuaries all round the coast, and though many, if not most of these, had for their primary purpose the defence of naval bases or anchorages, the greater number of them were almost equally important as providing for the security of merchant vessels at anchor, or in the narrow and crowded approaches to the great commercial ports. All round the British and Irish coasts, moreover, the destroyer flotillas and the units of the Auxiliary Patrol were on the alert to intercept submarines on their passage North-about, to harry them on their appearance at any point on the coastline, or to give assistance to ships attacked.

It was, of course, some time before this complex machinery of defence settled down into smooth working order and the new methods of anti-submarine warfare became fully effective. Meanwhile the enemy continued to operate actively in the areas in which they had made their appearance at the end of January—the English Channel and Irish Sea. On February 18th, the date announced for the opening of the submarine blockade, the French steamer *Dinorah* (ex-Austrian) was damaged by a torpedo in the Channel; on the following day the *Belridge* was torpedoed.[1] On the 20th two British steamers were

[1] See p. 12, *supra*.

sunk in the Irish Sea, and on the 23rd and 24th five, ranging from 1,100 to 5,800 tons, were torpedoed off Beachy Head.

In consequence of these losses, reiterated warnings were issued to merchantmen to keep well away from prominent headlands and to keep in mid-Channel except between Folkestone and Boulogne. These instructions, however, proved unsatisfactorily vague, as they were interpreted by masters to imply following a fixed track exactly half-way between the English and French coasts, and they were accordingly modified by instructions to spread across the Channel with wide intervals, but still giving prominent headlands, especially Beachy, a wide berth. At the same time measures were taken to avoid, as much as possible, the congestion of traffic in exposed neighbourhoods. The Committee for the Diversion of Shipping had already drawn attention to the risks run by ships detained outside Havre by the congested state of the port, and arrangements had been concerted with the French Government and the shipping companies concerned, for facilitating and safeguarding their entrance, and for the detention in other Channel ports of vessels awaiting news that a berth at Havre had been found for them. A still more important question, however, was that of the pilotage regulations in force.

In order to baffle the German submarines, then operating only against naval units, it had been decided in November 1914 to extinguish or alter the position of the principal lights and buoys between Lowestoft and the Isle of Wight, and these alterations had been completed during the following month. It then became necessary to provide additional pilotage facilities along this stretch of the coast, and a pilot station was accordingly established at St. Helens. Now that the weight of the submarine attack fell so heavily on merchant shipping, this arrangement was found to be inadvisable, as the concentration of shipping awaiting pilots between Bembridge and the Nab exposed a large target very difficult to protect, while the extinguishing of the principal lights tended to render the flow of traffic slow in the eastern portion of the Channel. On February 25th Beachy Head light was permanently relit and by the end of the first week in March all the main coast lights between Selsea Bill and Deal were again working in their normal positions. It thus became possible to remove the pilot station from St. Helens to the Downs, where ample protection could be afforded to vessels awaiting pilots. From thence to Yarmouth, however, pilotage was made compulsory for all vessels other than coasters of less than 500 tons gross, passing between the Downs and Yarmouth or Gravesend, and for all vessels other than ships of less than 3,500 tons trading coastwise, between Gravesend and Yarmouth. The object of these regulations was to prevent vessels from blundering into the minefields and net defences, or running over the boom in the Gull Stream, as to all of which there were constant complaints; but the supply of pilots proved unequal to the demand, and on March 27th compulsory pilotage from the Downs was restricted to vessels of 3,500 tons and upwards, though all ships were strongly advised to take pilots if possible.[1]

Concessions were also made as regards the movements of shipping in the Thames Estuary, the navigation of which was now confined to the Edinburgh and Black Deep Channels, and in the following month certain of the gas buoys in the Estuary were relit. At all the principal ports on the coast, and especially at those employed as naval bases, the navigational and pilotage regulations at this time represented an inevitable compromise between the requirements of the defence and examination service, and the necessity of avoiding congestion of traffic outside the port; but so far as possible, and even in opposition to the representations of the local naval and military authorities, the Admiralty adhered to the policy of regarding an uninterrupted flow of traffic as the first consideration. Many of the East Coast navigation lights were gradually replaced, and the examination rules were modified to avoid the necessity of checking the speed of ships until their arrival at a safe anchorage. Instructions were also given to the patrols that in warning ships off dangerous areas, or passing on information and advice, they were to communicate by megaphone or signal, without ordering ships to an exposed anchorage, or compelling them to reduce their speed.

In spite of all these precautions and of the activity of the patrols, the tale of losses continued, and the range of the attack soon spread beyond its original points of

[1] Notices to Mariners, Nos. 1795 and 1823 of 1914, dated 4, 15 December; Nos. 164 and 239 of 1915, dated 8, 27 March.

impact. During the month of March casualties and attacks were reported from points all along the English Channel between the Downs and the Lizard, from the North Sea, the west coast of Ireland, the Irish Sea, the entrance to the Bristol Channel, and the neighbourhood of the Scillies. At one period three submarines at least were operating simultaneously in the Irish Sea and the approaches to the Bristol Channel, and on March 27th and 28th, U 28 sank four vessels in the neighbourhood of Lundy and the Smalls. No ship, however, was lost in the Irish Sea itself after March 13th, and it appeared that the measures adopted for the defence of this area had rendered it more or less immune from attack. On the other hand, every week saw two or three vessels sunk or molested in the Channel, and there was ample evidence that submarines were still able to pass through the Straits. Scarcely less disconcerting was the knowledge that submarines were passing down the west coast of Ireland to attack shipping in the crowded waters of the South-Western Approach.[1]

Nevertheless, there was little indication of any diminution in the flow of trade. The premiums under the State Insurance Scheme were maintained at the same low rates ($\frac{3}{4}$ per cent. for hulls, 1 per cent. for cargoes) at which they stood at the beginning of the year, and the security thus afforded to shipowners and to the financial interests was quite sufficient to avert any interruption of the movement of commerce. By the men who ran the personal risk—the masters, officers, and crews of the Mercantile Marine—it continued to be regarded with a superb indifference which deprived the submarine menace of any effect as a deterrent.

Nor was neutral shipping greatly affected. The rates on cargoes in neutral bottoms were raised by underwriters from 25s. to 80s. per cent.,[2] but this was no appreciable impediment to commerce, and though the American War Risks Bureau increased the premium on cargoes to and from the United Kingdom at the end of February, the new rate was only 1 per cent., and hulls could be covered for the round voyage at $1\frac{1}{2}$ per cent.[3] In fact, the figures of foreign tonnage entered at British ports during March

---

[1] This title has been adopted as a short and convenient form of reference to the waters south and south-east of Ireland, comprising the approaches to the St. George's, Bristol, and English Channels.
[2] *Times*, 1 March, 1915.
[3] *Ibid.*

compared much more favourably with the preceding year than in any month since November 1914.

This activity of neutral shipping in the trade of the United Kingdom was the more striking since it was soon evident that the warning contained in the German announcement of February 2nd and 4th was no empty threat. The torpedoing of the *Belridge* was soon followed by incidents of even graver significance. On March 13th the *Hanna*, a Swedish steamer carrying coal from the Tyne for Las Palmas, was torpedoed without warning off Scarborough, and sank with the loss of nine lives, and on March 25th the Dutch steamer *Medea* was captured and sunk by U 28 in the English Channel. The sinking of the *Medea* gave rise to an interesting case in the German Prize Courts, in which the decision was very prejudicial to neutral interests. She was laden with oranges from Spain for London, and the Prize Court at Hamburg decided on August 13th that her cargo was conditional contraband, but that it was not liable to seizure as there was no evidence that the oranges were likely to be bought by the British Government. Nevertheless, they fully approved the action of the commander of U 28, holding that as he " was not in a position to investigate the facts of the case on the commercial side," he was justified in destroying both ship and cargo " because the proximity of the enemy Power gave reason to apprehend the recapture of the ship." They did, however, admit the right of the ship and cargo-owners to compensation; but in this respect their judgment was subsequently reversed by the Supreme Prize Court at Berlin.

Meanwhile, the deliberate destruction of the *Medea*, in which there was no question of mistake or doubt as to the nationality of the ship, stood out as a serious menace to neutral shipping, the more so when considered in connection with the treatment accorded to two other Dutch steamers, the *Batavier V.* and *Zaanstroom*, which had been intercepted by U 28 on March 18th, on their way from Rotterdam to London, and taken into Zeebrugge. Here the proceedings of the Germans were, for once, in accordance with established precedent, yet in these cases also, the subsequent decision of the Prize Court gave ground for legitimate uneasiness. Both ships carried foodstuffs as part of their cargo, and both were condemned on the ground that London was a base of supply for the

British forces—a claim against which the British Government had already vainly protested—and that Cape Town and other ports to which part of the cargoes were consigned on through bills of lading, fell in the same category. The most interesting point in the judgment, however, was the explicit declaration that the German Prize Courts sat to apply national and not international law, and that " the view partly upheld in the older literature on the subject to the effect that the Prize Court had to apply international law, even where the same had not become incorporated in the national law, had to be rejected on principle." [1] It is hardly necessary to point out how completely this view of the functions of a Prize Court was opposed to that maintained by British jurists.[2]

The risk run by neutral shipping was thus twofold. They were liable to be sunk with full deliberation if they carried cargo for the United Kingdom which could by any stretch of imagination be described as contraband, for it was almost impossible to find a British port which would not come within the German definition of a base of supply. They were liable to be torpedoed without warning in mistake for a British ship, or through sheer recklessness, on any voyage which took them through the German War Zone, whether or no they were bound to or from a British port.

Nevertheless, the improvement in the figures of neutral tonnage entered was fully sustained during the month of April. Not only were the arrivals of Spanish steamers which were as yet little affected by the submarine menace, unusually numerous, but Scandinavian shipping, though particularly exposed to attack, was very busy both in the North Sea and in the general carrying trade. Only in the tonnage under the Dutch flag was there a marked decrease, and this decrease was the effect of a combination of adverse conditions in which the submarine campaign was only one of many factors.[3]

---

[1] Article in *Neue Hamburgische Börsenhalle*, quoted in *Lloyd's List*, 7 August, 1915. The article proceeds: " It need hardly be elaborated that there is a possibility of certain axioms, which up to now were regarded as the customary law of nations, being affected and becoming invalidated owing to the appearance of new forms of warfare, such as the submarine war."

[2] See, for instance, the judgments of Sir Samuel Evans, in the *Marie Glaeser* (delivered 16 September, 1914) and *Odessa and Cape Corso* (delivered 21 December, 1914), *Lloyd's Reports of Prize Cases*, vol. i, at pp. 122 and 326. [3] See pp. 111-3, *post*.

The indifference to the German threats displayed by the Scandinavians was, indeed, remarkable; but it was only what might have been expected from their previous record. The running of war risks was no new thing to the Norwegian, Danish, and Swedish shipowners and mariners. From the first, their vessels had been exposed to sudden destruction by the German minefields, but they had never been deterred thereby from making the voyage to and from British ports. This danger, at least, was now less than of old, thanks to the activity of the British mine-sweeping service, and, above all, to the maintenance of the Swept Channel, which now ran all down the east coast of England from the Tees to the Thames. The limits of the original minefields were well known and the strength of the patrols rendered it difficult for the Germans to add to their number. It is possible also, that they were somewhat chary of laying additional minefields off the British coast which might hamper the operations of their own submarines. Losses either of British or neutral shipping due to the explosion of mines were, in any event, very few during the early months of the submarine campaign. Of such casualties as occurred, three or four were due to vessels striking mines which had drifted from the British minefield, or blundering into that minefield through failure to receive instructions or neglect of those received.

Moreover, the neutral ships which fell victims to mines in the North Sea during February, March, and April included three vessels engaged not in British, but in German trade, and two of these, in particular, were laden with cargoes of which the enemy were sorely in need. The Foreign Office declaration in October, 1914, that cotton for Germany would not be regarded as contraband, led to considerable activity at American ports. The attempt to use for this purpose German steamers nominally transferred to the American flag had been checked by the capture of the *Dacia*,[1] which was taken into Brest on March 1st, and subsequently condemned by the French Prize Court; but several genuine American steamers were chartered for Germany, and among these were the *Evelyn* and *Carib*, both bound for Bremen, which were sunk on February 19th and 23rd respectively, through striking mines as they approached the German coast. On April 2nd

[1] See Vol. I, p. 364.

the *Greenbriar*, another American steamer, homeward bound from Bremerhaven, met the same fate. The effect of such disasters upon the reviving intercourse between Germany and the United States could not fail to be serious. So unfavourably, indeed, was the voyage to German ports regarded by the United States War Risks Bureau that the premiums were fixed at 6 per cent. on hulls and 5 per cent. on non-contraband cargoes respectively, four or five times the rate charged on a voyage to the United Kingdom.[1]

In the Baltic, also, the minefields claimed a toll from German trade. The Norwegian steamer *Nordkyn* was blown up while carrying a cargo of herrings to Königsberg, and two German steamers fell victim either to German or Russian mines.

Trade between Baltic ports and the United Kingdom was still hampered by the activity of German cruisers and torpedo craft off Falsterbö, but the quiescence of the High Seas Fleet in the North Sea was even more marked in the spring of 1915 than during the earlier months of the war. No cruiser or armed liner put out from a German port to prey on British commerce, and no further raids were made on the British coast. Submarines, on the other hand, showed increased activity in the North Sea during the month of April, and though they claimed only two British ships as victims, eight neutral merchantmen were sunk or damaged. Most of these were engaged in British trade, but two, the Dutch steamer *Katwijk* and the Greek *Ellispontos*, were torpedoed without warning while on voyages between neutral ports.[2] For these compensation was subsequently offered.[3] In this month also the submarines began to attack the fishing fleets, and eight trawlers were sunk in the North Sea, two of these being torpedoed without warning. One other was captured and taken to Germany, and yet another sunk by a German torpedo-boat.

Outside the North Sea submarines were active in the Channel and the South-Western Approach, and the destruction of the Norwegian steamer *Caprivi* off the north coast of Ireland on April 23rd showed that the

---

[1] *Times*, 1 March, 1915.
[2] *Katwijk*, Baltimore for Rotterdam; *Ellispontos*, Amsterdam for Montevideo.
[3] *Times*, 25 April, 11 May, 8 June, 1915.

Tory Island minefield was still in some degree a menace to shipping, in spite of the devoted work carried on by the mine-sweepers in that stormy area. It was, however, in the Mediterranean that April brought the most important new development in the war at sea, for during February and March the Allied fleets were engaged in the attempt to reduce the Dardanelles defences, and on April 25th the army under Sir Ian Hamilton effected a landing in Gallipoli.

This new extension of the military commitments of Great Britain had, as we shall see, a serious effect on the shipping position, by reason of the large number of additional ships withdrawn from commercial employment to act as transports or auxiliaries to the Mediterranean fleet. On the other hand, apart from the strategical and political results which might be expected from the forcing of the Straits and the occupation of Constantinople, the prospect of reopening communication with the Black Sea ports was, commercially, of very great importance.

It is true that the opening of the Straits could not be expected to restore at once the position which existed before the situation was so disastrously changed by the arrival of the GOEBEN at Constantinople. The stocks of grain at the Russian ports on the Black Sea and Sea of Azov had been seriously depleted since that date; for the mobilisation of the Russian armies had the inevitable result of greatly increasing the consumption both of foodstuffs and fodder. Wheat and oats had been drawn in large quantities from the ports, and the practical exhaustion of the oat supply led to heavy purchases of barley as an alternative feeding stuff. Owing to the suspension of exports, the grain thus drawn from stock had not been replaced, and though great quantities of grain were lying in the interior, the poverty of the internal communications rendered it doubtful how far they could be made available for immediate shipment. There was also some apprehension as to how far requisitioning or fixing of prices by the Russian Government might interfere with the operations of dealers.[1]

At the same time, there could be no doubt that wheat and maize would be forthcoming in sufficient quantities to affect appreciably the course of the grain markets, and it must be remembered that, in addition to the Russian

[1] *Lloyd's List*, 6 April, 1915.

crops, those of Roumania would be available. If even a moderate supply were forthcoming, the effect on the price of wheat could not fail to be considerable. The main cause of the high level to which grain prices had risen was the concentration of demand on the North American market, and whether or no much wheat was shipped from the Black Sea to Great Britain, the opening of the Straits would automatically relieve the North American market of a part at least of the French and Italian demand. Moreover, by July and August, the 1915 crops would be ready for shipment from the Black Sea ports, and in view of the inability of Australia to export before January or February 1916, it was very desirable that, if possible, this great alternative source should be rendered available, not only in order to ensure a sufficiency of supplies, but in order to discourage wild speculation and restore the market to a healthy condition.

This in itself was an important matter, for the increased cost of living was already causing anxiety and discontent; but the advantages to be expected from the reopening of the Straits did not end there. The resumption of export from the Black Sea and the effect of the big financial operations involved was bound to react favourably on other trades, while to Russia herself the restoration of the exchanges by a resumption of grain shipments, and the opening of ice-free ports for the reception of imports, were alike matters of primary importance. From the economic point of view the "Gallipoli gamble" was at least a gamble for high stakes.

It was not, however, the Dardanelles Expedition alone which, in the Eastern theatre of war, had a profound commercial significance. While the Allies were on the offensive in Gallipoli the British forces in Egypt were charged with the protection of the most vital and most vulnerable link in the maritime communications between Europe and the East.

Although war had been formally declared against Turkey on November 5th, it was not until some three months later that the Turkish preparations were sufficiently advanced to permit of their attacking the Suez Canal. The intervening period was utilised by Major-General Sir A. Wilson, commanding the Canal Defences, to establish posts covering the more important ferries, and dig trenches for the purpose of resisting a crossing.

SUEZ CANAL ATTACKED

A flotilla of armed launches, manned by the Royal Navy, was organised for canal patrols, and plans for the control of shipping were worked out in consultation with the Canal Authorities.

On February 3rd the long-expected attack was made, and was everywhere repulsed. The losses of the Turks were heavy, and during the next few days their whole force retreated in a demoralised condition to the Sinai Peninsula.

Although the operations in this quarter were on a relatively insignificant scale, and the actual Turkish attack was not pressed with much determination, Sir A. Wilson's victory was an event of first-class importance in the history of the war, since it averted once and for all the danger of a permanent interruption of the sea-route to the East. It is true that small raiding parties of Turks and Arabs continued for some time to menace the Canal, and on several occasions mines were laid by men who succeeded in evading the posts and patrols, and wading out into the channel. The danger arising from these mines was serious, for the sinking of a ship in the fairway might block navigation for a considerable period; but it was met by increasing the patrols and by instituting a search of the canal bank at daylight every morning for traces of mine-laying. So successful were these measures, that it was not until June 30th that a British steamer, the *Teiresias*, struck a mine at the south end of the Little Bitter Lake, and sustained serious damage. She was not sunk, however, being subsequently towed into Alexandria for repair, and thanks to the skilful handling of the ship, and the prompt action of the Canal Company's officials, navigation was held up for no more than fourteen hours. Moreover, this was the last time that a mine was placed in the Canal without being immediately discovered, and except on this occasion, and during the progress of the actual attack at the beginning of February, traffic in the Canal proceeded practically as in times of peace.[1]

Meanwhile the German cruisers on the trade routes had been finally disposed of by the destruction of the DRESDEN and the internment of the KRONPRINZ WILHELM and PRINZ EITEL FRIEDRICH,[2] and the only sign of any attempt to

[1] *Naval and Military Despatches*, vol. vi, Despatches from Lieutenant-General Sir J. G. Maxwell, 16 February, 1915, 19 August, 1915, 1 March, 1916.

[2] See Vol. I, Chapter XXII.

interfere with British trade outside Home Waters was the discovery of incendiary bombs placed by German agents on board two or three British ships which sailed during April from American ports. Best of all, a distinct check had been administered to the submarine attack.

Although, as we have seen, the German submarines were by no means inactive during April, only eleven British merchantmen were sunk, as against twenty-one in March. Since March 13th no ship had been sunk in the Irish Sea, though the presence of submarines was from time to time reported on evidence of varying credibility. Shipping to or from Liverpool and the Clyde was still exposed to attack in the southern approaches, but traffic within the Irish Sea itself was thenceforward undisturbed for a period of some months.

More important still was the immunity attained, after the first week of April, in the English Channel. Submarines operating in the South-Western Approach continued to make occasional attacks on shipping off Land's End and the Lizard, but for several months subsequent to April 8th no vessel was molested between Start Point and the Downs. The net barrage in the Straits had proved its efficacy. At the beginning of the month U 32, under one of the ablest of the German submarine commanders, was caught in the nets while endeavouring to enter the Channel, and though she succeeded in escaping destruction, the German Admiralty were sufficiently impressed by the report of her experiences to forbid further attempts to enter the Channel from the North Sea. The effect of this order was to exclude the German submarines from the Channel as a whole, for their fuel supply was too small to permit of their passing far up the Channel from the West and returning by the North-about route.

Thus, though an increasing number of submarines were reported, at the end of April, to be passing North-about, the steps taken to protect shipping had met with a large measure of success, and, as the defensive organisation improved, good hopes might be entertained of setting bounds to the new attack on commerce. The results which it had hitherto attained, though considerable in themselves, fell far short of the wholesale destruction which had been foretold by the enemy. During the whole period from February 18th to April 30th the losses of British shipping through submarine attack, amounted to

ARMING OF MERCHANTMEN

39 steamers of 105,000 tons—about two-thirds of the tonnage sunk by surface cruisers during the two months of September and October, when the EMDEN and KARLSRUHE were at the height of their activity. Moreover, while 39 steamers were sunk, no fewer than 40 which were attacked by submarines reached port in safety. Of these, six sustained more or less damage, but were successfully beached or towed into port and afterwards repaired; in nine instances the torpedo missed; the other vessels attacked, with one exception, owed their escape to their own speed. These included the great majority of the larger ships. The one exception was *La Roserina*, of the British and Argentine Steam Navigation Co., one of the few liners provided with a pair of guns at the stern for self-defence. Attacked off the south of Ireland on April 17th, she had the distinction of being the first merchantman to beat off a submarine by gunfire.

The desirability of more general arming of merchantmen had, indeed, already been urged, but the question was complicated not only by the great demand made by the development of the Auxiliary Patrol on the output of the armament firms, but by doubts as to how far neutral Powers would accord to defensively-armed vessels the privileges of their ports. The only ocean-going steamers already armed were liners running to and from British ports abroad, with regard to which the diplomatic question did not arise, and those trading to the South American Republics, the Governments of which had been induced to waive their objections. Even for these the supply of guns was short, and early in April it was arranged that outward-bound Orient liners should pass their guns to homeward-bound vessels at Gibraltar in order that as many ships as possible might be armed while passing through the danger zone. The only other step in this direction taken at the time was the mounting of one 12-pr. gun in each of twenty-five Admiralty colliers and storeships carrying supplies to France, and the same number of steamers in the coasting trade. How much was possible even to an unarmed merchantman in the way of resistance and escape was shown so early as February 28th, when the *Thordis*, attacked in the Channel, ran straight for her assailant and compelled her to dive, not undamaged; nor were many similar instances wanting of the pluck and resource possessed by officers and men of the Mercantile Marine.

36 OPENING OF THE SUBMARINE CAMPAIGN

Allied shipping, as was natural from its smaller volume, suffered less severely, the total number of ships sunk being only 5 steamers and 2 sailing vessels, with a tonnage of 12,000 [1]—a smaller loss than that inflicted on Allied shipping by the KRONPRINZ WILHELM, during the same period, in her capture of the *Floride* and *Guadeloupe*. Neutrals lost rather more heavily, 10 vessels being sunk, with a total tonnage of 12,000. Of these, 3 were Norwegian,[2] 3 Swedish, 2 Dutch, 1 Greek, and 1 Portuguese. In addition, the *Belridge* was damaged.

Taking into account the disappearance of the German raiders from the trade routes, and the diminution in casualties caused by mines,[3] there was much in the position to call for congratulation, yet it had to be recognised that the new form of attack was as yet only in its initial stage, and that, owing to the ability of the submarine to operate from a home base, this attack was likely to be more vigorously and persistently sustained than the spasmodic operations of the German cruisers in distant seas. Moreover, there was ample evidence that no scruple of humanity or international law would prevent the enemy from developing the full power of their new weapon. Of the 39 British ships which had been sunk, 20 were torpedoed without warning, and several of those which escaped were attacked in the same way. In the notorious case of the *Falaba*, although a warning was given, insufficient time was allowed for the passengers and crew to take to the boats before a torpedo was fired, and 104 lives were lost in consequence. Altogether, no fewer than 231 lives were lost in British merchantmen and fishing-craft during this period, as a result of submarine attacks.

---

[1] French, 2 steamers, 2 sailing vessels; Russian, 3 steamers, one of them in the Baltic.
[2] All these were small sailing vessels.
[3] The total losses of merchant tonnage due to mines during February, March, and April were as follows:

British, 2 s.s., 4,235 tons, and 2 fishing vessels (4 steamers damaged).
Allied, 1 s.s., 1,727 tons.
Neutral, 11 s.s., 19,000 tons (1 s.s. damaged).

CHAPTER III

TONNAGE AND TRANSPORT AT THE BEGINNING OF 1915

HEAVY as were the losses of British shipping during the opening weeks of the submarine campaign, the casualties suffered were not yet on such a scale as to cause any serious alarm as to the tonnage position. During the three months February, March, and April 1915, the losses of ships entered in the War Risk Associations, including those sunk by mines, and the last few victims of the KRONPRINZ WILHELM and PRINZ EITEL FRIEDRICH, amounted to no more than 1 per cent. of the number of entered vessels, and for the whole nine months of war to April 30th, the percentage of loss was only 2·58.[1] Down to the end of March 1915, the output of new tonnage since the beginning of the war was well in excess of the total losses due either to war or to marine risks. In addition, a large number of German and Austrian vessels, captured at sea or seized in British ports at home or abroad, were now under the British flag. The tonnage available for all purposes was thus appreciably in excess of that on the Register at the outbreak of war, and though the shipbuilding output for the March quarter was less by nearly 40 per cent. than for the last three months of 1914, there was no immediate prospect of the rate of wastage increasing to such an extent as to become dangerous. Nor was there, as yet, any sign of the so-called submarine " blockade " driving many neutral ships away from British ports.

Nevertheless, an appreciable and increasing shortage of carrying power for commercial purposes was visible during

[1]

	Number s.s. lost.	Percentage of numbers entered.
6 months to January 1915	70	1·58
February	10	·23
March	24	·54
April	10	·23
	114	2·58
Heaviest month previous to April 1915, September 1914	23	·52

the early months of 1915. This shortage was due in part to the requisitioning of British vessels for naval and military employment, and in part to causes which affected British and neutral shipping alike—the redistribution of trade and the congestion of the ports. The new channels into which trade had settled by the end of 1914 involved, as a general rule, the substitution of longer for shorter voyages, with a consequent reduction in the number of voyages made in a given time. The congestion of the ports led to long delays in loading and discharge, and thus still further reduced the annual carrying power of the ships.[1]

During the earlier months of the war the requisitioning of some 20 per cent. of the ocean-going steam tonnage on the Register of the United Kingdom had been roughly balanced by the diminution in the volume of trade to be carried; but the equilibrium thus set up was dangerously unstable. By the beginning of 1915 the revival of trade on the one hand, and the diminution in effective carrying power per ton of shipping on the other, had produced an excess of demand over supply which was reflected in the rapid rise of freights to an altogether abnormal level, and had already begun to give grave concern.

To some extent the shortage in tonnage was made good during the early months of 1915 by bringing into active employment the prizes and detained vessels lying in British ports. The utilisation of these vessels had been hampered by lengthy Prize Court proceedings, especially in the Oversea Courts; but by the end of January 1915 all had been condemned or requisitioned, and those in oversea ports were being brought home by the Oversea Prize Disposal Committee, appointed in November 1914, under the chairmanship of Vice-Admiral Sir Edmond Slade, in order that they might be utilised to the best advantage. Ships which, under the Sixth Hague Convention of 1907 were subject only to detention, could not be transferred to private owners, nor could they be generally employed in foreign trade, as there were difficulties with regard to their reception in neutral ports.[2] The right of requisition, however, was unquestionable, and practically all the ships detained in home ports were ultimately employed, under the supervision of the Oversea Prize Disposal Committee,

---

[1] See Vol. I, pp. 398–405.
[2] Holland, for example, refused to receive such ships in any of her ports. See *Correspondence with the Netherlands Government* [Cd. 9026], 1918.

in coasting traffic, especially in the supply of coal to London.[1] A few of the prizes condemned by the Courts were sold outright to British firms, by whom they were employed in their ordinary trade. The remainder, together with the larger detained vessels, were either let out on time charter on Government account, for service in the trade of the Empire, or employed in the service of the Transport Department or the Dominion Governments.

Great difficulty was at first found in manning the vessels, as the supply of seamen was very short, owing to the effects of recruiting and the calling up of the Naval Reserves. This difficulty, however, was overcome by signing on neutral aliens for the ships placed in commercial employment, and by one means or another crews were found for all the available ships.

The relief thus given was very appreciable, for even those German and Austrian ships which were not directly employed in trade contributed to keep up the supply of tonnage by replacing British vessels which must otherwise have been requisitioned. Nevertheless, the demands of the Transport Department showed no tendency to decrease. Of 627 ships taken up at various times by the Transport Department and the Indian and Dominion Governments for military service, 315 had been discharged by the middle of January, but 312 were still on pay, and naval service absorbed as colliers, oilers, supply ships and auxiliaries, very nearly 800 vessels, making a total of 1,100 in naval or military employment, exclusive of prizes. This total included some 50 yachts attached to the Auxiliary Patrol, and a number of small, fast, passenger steamers employed in cross-Channel trooping; but the great majority were cargo-carriers, and of these, about 60 per cent. were drawn from the restricted pool of some 3,700 vessels of 1,600 tons gross and upwards, on which the foreign trade of the country depended.

Moreover there was, as yet, no sign that the limit of requisitioning had been reached. The strength of the armies in France was steadily increasing, and apart from ships actually employed in the carriage of reinforcements and drafts, this involved a continual increase in the monthly total of foodstuffs, munitions, and equipment to be landed at French ports. The campaigns in East and West Africa were still in progress, and the Mesopotamian Expedition

[1] See Vol. I, pp. 399, 402.

was developing into an undertaking of some magnitude. To add to the strain on the Transport Department, the War Office had requested requisitioned tonnage to be provided for the carriage of 170,000 tons of coal for the Egyptian State Railways by July 31st, and the Home Office had indented for space to bring home in February 50,000 tons of sugar purchased by the Royal Commission.

The Allies, too, were beginning to press for assistance. A great part of their essential imports was already carried by British shipping, and the dependence of France on British tonnage was increased by the difficulty in manning her own ships arising from the law of *Inscrit Maritime*, which prevented the substitution of men who did not comply with its provisions for those called up on the mobilisation of the fleet. So far as possible, ships on Allied charter were exempted from Admiralty requisition, and some assistance to France in the carriage of military stores had also been given by requisitioned vessels; but no large block of requisitioned tonnage had hitherto been allocated to an Allied service. Towards the end of 1914, however, an urgent request was received from the French Government for direct help in the provision of fuel for the State Railways. The output of the French mines was seriously reduced by the German occupation of the north-eastern coalfields,[1] and it was essential that the imports from Great Britain should be maintained at the highest possible level. Now that the northern ports had been secured, and St. Nazaire was no longer choked by transports, both the cross-Channel and the Bay of Biscay traffic were again in full swing; but the reduction in British output due to enlistment of miners, the demands of the British Admiralty on the supply of Welsh fuel, and the shortage of collier tonnage caused by requisitioning reduced the amount and raised the cost of the supplies available. In view of the paramount military importance of the French State Railways, the French Government now asked that the British Admiralty should undertake both the purchase and the transport of coal for this purpose, in order to ensure a steady supply at a fixed and reasonable price.[2] Some assistance also was asked

[1] Output of coal and lignite: 1913, 40,844,218 metric tons; 1914, 29,786,505 tons; 1915, 19,908,892 tons.
[2] Coal for the French Navy had been purchased through the Admiralty Contracts Branch since the latter part of 1914, but tonnage was provided by the French themselves.

for the Nord and Est Railways, and for the French Gas Companies.

In face of these new demands, it was of the first importance that all requisitioned tonnage should be managed to the best possible advantage, in order that the necessary services should be carried on by a minimum number of ships, and in a Memorandum dated January 11th, 1915, the President of the Board of Trade suggested that expert civilian assistance should be provided for the Transport Department, with the object of avoiding any unnecessary waste. In commenting on this memorandum, the Director of Transports, Mr. Graeme Thomson, pointed out that the responsibility of the Department was limited to supplying and fitting out tonnage demanded for specific purposes by the naval and military authorities, and that it lay altogether outside its scope to decide upon the necessity of the various services demanded. This, of course, was true, and it was equally true that the employment of shipping for naval and military purposes could under no circumstances be conducted with the same regard for economic considerations as commercial traffic. Nevertheless, the work of the Transport Department had developed so far beyond anything anticipated before the war that some corresponding development of its organisation had become inevitable.

The Transport Department of the Admiralty, like so many other sections of our war organisation, had been profoundly affected by the political developments of the years immediately preceding the war. It was in 1910 that it was first asked to consider the means whereby the Expeditionary Force could be landed on the Continent in the event of the Franco-British understanding ripening into an alliance under the pressure of a European war. This was a movement on a much bigger scale than had ever been required at any one time in our military history, and it presented problems of such difficulty that, in December 1912, the War Office and Admiralty decided to call in one or two experienced shipowners to advise on the whole question of embarkation, transport, and disembarkation. They accordingly approached Mr. Lionel Fletcher, a Manager of the White Star Line, and Mr. Thomas Royden, Deputy-Chairman of the Cunard Steamship Company, with a request for assistance. After very full and careful consideration of the problem, in conjunction with representatives of the War Office and the Transport Department, these gentlemen presented, in April 1913, a detailed, confidential report, which was adopted by the Departments concerned as a working basis. During the remainder of the year, this report was under discussion and consideration, and in February 1914, an Interdepartmental Committee, under Admiral Slade, was appointed to frame working instructions for giving effect to its proposals. This Committee was still sitting when war broke out; but it had already covered the greater part of the ground, and it was possible to bring the scheme outlined in the *Royden-Fletcher Report* into immediate operation.

With the military side of that report—invaluable though this timely preparation proved in 1914—we are not here concerned; but among the questions with which it dealt was one of primary importance in the development of the shipping problem under war conditions. This question related to the manner of taking up ships for naval and military service.

In earlier wars, ships required for the carriage of troops and stores or the auxiliary services of the Army and Navy had, like the colliers and supply ships employed in time of peace, been chartered by the Transport Department in the open market. So long as the requirements of the fighting services were not too great, and reasonable notice of those requirements could be given, this method worked well enough; but the operation now contemplated was of unprecedented magnitude, and no long notice could, in the nature of things, be expected. The situation thus created was serious, for so large and sudden an addition to the demands of the freight markets must inevitably force up freights, with the result that very high rates might have to be paid for the hire of transports and auxiliaries; nor was this the only, or even the most important consideration. While the Admiralty might reasonably rely on the patriotism of shipowners to ensure that an adequate supply of tonnage should be offered, the negotiation of charters with individual shipowners could not but cause delays at a time when delay might be fatal to the success of important military operations. It was thus necessary to consider whether, in the contingencies now contemplated, it was safe to rely any longer on the old precedure, or whether the ships required should be requisitioned by virtue of the prerogative of the Crown.

THE RIGHT OF REQUISITION

The prerogative right to requisition shipping for the defence of the realm had the sanction both of ancient usage and legal authority. In mediæval times, when there was, outside the Mediterranean, little or no distinction between the trading vessel and the man of war, all naval armaments were provided mainly by the issue of writs for the arrest of merchantmen belonging to private owners; but, with the growth of differentiation between the trading and fighting fleets which began in the sixteenth century, the custom fell gradually into disuse. The cognate right to impress seamen for service in the fleet was constantly exercised until it was rendered superfluous by the creation of a permanent establishment for the naval personnel; but, after the end of the seventeenth century, the right to requisition shipping was rarely, if ever, exercised.[1]

Nevertheless, the power of the Crown to requisition British merchantmen in time of war, whether in British ports or on the high seas, remained uncontested, and was, indeed, expressly acknowledged and confirmed by the Courts on more than one occasion.[2] It was to this prerogative right that the Admiralty now turned, and the Interdepartmental Committee decided, on the advice of Messrs. Fletcher and Royden, that, in the event of war, the ships required for naval and military service should be requisitioned rather than chartered.

So high was the prerogative put that, until the decision of the House of Lords *In re a Petition of Right of De Keyser's Royal Hotel, Limited*, it was held that a subject whose property was requisitioned by the Crown for the defence of the realm had no right at common law to any compensation for the property so taken.[3] Nevertheless, it

---

[1] See M. Oppenheim. *A History of the Administration of the Royal Navy*, passim, and *Victoria County Histories: Suffolk*, vol. ii, p. 203; Leslie Scott and Alfred Hildesley, *The Case of Requisition*, Oxford, 1920, pp. 148-57.

[2] There appears to be some doubt as to how far the prerogative extended to the requisitioning of vessels otherwise than within the British Isles or the waters adjacent thereto. See Bailhache, J., in *Russian Bank for Foreign Trade v. Excess Insurance Co.*, 1918, 2 K.B., 123. The point was not fully argued in that case, but the Crown lawyers were prepared, had it been necessary, to maintain the right. Ships were "imprest and taken up" in Virginia during the seventeenth century. See *The Case of Requisition*, p. 154.

[3] See *per* Avory, J., *In re a Petition of Right*, 1915 (The "Shoreham Aerodrome" Case), 3 K.B., 649; 31 Times Law Reports, 596, and *Rex v. Broadfoot* at p. 161. For a full discussion of the whole question and the effect of the decision in the De Keyser Hotel Case, see *The Case of Requisition*.

had undoubtedly been customary from time immemorial to pay a fixed rate of hire for vessels requisitioned to serve as warships or transports,[1] and there was no intention now of departing from this practice. In the spring of 1914, Mr. Lionel Fletcher drew up for the Interdepartmental Committee, a scheme for an Arbitration Board to fix the rate of hire for various classes of ships. This scheme was adopted by the Director of Transports, and we have already seen that, in practice, vessels taken up under the Proclamation of August 3rd, 1914, were paid for at rates fixed by agreement with the shipowners themselves.[2] These rates were, at the time, sufficiently generous, and it is possible that, during the first month or two of the war, tonnage could have been obtained at equal or smaller cost by chartering on the market, though the effect on current rates of Admiralty chartering on so large a scale cannot be precisely estimated. The point of primary importance, however, was the avoidance of delay. It was essential that the Admiralty should be able in an emergency to lay their hands at a moment's notice on the ships they required, and by the decision to requisition instead of chartering, this was attained.

By the date when the Cabinet decided that the Expeditionary Force should be sent to France the Transport Department were prepared to meet the emergency. They had calculated the amount of tonnage required for the transport of each division; they had worked out their plans for embarkation and disembarkation in concert with the military authorities; they knew where to lay their hands on the ships required.

At that time the organisation of the Department was in four branches. Two of these were concerned with the actual work of requisition. The Military Executive Branch dealt with the taking up and running of tonnage for the transport of troops and military stores. The Naval Executive Branch was responsible for vessels required by the Admiralty as colliers, oilers, supply ships, or auxiliaries. They acted, as regards the taking up of colliers, through Messrs. Mathwins of Cardiff, the Admiralty coal agents. To assist these two branches in their work there was a third, the Naval Assistant's, charged with the supervision

---

[1] See Oppenheim, *Naval Administration*, passim, and *The Case of Requisition*, loc. cit. and Appendix G.
[2] Vol. I, p. 188.

of fitting out requisitioned vessels and their suitability for the service on which they were to be employed. It was by the Naval Assistant's Branch that the roster of vessels suitable for naval or military employment was compiled and kept up to date. Finally, the Financial Branch dealt with all accounts, claims, and estimates arising from the action of the Executive Branches. The whole staff of the Department numbered forty-four.

It was on August 5th, 1914, that the Military Branch of the Transport Department began to requisition. The despatch of the Expeditionary Force to France—decided upon at short notice and carried out under circumstances of extreme urgency—threw a heavy strain on the staff of the Department. Working at high pressure, many of them for thirty-six hours at a stretch, they succeeded in fulfilling every requirement. Meanwhile the Naval Branch were taking up ships in ever-increasing numbers as armed merchant cruisers, boarding and examination steamers, colliers, oilers, and supply vessels. Within a few weeks it became clear that the responsibilities of the Department would be far greater than had ever been contemplated in peace. Here, as everywhere, the early disasters in France dislocated the war plans and complicated every problem, by involving Great Britain in the necessity of multiplying her military commitments, while increasing rather than diminishing her naval and economic effort. The shift of base to St. Nazaire, the operations on the Belgian coast, the second shift of base back from St. Nazaire to Havre, all necessitated the continued employment of a large body of tonnage. Still greater were the demands of the Imperial Concentration which not only brought the Indian, Australian, and Canadian contingents to Europe, but involved the withdrawal of the foreign garrisons and their replacement by Territorials from home. Above all, the conception of a limited Expeditionary Force was now replaced by the vision of a constantly expanding Army on the continental scale, involving the permanent withdrawal from commerce of the ships necessary for its transport, reinforcement, and supply. All the time, too, and to a great extent as the corollary of the military developments, the demands of the Navy for colliers and auxiliaries steadily increased.

It is small cause for wonder that, in the execution of a task of such magnitude and difficulty, mistakes were made.

The demands on the Transport Department were so numerous, so urgent, and in many respects so unexpected, that the overworked and overburdened staff could but just keep pace with them and could pay little attention to commercial and economic considerations. So far as possible the ships were taken up with a minimum of disturbance to trade, but there were undoubtedly instances of special hardship. Some ships were taken up for services for which they were ill suited; some important services were unnecessarily dislocated; space was wasted and much inconvenience caused to merchants by the requisitioning of vessels with part cargoes still on board. Under more normal conditions these things might have been avoided; but tonnage, at the time, was plentiful, and military considerations were paramount. It was no small feat that every essential requirement of the military situation was fulfilled.

By the beginning of 1915, however, the situation had changed. The freight markets had begun to show a demand for tonnage in excess of the visible supply; the course of the war indicated a probable increase rather than a diminution of the naval and military demands. It was now essential that the fulfilment of those demands should be accompanied by some regard for economy in the use of carrying power. Already the Transport Department had begun to use colliers returning to this country from foreign stations for the carriage of Government stores, in order to avoid the waste of carrying power involved in long ballast voyages. In some few instances they had even released the ships temporarily to their owners, for the purpose of carrying commercial cargoes on the homeward voyage. It was obvious, however, that the whole question of economic utilisation of requisitioned tonnage was now of vital importance, and, as a result of the Report presented by the Director of Transports on Mr. Runciman's Memorandum of January 11th, the First Lord of the Admiralty desired the Fourth Sea Lord to assemble a conference of representatives from the Departments concerned, for the purpose of inquiring into the possibility of relieving the tonnage situation.

This Conference under the Fourth Sea Lord held two meetings during January 1915 at which certain minor economies were suggested, and, where these economies could be effected by direct Admiralty action, good results followed; but the relief to be obtained was restricted both by service requirements and by the limits of Admiralty jurisdiction. The Conference were of opinion that, in the early days of the war, neutral shipping, thrown out of employment by the dislocation of trade, might advantageously have been chartered at low rates for Government service; but at that time the Departments concerned had objected to the measure, and now that freights had risen to an abnormal level it could no longer be economically applied. The use of empty colliers for homeward cargoes was approved; but the long ballast voyage from South America could not always be avoided, since the South American Governments made difficulties about recognising the commercial status of ships which had been used as fleet auxiliaries. The Transport Department were, however, endeavouring to supply from this source the Home Office demand for space for 50,000 tons of sugar from Cuba.

To the Fourth Sea Lord's Conference it appeared that the actual economies which could be effected in the Government services were comparatively small, and that the only real hope of alleviating the situation lay in increasing the supply of labour at the docks and thus providing an efficient remedy for port congestion. This point had not been overlooked by the President of the Board of Trade in his Memorandum of January 11th, and a few days later its importance had been strongly urged upon him by a representative deputation of shipowners.[1] It was felt, nevertheless, that some further effort should be made to ensure that requisitioned tonnage was utilised to the best possible advantage and that every vessel which could be spared should be speedily released. The Director of Transports and his staff were already employed to the fullest extent of their powers. Although the staff had been more than doubled during the first six months of war, the strain thrown upon them by their current work was exceedingly heavy, nor, if they had the time, had they a sufficiently wide knowledge of shipping and commercial affairs to review effectively the possibilities of economy and the conflicting demands of the fighting services and the trade of the country. Even in its normal activities, the Department relied, to a great extent, upon the shipowners whose vessels it had taken. But for the alacrity with which the owners of requisitioned

[1] See Vol. I, pp. 404–5.

ships undertook, at the request of the Department, to co-operate in manning, provisioning, and to a certain extent, running the ships, the ships themselves would have been useless and the work of transport impossible. It was to the shipowners that the Government now turned for assistance in the solution of the problem with which they were faced. By a Minute of the Prime Minister, dated February 10th, 1915, three prominent owners, Mr. Thomas Royden, Mr. Ernest Glover, and Mr. Richard Holt, M.P., were appointed to assist the Director of Transports as an Advisory Committee, " to examine the employment of cargo vessels under requisition in conjunction with the Director of Transports, and to obtain the speedy release of such as could be spared."[1] The powers of the Committee were advisory only; but, by reason of the long experience and wide knowledge of shipping affairs possessed by its members, it provided the Director of Transports with the necessary machinery both for reviewing the work of the Department in connection with the tonnage situation and for supervising that work itself, especially in respect of the heavy demands now being made for the carriage of commercial cargoes.

An additional reason for the appointment of the Advisory Committee was the necessity of taking steps to equalise, so far as possible, the incidence of requisitioning as between owner and owner. In the early days of the war when the demand for shipping was slack and freights were low, the Blue Book rates for the hire of requisitioned steamers were sufficiently attractive for owners to welcome the notices of requisition; but the rapid rise in freights which set in towards the end of 1914 had already produced a complete change in the situation. The rates which free ships could obtain in the open market were far above those paid for requisitioned vessels, and an owner who had three-quarters of his fleet running in Government service at Blue Book Rates was at an obvious disadvantage compared with a business rival, half or more of whose ships

---

[1] Mr. Thomas Royden was Deputy-Chairman of the Cunard Steamship Co.; Mr. Ernest Glover was a partner in Messrs. Glover Bros., Shipowners, Ship and Insurance Brokers, London; Mr. Richard Holt, M.P., was a Director of Messrs. Alfred Holt & Co., the Blue Funnel Line, China Mutual Steam Navigation Co., and the Ocean S.S. Co. Sir Edward Hain, of the Hain Steamship Co. Ltd., Mr. F. C. Gardiner of Messrs. James Gardiner & Co., and Mr. James Groves, of Messrs. Farrar, Groves & Co., joined the Committee at a later date.

were free to compete for charters in the markets of the world. Nor was it only that the much-requisitioned owner had to see his competitors making profits which were denied to himself. If his ships were running on a fixed service, or if he were bound by forward contracts for the provision of tonnage, it was necessary for him to find other vessels as substitutes for those requisitioned. These he could only obtain by chartering at the current market rates, and the loss thus involved frequently absorbed all the profits earned by his remaining free ships.

This inequality in the incidence of requisitioning was known and regretted by the Transport Department. The two main considerations present to their minds in taking up a vessel were, naturally and properly, its character and position. The ships requisitioned were those considered most suitable for fulfilling the requirements of the various services, and most readily available to be put on service. With these considerations the interests of shipowners could not be allowed to interfere, but something might be done to equalise the demands on owners whose vessels were of roughly the same type, and to secure this, was one of the most important functions of the new Advisory Committee.

No time was lost by the Committee in entering upon its important duties. From the first its members adopted the rule that one or more of their number should be in daily attendance at the Admiralty, in order that the questions of detail arising from day to day might receive the promptest possible attention; nor were they long in laying down principles on which to deal with the broader problems of requisitioning. Their first task was to equalise, so far as possible, the incidence of the burden. For this purpose the Committee prepared tables showing in respect of each shipowner the proportion of his ships under requisition and the number of days during which each ship had been on service. In this way they were able to work out the proportion of ship-days' service performed by the fleets of each owner.[1] Armed with this evidence as to the incidence of requisitioning, they were able to advise the Director of Transports both as to the taking up of new

[1] For example, a shipowner possessing a fleet of 9 steamers, 3 of which had been continuously in service for 100 days, and an owner of 9 ships, of which 6 had been under requisition for 50 days out of the 100, would each be credited with the service of one-third of their fleet during that period.

vessels and the release of those no longer required. The suitability of the vessels remained, of course, the paramount consideration; but, as between owners of ships of approximately the same class and description, it was found possible to secure a considerable degree of equality. Ships belonging to an owner who had been over-requisitioned were the first to be released. Ships belonging to an owner who had hitherto escaped his fair share of the burden were the first to be taken. Vessels belonging to an owner with a low record of service were, from time to time, taken up in substitution for those belonging to the over-requisitioned fleets. To assist in securing this equality, a circular was sent out in April to all important shipowners, requesting them to keep the Admiralty informed of the movements of their vessels, in order that the Transport Department, being fully informed as to the position of available tonnage, might more readily adjust its demands to the size of the fleets.

It was, of course, some time before the system of " proportionate requisitioning " was fully under way, and longer still before its effects could be fully discerned; but steady progress was made, and, while nothing could prevent requisitioning from being other than a burden to the shipowner, so long as the disproportion between the earnings of " free " and requisitioned ships continued to be what it was, the greater equality obtained in the incidence of the burden removed a sense of injustice which had undoubtedly been severely felt. There were, too, other ways in which the Advisory Committee were able to bring the shipowner much needed relief. Many complaints had been made as to the requisitioning of vessels which had just been fixed for a voyage, although such vessels had previously been offered to the Transport Department and refused by them as unsuitable or not wanted. In view of the constant fluctuation in the requirements of the Departments using requisitioned tonnage and the very short notice of those requirements frequently given to the Transport Department, it was impossible altogether to prevent such occurrences; but after the establishment of the Advisory Committee this particular source of annoyance was appreciably reduced, the information obtained from owners as to the employment and position of their vessels being used, as far as possible, to secure that requisitioning should involve a minimum of dislocation.

Meanwhile, the Transport Department had been obliged to shoulder the burden of the additional demands put forward at the end of 1914. The request for assistance in the supply of fuel to the French State Railways had been acceded to by the British Government. The Contracts Branch of the Admiralty undertook the purchase of the coal, and the tonnage required for the purpose, so far as it could not be carried by the French themselves, was requisitioned by the Collier Section of the Transport Department, Naval Executive Branch. Similar arrangements were made for fulfilling the requirements of the War Office in connection with the Egyptian Railways. For Egypt three or four steamers monthly sufficed, but the supply of the French Railways was a much bigger business. When the service was fairly in working order, the shipments ran into 100,000 to 150,000 tons per month, and in every month from March onwards some thirty to fifty steamers were allocated to the service. Moreover, although the Nord and Est Railways were left to arrange their own purchases they were given the assistance of requisitioned tonnage for the carriage of the coal. Fortunately the colliers required were of the same size and type as those employed in the supply of fuel to the British Expeditionary Force, the fleet, and the naval bases. The vessels on all these services could thus be regarded as interchangeable, and diverted from one service to another according to the needs of the moment, the cargoes in readiness, and the condition of the ports.

The Home Office demand for tonnage to lift 50,000 tons of sugar was met in part by directing to Cuban ports colliers returning from the South American station, in part by sending requisitioned shipping from home ports or elsewhere. This allocation of requisitioned tonnage to the carriage of commercial cargoes marked the first step in a gradual extension of the functions of the Transport Department which was to have far-reaching effects as the war went on. At the time, the Advisory Committee were strongly opposed to the measure. They held that tonnage employed in the carriage of civil requirements could only be operated to the utmost economic advantage under the conditions of ordinary commerce, and that, while it might at times be necessary to direct shipping to lift cargoes of special importance to the national interests, the shipowners should be left free to fix their vessels on the freight markets in the ordinary way. Ships in naval and military employment could not, in any circumstances, be operated with the same regard to economic considerations as those employed in trade, and for these, the flat Blue Book rate of hire per month was a convenient and equitable method of remuneration; but the application of Blue Book rates to ordinary commercial voyages at once removed the normal stimulus to efficiency and despatch by substituting a time rate for a voyage basis of payment, and removed the ordinary economic checks on delays and inefficiency in loading, running, and discharging the ships. In face of this opposition the Home Office held strongly to their demand. In the early days of the war the Sugar Commission had been able to secure tonnage from Java at a low rate of freight by centralising the chartering through Messrs. A. Holt & Co; but, now that freights had risen, it was obvious that, if tonnage were fixed on the freight markets to lift the West Indian supplies, much higher rates would have to be paid, and the Commission were apprehensive as to the effect on prices in the United Kingdom. Thus Government purchase of the supplies led directly to the demand for carriage of the cargoes in requisitioned tonnage, and as the claims of the Home Office were backed by the Transport Department itself, the Cabinet decided in their favour. From this time onwards all sugar [1] imports were carried at Blue Book rates with the exception of a few cargoes in chartered neutrals, and as the season advanced, the Department was required to find tramp tonnage or to requisition space on liners for the imports from the United States and British West Indies, Java, Mauritius, and South America, as well as for large further supplies from Cuba itself.

Although the Committee thus opposed the carriage of commercial cargoes at Blue Book rates, they were keenly alive to the desirability of avoiding the waste of carrying power involved in the return of requisitioned ships to this country in ballast. With their co-operation and, to a great extent, on their initiative, the system of " tem-

---

[1] Sugar from South America was carried mainly by liners; from the West Indies and Mauritius mainly by requisitioned tramps. Liners carried part of the Java crop, but the greater proportion was lifted by tramps. The Netherlands Government raised no objection to the employment for this purpose of ships which had previously acted as Admiralty colliers, so long as they were unarmed. (See *Correspondence with the Netherlands Government* [Cd. 9026], 1918.)

porary release" which had already been tentatively applied to a few ships, was greatly extended during the spring of 1915. Under this system, ships which had completed an outwards voyage on Government service and were not required for such service on the homeward run, were released to their owners in the foreign port subject to stipulations as to service and redelivery. The usual stipulations were that the ship should be redelivered to the Transport Department for further Government service by a certain date, and that on the homeward voyage she should lift cargo of a particular description. It was mainly to colliers returning from the Mediterranean that this system was, at first, applied. The Spanish ore trade was, at that time, in some disfavour with shipowners, as the freights then ruling and the conditions of the trade rendered it unremunerative in comparison with other branches of commerce. So averse were both British and neutral owners from the traffic that manufacturers of munitions found it difficult to procure as much ore as they required, and in view of the constantly expanding demands of the Army, the position was serious. It was to a great extent by the system of "temporary releases" that the problem was solved. Colliers which had taken coal to the Mediterranean depôts were released to their owners at Malta, Alexandria, or Port Said, on condition that they were fixed for a return voyage from the Spanish ore ports, and redelivered to the Transport Department on completing discharge of the ore in this country. As the current rates, though low in comparison with other trades, were substantially above Blue Book rates, the owners were usually glad enough to take advantage of the opportunity. If they refused, as occasionally happened, the vessel was continued on requisition and the Transport Department itself sub-chartered the vessel to ore importers at the current market rate.

While the Advisory Committee were thus doing their utmost to equalise the incidence of requisitioning and to ensure the best possible use of requisitioned tonnage, the Transport Department was obliged to meet a new and serious extension of the military demand. About the middle of February the Director of Transports was informed that he must be prepared to provide tonnage for the troops sent out to occupy the Dardanelles defences after the expected reduction of the forts by the fleet. There was, at the time, no anticipation that the expedition would involve a prolonged campaign on a large scale; but during March and April the Royal Naval Division, the 29th Division, and the 2nd Mounted Division were sent out, and for this movement forty-seven vessels of some size had to be allocated. Thus the movement of the divisions, together with the necessary provision of supply and hospital ships, and of the additional colliers necessitated by the naval concentration at the Dardanelles, constituted an appreciable addition to the drain on the shipping resources of the country. Those resources were, as yet, far from exhausted, but the emergence of so considerable and so unexpected a demand showed how legitimate was the anxiety of the Board of Trade, and how timely were the measures taken to ensure economy in the use of requisitioned tonnage.

CHAPTER IV

THE PROBLEM OF IMPORT DISTRIBUTION
TO MAY 1915

IN view of the new demands which the Transport Department had to meet, there was little hope of a reduction in the total number of ships on service. Any economies which might be effected were bound to be offset by the additional commitments undertaken, and the utmost that could be hoped was that the total tonnage withdrawn from commercial employment might not be greatly increased. Even this was most uncertain, and it was proportionately desirable to take every possible measure for securing that the tonnage left in commercial employment should be utilised to the full extent of its maximum carrying power. Had the diminution in imports received corresponded to the decrease in tonnage entered, the effects of requisitioning would already have been reflected in a serious shortage of supplies; but the weight of cargoes carried per 100 tons of shipping entered was still rising, and in April showed an increase of no less than 40 per cent. on the figures of the same month of the previous year.

So far all was well, but though ships were carrying heavier cargoes than in time of peace, they were not, unfortunately, making so many voyages in a given time. To some extent this was inevitable, since supplies formerly obtained from the Continent had now to be brought from more distant sources; but the increased average length of voyages was not the only factor. Of equal, perhaps of greater importance, was the reduction in the time spent at sea, caused by delays in port.

To the Fourth Sea Lord's Conference, as we have seen, the question of port congestion appeared to be the most important of all which concerned the supply of tonnage, and the one whose solution would contribute most effectively to restoring the equilibrium between supply and demand. It was indeed no new factor in the situation. From a very early period of the war the congestion of the French ports had involved a serious reduction in the carrying power of all vessels taking coal to France or stores for the British Expeditionary Force, and by the winter of 1915 the effects of congestion were hardly less noticeable in the ports of the United Kingdom itself.[1]

The full extent of the danger was not as yet widely appreciated. The voyage between port and port, though it forms only one link in the chain of communication between the foreign producer and the consumer in this country, is so much the most obvious and easily comprehended that the other links, equally essential, are apt to be overlooked. In the study of war problems before 1914 it was the protection of the ocean voyage and the encouragement of shipping to which attention had been chiefly directed. This had in large measure been secured by the naval dispositions, the Admiralty instructions to shipping, and the State Insurance Scheme. The problem of maintaining the flow of supplies had to a great extent been solved; but to make those supplies effective, rapid distribution from the ports was also necessary.

This problem, too, had been the subject of investigation before the war, though its consideration had been mainly confined to a particular aspect of the question which did not, in fact, arise in an acute form until a comparatively late period of the struggle. It was in January 1909 that the question was first officially raised. In that month Sir Frederic Bolton, a shipowner, underwriter, and insurance broker, who had been Chairman of Lloyd's in 1906, wrote to the Prime Minister, Mr. Asquith, drawing attention to various aspects of the probable effect of war on oversea trade, and in particular to the possibility that the traffic of some of the principal ports might be temporarily suspended, or diverted to other ports, whose capacity to receive and distribute it was uncertain. This letter was referred by Mr. Asquith to the Committee of Imperial Defence, who were seriously impressed by the possible danger arising from a total or partial stoppage of trade, especially at London and the East Coast ports, and considered it desirable to investigate the capacity of ports on the South and West Coasts to deal with the diverted traffic. They accordingly requested Sir Frederic Bolton to undertake a general inquiry into the volume of traffic

[1] Vol. I, pp. 197, 287, 361, 399–405.

passing through the principal ports of the United Kingdom, the means by which it was distributed, and the extent and population of the areas served by the ports.

Such an inquiry was the very point at which Sir Frederic had been aiming, and he readily undertook the task. The Defence Committee accordingly placed him in touch with the Admiralty, who recognised the importance of the investigation, and detailed Captain T. H. Hawkins, R.M.L.I., to assist in carrying out a preliminary inquiry.

The first result of their investigations was to reveal the complexity and magnitude of the task undertaken. The official statistics of imports at each port gave weights for the majority of the articles, but in a large number of classes values only were shown, and in each such instance it was necessary to estimate the weights. Statistics for the coasting trade, which played a most important part in the work of distribution, and formed a large proportion of the total volume of traffic at many of the ports, were exceedingly imperfect. In the absence of tabulated statistics, the investigation into the Port of London alone involved the examination of 28,000 separate transires for the year 1908, and, even then, a very large proportion of the weights had to be estimated. In addition to the volume of traffic, it was necessary to investigate the accommodation, equipment, and labour supply of the ports, their facilities for distribution by road, railway, river, or canal, and the extent to which these facilities would enable them to handle a large volume of trade, or to serve more distant centres of population than those to which they were accustomed.

By the end of 1909 Sir Frederic Bolton had become convinced that a position of greater authority and the provision of an adequate staff were essential to the successful prosecution of his task. On December 7th he presented a short interim report, recording the progress made and the difficulties encountered, and asked to be placed in a position to continue the work effectively.

This interim report was referred by the Prime Minister to a small Sub-Committee of the Committee of Imperial Defence, under the chairmanship of Lord Esher, who reported in March 1910 that the inquiry ought to be continued under the immediate supervision of the Committee itself. Accordingly, a further Sub-Committee was appointed under the chairmanship of Colonel J. B. Seely, then Under-Secretary for War, to consider and advise on "the local transportation and distribution of supplies in time of war." Sir Frederic Bolton became a member of this Sub-Committee, and Captain (now Major) Hawkins was appointed Secretary.

After a prolonged investigation Colonel Seely's Sub-Committee presented a Report in August 1911. For the purpose of their investigation they divided the United Kingdom into twenty-one areas grouped around the leading ports, and for each of these areas they compiled statistics showing the estimated population, the value and estimated weight of imports, exports, and re-exports, the interchange of commodities with other areas, coast-wise or by rail, and the local home production of some of the principal foodstuffs. In respect of three of these areas, covering London and the greater part of the East Coast, they had completed an exhaustive inquiry into consumption, supplies, means of distribution, and the possibility of maintaining adequate supplies through substituted ports. Their report indicated that any extensive diversion of traffic would throw a great strain on the railway facilities of the country, and that unless " special preparations for the general transit of supplies, and for proper distribution of necessaries " were made in time of peace, the dislocation caused by war might be extremely serious. For this reason they recommended that a permanent Sub-Committee of the Committee of Imperial Defence should be appointed to consider the whole question of " the despatch, transport, receipt, and distribution of supplies and production in time of war," and should use the materials contained in their own Report and its Appendices as the basis of continued detailed investigation.

The next step was taken in November 1911, when the Standing Sub-Committee of the Committee of Imperial Defence, under the chairmanship for this purpose of Colonel Seely, was directed to inquire into " the probable extent to which the demands of the civil population, and of the naval and military services, will require mutual adjustment in the event of any dislocation of the normal routes of supply of food and raw material." The Report of the Sub-Committee, dated June 20th, 1912, dealt entirely with the arrangements for the control of railways, and recommended the appointment, on the outbreak of war, of an Executive Committee of Railway Managers under the

Board of Trade. This recommendation was on the lines of a proposal contained in the Report of the previous Sub-Committee, and was followed, in 1914, in the appointment of the Railway Executive Committee.

In August 1912 a Sub-Committee under the chairmanship of the Rt. Hon. Walter Runciman, President of the Board of Trade, was instructed to take up a particular section of the further inquiry recommended by Colonel Seely's Committee in 1911. Among the points submitted to their consideration were the probable diversion of shipping from the East Coast ports in the event of war with Germany, and the capacity of ports on the South and West Coasts to handle such diverted traffic.

The work involved was heavy, and it was not until February 1914 that the Sub-Committee presented its Report. Its effect, when presented, was to emphasise the necessity for further study of the question, as in making their recommendations, the Sub-Committee stated that they had " no means of judging whether the railways are capable of dealing with the additional trade which might be transferred to the western ports." They had accumulated valuable material as to the actual accommodation and equipment of the ports, but before the problem of internal distribution could be regarded as definitely solved, it was still necessary to obtain more detailed information with regard to the requirements of various definite areas, the interchange of commodities between them, and the transport facilities by which they were served.

It was obvious that further investigation was required, and the Sub-Committee accordingly recommended that the Board of Agriculture and Fisheries should be asked to obtain fuller information as to the seasonal stocks of foodstuffs, that further consideration should be given to the problem of London's food supply, and that the Board of Trade should ask the Railway Communication Board to report as to the capacity of the railways to handle additional traffic from the West Coast ports. Further, they proposed that a General Manager at each of the principal South and West Coast ports should be requested by the Board of Trade to form plans for the expansion of its trade in time of war, and the co-ordination of increased commercial traffic with the demands of the Admiralty and War Office. They also recommended the appointment of a small permanent Committee, including representatives of the Admiralty, Board of Trade, Lloyd's, and shipowners, to consider questions relating to the diversion of shipping from East Coast ports.

Thus, although the Report of Mr. Runciman's Sub-Committee was, like that of Mr. Huth Jackson's Sub-Committee on War Risks, timely in its presentation, it was not like the Insurance Report a complete and final solution of the problem with which it dealt, and war broke out, unfortunately, before there was time either to complete the further investigations which were required before such a solution could be reached, or to complete the organisation by which it could be carried into effect.

It is true that the problem of distribution, as it was actually presented in the early stages of the war, was not complicated by the existence of such extreme emergency as had been assumed for purposes of inquiry. There was no question of London and the East Coast ports being closed completely by enemy action. The navigation of the Thames and Humber was impeded by minefields and by the restrictions arising from the examination service and measures of port defence [1]; Harwich and Immingham were partly closed by their use as naval bases [2]; and in December 1914 the closing of the Firth of Forth above the bridge diverted the traffic of Grangemouth and Bo'ness [3]; but there was nothing approaching a blockade of the Thames or a general suspension of trade on the East Coast. On the other hand, the general dislocation caused by war demands on the facilities of the ports was far greater than had been contemplated. In their estimate of the probable situation the Sub-Committee had taken account of the strain thrown on the railways and ports by the coaling of the fleet in home waters, by reservists joining their ships and units, by the mobilisation and despatch of the Expeditionary Force, and by the mobilisation of Territorial divisions for home defence. On this calculation the period of acute strain was expected to be very short, and the Sub-Committee were of opinion that the supply of drafts and stores to the Expeditionary Force after its despatch would be only a minor factor in the situation.

Here, as in every other department of war activity, the

[1] Vol. I, pp. 187, 280.   [2] Ibid., p. 280.   [3] Ibid., p. 358.

whole situation was profoundly changed by the results which followed the opening moves of the war on land. Within the first two months of the war the scope of the British military effort was indefinitely extended. By the end of September 1914 orders had been issued for the raising of no less than eighteen new divisions; nor could even this be regarded as a final limit. The outlying garrisons were on their way home for service in France; Territorial divisions and battalions were on their way to India, Egypt, and the oversea bases, to replace the troops withdrawn; the first Canadian contingent was about to embark for the United Kingdom, there to train for service in France.

This extension of Great Britain's military obligations had a direct and important bearing on the problem of internal distribution of supplies. In raising the new armies an appeal was made to the patriotism of the workers to which they readily responded, and in those days of stress the future course of the war was not foreseen with sufficient clearness for any check to be placed on that response, in the interests of essential industries. Railway men and transport workers were freely enlisted, and at some of the larger ports a large percentage of the strongest and most efficient workers were withdrawn from their employment. But the effect did not end there. Instead of merely keeping the original six divisions of the Expeditionary Force up to strength by a stream of drafts, it became necessary to reinforce them at once by every man that could be spared. In so far as the reinforcements were drawn from overseas a double strain was imposed. The troops had to be landed in Great Britain, collected at a home base, and afterwards taken to the coast and embarked for France. During the early months of 1915 the scale of reinforcements increased. The first Territorial division crossed in February; the first division of the new armies in May. But it was not only the demands of the Army in France that had to be met. In February came the decision to send troops to the Dardanelles, and by April the original conception of a purely naval attack supported by military occupation of the forts after their reduction, had given place to the scheme of a combined operation on a large scale. Thus, so far from the military strain on transport facilities ceasing to be serious after the first two or three weeks of mobilisation, it had become

62 THE PROBLEM OF IMPORT DISTRIBUTION

a permanent factor in the war, and the demands of the military authorities on the accommodation, equipment, and railway facilities of the ports tended to increase rather than to diminish.

It was not, of course, merely a question of moving troops. The new divisions had to be fed and supplied with guns, munitions, horses, motor-transport, entrenching tools, barbed wire, and all the thousand requisites of modern war. We have already seen how severe was the strain on the resources of the mercantile marine, and the pressure on the railways was hardly less serious.

Further, the needs of the Navy steadily increased. From the first the supply of the naval coaling bases involved a large amount of additional coal haulage, which was greatly increased by the necessity of accumulating stocks for bunkering transports at Avonmouth and other ports used in the despatch of troops. To this had to be added the requirements of the mine-sweepers and Auxiliary Patrols, and the rapid expansion in the number of auxiliary craft soon rendered this addition to the naval demands a very serious factor in the situation. So far as possible the auxiliary bases were supplied from the nearest coal port; but the problem was complicated by the fact that the various classes of auxiliaries required to be supplied with coal of the same kind as they had been accustomed to burn in time of peace. The Grand Fleet and destroyer flotillas, the armed merchant cruisers of the Tenth Cruiser Squadron, the trawlers and drifters of the Auxiliary Patrol, had to be dealt with as separate services.

While the coal supply of the auxiliaries added to the strain on the railways, the provision of base accommodation for the patrols, mine-sweepers, boarding and examination steamers, made a heavy demand on port accommodation. Further, as the submarine campaign developed, the requirements of port defence and of the examination service imposed greater and greater restrictions on navigation in the approaches to the ports. As the control of enemy trade grew more and more stringent, the number of berths and quays occupied by ships and cargoes brought in as prizes or for examination steadily increased.

This was a serious matter, for these steamers and their cargoes tended to occupy berth and quay space for long periods. Even if only a small part of the cargo was contraband, it was frequently necessary to unload the greater part of the innocent cargo in order to get at the goods to be seized. The whole operation of unloading and reloading frequently took three or four weeks, during which time the berth occupied by the steamer together with a considerable space on the quays or in the transit sheds was withdrawn from commercial employment. Moreover, when suspicious cargo was once landed, there was a tendency for it to remain a long time in the ports, awaiting either the final judgment of the Prize Court, or a favourable moment for sale. Ships, too, which were awaiting the result of Prize Court proceedings were sometimes allowed to occupy space in the docks for weeks after their discharge, though vessels with valuable cargoes were awaiting berths.

Another unexpected factor in the situation was the steady diminution of coasting traffic. Not only were a large number of coasting steamers requisitioned for collier or other service, but the decision of the Government to prohibit any advance in railway rates placed the owners of coasters at a grave disadvantage. Increased working expenses combined with the effects of requisitioning to send up coasting freights, and the cost of insurance against war risks both for hulls and cargoes bore heavily on coasting traffic. With these additional charges added to the normal freights they were greatly hampered in competing for traffic against railways which were still carrying goods at antebellum rates. We have seen that the latter months of 1914 were marked by a serious decline in the volume of coasting traffic as compared with the previous year,[1] and by April 1915 this decrease amounted to over 25 per cent. The result was that additional traffic was thrown on to the railways, already barely able to cope with the volume to be carried, and the ports were blocked by accumulations of goods which should normally have been distributed by coaster, and which the railways were unable to handle.

Thus the actual problem to be solved was not the wholesale transference of trade from East to West Coast ports, but the more general problem of maintaining the even flow of trade through ports whose accommodation, equipment, supply of labour, and facilities for distribution had, in many instances, been seriously impaired. But the

[1] Vol. I, p. 402.

64 THE PROBLEM OF IMPORT DISTRIBUTION

problem was complicated by a redistribution of trade which, though it was less drastic than had at one time been contemplated, was sufficiently serious. For, apart from the closing, or partial closing, of Southampton, Newhaven, Dover, Harwich, Grangemouth, Bo'ness, and a number of minor ports, there was a general shifting of trades from the smaller to the larger ports, due to the replacement of the nearer by more distant sources of supply and the consequent increase in the average size of vessels employed in the import trade. Even in time of peace twelve great ports—London, Liverpool, Hull, Glasgow, Cardiff, Manchester, Bristol, Newcastle, Leith, Grimsby, Southampton, and Dundee—handled 69 per cent. by weight of the total imports, or, if ore and timber be excluded, 80 per cent. This proportion was now increased; Southampton was practically closed to ocean traffic, but the others, especially London and the four great West Coast ports, Liverpool, Glasgow, Manchester, and Bristol, had now to receive much of the long-distance traffic substituted for the continental trade formerly carried on by the smaller ports. The total volume of imports was, it is true, reduced; but this reduction was due in large part to decreased arrivals of timber, of which these ports normally received only a small percentage. Moreover, the West Coast ports were in truth unable to deal effectively with even the normal volume of traffic. The establishment of the military Home Supplies Depôt at Avonmouth, the use of Liverpool as a base for the armed merchant cruisers of the Northern Patrol, the demands of the Transport Department on Avonmouth, London, and Liverpool, the depletion of the labour staff, appliances, tugs, rolling stock, lorries, horses and carts at all the ports, and the decrease in coasting traffic, seriously impaired their power of rapid distribution.

The evil of this concentration of trade at the larger West Coast ports was increased by the obstacles imposed by war conditions to the regularity of its flow. The shifting of the sources of supply of many bulky commodities tended to shift the periods of greatest pressure in respect of such articles; the disturbed financial conditions abroad and the operations of the enemy's cruisers and submarines led to irregularity in arrivals. The arrivals of sugar cargoes afford a striking instance of the effect of redistribution of trade. During August and September 1914 comparatively few cargoes arrived owing to the cessation of imports from the Continent, but during the autumn West Indian and Java sugar was received in large quantities, and in the winter months the heavy purchases made by the Royal Sugar Commission with a view to building up stocks in this country came to hand. For the four months October to January inclusive, the sugar imports amounted to 943,000 tons, as against 692,000 in the same period of 1913–14—an increase of 251,000 tons, or over 36 per cent. Unfortunately the Government sugar purchases went into consumption very slowly. The Royal Commission considered it inadvisable to sell until the stocks previously imported by private buyers at a lower rate had been worked off, and in the meantime their purchases made a serious demand on the storage capacity of the ports. The Transport Department, who were alive to the necessity of clearing the ports, urged that the sugar should be removed to inland distributing centres, but this the Commission declared themselves unable to do, owing to labour and railway difficulties. They held, moreover, that the farther inland the cargoes were brought, the greater would be the amount of unnecessary haulage due to inevitable error in distribution. The inland storage available was, in fact, small. In the ordinary way, sugar passed rapidly into consumption, and now that imports were, temporarily, so much in excess of the normal, the accumulations contributed very materially to the blocking of the ports.

The conditions were, naturally, worst at ports such as Liverpool, which were built and equipped for the purpose of rushing through imported food and materials as quickly as possible to inland centres. Though Liverpool in 1913 handled 13·8 per cent. by weight of the total imports of the United Kingdom, only 4·2 per cent. of the total population lived within a fifteen-mile radius of the port. It was pre-eminently a through transit port for the great industrial district of southern Lancashire, and had little storage capacity in comparison with the volume of traffic. Thus, when distribution was hampered by the effect of naval and military demands on labour, accommodation, and equipment, the shortage of railway trucks, and the irregular flow of trade, the storage facilities were speedily exhausted. The worst result of this congestion was the accumulation of goods in the transit sheds, owing to the impossibility of finding warehouse space to which they could be removed. These sheds are an indispensable part of the equipment of a port built for a liner trade. The tramp with a whole cargo of ore or grain can discharge direct into the trucks or silos; but the typical liner cargo consists of a great number of parcels of many kinds of goods for many consignees, and before they can be forwarded these parcels must be sorted and checked. It is for this purpose that the transit sheds are provided, and if they are piled high with goods for purposes of storage, the work of sorting and checking becomes difficult and slow, and distribution from the port is blocked. In their 1914 Report the Standing Sub-Committee of the Committee of Imperial Defence referred to the congestion of the transit sheds as the greatest difficulty likely to arise at Liverpool in any period of strain, and their forecast was now abundantly justified both there and at all ports doing a big liner trade. Discharge was retarded, and newly arrived vessels had to wait many days before a berth for them could be cleared.

It was this specialisation in the trade of the ports which rendered substitution so difficult. The great coal and ore ports on the Bristol Channel were now doing considerably less than their normal trade, but they were ill-equipped for dealing with general traffic. They had abundant facilities for loading coal cargoes, or for receiving ore direct into trucks and timber into lighters, but they had no sufficient provision of transit sheds for dealing with a large liner traffic, few silos for the reception of grain, and little cold storage accommodation for meat and dairy produce. Nor had they the warehouse accommodation which would enable them to give much relief to London, the greater part of whose imports were absorbed by the dense population clustered round the port, and required ample storage space from which deliveries could be made direct to the merchant. At the smaller coal, ore, and timber ports these limitations were even more severely felt. Many other minor ports were suffering from the diminution of the continental traffic; but the extent to which they could be used for ocean traders was limited by the size of vessel they could take, their accommodation and equipment, their supply of labour, and the scanty housing accommodation for imported workers. Moreover, extensive diversions in any direction were prohibited by the difficulty, in the congested state of the railways, of supplying any area from ports at a much greater distance than those by which it was ordinarily served.

Had the detailed investigation of the system of internal distribution begun by the Seely Committee been completed, or had there been time for the implications of the 1914 Report to be thoroughly digested, much of the trouble might probably have been avoided; but the outbreak of war followed so closely on the presentation of the Report that there had been no time for completion of the inquiries, and the machinery for co-ordinating naval, military, and commercial demands was still imperfect.

By January 1915 the Board of Trade were, as we have seen, becoming alarmed as to the effect of port congestion, and their anxiety was shared by the Director of Transports and by the Admiralty.[1] It was felt still more strongly by the shipowners, and in their Memorandum to Mr. Runciman of January 22nd[2] they emphasised very strongly the need for remedial measures. Their chief proposals were four in number. First, the trucks belonging to all the railway companies should be pooled in order to avoid unnecessary journeys of empties. Secondly, the naval and military requirements for port accommodation, railway facilities, tugs, barges, and appliances should be carefully reviewed, and, if possible, cut down. Thirdly, the use of quays and transit sheds for storage purposes should be forbidden, and the prompt removal of cargoes enforced by penal rents. Fourthly, inquiries should be made from each port as to the sufficiency or otherwise of the available labour supply.

During the same month the Committee for the Diversion of Shipping also turned its attention seriously to the consideration of port problems. This Committee was appointed by the Admiralty in accordance with the recommendation made by the Sub-Committee of 1912, for the purpose of directing such diversion of shipping as might be necessary owing to the state of hostilities with Germany, and the dangers of navigation in the North Sea. Its Chairman was Vice-Admiral Sir Edmond Slade, a member of the 1912 Committee, and its Secretary, Major T. H. Hawkins, the officer originally deputed by the Admiralty to assist Sir Frederic Bolton in his investigations, and subsequently appointed Secretary to the Seely Committee. Sir Frederic Bolton himself was a member of the Diversion

[1] *Supra*, p. 47.   [2] Vol I, p. 404 and *supra*, p. 47.

68 THE PROBLEM OF IMPORT DISTRIBUTION

Committee, which also included representatives of the Admiralty, War Office, Board of Trade, Committee of Imperial Defence, and the leading shipowners' organisations.[1]

Almost from the first the Diversion Committee became involved in work which differed considerably from that for which it was originally appointed. Ships bound for German ports, or ports in the danger zone, and ships carrying contraband cargoes to countries contiguous to Germany were promptly and easily diverted by the cruisers at sea, or through the instructions communicated to Lloyd's and the War Risks Clubs. The State Insurance Scheme enabled the Government to control the movement of shipping and prevent vessels from sailing on unsafe or undesirable voyages. No general transference of trade from the East Coast ports proved to be necessary. A small special Committee under the Board of Trade was set up to deal with British or neutral ships diverted on the ground of contraband cargo, for the purpose of securing their speedy release, and thus preventing the blocking of the ports. A large part of the Committee's work was thus gone, and it possessed no executive powers over any vessels other than those brought in by the naval patrols and coming under the jurisdiction of the Admiralty Marshal. On the other hand, the strength and representative character of the Committee enabled it to make effective representations on many shipping questions

---

[1] Composition of the Committee:
  Vice-Admiral Sir E. J. W. Slade, K.C.I.E., K.C.V.O. (Chairman).
  Captain Richard Webb, C.B., R.N., Admiralty.
  Brig.-Gen. S. S. Long, C.B., subsequently replaced by Brig.-Gen. A. R. Crofton Atkins, C.M.G., War Office.
  Lt.-Col. Sir M. P. A. Hankey, K.C.B., Secretary, Committee of Imperial Defence.
  Mr. H. Booth, Board of Trade.
  Sir Frederic Bolton, Lloyd's.
Liverpool and London War Risks Insurance Association:
  Sir Alfred A. Booth, Bart.
  Capt. H. A. Sanderson, R.N.R.
  Sir Norman Hill.
London Group War Risks Association:
  Sir Edward Hain.
  Mr. Howard Houlder.
  Mr. H. R. Millar.
Newcastle Group War Risks Association:
  Mr. A. Ritson.
  Mr. J. H. Warrack.
  Mr. Stanley Todd.
    Major T. H. Hawkins, R.M.L.I., Secretary.

THE DIVERSION COMMITTEE

outside its original terms of reference. During the first six months of the war it advised the Admiralty and the Government on such matters as the premiums fixed under the State Insurance Scheme, the voyages to be excluded from the operation of that Scheme on the ground of undue risks, instructions for deviation, and routes, and the prevention of trading with the enemy. In general, it acted as a link between the Government and the shipowners in all questions affecting British shipping.

Closely in touch as they were with every department of the shipping industry, the members of the Committee could not fail to observe with anxiety the growing congestion of the ports, and in January 1915 Major Hawkins was instructed to proceed in person to the chief West Coast ports and report on their position. During that month he visited Bristol, Liverpool, and Manchester; and during February, Glasgow, Greenock, Ardrossan, Silloth, Barrow, Maryport, Fleetwood, and the remaining Bristol Channel ports. His reports dealt in great detail with the equipment, labour supply, and class of trade at each port, the nature and extent of the naval and military demands, the condition of the warehouses and transit sheds, and the possibilities of relieving existing congestion or handling additional traffic. In addition to special recommendations relating to each port they contained a number of general suggestions some of which, at a later period, were to bear important fruit. Among the points dealt with were the removal of Government sugar to inland storage centres, the erection of temporary sheds for Government purposes in order to relieve the strain on the permanent accommodation of the ports, and special rates for war risks insurance on coasting vessels. The most important recommendations, however, were three in number.

Two of these, the pooling of railway trucks and the imposition of penalty rents for cargoes not promptly removed, were on the same lines as suggestions made by the shipowners in their Memorandum of January 22nd, 1915. The suggestion as to penal rents was the more important as in a time of rising prices there was a strong temptation for merchants to leave cargoes on the quays until sold, in order to save the cost of double handling and of warehousing away from the quays.

The third point related to the organisation of dock labour.

Large as was the number of men recruited for military service, it was not actual shortage of labour which was the greatest difficulty. The organisation of employment at the ports was bad, and the casual nature of much of the work did not tend to efficiency, especially now that so many of the strongest and most skilful workers had enlisted. In order to raise the status of the workers and to enable them to feel that by remaining in their normal employment they were serving their country as effectively as if they were fighting, Major Hawkins proposed a simple declaration of service and the issue of a special badge. The greatest difficulty of all, however, arose from the fluctuating demand for labour at the ports, and the difficulty of transferring labour from one port to another to meet the fluctuations of demand. Not only did transfer on a large scale raise the possibility of trouble with the workers at the ports affected, but there were many practical difficulties in the way of housing, organisation, and the selection of the right moment for transfer and return. Major Hawkins suggested, therefore, that a small corps of workers should be enlisted as soldiers for Home Defence only, with an obligation to perform transport work on occasion at seriously congested ports. Such a body would form a mobile, central reserve of labour which could be directed to any port in time of emergency, and if it was made clear that it would be used only for supplementing existing labour when clearly necessary, and not to compete with that labour or for the purpose of strike-breaking, it need not come into conflict with Labour interests.

In the meantime, the President of the Board of Trade had appointed a Committee " to consider and recommend the adoption by the various dock authorities in Great Britain, either separately or in co-operation, of such measures as appear best calculated to remove or diminish the existing congestion in the docks and to deal with the traffic of the ports in the public interest in the most expeditious and advantageous manner possible." With the exception of the Chairman, Lord Inchcape, and the Secretary, Sir Frederick Dumayne, this Committee was composed entirely of representatives of the Dock Authorities at the principal ports.[1] In so far as questions

[1] The composition of the Board of Trade Committee on Congestion at Ports was as follows: Lord Inchcape, G.C.M.G., K.C.S.I., Chairman; Mr. J. G. Broodbank, Lord Devonport, and Mr. H. T. Moore, London; Mr. Alfred Chandler and Sir Helenus R. Robertson, Liverpool; Mr.

relating to the facilities provided by the Dock Authorities were concerned, the Committee was very strong; but its ability to deal with the general problem of port congestion was limited by the fact that, with the exception of the Chairman, it contained no representative of the other interests concerned in or using the ports. Moreover, the extent to which the Dock Authorities controlled the labour and facilities employed in the discharge of the ships and the transport of goods to and from the quays varied very widely as between port and port. Thus, the Port Authority at Manchester owned a large proportion of the storage accommodation, and was the sole employer of the transport workers employed on the quays. In London the Port Authority owned a substantial part of the warehouse accommodation and employed a large, but not the larger part, of the labour. At Liverpool the Port Authority controlled less than 12 per cent. of the storage accommodation ; 85 per cent. of the whole traffic of the port was worked over quays rented from the Authority by the shipowners, and hardly any of the labour was employed by the Authority.

For these reasons the Committee on the Diversion of Shipping, while welcoming the appointment of Lord Inchcape's Committee, felt it incumbent upon them to continue their own investigations. Major Hawkins's Reports on the West Coast ports were adopted by the Committee, and copies were sent to the Board of Trade Committee. They were also forwarded through the Admiralty, to the Committee of Imperial Defence, with a Memorandum calling attention to the need of executive action to relieve the position.

As a result of this step Admiral Slade, the Chairman of the Diversion Committee, was requested to talk over the matter with Lord Inchcape, and it was finally decided by the Board of Trade Committee to ask the various Government Departments using the ports to accept Sir Frederick Dumayne as an independent expert to advise on the economical utilisation of the space and facilities requisitioned for Government service. They also made certain recommendations with regard to the working of the ports,

Ernest Latimer, Manchester; Mr. D. Shields, Glasgow; Mr. D. Ross Johnson, Bristol; Mr. C. S. Denniss, Cardiff; Sir Sam Fay, Immingham; Mr. E. C. Geddes, Hull; Mr. W. J. Noble, Newcastle; Mr. P. J. Pringle, Leith; Mr. J. Hannay Thompson, Dundee; Sir Herbert A. Walker, Southampton; Sir Frederick G. Dumayne, Secretary.

the most important of which was that a small working Committee should be established at each of the larger ports to co-ordinate the requirements of the various departments and interests concerned. This recommendation, however, was not adopted, and, though various minor improvements were effected, no immediate step was taken to deal with the larger problems of congestion.

During April, Major Hawkins, on behalf of the Diversion of Shipping Committee, visited and reported on the North-Eastern ports from Dundee to the Humber, where the conditions differed widely from those on the West Coast. The trade of these ports had greatly decreased as a result of the war, and the greatest difficulty arose from the number of prize and diverted vessels to be dealt with. The number of such vessels was greatly increased by the Retaliation Order in Council of March 11th, and having regard to the length of time for which berths, quay space, and sheds were occupied by their cargoes, the prospect of a continued increase in the number of diversions gave grounds for considerable anxiety. The Committee accordingly recommended that all prize and diverted ships should be removed from the docks immediately after discharge; that wherever possible, cargoes the subject of Prize Court proceedings should be sold without waiting for the final judgment; and that when this was not possible, the goods should be removed to storage outside the dock premises, or stowed in temporary sheds, so as to set free the permanent storage accommodation for commercial use.

This question of the diversion of contraband cargoes was, indeed, becoming pressing. By May 7th seventy-four ships had already been sent in under the Retaliation Order, and very careful provision was needed to prevent grave interference with the ordinary traffic of the ports. Fortunately the relations between the Admiralty Marshal and the Diversion Committee were close and cordial. From the date of the Order the Marshal consulted the Committee in respect of every diverted vessel for which port accommodation was required, so that they might be sent to the ports where they could be handled with the minimum of dislocation to commercial traffic, and thanks to this co-operation, the work was accomplished without friction, and with surprisingly little difficulty.

The state of the West Coast ports, however, was

going from bad to worse, and by the beginning of May the anxiety of the Diversion Committee became acute. Large Government purchases of Indian wheat were about to arrive; much Java sugar was on its way; and nitrate to the extent of some 100,000 tons was expected within the next few months. There was thus every prospect that the strain on the larger ports would be increased rather than diminished, and on May 7th the Committee forwarded to the Admiralty, for communication to the Committee of Imperial Defence, a strong resolution urging that steps should be taken without loss of time to place the dock and transport facilities of the country under such control as would secure their use to the best advantage to meet naval, military, and commercial requirements.

For the time being, however, this resolution had no effect. The attention of the Admiralty and the Government was absorbed by the development of the submarine campaign, and the dangers arising from port congestion were themselves cloaked, to a great extent, by the success with which the volume of imports was maintained.

CHAPTER V

IMPORTS AND FREIGHTS IN THE SPRING OF 1915

DESPITE the activities of the German submarines, the volume of traffic at British ports was actually on the increase in the early months of 1915. Ever since October 1914 the monthly imports of foodstuffs had exceeded in volume those brought in during the last corresponding month of peace, and in March and April 1915 the imports of raw materials were so heavy that, for the first time since the beginning of the war, the total import weights showed a similar increase. With supplies thus pouring into the ports, it was easy to overlook the extent to which the future course of trade was prejudiced by the withdrawal of British ships from commercial employment and the clogging of the machinery of distribution, the more so as the cumulative effect of these factors took some time to become clearly manifest.

It was indeed evident that tonnage for commercial purposes was becoming short, but the effect of this shortage was felt as yet in enhanced cost of transport rather than in restriction of supplies. Space for all essential imports could still be secured, but only at a heavy price. The place of ships taken up as transports or auxiliaries had to be supplied by attracting into the trade of the United Kingdom vessels previously engaged in commerce between foreign ports, and the place of these vessels in the interforeign trade was apt to be filled by neutral steamers, hitherto engaged in British trade, unless such vessels could be retained by the offer of enhanced rates. Tonnage, whether British or neutral, required for British trade, could be procured only in competition with the demands of charterers abroad, and, as the pressure on the available shipping increased, freights rose well above even the abnormal level which they had reached at the beginning of the year. The total carrying power available was probably still adequate to the world's requirements, but

Allied and neutral countries, as well as Great Britain, were affected by the partial paralysis of the continental trades, and were compelled to draw a larger proportion of their supplies from more distant sources, so that on the longer routes the competition for tonnage was keen. By March 1915 the average grain freights from North America to the United Kingdom, which had stood at 29s. 10d. in January, had risen to 37s. 7d. per ton, and with the beginning of the Indian export season, rates from Karachi showed an even greater advance. Plate rates remained at some 200 per cent. above the normal, and all inward freights were abnormally high.

The rich harvest thus reaped by the tramps was shared by the owners of sailing tonnage. Insignificant as that tonnage now was when compared with the number of merchant steamers, it still played a considerable part in certain trades, notably in the import of grain, lumber, and nitrate from the Pacific coast of America. With the available steam tonnage so much reduced, vessels of the older type came into unwonted demand, and their owners had no difficulty in fixing remunerative charters. At the Puget Sound ports freights of from 100s. to 112s. were offered for lumber cargoes to the United Kingdom as compared with a normal rate of 60s. to 65s., and even at these figures shippers found it difficult to procure tonnage, owing to the great demand for space for flour and grain. Still greater was the advance in freights from the nitrate ports, which had risen by the beginning of March to 65s., as compared with 20s. in August 1914.[1]

On outward cargoes generally the advance on peace quotations varied from 15 to 25 per cent. Beyond this they seldom went, for the export trade had been seriously affected by the diversion of effort in Great Britain and by the diminished purchasing power of foreign markets, so that the demand for space was less insistent than in the homewards traffic. Moreover, the exports other than coal were mostly handled by liners running on a regular service. The majority of these lines were grouped in some form of Conference organisation, and while the tendency of these Conferences was to maintain the level of freights in normal times, the regulated rates, only varied by a decision of

---

[1] *Lloyd's List*, 17 February, 1915, Report of Annual Meeting of Clyde Sailing Ship Owners' Association; 10 April 1915 (Seattle report of 18 March).

the Conference, were less liable to sudden and violent fluctuations than quotations in the open market. Thus, while the outward rates on cargoes carried by vessels in the Indian Conference were raised from 20 to 25 per cent., and homeward rates from Colombo showed an advance of 30 per cent., homeward freights from Rangoon, Calcutta, and Vladivostok, which the Conference did not fix, had risen by over 100 per cent.[1]

Coal exports, on the other hand, were carried in vessels of the tramp class, and as the volume of exports was still large, especially to ports where big bunker depôts were maintained, outward coal freights rose to an unprecedented level. By the beginning of March the rate to the Canaries was thrice, and to Port Said four times the normal, and the general rise in coal freights since the beginning of the war was estimated at not less than 100 per cent.[2]

One result of this continuous rise in freights was to accentuate the inequality between the Blue Book rates paid to the owners of requisitioned vessels and the earnings of free tramps. The tramp shipowners accordingly put in a claim for a 33 per cent. advance on the Blue Book rates, and on March 1st a conference on this claim took place between the Representative Committee of Tramp Steamer Owners and the Director of Transports. As a result of this Conference the owners received a partial, but only a partial satisfaction of their demand. The flat rate of increase was very small—1s. 6d. per month per ton gross register—but certain additional allowances were made in respect of vessels employed on services calling for special equipment, or involving exceptional wear and tear, and taking these concessions into account, the average increase amounted to about 16 per cent. Special arrangements were made at the same time for the remuneration of vessels of less than 1,300 tons deadweight capacity (about 900 tons gross). Tank steamer owners, who had asked for an advance ranging from 11 to 39 per cent. according to size and service, were granted an increase of from 8 to 22 per cent. Liner rates remained unchanged.[3]

Even with these increases, which were dated back to January 1st, the Blue Book rates for tramps remained some 50 to 70 per cent. below the rates obtainable on the

[1] *Times*, 2 March, 1915.
[2] *Ibid.*, 4 March, 1915. Report of Houlder Bros.' Annual Meeting in *Lloyd's List*, 13 April, 1915.
[3] *Hansard*, 20 April, 1915 (Dr. Macnamara).

open market for long term charters, but on the whole they were accepted without grumbling by the shipowners. It was not so much the lowness of the Blue Book rates as the unequal incidence of requisitioning as between owner and owner which constituted their main grievance, and this was now in process of rectification.[1]

The general problem of abnormal freights remained, and had already begun to cause serious anxiety to the Government. Prices were steadily rising. By April 1915 the *Statist* Index Number for food prices, which stood at 74·8 in June 1914, had risen to 108·4. The increased cost of living was already felt as a heavy burden by the working classes, and as early as February the importance of the subject was recognised by a debate in the House of Commons in which very grave views of the situation were expressed. The course of that debate reflected strongly the widely prevalent view that high freights were an important if not the most important factor in the increase. This view was not shared by the Government, and in the course of the debate the Prime Minister made it clear that in their view the rise in freights, though a contributory cause of the rise in prices, was by no means the determining factor.[2] Nevertheless, the abnormal level both of freights and prices was too important an element in the economic and psychological situation to be overlooked, and various measures were taken by the Government during the spring of 1915 with the object of ameliorating the situation.

The first step in any attempt to reduce freights was obviously to increase the supply of available tonnage, and we have already seen that something at least was being done in this direction by the employment of interned ships and prizes, and by an endeavour to minimise the tonnage on naval and military service, and to employ for bringing in commercial cargoes, requisitioned vessels returning to this country. The appointment of Lord Inchcape's Committee gave some hope also that the condition of the ports might be sufficiently ameliorated to reduce the delays which militated so seriously against the efficiency of shipping. Meanwhile the question of employing requisitioned tonnage for the carriage of commercial cargoes had again

[1] *Hansard*, 20 April 1915, (Dr. Macnamara).
[2] *Ibid*. 11 and 17 February, 1915. Debate on "The Necessaries of Life (Prices)," *passim*.

come to the front. With the object of ensuring supplies for the Armies and providing a reserve to secure the civil population against a possible interruption of traffic, the Cabinet Committee on Food Supplies made large purchases of wheat in Argentina during December 1914 and the spring of 1915. These purchases were effected through a Joint Committee comprising representatives of the War Office, Admiralty, Board of Trade, Board of Agriculture and Fisheries, and the Treasury, and space for the imports was chartered on the market in the ordinary way by agents appointed by the Committee. As with sugar, Government purchase led to the suggestion of requisitioning ships to carry the imports at Blue Book rates, and this course was strongly urged by the Transport Department. The Advisory Committee were as strongly opposed. In addition to the arguments already unsuccessfully urged with regard to the purchases of the Sugar Commission, they pointed out that the Government purchases of wheat affected a part only of the supply, and that if these cargoes were carried at artificially restricted rates, the position of the private importers who were still responsible for the bulk of the imports would be very difficult and the mechanism of the markets would be upset.

It was, however, in connection with Indian wheat that the controversy came to a head. The Indian harvest was expected to be large, and with a view to checking wild speculation and defeating the native tendency to hoard, the Government of India decided to take control of the exportable surplus. They accordingly announced that, as from April 1st, no wheat would be allowed to be exported save on Government account. The leading export firms were appointed as agents to buy in quantities and at prices indicated by the Government, being remunerated by commission only. In order to discourage hoarding and place a premium on early threshing and delivery, the initial prices were fixed relatively high, and it was announced that these prices would be gradually reduced. From the first, however, the price paid to the producer was kept artificially low in comparison with world rates, in order to protect the Indian consumer by keeping down the price of wheat internally consumed. Tonnage for exports was chartered through an agent.

On the first intimation that the export of Indian wheat was to be made a Government monopoly, the Transport

Department renewed their proposal for the use of requisitioned tonnage. The Advisory Committee again dissented. Although the Government of India were thus acquiring a monopoly of the Indian wheat surplus, this was only a part of the British supplies, and, in the opinion of the Committee, the arguments against any interference with the normal course of the freight markets retained their force. Before the question could be decided, further information came to hand which made it plain that the Viceregal Government had no intention of putting the wheat on the British market at rates below the current world prices. The difference between these prices and the artificially restricted price paid to the Indian producer was in fact to be retained as a profit by the Indian Government and ear-marked for certain special purposes. In these circumstances, any saving in freights would go, not to cheapen bread in the United Kingdom, but to swell the profit of the Government, and the Transport Department accordingly decided not to press further the use of requisitioned tonnage. By centralising chartering through a single agent the Government did, however, succeed in fixing the space required at somewhat lower rates than were indicated by the general course of the markets.[1]

In respect of imported meat the action taken went a good deal further. The Board of Trade had originally been drawn into the meat market as a purchaser by the breakdown of financial arrangements in Argentina at the beginning of the war,[2] and had continued, under contracts arranged in August 1914, to import 15,000 tons of frozen meat a month for the supply of the British Armies. In these transactions Sir Thomas B. Robinson, K.C.M.G., Agent-General for Queensland, who had a large experience in the meat trade and in shipping, acted as agent for the Board, and Messrs. Anderson, Anderson & Co., acted as intermediaries and nominal purchasers of the meat, in order to obviate any difficulties arising from direct purchase by the British Government in a neutral country. For the supervision of the contracts a special Branch was formed within the Board, under Mr. George Barnes (later Mr. Garnham Roper), with Mr. H. W. Macrosty as

[1] *Times*, 24 March, 1915; *Statist*, 17 April, 1915; *Lloyd's List*, 7 June, 1915.
[2] See Vol. I, pp. 76-7.

administrative officer. It was anticipated at first that about a third of the 15,000 tons would be available for civil consumption in the United Kingdom; but, owing to the dislocation of sailings during the early months of the war, the entire deliveries under the contract were absorbed by the War Office demands, and during the autumn it became necessary to place additional contracts in Australia.

In January 1915 the responsibilities of the Board were considerably increased. The decision of the French Government to import frozen meat for their troops had seriously disorganised the trade. At first the French supplies were procured through the Commission Internationale de Ravitaillement,[1] to which body Sir Thomas Robinson was adviser, but after a short time the French military authorities began to buy direct. The French, however, had no previous experience of the frozen meat trade, and were frequently unable to secure satisfactory terms, cargoes being purchased for future delivery at prices well above those paid by the Board of Trade. French shipping, moreover, in consequence of the absence of imports before the war, was incapable of dealing with the purchases. There were, in fact, only five ships fitted with insulated space under the French flag, and their aggregate capacity did not exceed 6,000 tons. Thus the new French purchases brought them into the freight markets as competitors for the services of the British liners running from Plate ports. It must be remembered that the carriage of frozen meat, which requires specialised and costly equipment, is purely a liner trade; there was no floating reserve of tramp tonnage which could be drawn into the trade to meet a new demand, and tonnage could only be procured by diversion from the accustomed services. There was thus a serious danger that the operations of the French War Office would, without securing adequate fulfilment of their own requirements, raise freights and prices against the United Kingdom and lead to friction between the Allies. The Board of Trade accordingly urged on the French authorities the necessity of centralising all operations in meat, and in January 1915 it was arranged that all future purchases for the French Government in

[1] The Commission Internationale de Ravitaillement was an Inter-Allied organisation established for the purpose of centralising and supervising purchases by the Allied Governments in the United Kingdom.

Argentina, Uruguay, Australia, or New Zealand should be made through Sir Thomas Robinson, independent operations by the French being confined to minor sources of supply, such as their own Colonies and Venezuela. In return, the Board of Trade guaranteed to the French Government an average supply of about 20,000 tons a month, and undertook to find the tonnage required for transport of this amount. As part of the arrangement they took over all French contracts already signed, and agreed to purchase whatever meat was required to make good the deficiencies under such contracts.

Meanwhile, the Board were informed by the War Office that by the spring their requirements would rise to about 30,000 tons a month. It appeared probable that this increase in requirements would lead to a serious rise in prices, and with the object alike of stabilising prices and ensuring supplies, it was decided to acquire the whole of the exportable surplus of frozen meat in Australia and New Zealand. Early in February the Governments of the Commonwealth and Dominion and of the several Australian States were approached, and their co-operation obtained. The Governor-General of New Zealand, by an Order in Council dated February 23rd, prohibited all exports of meat to any destination other than the United Kingdom, and created an Imperial Government Meat Supply Branch of the New Zealand Government, to arrange for the purchase, at fixed prices, of all stocks available for export, and by this Branch the shipments were consigned direct to Sir Thomas Robinson for the Board of Trade.[1] In Australia, where all exports of meat were already prohibited except under licence,[2] similar arrangements were made with the Governments of the several States, who were more closely in touch with the producers than the Commonwealth Government itself. So early as August 1914, the Queensland Government had passed an Act bringing all meat supplies under control, and their example was speedily followed by New South Wales. Both in Australia and in New Zealand, however, amicable arrangements were made with the meat-freezing and other interests, by which reasonable f.o.b. prices were

---

[1] *Lloyd's List*, 17 April, 1915 (Wellington, 4 March).
[2] *Commonwealth of Australia, Manual of Emergency Legislation*, January 1916, pp. 145, 153.

fixed, having regard to the general price advance since the outbreak of war.¹

So far as the Australasian markets were concerned, the Board of Trade had thus acquired a water-tight monopoly. The next step was to find tonnage to bring forward the supplies. From the time when the Board began to purchase meat in August 1914 they had been in close touch with the liner conferences; and in December 1914 they had called a meeting of all the Lines engaged in the Plate, Australian, and New Zealand trades, for the purpose of explaining the situation and securing the best use of the insulated tonnage available. They had also arranged with the various dock authorities to give priority of discharge to ships carrying frozen meat. Tonnage in the Australian and New Zealand trade was, however, very short. No fewer than twenty-eight insulated steamers had been requisitioned by the Australian Government as transports, and by February 1915 the shortage of insulated tonnage was acute both in Australia and New Zealand. At the end of January the Commonwealth Government agreed to cease requisitioning ships of this class, and they further endeavoured to relieve the situation by putting into commission interned German steamers fitted with refrigerating machinery, and by allocating to shippers insulated space on the transports themselves. This use of transports was not, however, entirely satisfactory. Coming forward in convoy, the ships arrived at irregular intervals and in large batches, causing long delays in berthing and unloading, and congestion of the cold-storage accommodation. Meanwhile the New Zealand Government, with less tonnage immediately available, entered into negotiations with the Commonwealth for release of transports, and endeavoured both by direct pressure and by payment of compensation for sending ships out in ballast, to obtain additional carrying space.²

In spite of these endeavours the lack of tonnage was very serious. Hitherto there had been no great rise in

¹ Specimen prices

	June to July 1914.	New Contracts.
	d.	d.
New Zealand Prime Ox Beef	3⅝	4¾
Muttons, Wethers, 1st quality, under 72 lbs.	3¾	4½
Lamb, 1st quality, under 42 lbs.	4⅞	5¼

² *Lloyd's List*, 13 January, 1915 (Sydney, 25 November); 20 January (Hobart, 9 December); 15 March (Wellington, 29 January); 7 April (Wellington, 12 February); 9 April (Wellington, 20 February); 10 April (quoting *Melbourne Age*).

freights, and the New Zealand lines, in particular, were bound by long term contracts which forbade any immediate advance. There was, however, the possibility of a serious increase in the future, and, apart from this, it was necessary to secure some system of unified control which would permit the diversion of ships to ports where tonnage was specially short and enable the whole trade to be run as a single unit. Two conferences were accordingly held in February and March with the owners of insulated ships in the Australian and New Zealand trade, as a result of which the shipowners agreed to charter to the Government for the period of the war all insulated space on their ships at the rate of 72*s*. 6*d*. per 40 cubic feet, which represented only a slight increase on the current rates. An agreement was arrived at with regard to the right of diversion, and a Shipowners' Committee, with Lord Inchcape as Chairman, was appointed to supervise the running of the ships and the allocation of tonnage to the various ports. Sub-Committees in Australia and New Zealand, on which both shippers and shipowners were represented, were also appointed to attend to the details of allocation.[1]

In order to protect the shipowners against claims for breach of contract, an Order in Council was issued on April 13th, requisitioning for the carriage of refrigerated produce all insulated space in British steamers usually engaged in the Australian and New Zealand trade, thus rendering the Government responsible for any action taken in breach of existing agreements.[2] The agreement with the shipowners was, however, brought into effect with their consent as from March 8th without waiting for the Order. With regard to the ships in use as Australian troopships, special arrangements were made with the Commonwealth Government by which, though the whole insulated space on these ships was included under the Requisitioning Order, the Commonwealth Government only charged the British Government for space actually used for meat, making itself responsible for all space otherwise occupied.

Meanwhile difficulties had arisen in the Plate trade. In that trade, too, the rise in freights had hitherto been small, less, in fact, than $\frac{1}{2}d$. per lb., but there were indications of a further rise, and a still more serious danger arose in

---

[1] On the New Zealand Sub-Committee the Dominion Government was also represented.
[2] *Manual of Emergency Legislation, Supplement No.* 3, pp. 362–4.

connection with the f.o.b. price. The bulk of the Argentine production was controlled by the American Meat Companies, whose headquarters and organisation lay outside British jurisdiction. With the strong demand due to the expansion in War Office requirements and the appearance of France as an importer on a large scale, these Companies held a favourable position to enforce their own terms, and there could be little doubt that full advantage would be taken of the opportunity.

The danger was serious, but an effective remedy was quickly found. To the partial monopoly of production, the Board of Trade resolved to oppose a complete monopoly of carrying power. Practically all the insulated tonnage in the Plate trade was under the British flag. Indeed, the total insulated tonnage under foreign flags in any trade was inconsiderable.[1] Accordingly the Board of Trade entered into an agreement with the Lines engaged in the Plate trade similar to that already made with the Australian and New Zealand shipowners, and on April 29th an Order in Council was signed, formally requisitioning the space.[2] The terms agreed upon were 50s., 55s., or 60s. per 40 cubic feet according to the class of ship, representing an average advance of rather less than a halfpenny per lb. on ante-bellum rates.

The Board of Trade had thus acquired a complete monopoly of the Australian and New Zealand supplies both as regards purchase and transport, and in the Plate trade they had a monopoly of carrying power which enabled them to negotiate with the meat companies on equal terms. In view of the urgency of the Allied demands, which required practically the whole exportable surplus of all producing centres for their fulfilment, it was impossible to prevent a rise in prices[3]; but that rise was certainly much smaller

---

[1] Of the little insulated space under foreign flags a large proportion was only suitable for the carriage of fruit, and produce other than meat.

[2] *Manual of Emergency Legislation, Supplement No. 3*, pp. 365–7. The Plate Lines were scheduled in detail. The Nelson Line was excepted from the arrangement, as they were bound by long-term contracts at lower rates than those now fixed. (See *Hansard*, 10 June, 1915, cols. 423–4.) As these contracts expired, their vessels were subsequently placed on the same basis as other South American steamers, at somewhat lower rates.

[3] Price, average fores and hinds, under old contracts, $5\frac{13}{16}d.$–$6d.$ per lb; at end of April, $6\frac{7}{16}d.$ per lb; under new contracts, May 1915, for 25,000 tons a month, $6\frac{1}{2}d.$ per lb. These were c.i.f. prices, but under the new arrangements the Board paid the meat companies only the f.o.b. value of the meat, plus cost of insurance, and paid the agreed freight direct to the shipowners.

than it would have been had not the hands of the Board been strengthened by their control of the means of transport. It was this aspect of the matter which did more than anything else to reconcile the shipowners to the limitation imposed on their profits. The position of the Government in respect of meat was very different from that which they occupied in respect of grain. Their monopoly of insulated tonnage was an effective weapon for keeping down f.o.b. prices as well as for regulating freights, and they controlled so large a proportion of the imports that they were able to pass on to the consumer the benefits of any saving either in f.o.b. prices or in cost of transport. At the same time, the specialised character of the shipping affected and its retention in its accustomed trade, prevented any injurious reactions on the world's freight markets.[1]

The general idea underlying the purchase of the entire Australian and New Zealand surplus was that the beef, or the greater part thereof, would be appropriated for military purposes, and that all the lamb and practically all the mutton would be available for civil consumption. Arrangements were made to place all supplies not required for the fulfilment of War Office or French requirements, on the British market, through the agency of the ordinary meat importers and commission agents, who received a fixed commission for their services. In order not to disturb the accustomed channels of trade, these firms were instructed to do business as far as possible with their ordinary buyers, but sales to speculators were forbidden, and the Government agents were instructed to keep prices steady and moderate. The wholesale distributors who purchased from these agents were allowed to sell only to *bona fide* retailers, and at prices not more than a halfpenny per lb. above the price which they themselves paid. In the Plate trade, the firms who acted as agents for the meat companies were permitted to import each month a certain amount of chilled beef on their own account, for which they were charged a freight equivalent to the actual payment to the shipowners.

By the arrangement with the Lines the freight paid by the Government was fixed at a definite rate per cubic foot

[1] *Hansard*, 10 June, 1915, cols. 399-400 (Mr. Houston); Sir Owen Phillips, at Annual Meeting of the Royal Steampacket Co., *Times*, 13 May, 1915, *Lloyd's List*, 13 May, 1915; *Liverpool Steam Ship Owners' Association, Annual Report* for 1915, p. 14.

of insulated space, whether filled or not, for each homeward voyage. When full cargoes of meat were not obtainable the Board of Trade accepted from private shippers other refrigerated produce, such as rabbits, dairy produce, or fruit, and in the last resort filled up with non-refrigerated cargo. For such outside shipments the Board charged to the merchant a freight roughly equivalent to the meat rate. As regards outwards cargo and imports not requiring insulated space the shipowners were left to make their own arrangements.

It will be observed that, under the terms of the two Orders in Council, it was only the insulated space in the ships, not the ships themselves, that came under requisition. In practice, however, the requisitioning of insulated space gave the Board of Trade absolute control over the movements of the ships, and, in fact, the Requisitioning Orders only gave formal effect to agreements already arrived at with the shipowners. So far as possible the Board abstained from interfering with the regular routes and sailings of the Lines, and in the Australasian trade it was agreed that passenger steamers should not be diverted without the owners' consent. Nevertheless, the Committee appointed to supervise the running of the Lines were able to a great extent to pool the ships belonging to the various companies so as to adjust the services to the demands of the various ports of shipment, and arrange for steamers to call at ports which they did not usually visit.[1] This was not always an easy task, and the New Zealand Government, who were represented on the New Zealand Sub-Committee, almost immediately found themselves involved in a lively controversy with the South Island shippers, who complained that the North Island was unduly favoured in the allocation of space.[2] On the whole, however, little difficulty was experienced; the shipowners themselves co-operated cordially, and the problem of local shortages was so successfully overcome that all refrigerated produce on offer during the year in Australia and New Zealand, whether on Government or private account, was lifted, the Plate contracts were successfully fulfilled, and assistance was given to the French

---

[1] *Hansard*, 10 June, 1915, col. 423. In some instances, but not in all, reasonable expenses of deviation were paid.
[2] *Lloyd's List*, 2 June, 1915 (*Wellington*, 18 April).

in the carriage of supplies from Madagascar, China, Venezuela, and Brazil.

In respect both of meat and sugar the Government had now acquired a practical monopoly of imports, and arranged for carriage of their purchases in requisitioned ships or requisitioned space. On all other commodities freights were left to be fixed as between merchant and shipowner, and shared in the general rise brought about by the disproportion of supply to demand. Great as was this advance, the burden of freights represented as yet only a small proportion of the increase in prices due to the growth of war demands and the redistribution of trade. But neither increased freights nor increased f.o.b. prices in the country of origin were sufficient to check the volume of supplies. On the other hand, the comparatively small increase in outward freights was a considerable burden on the export trade, for the purchasing power of foreign markets was generally diminished and their demands for British products were less urgent than British requirements for food and raw materials. Nevertheless, the monthly figures of export values showed a steady increase during the early months of 1915, and while this increase reflected, to some extent, the general rise in prices, in the main it represented a real and substantial increase in the volume of exports. By April the worst of the crisis in the cotton trade was over. The Indian demand was still weak owing to excessive imports during 1913 and the early months of 1914, but China, Egypt, and the Dutch East Indies were now buying more freely, and the war had created a new demand in France. Manufacturers of woollen goods were not only busy in the supply of the British Armies, but found an ample outlet for their exportable surplus, as France and America were buying very heavily, and some of the continental neutrals were placing in this country orders which would normally have gone to Germany. Exports of iron and steel manufactures and machinery were naturally restricted by the demands of the war industries, but many miscellaneous manufactures were now finding a better market. The shipments of coal, too, were steady at about 60 per cent. of the normal.

Satisfactory as was the increase in export values, it was far from keeping pace with the expansion in imports. During the first four months of 1915 the excess of import over export values amounted to £133,000,000, as compared with £45,000,000 in the same period of the previous year. To this must be added money expended by British troops abroad and Government purchases of military material and other articles which did not appear in the ordinary trade returns. On the other hand, the invisible exports—interest on capital invested abroad and payment for shipping, banking, insurance, and other services—had increased rather than diminished, owing to the high freights earned by British ships. Even so, it was estimated that, taking into account loans made to the Allies and the Oversea Dominions for war purposes, there was an adverse balance of roughly £30,000,000 a month to be provided by drawing in capital and borrowing from abroad.[1] Hitherto no great difficulty had been found in financing this balance, but some anxiety was already felt as to the effect on the gold reserves of a continued expansion in imports, and it was realised that only a large increase in exports could effectually restore the equilibrium.

Desirable as it was to foster the export trade, it was equally necessary to regulate it. The first object of the various export restrictions was, of course, to prevent undue depletion of the stocks of commodities required in the conduct of the war; but, beyond this, it was essential to prevent the export to neutral countries of goods likely to be passed on by the neutral buyer to the enemy. For this purpose, among others, a Trading with the Enemy Committee had been set up, thanks to the foresight of the Committee of Imperial Defence, on the first day of the war, and the list of prohibited or restricted exports was already lengthy. The machinery by which licences for exports to approved neutral firms were obtained from the Privy Council was unnecessarily cumbrous, and traders complained bitterly of the incidental delays. On the other hand, there was little doubt that many cargoes shipped from British ports to neutral countries ultimately reached the enemy's hands. A clearer policy based on more exact information was urgently required, and early in 1915 the Government decided that work of such complexity and delicacy could only be adequately performed by a special, well-equipped Department. A War Trade

---

[1] *Statist*, 8 May, 1915.

Department, responsible to the Treasury, was accordingly created, and on February 19th the Government announced that all applications for licences to import or export prohibited or restricted commodities should in future be addressed to this new authority.[1]

From this date the War Trade Department took over, as regards the regulation of exports, the functions of the Trading with the Enemy Committee and the Privy Council. Within the Department were formed a Main Licensing Committee and a number of Licensing Sub-Committees dealing with special commodities. To provide material for its decisions the War Trade Intelligence Department, with a strong, expert staff, was formed in March, and during April the machinery was completed by the addition of the War Trade Statistical Department. The utility of these additions went far beyond their immediate purpose. Acting as a clearing-house for the collection, analysis, and dissemination of economic data relating to enemy and neutral trade, they furnished a reliable intelligence and statistical basis for the development of the whole blockade policy.[2]

Thus, in many respects, the early months of 1915 saw the seaborne trade of the United Kingdom settling down into the new channels imposed by war conditions. Imports were regaining their normal volume, exports were increasing, and the necessary control of the export trade had been centralised and provided with a much-needed Intelligence Section. A beginning, too, had been made in the more careful allocation of the shipping resources of the country, and the adjustment of military and commercial requirements. The last of the German surface raiders had been hunted from the seas, and three months of the new form of attack on commerce had not checked the flow of trade or involved a critical percentage of loss. Nevertheless, the situation was still full of peril, and if any undue hopes had been excited they were about to be rudely shaken.

[1] *Manual of Emergency Legislation, Financial Edition,* June 1915, p. 150.
[2] The employment of the word "blockade" here and elsewhere to describe the whole machinery for the interception of enemy trade is technically incorrect; but the convenience to writer and reader is great, and though misleading in some respects, it has the sanction of general usage.

CHAPTER VI

EXTENSION OF THE SUBMARINE CAMPAIGN
MAY—SEPTEMBER 1915

THE apparent check administered to the German submarines during April was not, unfortunately, followed by any permanent diminution in their activities. While traffic in the Irish Sea and English Channel remained free from molestation, the vigour of the attack was intensified during May in the North Sea and the South-Western Approach.

In the North Sea, the majority of the victims, other than fishing craft, were neutrals bound from Scandinavian ports with wood cargoes, or carrying to Scandinavia cargoes of contraband, such as coal or grain, which the Germans suspected to be intended for ultimate delivery to Russia. British merchantmen on the Norwegian tracks were too few and too widely scattered to present a very vulnerable target, and those engaged in the Dutch and coasting trades enjoyed a considerable measure of protection from the minefields and patrols, within the line of which they moved for the greater part of their course. Thus, while the fishing fleets suffered heavy losses, casualties to British merchantmen were few and comparatively unimportant.

In the South-Western Approach, on the other hand, the Germans had found an almost ideal field of operations. Through this area passed practically the whole ocean traffic of the United Kingdom. From the west, the all-important North American tracks followed the line of the Irish coast, to pass through the St. George's Channel for Liverpool and the Clyde, or struck straight across the area for the entrance to the English Channel. From the south-west and south came the tracks from South America, Africa, Australia, India and the Far East, the Mediterranean, Spain and Portugal, and the French Atlantic ports. To the north-east and east of the area, the entrances to the

THE DANGER IN THE APPROACHES

St. George's, Bristol, and English Channels confined the course of shipping within limits less narrow than those imposed by the North Channel or the Straits of Dover, but definite and incapable of extension. To the south and west were open waters which provided for the submarine a safe line of approach or departure; but for merchant shipping the possibilities of deviation, though considerable, were limited by the necessity under which the majority of vessels lay of making such landfalls and seamarks as the Fastnet, the Tuskar, the Smalls, the Scillies, or Ushant. The problem of trade defence in this area was thus extremely difficult. The open waters to the south of Ireland and west of the line Scillies–Ushant were too broad to be effectively controlled except by a very large number of fast, armed vessels, and the difficulty of providing for effective dispersal of shipping was increased both by the inevitable tendency to concentration off the principal landfalls and at the entrance to the defended passages, and by the crossing of the tracks from north to south and from east to west. Moreover, while the course to be followed by particular branches of trade could be laid down, the volume of shipping was too great to allow of any effective system of individual dispersal. The most that could be done, at any rate in the initial stages of the anti-submarine campaign, was to guard the entrances to the channels, the chief focal points, and the inshore course along the Irish coast, and to provide armed escort through the danger area for vessels of special naval or military importance, such as oilers and munition ships.

During May the activity of German submarines in the South-Western Approach was revealed by attacks on shipping at almost all the focal points of the area: off the south coast of Ireland from the Fastnet to the Old Head of Kinsale; at the entrance of the St. George's Channel near the Tuskar; off Trevose Head, an important landmark for shipping approaching the Bristol Channel from the south-west; within a radius of some 50 to 60 miles from the Scillies; in the western entrance of the English Channel, 40 to 50 miles south-west of Start Point; north of Ushant at a similar distance from the land. In the area of the South-Western Approach itself nearly half the ships attacked succeeded in making good their escape, including most of the larger and faster vessels molested. Three at least, the liners *Ping Suey* and *Demarara*, and the *Garmoyle*, one of the coasters which had recently received a defensive armament, beat off their assailant by gunfire. Nevertheless, the tale of losses was heavy; but all other individual casualties were overshadowed by the sinking of the 30,000-ton Cunard liner *Lusitania*, torpedoed without warning off the Old Head of Kinsale on May 7th, with a loss of nearly 1,200 lives.[1] Prior to her departure from New York warnings had been published in the American press, and sent by telegram to intending American passengers, that a special attempt would be made to sink her on this voyage, and the universal horror excited by the disaster was increased by the deliberation of the attack and the hysterical rejoicings with which it was welcomed in the German press. By the Germans, indeed, the sinking of the *Lusitania* appears to have been regarded as the equivalent of a great naval victory; but a clearer understanding of the nature of British trade would have shown that these rejoicings were misplaced. It was not the small group of crack liners, of great size, high speed, and luxurious accommodation, which formed the strength of Great Britain in the carrying trade. That strength was distributed over some 8,700 ocean-going steamers of 1,600 tons gross and upwards, many of which were capable of performing still more valuable service as cargo carriers than the *Lusitania* herself. As a piece of calculated "frightfulness," the sinking of the *Lusitania* failed, for there is not the slightest evidence that it did anything to deter the men of the Mercantile Marine from taking the risks, to which they were now already hardened, of an ocean voyage. As a direct blow to British trade, it was but one among many casualties which, serious as was the aggregate of tonnage lost, bore as yet but a small ratio to the total of British shipping or the volume of British trade.

Moreover, in sinking deliberately an unarmed vessel, crowded with passengers, among whom were many American citizens, the Germans embarked definitely on the dangerous course of provocation and defiance which was, in the end, to lead them into conflict with the great Western Republic. The indignation excited in America was naturally great, and it was intensified by three other incidents which took

---

[1] For the circumstances of the attack see Corbett, *Naval Operations*, vol. ii, pp. 394-1, and Archibald Hurd, *The Merchant Navy*, vol. i, pp. 310-28.

place about the same time. In their anxiety to impede the trade between Holland and the United Kingdom, the Germans had resorted during March and April to a form of attack even more unprecedented and less legitimate than the operations of the submarines themselves. On about a dozen occasions ships on passage between Dutch and British ports were bombed by German aeroplanes, and, once at least, man-killing steel darts and machine-gun fire were also employed. The German practice was poor, and no damage was done; but the attacks had the effect of still further embroiling Germany with neutrals, for on March 23rd the Dutch steamer *Zevenbergen*, and on April 28th the American *Cushing* were attacked in mistake for British ships. The same plea of mistaken identity was put forward once more in the course of the submarine operations in the South-Western Approach. On May 1st the *Gulflight*, a tank steamer of the latest type, bound from Port Arthur to Rouen, was torpedoed without warning south-west of the Scillies. She did not sink, and subsequently struggled into port; but the wireless operator and a seaman dived overboard and were drowned, and the captain died of heart-failure caused by the shock. Thus, even before the torpedoing of the *Lusitania*, there was occasion for considerable friction between the German and American Governments, and before May was out another American steamer, the *Nebraskan*, homeward bound from Liverpool to the Delaware, was torpedoed off the Fastnet and compelled to put back to port.

Firmly as the United States, at this period, adhered to a rigid neutrality, no Great Power could tolerate such attacks upon the lives and property of its nationals, and on May 13th, after the sinking of the *Lusitania*, the American Government delivered to the German Ambassador a strong note, protesting against the methods adopted in the submarine campaign, emphasising the necessity of visit and search as a preliminary to destruction, and insisting that no ships must be destroyed unless the safety of their crews and passengers could be fully assured. The German Government replied, in effect, by claiming an unlimited right of reprisal for the alleged illegality of the measures adopted by Great Britain to restrict German trade. They contended, further, that all British steamers had been armed and ordered to attack every submarine they met, and had thus forfeited the protection afforded by their status as merchantmen. In particular, they claimed that the *Lusitania* had a concealed armament, that she was carrying troops, and that her cargo was illegal according to American law. These allegations the American Government had no difficulty in refuting, and in two further notes they strongly reasserted their original contentions. No definite satisfaction was obtained from Germany, but the effect of the protest was to induce the submarines to adopt, for the time being, more cautious methods, especially in dealing with passenger steamers and vessels under the American flag. A still more important result was the beginning of a gradual but steady intensification of anti-German sentiment in America which was, even at the time, not without its effect on the attitude of the American Government.

Meanwhile, the loss of the *Lusitania* and the numerous other casualties in the South-Western Approach naturally led to a demand for the reinforcement of the patrols in that area; but with this demand it was very difficult to comply, as the trawler fleets had already been depleted to an extent which reacted seriously on the fish supply of the country. Large as were the numbers already requisitioned, they were far from adequate for the work to be performed. Moreover, the armed trawler, though a useful craft, was by no means an ideal one for the purpose of trade defence against the latest type of German submarine, with a surface speed of 19 knots. As support to a net line or as an escort for slow vessels, the trawler was invaluable, but as an escort to the faster merchantmen she was unsatisfactory. The necessity of reducing speed to allow the trawlers to keep company not only kept the escorted vessel longer in the danger area—a risk counter-balanced by the protection provided—but might very easily involve her arrival during daylight, at a danger point, such as a prominent headland, outside the patrolled area, which she might otherwise have passed during the hours of darkness. Could a sufficient number of destroyers have been set free to permit of their being freely employed as patrols or to allow the formation of special flotillas for the purpose of a vigorous counter-offensive, the problem of trade defence would have been greatly simplified; but the paramount claims of the Grand Fleet, and the importance of ensuring the maximum protection to the passage of reinforcements and supplies to France, left too few disposable for general purposes to permit the adoption of this policy.

All that could be done was to send down a small squadron of armed yachts, but even so limited a reinforcement enabled one serious gap in the defensive organisation to be at least partially filled. The instructions to merchantmen to keep in mid-channel and avoid prominent headlands and sea-marks were well conceived for the purpose of avoiding a concentration of shipping at points specially likely to attract the enemy's attention, but they had the serious disadvantage that, in order to observe them, shipping was obliged to remain well outside the limits of the patrolled areas. Thus, when a merchantman was actually attacked or chased by a submarine, the prospects of rescue were small. The majority of the vessels sunk were destroyed at leisure, with little thought of interference, and it was not until the crews had pulled some miles in their boats that they sighted a British patrol. With the arrival of the yachts it became possible to extend the area of protection. The Yacht Squadron was ordered to patrol at a distance of 40 miles from the Irish coast, where they could afford some support to ships following the main trade routes passing through the South-Western Approach, and it was not long before they made their presence felt. At about the same time a new and important method of anti-submarine warfare—the employment of armed decoy-ships cruising under the merchant flag, but ready at a moment's notice to hoist the White Ensign and open an effective fire—came into more general use.

During May, also, the instructions to merchant vessels with regard to the use of wireless telegraphy were thoroughly revised and consolidated. All British merchantmen were strictly forbidden to send out any wireless messages, other than emergency signals, within 100 miles of the coast. Outside that limit they might report their arrival on getting into wireless touch, so long as they were careful not to give away their true position. If a position was given it was to be a false one, to be corrected on receipt according to a prearranged code. On their own part, the Admiralty arranged to send out, when desirable, at 8 and 9 a.m. and 3 and 9 p.m., general warnings in merchant code as to danger areas; but in order to avoid the possibility of false orders being sent out by German agents, masters were directed to disregard all positive orders unless

96 EXTENSION OF THE SUBMARINE CAMPAIGN

addressed to individual ships. At a later date (August 1915) it was decided to send out the general messages *en clair*, in order to avoid a possible betrayal of the code.

The whole organisation of anti-submarine defence was thus rapidly becoming more effective; but the submarines themselves were growing in daring and efficiency, and despite all the precautions taken by the Admiralty, and all the devotion and energy of the patrols, the attack continued through June and July with unabated vigour. In the South-Western Approach alone between forty and fifty ships, thirty-one of which were British, were sunk during these two months. Casualties were reported from all the old danger areas and, in addition, several vessels were sunk within a radius of about fifty miles from the Smalls, and some sixty to seventy miles west and south-west of Lundy Island. Within the line of drifters and patrols maintained between the Smalls and the Tuskar there were, however, no casualties, and by the beginning of July the arrival of additional drifters permitted a continuous line of nets between these two points to be maintained permanently. The weight of the attack still fell mainly on ships of small or moderate size, but three or four large liners were also attacked, and the Leyland liner *Armenian*, of 8,825 tons, was sunk off Trevose Head on June 28th, after a chase in the course of which twenty-nine of her people were killed by gunfire. On the other hand, the great P.S.N. liner *Orduna*, which was twice attacked, escaped each time. On the second occasion she owed her safety entirely to her own speed, but when first attacked, on June 28th, off the Smalls, her S.O.S. call brought up the armed yacht BACCHANTE II, who beat off the submarine by a well-directed fire. On the previous day the *Kenmare*, attacked off the south coast of Ireland, was rescued by trawlers of the Queenstown patrol, and on several other occasions during June and July submarines were sighted and chased or engaged by the patrols. For the most part, however, the attacks on merchantmen took place at a considerable distance from the coast, where, save for the half-dozen units of the Yacht Squadron, few British men-of-war were likely to be encountered.

One effect of this gradual shifting of the zone of operations to a greater distance from the defended waters was a very notable reduction in the percentage of vessels sunk without warning. In view of the controversy with the United States which had arisen over the sinking of the *Lusitania*, the Germans had strong reasons for modifying the policy of sinking at sight, which had, moreover, proved singularly unsuccessful as a deterrent to British shipping, and the larger and faster craft now employed could well afford, when operating many miles from land, to abandon this method of attack, except against the fastest merchantmen. There were, indeed, military reasons for preferring capture, where possible, as a preliminary to the destruction of a vessel. Although some captured ships were subsequently torpedoed, the greater number were destroyed by shells, bombs, or fire, and this economy in the use of torpedoes had its effect in increasing the number of victims for which a submarine could account on a single cruise. In dealing with neutrals also, compliance with the doctrine of visit and search rendered it possible to destroy vessels carrying contraband cargo, without any serious risk of international complications. Thus, while the gradual change in the usual method of attack greatly reduced the personal danger to merchant crews, it added in an almost equal degree to the efficiency of the submarine as a commerce-destroyer.

Against an attack conducted on these principles the defensive position in the South-Western Approach was still thoroughly unsatisfactory. The great obstacle to its improvement lay in the insufficient number of really fast, armed vessels available. All that could be done was to strengthen the Yacht Squadron and to make the best possible use of the material at hand. The Auxiliary Patrols were accordingly reorganised in such a way as to provide for the greatest possible centralisation of command and concentration of effort, and their efficiency was increased by the despatch of aeroplanes to Ireland for use in detecting the presence of submarines off the coast.

It was not, however, only in the South-Western Approach that submarines were active during June and July. On their passage to and from this area they inflicted many casualties among ships passing north-about or along the West Coast of Ireland. In addition to coasting traffic and vessels bound to or from North Sea ports, many steamers, British, Allied, and neutral, were now on their way to Archangel with coal, munitions, and military stores, or returning with Russian produce. Of these ships several were sunk, among them an American steamer, the *Leelanaw*, bound from Archangel to Belfast with a cargo of flax and hemp.

In the North Sea itself submarines were vigorously at work. From Lowestoft to the Shetlands the fishing fleets were harried with merciless severity. So heavy were the losses of the Scottish fishermen in June that they could no longer face the risks without some measure of direct protection, and it became necessary to send armed drifters to sea with the fleets. The adoption of this measure was followed by a marked diminution in the number of casualties off the Scottish coast, but the total of fishing craft destroyed during June and July fell little short of a hundred.

Neutral merchantmen also continued to suffer heavily, but, out of a score of neutral victims, more than half were small sailing vessels laden with wood cargoes from Scandinavia. The actual loss of tonnage on the Scandinavian tracks was, indeed, comparatively small. Much more serious was the menace to trade in the southern area of the North Sea, where daring submarine commanders succeeded, on several occasions, in penetrating the line of patrols which protected the approaches to the Thames and sinking some half-dozen merchantmen at the entrance to the estuary, or on the inshore route along the coast of Suffolk. Operating in so dangerous an area, often within a mile or two of the land, the submarines took no risks, and all these vessels were torpedoed without warning of any kind.

The danger thus disclosed was serious in view of the great volume of shipping (some sixty vessels each day) using the Swept Channel, and the still greater concentration of trade at the mouth of the Thames. Unhappily it was not the only, perhaps not even the most alarming menace to navigation in this vital area. The last attempt of the German battle-cruiser squadron to carry on operation in the North Sea had been so severely punished by Admiral Beatty on January 24th that no further raids had been made on the English coast, and the organisation of the British patrols was by now too efficient to allow much hope of successful mine-laying by surface vessels unprotected by a covering force. A new and formidable weapon had, however, been developed by the enemy, in the mine-laying submarine. The boats of this class were smaller than those used for commerce-raiding, and were not, at first, armed with torpedo-tubes, but they each carried a dozen mines, and, while much inferior to the surface mine-layer in their capacity for laying a large field, their superior powers of evasion gave them an incalculable value for work on a well-defended coast. During June and July they succeeded in mooring small groups of mines off such prominent lights and sea-marks as the South Goodwin, the Kentish Knock, the Gull, and the Elbow Buoy, where they could easily be avoided by the larger German submarines, but were excellently placed for causing the greatest possible damage to merchantmen, whether British or neutral engaged in the trade of the United Kingdom.

The importance of defending these points of concentration for shipping had not been overlooked by the British Admiralty, who had for some time past been experimenting with deep minefields, moored at a depth which rendered them innocuous to merchant shipping, but at which they might be expected to prove fatal to a submerged submarine lying in wait for her prey off a prominent headland or sea-mark. Such deep minefields had by this time been laid off Beachy Head, Dartmouth, the Kentish Knock, and Tod Head, Kincardineshire; but the results were not, at present, very satisfactory.[1] The mines showed a tendency to come to the surface, and during June two friendly vessels were actually sunk in this way, while the Kentish Knock minefield proved no impediment to the operations of the submarine mine-layer in this area.

Thus, in addition to the risk of being torpedoed without warning, ships approaching London or passing up or down the East Coast were now exposed to a renewed and intensified mine peril. On several occasions mines which had either been newly laid, or drifted from previously existing fields were discovered in the Swept Channel itself, and more than once shipping had to be temporarily held up or diverted in order to avoid the risk of serious disasters. So effective, however, were the precautions taken, and so energetic the work of the minesweepers, that actual casualties were few, and within a very short time the menace presented by the irruption of German submarines into the Swept Channel was also effectively countered. The control of navigation was tightened, and all vessels passing up or down the coast of Essex and Suffolk were

[1] The first deep minefield was laid off Beachy Head in April 1915.

compelled to use a single channel lying behind the sand-banks with which that coast is fringed. In the intervals between those banks a net barrier was maintained by drifters, and, thanks to the efficiency of the drifter patrols, the daily stream of traffic passing up and down the Swept Channel was secured against any but rare and exceptional losses, without appreciable hindrance to the flow of trade.

The still greater and more important traffic of the English Channel continued to be immune from attack. The larger submarines, as we have seen, were now prohibited from running the gauntlet of the Straits, and though four smaller vessels of the new coastal type were permitted to make the attempt during June, their experiences were not sufficiently encouraging for the experiment to be repeated. Mines presumably laid by a submarine mine-layer were discovered off Calais during July, but they were swept up before any damage had been done, and even for the mine-laying submarines it was now no easy task to enter the Channel from the North Sea. The netted area across the Straits of Dover was extended during June and July very nearly to the edge of the British mine-field, which was itself enlarged, and, with a view to increasing the efficiency of the barrier, nets with mines attached were now used for the outer lines. Thus, the only real danger point in the Channel lay at its western entrance. Here the gateway was too wide to be effectively closed; but, in order to increase the difficulty of submarine navigation, the French fog-bells at Ushant and the Channel ports were discontinued at the end of June, and during the following month the same precaution was taken all round the British Isles. The chief lights, however, were retained in full working order, both in the Channel and elsewhere, and so great was the importance attached by the Admiralty to assisting the free flow of merchant shipping that they refused to allow any further coast lights to be extinguished even for the purpose of defence against the Zeppelin raids which had now become a feature of the war.

Another problem which became urgent during June and July was the protection of the sailing trade. Of minor importance as compared with steam traffic, the big sailing vessels from the Pacific, with their cargoes of grain, lumber, and nitrate were too valuable for their safety to be disregarded; but it was very difficult to defend them against submarine attack, since the prevalence of easterly winds might keep them for many days, even for weeks, in the danger area at the approaches to the Channel. Vessels carrying cargoes consigned " to order " and obliged to beat up the English or St. George's Channel after putting in for instructions, were specially liable to destruction, as they were exposed to a double risk.

Several large sailing vessels, British and Norwegian, were sunk or damaged during May and June, and towards the end of June the whole question of protection for the sailing traffic was brought into prominence by the loss of the *Dumfriesshire*. The *Dumfriesshire*, a four-masted barque laden with 4,100 tons of barley from San Francisco put into Falmouth for orders on June 25th. From Falmouth she was sent on to Dublin, but while working up the St. George's Channel she was torpedoed on June 28th, twenty-five miles S.W. of the Smalls, and carried her valuable cargo to the bottom.

Some six weeks before the loss of the *Dumfriesshire* the Mercantile Marine Association had suggested to the Admiralty that, in view of the increasing use of sailing vessels, especially for the carriage of foodstuffs, free towage should be provided through the danger area. This was impossible, for almost all the powerful tugs not already requisitioned for naval or military use were stationed at Liverpool or ports on the North-East Coast; but it was clear that some attempt must be made to minimise the risks, and in response to an appeal for instructions from Lloyd's, enclosing a list of 138 sailing vessels homeward bound from America, and seven from Australian ports,[1] the Admiralty called a special conference to consider the question on July 16th. At this conference the Fourth Sea Lord, the Director of the Trade Division, and representatives of the Transport Department and the Board of Trade met the representatives of Lloyd's, the Liverpool and London War Risks Association, the Sailing Ship Owners' Association, and leading individual owners.

As a result of the conference, a memorandum was sent out to all sailing ship owners advising them always to obtain from charterers definite instructions as to the port of destination, so as to avoid the necessity of putting in for orders. Further, as the supply of tugs was inadequate to the demand, they were urged to accept no charters

[1] The cargoes of 64 of these vessels were given as follows : grain, 41 ; nitrate, 15 ; timber, 8.

except for West Coast ports to which the vessels could proceed direct. Outward-bound vessels unable to procure tugs might, when necessary, apply for towage to the local Naval Authority.

At the same time a telegram was sent to all Naval Intelligence and Reporting Officers, and all Consular Officers abroad, instructing them that sailing vessels unable to obtain instructions as to their port of discharge before sailing were to be advised to call for orders at the Azores, Canaries, Cape Verdes, Madeira, or Gibraltar, and not to proceed to the United Kingdom until a port had been fixed; but, in view of a possible extension of the danger area, owners were urged to avoid so far as possible calling for orders even at these distant ports.[1] There were, however, many vessels already on their way home which would reach the danger zone without touching at any intermediate point. Outward-bound ships were accordingly instructed to communicate with any homeward-bound sailing vessels encountered and advise them to proceed direct to their port of discharge, or, if their destination was not settled, to proceed to Queenstown on a westerly wind, and then await further orders, inside the harbour.

While the double risk entailed by calling for orders was thus eliminated, the possibility of long detention in the danger area by contrary winds was a serious matter for vessels proceeding direct to a fixed port. Instructions were therefore given that all sailing vessels bound for British ports should remain well outside the 100-fathom line until they obtained a favourable wind enabling them to set a direct course for their destination.

At the most, however, the destruction of sailing vessels formed only a minor feature of the submarine campaign, and that campaign was now being pressed with greater activity than ever before. Heavy as were the losses of shipping during May, June, and July, they were far exceeded in August, when no fewer than 60 British ships were attacked by submarines, and 42, with an aggregate tonnage of over 135,000 gross, were sunk. Including losses due to mines, the number of victims was 49 and the tonnage 148,000, and, whether the losses be measured by tonnage or by numbers, no such black month for British shipping had as yet marked the course of the war.

---

[1] These instructions were sent to the Naval Intelligence Officers on July 22nd, and by August 5th they had gone out to all the Consular Offices.

A BLACK MONTH

By far the greater number of casualties took place in the South-Western Approach, where, at one period, four enemy submarines were simultaneously at work. Within the limits of the area 32 British, 4 Allied, and 5 neutral merchantmen were destroyed, and among them was the largest and most valuable vessel which had fallen a victim since the destruction of the *Lusitania*. This was the great White Star liner *Arabic*, of 15,801 tons, which was sunk twenty miles from the Smalls on August 19th, with a loss of 44 lives. She was the only vessel in this area torpedoed without warning during August, for, as during the two previous months, the submarines were now mostly operating far out from land.

The loss and damage caused by submarines operating in the South-Western Approach did not, however, end here. During a week of exceptionally heavy weather it proved impossible to maintain unbroken the line of drifters between the Tuskar and the Smalls, and, taking advantage of this opportunity, a submarine succeeded in slipping through into the Irish Sea, where she sank three steamers off Bardsey Island and the South Arklow Light Vessel.

On the North-about Route there were few casualties, but in the North Sea five British merchantmen and over thirty fishing craft were destroyed. A dozen neutral vessels were also sunk, among them the Swedish steamer *Malmland*, bound from Narvik to Rotterdam, for whom, in view of her destination, the German Government agreed to compensate the owners. The larger German warships remained quiescent, but the armed auxiliary METEOR [1] broke out into the northern waters of the North Sea, captured and burnt a little Danish schooner, the *Jason*, laden with pitprops for Granton, and laid a new minefield off the Moray Firth. This daring raid did not go unpunished, for the METEOR failed to escape detection and was blown up by her own crew in order to escape certain capture. Nevertheless, her work had been done, and, though the Moray Firth minefield was swept up before the end of the month, it had already claimed a couple of victims. Some half-dozen other vessels were also sunk in the southern area, where the submarine mine-layers had been at work.

Great as were the resources of British shipping, a con-

---

[1] The METEOR was the British steamer *Vienna* of 1,912 tons and 14 knots, which had been detained at Hamburg on the outbreak of war and subsequently converted into an armed auxiliary and mine-layer.

tinuation of losses on the scale suffered in August could not be lightly regarded, and the apparently unchecked operations of the enemy in the South-Western Approach threatened yet further havoc to an extent never before approached during the war. Yet the development of the campaign during August was marked by some features encouraging to the defence. The net barriers across the Straits of Dover, the North Channel, and the St. George's Channel were fulfilling their purpose well.[1] The new line of nets laid between the East Coast sandbanks had proved equally successful, and the crowded waters of the Swept Channel were, generally speaking, immune from attack.[2] Even in the South-Western Approach itself the activity of the submarines was hampered. As the strength and efficiency of the patrols increased, they were gradually pushed farther and farther out from shore.[3] Both armed trawlers and net-drifters were now operating well out from the coast-line at various points, and the submarines were forced more and more into the open sea. Nor even in the open sea was their task free from danger. The decoy-ship BARALONG claimed her first victim on August 19th, when she sank U 27, then engaged with the Leyland liner *Nicosian*, more than seventy miles from the Irish coast. During the same month the arrival of a Sloop Squadron from the North Sea added greatly to the efficiency of the deep-sea patrol, and by September the route given to merchant vessels from North America was identical with that followed by transports from Canada, and thus received some measure of protection from the escorting destroyers.

Four other vessels besides the *Nicosian* were rescued during August in the South-Western Approach, and encounters between submarines and patrols were numerous.

[1] The submarine which penetrated into the Irish Sea sank, on her way, two steamers just inside the Smalls-Tuskar line which have been counted among those destroyed in the South-Western Approach. One of these was the *Isodoro*, bringing iron ore from Bilbao to Cardiff, the first Spanish steamer to be sunk in the war.
A single submarine mine-layer penetrated the Straits of Dover on August 20th, and on the following day the small steamer *William Dawson* was blown up off Boulogne; but this was the only casualty in the English Channel during the month.
[2] Two vessels were torpedoed at the beginning of August off Palling, Norfolk, and Blakeney Buoy, respectively; but there is no record of the net line between the Longsand and the Shipwash Bank being penetrated.
[3] By August 30th the strength of the Auxiliary Patrols operating in British waters was 79 yachts, 691 armed trawlers or drifters, 786 net-drifters, 270 mine-sweepers, 156 motor-boats, and 198 trawlers and drifters for boom defence, actually on station.

By the end of the month the Germans had lost twenty submarines in all areas, and by various means, since the beginning of the war. Exactly half of these had been destroyed during the last three months. Sixteen of the twenty were of the ocean-going class, and they represented a large proportion of the effective force actually available. Moreover, the attitude of the United States rendered it dangerous for the submarine campaign in British Home Waters to be continued on the lines which had resulted in the sinking of the *Lusitania*, and on no other lines did the German Admiralty believe that it could be effective.[1]

Had no alternative field of operations been available, the Germans might have been willing to accept all risks in order to continue their attack on British shipping at its most vulnerable point; but the progress of events in Gallipoli and the incalculable consequences to be apprehended from the reopening of the Dardanelles had already attracted their attention to the Mediterranean as a still more vital theatre, and much of the havoc in the South-Western Approach during August was wrought by submarines on their way out to that sea.

Apart from the slow progress of the Dardanelles operations and the possibility of their disturbance by submarine attack, the naval situation within the Straits was satisfactory. No further serious attempt had been made on the Suez Canal, and the great highway to the East remained unmolested save for a threatened attack on Aden, which came to nothing, and an intermittent shelling of Perim Harbour from Sheikh Saiyad. On the other hand, the effectiveness of economic pressure on the Central Powers had been greatly increased by the entrance of Italy into the war. For some time past the Italian Government had taken steps, by export prohibitions and drastic supervision of railway traffic, to restrict the passage of contraband to Germany, either direct or through Switzerland. Their action was reinforced, after the publication of the British Order in Council of March 11th, by that of the Italian shipping companies, who telegraphed to their agents in North and South America instructions to refuse transit cargoes of a nature likely to involve the diversion or detention of the ships by British cruisers. Thus, even while Italy remained neutral the volume of imports reaching Germany and Austria through Genoa and other

[1] Von Tirpitz (English edition), p. 416.

Italian ports was greatly diminished; but by May the sands of her neutrality were running out. On the 4th of that month she formally denounced the Triple Alliance, and on the 23rd declared war against Austria. The German Government promptly broke off relations, but the Italians were not ready for war with Germany, and refrained at first from seizing the German vessels lying in their ports. Both the export of Italian products to Germany and the transit trade were, however, reduced to a minimum. Meanwhile, over 80,000 tons of Austrian shipping had passed into Italian hands,[1] and on May 6th the Italian Government proclaimed a blockade of the Austrian and Albanian coasts.

On the other hand, there was ample evidence that at least one German submarine had actually passed through the Straits, for on May 16th a French cruiser was attacked, and towards the end of the month the battleships TRIUMPH and MAJESTIC were sunk off the entrance to the Dardanelles. It had now become a matter of primary importance to prevent the establishment of submarine bases within the Mediterranean, and the French squadron in the Levant were busily engaged in this task and in the interception of supplies intended to facilitate the movement of Turkish troops either against Egypt or towards the Dardanelles. The majority of the vessels sunk or captured off the Syrian coast were small Turkish and Greek sailing vessels laden with foodstuffs, but copper and oil cargoes were also captured. Meanwhile a formal blockade of the coast of Asia Minor from Samos to the Dardanelles was proclaimed by Great Britain as from June 2nd; the Russian Fleet in the Black Sea swept the Anatolian coast with such success that by August 2nd they were able to announce the capture or destruction of more than a score of Turkish steamers and some 450 small sailing craft carrying coal and stores to Constantinople; and from May onwards British submarines penetrated into the sea of Marmora and sank several Turkish and German steamers and many sailing vessels engaged in the transport of troops or stores.[2]

[1] Including three steamers in the ports of Eritrea and Italian Somaliland. Two of the Austrian steamers in Italian ports had previously been transferred to the Italian flag.

[2] Although these vessels were actually in belligerent employment, ample time was given before their destruction for the escape of those on board to the adjacent coast.

Actively as traffic with the Turkish ports was harried, the dominant motive of all these operations was military rather than economic, and it was chiefly as a threat to our military communications that the irruption of enemy submarines into the Mediterranean was regarded by the British Admiralty, and was in fact intended by the German Government. The reality of the threat was soon demonstrated, for on July 4th the French transport *Carthage* was sunk, and on August 13th the *Royal Edward*, a steamer of 11,117 tons, crowded with British troops, was torpedoed in the Ægean, with heavy loss of life. During September another transport, the *Southland*, was torpedoed but succeeded in reaching port, the *Ramazan*, laden with military stores, was captured and sunk, and the oiler *H. C. Henry* met the same fate.

Despite these initial successes, and though their activity threw a heavy strain on the naval forces of the Allies and involved constant dislocation of the transport arrangements, the German submarines proved totally unable to stop the flow of reinforcements and stores to Gallipoli; nor did they meet with any substantial further success against the Allied squadrons. The whole trade of the Mediterranean was, however, open to their attack, and this attack could be pressed simultaneously with that upon the transport routes. At first everything else was neglected in the attempt to disturb the Dardanelles operations, but, as further submarines arrived, the scope of the enemy's activity extended. Three British steamers homeward bound with commercial cargoes were captured and destroyed during September,[1] and their fate would have been shared by the *Antilochus* of the Ocean Steamship Company had she not carried a defensive armament and known how to use it. Two French steamers, an Italian steamer, and a small Italian sailing vessel swelled the list of victims.

By this time at least three German submarines had passed the Straits, and others were on their way out; nor was this all. Although Turkey possessed no effective craft of this description at the beginning of the war, it was ascertained that the Germans had sent two or three of small type overland, in sections, to be fitted together at Constantinople. Others had been despatched in the same way to Pola, to reinforce the Austrian flotilla.

[1] One of these was from Alexandria, the others from Indian ports.

The situation thus created was serious. The Austrian submarines, old and new, had a comparatively small radius of action, and showed little or no sign of activity outside the Adriatic, and the German boats sent overland to Constantinople were unlikely to be used far from the coast. Even so, they were a serious menace to the mass of transports in the Ægean, as well as to Allied shipping in the Black Sea, where the British steamer *Patagonia* was torpedoed without warning on September 15th. The submarines which had passed the Straits, on the other hand, were of the latest type, with a fair speed, and capable of a three weeks' cruise without renewing their supplies. It was now evident that not only transports and store-ships but the whole of the great volume of merchant shipping in the Mediterranean required protection against attacks, and such protection it was very difficult to provide. The Mediterranean is a long and broad sea having many focal points and channels of moderate breadth between the islands to compel concentration of shipping; but no waters so restricted that they could be barred to the enemy. The anchorage at Mudros had been rendered reasonably secure, and there were many defended ports, French, Italian, and Egyptian, in which vessels could safely lie; but for protection during the long passage of some 2,000 miles either to the Ægean or Port Said, transports and merchant vessels alike could rely only on direct escort or their own armament.

The Mediterranean thus afforded to the enemy a fair prospect of striking British trade a heavy blow, at much less risk to the material and crews employed than was involved in a continuance of operations round the British Isles, and with less danger of arousing neutral, especially American hostility. The volume of trade exposed to attack was, indeed, much smaller than that passing through the South-Western Approach, but it was large in itself, and, including as it did the whole commerce of the Oriental Route, it was of vital importance to Great Britain. Moreover, the attack could be combined with continued pressure on the communications of the British and French military forces in the Eastern theatre of war.

To carry on effective operations simultaneously in the Mediterranean and in British Home Waters would have required a larger number of ocean-going submarines than the Germans at this time possessed. They accordingly decided, for the time being, to concentrate the whole weight of the attack in the Mediterranean, confining themselves in Home Waters to the operations of the submarine mine-layers and the small coastal type in the North Sea. It is true that over a dozen vessels were sunk during September on the North-about Route or in the Atlantic, but these were mostly, if not all, casual victims of submarines either returning to their home base or on their way to a more distant cruising ground. One such boat, U 41, bound for the Mediterranean, fell a victim to the BARALONG, but two at least continued on their way to the Straits, and a third turned aside into the Bay of Biscay, where she sank three British and two French merchantmen off the mouth of the Gironde. In the North Sea, where the submarines had been sharply handled during the last few months, the attack also died down. Half a dozen small Norwegian sailing vessels laden with staves and pit-props for British ports were captured and destroyed off Lindesnæs, but there were few other casualties, except those caused by submarine mine-layers. These, indeed, were active. Early in the month UC 5 laid mines off Folkestone and Boulogne, and the Swept Channels in the Thames Estuary and along the East Coast were frequently penetrated. Nearly a dozen vessels were sunk or damaged in the Downs, in the Thames Approaches, or off the East Coast. Among these was the *Königin Emma*, of the Netherland Steamship Company, bound from Batavia to Amsterdam, which struck a mine off the Sunk Light Vessel on September 22nd, and sank shortly after. A steamer of 9,181 tons, she was the largest neutral vessel as yet destroyed in the war.

Serious as was the effect of the increased activity displayed by the submarine mine-layers, both in loss of ships and dislocation of traffic, it was kept within narrow limits by the untiring energy of the mine-sweeping service and the patrols. At its worst it was a small matter compared with the operations of the cruising submarines in the South-Western Approach during August. The total war losses of British merchantmen during September amounted, indeed, to over 100,000 tons, but they were little more than two-thirds of those suffered in the previous month. The future development of the attack in the Mediterranean gave ample ground for legitimate anxiety, but on the whole it might be hoped that, for the time being, the upward tendency of the curve of destruction had received a decided check.

CHAPTER VII

THE NORTH SEA AND RUSSIA
DURING THE SPRING AND SUMMER OF 1915

HEAVY as were the losses inflicted by German submarines during the spring and summer of 1915, the new form of attack on commerce showed as yet little sign of attaining its ultimate object, the economic isolation of the British Isles. Many fine ships and valuable cargoes had been sent to the bottom; but neither British nor foreign shipping had allowed itself to be terrorised, and there was little, if any, diminution in the stream of traffic from and to British ports. Startling as were their successes, the submarines had failed to check the flow of trade.

Nowhere was their failure more conspicuous than in the North Sea, and the continued activity of shipping on the North Sea tracks was the more notable because no other branch of British trade was so dependent on the assistance of neutrals. Although the Germans had not as yet hardened their hearts to an indiscriminate attack on neutrals, they no doubt hoped, when they issued their warnings of February 2nd and 4th, that the dangers threatened to ships entering the war zone would be sufficient to deter many shipowners from sending their vessels to British ports. More particularly might this expectation be entertained as regards vessels trading between Great Britain, and Holland or Scandinavia. The North Sea minefields and the German command of the entrance to the Baltic already made these trades sufficiently perilous. The new danger threatened by the submarine campaign was accentuated in this area by the proximity of the tracks to the German bases.

The opening incidents of the campaign emphasised the risk. The attacks on the *Belridge, Hanna, Katwijk,* and *Ellispontos* may have been due to mistaken identity, but they were suggestive of a calculated recklessness which might perhaps strike fear into the hearts of neutral shipowners and seamen. The treatment of the *Medea, Batavier V*, and *Zaanstroom*, showed how widely the Germans were prepared to stretch the definition of contraband and how drastically they were prepared to deal with vessels carrying " contraband " cargoes.

Fortunately, as we have seen, the effect of these incidents was far smaller than might have been anticipated, and the German warnings were simply ignored by the majority of neutral shipowners in the North Sea trade. Events proved that their attitude was justified. Whatever they might threaten, the German Government were too deeply interested in maintaining friendly relations with States from or through which valuable supplies were received, to permit indiscriminate torpedo attacks on Dutch or Scandinavian merchantmen. There were, indeed, a few instances in which the submarines displayed a complete disregard for neutral lives. For example, the Norwegian steamer *Svein Jarl* from Warkworth for Kirknes with coal, was torpedoed without warning on the night of June 9th and twelve of her crew were drowned. In general, however, neutral ships in the North Sea were sunk only when examination revealed them to be carrying cargoes of unmistakable contraband, and even then time was allowed for the crew to take to their boats before the prize was sunk or set on fire. Two or three were taken into German ports. Others were merely required to throw contraband cargo overboard.

It was Dutch shipping which was exposed to the greatest risks. The direct track from Dutch ports to the Thames Estuary ran through the most dangerous area of the North Sea. The British and German minefields, from both of which mines frequently drifted, were always a serious source of danger, and vessels following these tracks were now exposed also to the attack of submarines issuing from the advanced bases at Zeebrugge and Ostend. It was natural, therefore, that the German warning of February 4th should be taken seriously in Holland. The Dutch shipowners were alarmed at the possibility of mistakes arising from the use of neutral flags as a disguise by British merchantmen, and the Netherlands Government went so far as to intimate that no British ship known to have sailed under Dutch colours would be allowed to enter any port in Holland or her Colonies. Meanwhile, the regular services to the United Kingdom under the Dutch flag were temporarily suspended, and though the London services of the Batavier and Zealand Lines were resumed by March 1st,[1] there was a considerable falling off from April onwards, in the entrances of Dutch, and to a less degree of British, tonnage from Dutch ports.

The falling off in British entrances would have been still greater but for the steps taken by the Board of Trade to afford insurance at reasonable premiums. In view of the exceptional risks involved, the voyage to Dutch ports had, from the first, been excluded from the State Insurance Scheme, but in order to maintain the supplies of margarine and dairy produce from Holland the Board, early in the war, arranged to insure direct the General Steam Navigation Company's steamers, and in December 1914 a similar arrangement was made with the Great Eastern Railway Company. After the proclamation of the submarine "blockade" it became necessary to go further, as the rates quoted on the open market were such as to discourage traffic, and in May 1915 the Board agreed to insure all British vessels in the trade with Holland.[2]

In spite of this encouragement importers and shipowners had many difficulties to contend with. The position of Holland as the main gateway now open into Germany necessitated a drastic restriction of the passenger traffic which bore hardly on the regular services. Indeed, from April 21st to May 5th all traffic between the two countries was absolutely suspended by an Admiralty order issued at the request of the War Office to ensure secrecy for important military movements. Even had ample tonnage always been available imports must have dropped, for Holland had less to send. Not only was it necessary for Holland to conserve her own supplies of commodities such as sugar and rice, in view of the diminution of German exports and the laying up of German shipping, but Germany herself was a strong competitor in the Dutch markets. So high were the prices the Germans were now willing to give for butter and other foodstuffs that the proportion of the exportable surplus sent down the Rhine or over the land frontier, steadily increased at the expense of Great Britain.

It was this increase in the enemy's food supplies which

---

[1] *Times*, 1 March, 1915.
[2] *Government War Insurance Schemes. Preliminary Statement of Results.* [Cmd. 98.] 1919.

was the most important aspect of the shrinkage in imports from the Netherlands. As regards British supplies that shrinkage was not, in itself, a vital matter. The shipments of meat, butter, cheese, sugar, rice, potatoes, peas, tapioca, flour, tobacco, and petroleum all fell away by 50 to 100 per cent., but in respect of none of these commodities did Holland rank among the principal sources of supply. On the other hand, the really important supplies of condensed milk still came forward freely, and the imports of margarine, obtained almost exclusively from the Netherlands, increased by nearly 50 per cent. Large consignments of cured or salted fish helped to make good the dislocation of the British fisheries, and increased shipments of flax did something to compensate the diminution in Russian exports. In return, coal was shipped to Holland at the rate of 150,000 tons a month. The exports of manufactured goods fell away considerably owing to the restrictions imposed by the War Trade Department and the diversion of labour and plant in Great Britain to war uses, but the re-exports of foreign and colonial produce, and the consignments by parcel post were so large that the total trade balance was decidedly in favour of Great Britain. The increase in the parcel post was mainly accounted for by the number of parcels despatched to prisoners in the internment camps, but there was, unfortunately, little doubt that a large proportion of the re-exports—tea, coffee, cocoa, and tobacco—ultimately found its way to Germany. The shipments of nuts, kernels, oils, and oil-seeds stood on a somewhat different footing, for Great Britain had a strong and direct interest in maintaining the supply of materials to the Dutch manufacturers of margarine; but in this traffic, too, the enemy were concerned, for it was largely from and through Holland that the Germans drew their dwindling supply of oils and fats, and the increased production of margarine for domestic consumption in Holland had the effect of releasing butter for export to Germany.

On Scandinavian trade the submarine threat produced even less impression, though the number of ships sunk was greater. Had the Germans possessed sufficient submarines for a sustained offensive at the entrance to the Baltic, and had there been no political or economic considerations to limit their activity, they might, no doubt, have paralysed the Danish and much of the Swedish traffic.

But it was vitally important to Germany not to imperil her imports of iron ore from Sweden, of meat and dairy produce from Denmark. Even had the necessary force been available the Germans dared not go too far in disregard of Swedish or Danish interests. Their patrols in the Kattegat were busy, and large numbers of Scandinavian ships bound to or from British or Allied ports were taken into Swinemünde, but the definition of contraband was not unduly stretched, and the majority both of ships and cargoes were released. Moreover, many steamers with contraband cargoes were able to elude the patrols by keeping to territorial waters which the Germans could not violate without the risk of serious friction.

Once clear of the Skagerak, the open run from Lindesnæs to the British coast presented no overwhelming dangers. The German submarines at work in the North Sea were not very numerous, and the route was protected to some extent by the frequent southerly sweeps made by the British naval forces. For vessels following the tracks indicated by the Admiralty there was, therefore, no great risk, and, after arriving off the British coast, ships bound for the more southerly ports could run down the Swept Channel, inside the line of minefields and patrols, in comparative safety. From the more northerly Norwegian ports the voyage was even more secure, since the tracks led well clear of the entrance to the Baltic.

There was, however, one branch of Scandinavian trade which was peculiarly exposed to submarine attack. In the North Sea, as elsewhere, the shortage of steam tonnage was the opportunity of the sailing vessel. Even the older vessels which were approaching the limit of active service now found charters easy to obtain at the Norwegian ports, and during the spring and summer of 1915 the arrivals of Scandinavian sailing vessels laden with pit-props or timber were unusually numerous, particularly at the East Scottish ports.[1] These vessels were, of course, incapable of following the special tracks indicated to neutral steamers, and the losses among them were heavy. From March to September inclusive no fewer than thirty were destroyed; but they were mostly very small, and the total tonnage sunk on the Scandinavian tracks was insignificant in comparison with the volume of traffic.

Such as they were, the risks were far too small to deter

[1] *Lloyd's List*, 1 March, 1 April, 3, 18 May, 1915.

the hardy Scandinavian mariners from sailing, or to drive the Scandinavian shipowners out of a remunerative trade which could be covered by insurance at reasonable rates. Thus the flow of imports from Norway and Denmark was little smaller than in times of peace. The important supplies of bacon and butter from Denmark were maintained at little below the normal standard, and though eggs came forward less freely, owing to German competition in the Danish market, large supplies were still obtained. The Norwegian trade was still more prosperous. Imports of paper, wood-pulp, sawn timber, pit-props, and iron ore increased in volume. The import of fish oils went up with a bound, and though the import of fresh fish declined, owing to Germany's purchase of the entire herring catch, the decrease was compensated by larger shipments of cured and salted fish. In the exports from Great Britain to Norway and Denmark, coal was by far the most important item, whether as regards weight or value, and there was no sign of falling off in the shipments; in fact, they were even larger than usual, as the loss of German supplies had to be made good. Other exports, such as hardware and textiles, were also fairly maintained, and generally speaking, the Norwegian and Danish branches of the Scandinavian trade might be regarded as normal.

For Sweden, the problem of export to Great Britain was more difficult, inasmuch as ships coming from the Baltic ports had to run the gauntlet of the German cruisers and torpedo craft off Falsterbo, as well as that of the submarines and minefields in the North Sea. So great was the danger that, on the announcement of the German plan of campaign, the Swedish State Insurance Office doubled the premiums on voyages to British ports. Yet, despite all interference with the course of trade, the volume of traffic from Sweden to Great Britain was fully maintained. The imports of paper were equal to those of 1913, and those of wood-pulp considerably larger. Little iron ore or hæmatite pig-iron now came from Sweden, but the imports of other kinds of pig-iron increased. It was, however, the shipments of timber which formed, to Sweden, the most valuable portion of the British trade, and which employed the greatest amount of tonnage, and it was in respect of the traffic in timber that the German command of the lower waters of the Baltic gave rise to the greatest difficulty.

It will be remembered that so early as November 1914 great alarm had been excited in Sweden by a German proclamation to the effect that all wood and lumber would be considered as conditional contraband, unless so greatly increased in value by hand or machine working as to put its use for fuel commercially out of the question, and this alarm had been reflected by the refusal of the Swedish State Insurance Office to insure wood cargoes.[1] Since then things had gone from bad to worse. The proclamation of November 17th was followed in December 1914 and January 1915 by the decisions of the Kiel Prize Court in the cases of the *Alfred Hage* and *Belle Isle*, which interpreted both the definition of conditional contraband, and that of a belligerent base of supply in a sense very unfavourable to Swedish interests. In face of this attitude on the part of Germany, it was impossible to carry on the trade, and early in February a leading commercial organ in Sweden reported that loadings were at a standstill and that not a single steamer had been chartered for the coming season to carry timber to British or French ports.[2] By working the railways to Gothenberg and Norwegian ports to their fullest capacity, it was found possible to forward larger consignments than usual during the months in which the Gulf of Bothnia is frozen; but the capabilities of this alternative outlet were limited, and everything turned on the hope of some change in the situation before the break-up of the ice.

Happily for Swedish shippers, the importance to Germany of the ore-traffic and the transhipment trade supplied a lever which could be utilised effectively in obtaining consideration for Swedish interests. In respect of pit-props the German Government was not inclined to give way; but with regard to sawn timber an agreement was arrived at during March by which the Germans undertook that, for the time being, they would not interfere with wood cargoes of a description not considered as contraband prior to November 1914, subject to each ship obtaining a certificate from the Swedish Customs that the timber was of native origin, and that no firewood, pit-wood, or other contraband was included in the cargo. Accordingly, on March 23rd, the Swedish State Insurance

[1] Vol. I, pp. 358–60.
[2] *Kommersiella Meddelanden*, quoted by *Lloyd's List*, 5 April, 1915, from the *Journal of the Swedish Chamber of Commerce in London*, 25 March, 1915.

Committee announced that they were again ready to accept war risks on wood cargoes for any destination, and chartering was immediately resumed.¹

This revival of trade was not affected by a German proclamation issued on April 18th, which placed "all kinds of timber, rough or treated, especially hewn, sawn, planed, fluted, excepting mining lumber" in the list of conditional contraband.² The agreement made in March was still adhered to by the German Government, and as soon as the ice broke, trade was actively resumed. In only one instance was there any interference with this traffic. On June 15th the Swedish steamer *Verdandi* with a cargo of deals from Norrköping for Manchester, was sunk by the METEOR at the entrance to the Baltic; but for this incident the German Government at once apologised and offered compensation, and it had no effect on the course of trade.³ The position of shippers was, indeed, considerably strengthened on July 6th by the judgment of the Supreme Prize Court, Berlin, reversing the decision of the lower court in the case of the *Belle Isle*, as this judgment made it quite clear that ordinary sawn goods were not contraband at the date of the November Proclamation and were therefore exempt from capture, under the existing agreement. So thoroughly was confidence restored that the exports of sawn wood to Great Britain were greater, month by month, than in the last year of peace.

On the other hand, little comfort could be extracted from the judgment of the Supreme Court allowing the appeal in the case of the *Alfred Hage*, for this decision was based on evidence as to the commercial destination of a particular cargo of pit-props which, at the date of the seizure, were conditional contraband.⁴ By the Proclamation of April 18th "mining lumber" was removed into the "absolute" category, and it was evident that pit-props, sleepers, and all hewn wood could be sent forward only at considerable risk. Nevertheless, Swedish vessels laden with cargoes of this description continued to evade the German patrols by keeping in territorial waters as far as Lindesnæs. Other consignments were railed for shipment to Norwegian ports, and the total import of pit-props from Sweden was the same as in 1913.

¹ *Lloyd's List*, 7 April, 1915 (Stockholm); 15 April, 1915 (Foreign Office announcement).
² *Ibid.*, 13 May, 1915.
³ *Times*, 23 June, 1915.
⁴ Vol. I, p. 359.

It was not, however, only the export trade of the Scandinavian States which was subject to interference. Three or four steamers carrying coal to Scandinavian ports were sunk by submarines in the North Sea, and several homeward-bound Swedish vessels, mostly colliers, were taken into Swinemünde for examination. So serious was the inconvenience caused by the constant stoppage of vessels both inward and outward bound that, during May, the Swedish shipping companies running the regular lines to the United Kingdom decided to suspend their sailings from and to Stockholm and Norrköping, and to adopt the ports on the Sound (Hälsingborg and Malmö) as terminals.[1] In the following month, however, the German Government made a concession of great value to Swedish merchants and shipowners, by agreeing that, when a cargo consisted of goods the export of which from Sweden was prohibited, the ship should be allowed to pass, after examination of her papers off Falsterbö, without being taken in to Swinemünde.[2]

Satisfactory as this agreement might be to Swedish merchants and shipowners, it could not be regarded with equal complacency by the Allies, for it was expressly designed to discourage the transit trade through Sweden to Russia, one of the few avenues now left open for Russian imports and exports. The services between Stockholm and Raumo had been kept up as usual during the winter, by the aid of ice-breakers, and early in the new year a Finnish service under the Russian flag was opened between Stockholm and Abö, and was connived at by the German Government owing to the facilities offered for the return of invalid German prisoners sent home under exchange.[3] Nor were these services interfered with when active hostilities in the Baltic were resumed in the spring. Overmatched as it was, the Russian Baltic Squadron was sufficiently powerful to prevent the Germans from operating in the Gulf of Bothnia without employing a stronger force than could wisely be risked in minor operations. South of the Gulf of Finland, on the other hand, the Germans had an undisturbed command of the Baltic, and were free to embark on operations against the Russian coast.

[1] *Times*, 20 May, 1915.
[2] *Lloyd's List*, 1 July, 1915 (Stockholm, 19 June).
[3] *Ibid.*, 3 March, 1915.

The chief importance of these operations lay in the struggle for the Russian ports of Libau and Riga. Libau was finally evacuated on the night of May 8th, but the attack on the Gulf of Riga, which began early in June, ended in August with the retirement of the Germans.[1] The successful defence of the Gulf was greatly assisted by the presence of British submarines, which had succeeded in passing into the Baltic, and subsequently turned their attention, with excellent results, to harrying German trade with Sweden.

These operations in the lower Baltic did not, however, affect the services to Raumo from Swedish ports, and, though freights were very high, a considerable amount of traffic was carried on. Still more important was the railway traffic between Sweden and Finland. During the winter months, when the White Sea was closed to navigation and the passage across the Gulf of Bothnia was confined to the narrow track cut by the ice-breakers, this was almost the only line of communication left open between Russia and the Western Allies. Thanks to the assistance of the powerful ice-breaker *Canada*, Archangel was kept open for some three months beyond the usual period, but towards the end of January the *Canada* was disabled by an accident, and by the beginning of February the port was practically closed. With the Baltic and Black Seas both blocked, and the White Sea frozen up, the dependence of Russia on the transhipment route through Sweden became absolute. In view of the probable indefinite prolongation of the war, it was vital that she should be able to import the munitions, equipment, and material which she was unable to draw from her own resources, and though the closing of the Dardanelles prevented the shipment of the Russian harvests in payment, this difficulty had been overcome by the grant of large credits in France and Great Britain which enabled the necessary purchases to be made.[2] It was the carriage,

[1] On the evacuation of Libau five German steamers seized on the outbreak of war were abandoned to the enemy, together with one British steamer and a dozen small Russian sailing vessels. The steamers were all sunk prior to the evacuation, but were subsequently salved by the enemy. During August three of the British steamers detained in German ports were sunk to block the Channel off Pernau.

Several Scandinavian steamers were damaged during the bombardments of Libau on March 28th, and Windau June 28th.

[2] Statement by Mr. Lloyd George in House of Commons, *Hansard*, 15 January, 1915.

not the financing, of imports which presented the gravest problem.

Fortunately, the same month in which the White Sea was closed saw a great improvement in the railway facilities. The chief obstacle to the development of the transhipment route during 1914 had been the necessity of carting goods by road from the terminus of the Swedish railway at Karungi to Harparanda, where they were ferried across to Tornea, the total road journey involved amounting to some sixteen miles. In order to obviate this difficulty a new railway was commenced during the winter from Tornea to Karunki, opposite Karungi, on the Finnish side of the Tornea River. On February 7th the station at Karunki was opened, and the break in the railway journey was thus reduced to one and a half miles, goods discharged at Karungi being ferried across to the new Finnish terminus. The effect of this development was in great measure to relieve the congestion on the Swedish railways, and during the following months the rail traffic showed a considerable increase.[1]

Even with this improvement the transhipment route was a very restricted channel for Russian imports, but some relief was found in the rapid development of the trade of Vladivostok. Thanks to the undisturbed command of the China and Japan Seas established by the Allies early in the war, the products of British India and the East Indies, China, Japan, and the Philippines flowed freely into the Siberian port, and during the early months of 1915 very heavy shipments from North America began to cross the Pacific. Now that Admiral von Spee's Squadron had been destroyed, all danger of interruption to the traffic was gone, and with the closing of the White Sea by ice the importance of Vladivostok was greatly increased. The Russian Volunteer Fleet took large cargoes both from Puget Sound and from British Columbia, and the Royal Mail Steam Packet Company found it worth while to extend its Pacific services so as to share in the trade. Tramp tonnage was scarce, owing to the strong demand on other routes, and the British and Norwegian steamers which were usually to be found in the Northern Pacific had mostly been drawn away, but Japanese shipowners were able to fill the gap, and several Japanese tramps were fixed for the voyage. Many

[1] *Times, Russian Supplement*, 26 April, 1915.

thousand bales of cotton and large consignments of machinery formed the most important items in the cargoes, and during February alone, the exports from the American ports on Puget Sound to Vladivostok amounted to nearly £300,000 in value, considerably more than the exports to Asiatic Russia for the whole year 1914.[1] From all sources together the imports at Vladivostok during the first six months of 1915 amounted to over 200,000 tons, an increase of 33 per cent. on the figures for the same period of 1914.[2]

The diversion of trade to Vladivostok was, however, very uneconomical as regards the use of tonnage, for, though some heavy shipments of soya beans were sent to the United Kingdom, return cargoes in general were scarce, and many lengthy ballast voyages were thus involved. Moreover, the restricted capacity of the port and of the Siberian Railway, and the immense length of rail transport involved, rendered it impossible for the trade of Vladivostok to be, at best, more than a partial palliative for the closing of the European tracks. Nor could the transhipment route through Sweden, whether by rail or across the Gulf of Bothnia, take more than a small proportion of the traffic. For all bulky exports, such as timber, and for the larger proportion of the import trade, the White Sea was now the only available channel, and great efforts were made to open Archangel at the earliest possible date. In this matter the Allies of Russia were vitally interested, and during February the ice-breaker *Lintrose* arrived in the White Sea to take the place of the *Canada*, which had to go to Barrow for repairs. The old battleship JUPITER was also sent out by the Admiralty to assist in clearing a passage. On May 17th Archangel was declared open, but even before that date shipping had begun to arrive at the entrance to the White Sea, and by the end of the month the Sea was practically clear of ice.

It was, however, no easy matter to obtain tonnage. During 1914 the Russian Government Committee, established in London as a branch of the Commission Internationale de Ravitaillement, had found no difficulty in chartering through their agents, Messrs. R. Martens & Co., the ships required for carriage of their purchases. But by May 1915 the situation had changed. With plentiful employment on offer in trades more attractive

[1] *Lloyd's List*, 8, 10 April, 1915 (Seattle correspondent, 18 March).
[2] Official figures in *Times, Russian Supplement*, 17 December, 1915.

to the shipowner, neither British nor neutral owners were eager to accept White Sea charters. Time-charter rates rose rapidly, and even at high rates tonnage was far from plentiful. Russian shipping itself was quite inadequate to the fulfilment of Russian requirements, for a large proportion was locked up in the Baltic or the Black Sea. Munitions from France were shipped in vessels chartered by the Hudson Bay Company, agents for the French Ministry of Commerce, and for these shipments adequate tonnage was obtained; but there was a serious shortage of shipping to lift cargoes from Great Britain and colliers were particularly scarce. The Russian Government accordingly applied for the allocation of requisitioned tonnage, and their request was granted in June, when the Admiralty Contracts Branch undertook the purchase of Russian coal and the Transport Department began to requisition tonnage for its transport to the White Sea. From this time onwards all coal shipped to Russia in British bottoms was carried on Government account, and requisitioned tonnage played an ever-increasing part in the munitions and general trade. For the return voyage these vessels were either granted temporary release in order to bring home cargoes of wood, flax, and other Russian products, or fixed by the Transport Department with the Hudson Bay Company for the French import service.

Unhappily the resources of Archangel were deplorably inadequate to the handling of the trade now pouring into the port. The quay space was insufficient, and, in default of cranes, cargo had to be discharged by hand, with the aid of capstans. Yet, slowly as cargo was discharged, it was still more slowly removed. The railway station was on the southern side of the Dvina, and all goods had to cross the river before being loaded into trucks. From Archangel to Vologda there was nothing but a single line of narrow gauge, insufficiently equipped with rolling stock, and the break of gauge at Vologda necessitated rehandling the goods. From Archangel to Perm there was a river voyage of 400 miles before a railway was reached at all. The other White Sea ports, Soroka, Kem, and Kandalaksha were without railway facilities of any kind, as were the ice-free ports of Kola and Alexandrovsk on the Murman Coast. As regards the export of timber this lack of railways was of no consequence, for the materials were floated down the rivers to the port of shipment; but the effect on imports was very serious, and in the ordinary way the White Sea route accounted for only about 100,000 tons a year out of a total of nearly 7,000,000 tons of seaborne imports.

Even during the latter months of 1914 the port authorities had to struggle with imports arriving at ten times the normal rate, and this trade was now exceeded. So slow was the work of distribution that goods in enormous quantities accumulated at the port, and for these there was no proper warehouse accommodation; they lay about on the quays exposed to every kind of damage. So early as May 27th an official notice was issued that the Russian Government had been obliged to requisition almost the whole of the quays, and that, though the export of timber would be allowed to proceed, the import of private goods would be practically impossible. Even the import of government goods overstrained the resources of the port, and although the arrivals were very numerous, delays in the distribution of the cargoes greatly reduced the assistance thus rendered to the Russian armies.

The construction of a new railway to the ice-free ports on the Murman Coast had long been in contemplation, and appropriations for the survey of this line were actually made towards the end of 1914, but progress was exceedingly slow, and even the first section from Petrograd to Petrozavodsk on Lake Onega was not expected to be completed before the end of 1915. More immediate relief, however, was hoped for from the construction of a broad gauge line between Vologda and Archangel, parallel with the existing track. By the summer of 1915 the first stage of this line from Vologda to Niandarma, half-way to Archangel, was approaching completion, and great benefit was anticipated from it, as it would allow the whole of the narrow gauge rolling stock to be concentrated on the Niandarma-Archangel section.[1]

The difficulties of distribution from the port were not, however, the only impediments to trade on the Archangel Route. Vessels proceeding to and from the White Sea were liable to attack throughout almost the whole length of their voyage. Around the Orkneys and Shetlands, off Cape Wrath and the Butt of Lewis, there were almost always submarines in motion, on their way to or from the

[1] *Times, Russian Supplements*, 15 January, 26 April, 1915.

South-Western Approach, harrying the fishing fleets, or seeking for occasion to attack the Grand Fleet itself; all down the West Coast of Scotland and Ireland there was the risk of meeting enemy craft proceeding to or returning from their chosen cruising ground; and during August one submarine at least made its way into the lonely waters north of the Lofotens for the express purpose of attacking the White Sea trade. Hence, although special tracks were given to the masters, involving the minimum of risk, over a dozen steamers, British, Russian, or Norwegian, were lost between the end of April and the beginning of September.

Early in June, moreover, a new menace was revealed at the entrance to the White Sea itself; for on the 11th of that month, the British collier *Arndale* struck a mine as she rounded Cape Orlov, and ran ashore in order to save the lives of her crew. At the request of the Russian Government, six mine-sweeping trawlers, under Commander Bernays, R.N., were sent out to clear a passage, and by the beginning of July they were already at work. Their task proved to be exceedingly difficult. The mines —subsequently ascertained to have been laid by the METEOR during May—were numerous and widely scattered, and little assistance was received from the authorities at Archangel or from the Russian patrols, on whom fell the duty of warning incoming merchantmen and directing them into the safe channel. In spite of all obstacles, however, a channel was cleared, through which incoming or outgoing vessels were preceded by the sweepers. Even then occasional casualties occurred, mostly due to Russian mismanagement, and endless trouble was caused by the unnecessary delays to ships waiting off Svyatoi Nos for convoy or instructions. Nevertheless, the total losses down to the end of September, mostly incurred during the first few weeks before a channel had been cleared, amounted only to 6 British, 2 Russian, and 1 Norwegian steamer, and an American sailing vessel, sunk or damaged, including 3 British steamers salved and brought into Archangel. When regard is had to the difficulties under which the mine-sweepers worked and the extent of the traffic—some thirty vessels being more than once swept in in a single convoy—the record must be considered extremely creditable to the trawlers and their commander.

Thus, by one means and another, the communications between Russia and the Western Allies were to some extent kept open, and, in spite of all impediments, the essential supplies of munitions and war material were furnished to the Russian Government. As the effects of the improvement in the Finnish railway system, the development of the trade of Vladivostok, and the increasing traffic on the White Sea routes made themselves felt, the imports of the Empire showed a marked recovery. To the end of April the imports through all frontiers amounted only to about 38 per cent. in value of those received during the same months of 1914; by the end of June the proportion had risen to 44, and by the end of September to over 60 per cent. Much of this apparent increase was due, no doubt, to the advance in prices abroad and the continual fall in the Russian exchange; but, when all allowance is made for these factors a big actual increase is shown, due mainly to the success with which traffic was maintained on the White Sea and Scandinavian tracks, in spite of all the perils with which that traffic was menaced.

The position as regards exports was much less satisfactory; the transhipment route through Sweden, though it permitted the export of butter and eggs, was incapable of handling the bulkier commodities, such as wheat and timber, and afforded only a very limited output for flax and tow. With the opening of the White Sea, however, the timber export revived, and in addition to large quantities of eggs and butter, a little wheat was shipped from Archangel to France and Great Britain. By the autumn of 1915 Great Britain was receiving butter from Russia in even larger quantities than usual, and the supplies of flax and tow, so important for naval purposes, were also well maintained. The supply of eggs dwindled by more than two-thirds, and no oil-seeds were shipped, but some compensation for the loss of these seeds was provided by the shipments of the soya beans from Vladivostok. A more serious loss was that of the Finnish timber supplies. Despite the activity shown at Archangel, the closing down of the Baltic trade involved a great reduction in British wood imports from Russia. Yet even this was, to a great extent, made good by increased shipments of sawn timber from Norway, Sweden, and Canada. The biggest deficit was in pit-props. Increased supplies from Spain and Portugal were balanced by a falling off in those from France, and the Norwegian export, though it doubled the normal figures, did not go far to make good the deficiency in the Russian shipments. The only new source of supply available was British North America, and during the early months of the war, arrangements were made for the cutting of pit-props in Newfoundland; but, though the forests of Newfoundland and Canada were exploited with some success in 1915, the total deficiency amounted to 88 per cent. of the normal import, and it was necessary to resort to extensive cutting of home-grown timber in order to keep the collieries equipped.[1]

It was, however, on Russia herself that the diminution in the export trade bore most hardly. For the first nine months of 1915 the exports through all outlets and to all countries, were less than one-third in value of those recorded in the preceding year, and, in spite of the substantial support given to the Russian exchange by the British and French Governments, the value of the rouble shrank from 9·5 to the pound sterling in normal times, and 11·7 at the end of 1914, to 15·9 in the latter months of 1915. For the restoration of Russian credit, even more than for the supply of Russian needs, some less restricted avenue of trade than those now available was urgently required, and the progress of the Gallipoli operations was eagerly watched, in the hope that the Black Sea ports might once more be opened to traffic.

[1] Imports of pit-props in thousands of loads:

From	1911	1912	1913	1914	1915
Russia	1,286	1,277	1,539	737	61
Sweden	336	322	360	306	382
Norway	131	111	115	134	321
France	776	838	984	886	793
Spain	285	271	315	293	375
Portugal	70	80	103	95	132
Newfoundland	—	—	—	6	86
Canada	—	—	—	—	12
Other Countries	12	25	35	19	6
Total	2,896	2,926	3,451	2,476	2,168

CHAPTER VIII

THE COURSE OF TRADE TO THE AUTUMN OF 1915

SATISFACTORY as was the maintenance of trade on the North Sea tracks, it was on the ships following the ocean routes that Great Britain was chiefly dependent for the import of essential supplies and the distribution of her produce to the markets of the world; and it was on these ships, while they were passing through the area of the South-Western Approach, that the submarine attack fell most heavily. How great were the losses in this area we have already seen; but, great as they were, they bore as yet but a small proportion to the total volume of traffic. Down to July 31st, 1915, the end of the first twelve months of war, the total losses in all areas and from all war causes—cruisers, mines, and submarines—among British steamers of 1,600 tons gross and upwards, amounted to under 4 per cent. in numbers, and a little over $3\frac{1}{2}$ per cent. in tonnage. The cargoes lost were less than one-half per cent. in value of the cargoes carried.

So far there was no great reason for anxiety; but the havoc wrought in August was on a scale which suggested that the previous tale of losses afforded an inadequate criterion of the possibilities of destruction arising from the increased radius of action of the more modern submarines. For the first twelve months of war the average monthly loss, whether in numbers or tonnage, was under one-third of 1 per cent. In August the losses rose to nearly 1 per cent. in numbers, and over three-quarters per cent. in tonnage, and though the September sinkings showed a substantial reduction, they were still considerably above the previous average.[1]

Small as they were in comparison with the total volume of trade, these losses were far from insignificant. The demands on British ocean-going tonnage were so great that even a loss of 5 per cent. (to the end of September 1915) was by no means negligible, and the money value of the ships and cargoes destroyed ran into big figures. The value of all steamers entered in the War Risks Associations, lost during the first twelve months of war, was estimated at over £6,250,000; the value of cargoes lost in British ships at £7,240,000. These figures were almost insignificant in comparison with the total stake at risk, for the entered value of the ships was over £153,000,000, the estimated value of the cargoes £1,500,000,000; but, had it not been possible to spread the risks by insurance, the effect of losses aggregating over £13,000,000 must have been crushing to individual owners and merchants, and, these dragging down others in their fall, a crisis might easily have been precipitated fatal to the free flow of sea-borne trade. That such a crisis was averted was due to the State Insurance Scheme. Without that scheme, even had the initial difficulties arising from the outbreak of war been overcome, insurance facilities must have been uncertain and restricted, in view of the continual wide fluctuations in the measure of risk, and so sharp and sudden a rise in the curve of destruction as occurred in May or in August 1915.

The State Insurance Scheme was thus as important a factor in maintaining the flow of trade through the

[1] Estimates prepared by the Liverpool and London War Risks Insurance Association:

	Percentage Loss.		Monthly Average.	
	Nos.	Tons.	Nos.	Tons.
Six months to January	1·71	1·73	·28	·29
Six months to July	2·11	1·91	·35	·32
Twelve months to July	3·82	3·64	·32	·30
August	·92	·78		
September	·53	·47		
Total	5·27	4·90		

STATE INSURANCE SCHEME

vicissitudes of the submarine attack as it had been in averting the laying up of shipping on the outbreak of war. Indeed, the proportion of cargo business handled by the State Office increased steadily as the submarine menace developed. During the earlier months of the war, when the State Flat Rate was higher than the rates quoted by underwriters for all except the most dangerous voyages, the State Office did only a comparatively small part of the business of cargo insurance. In January, 1915, when the rate stood at 1 per cent., the equivalent of underwriters' quotations for the longer routes, the premium takings amounted to about £1,250 a day. By the middle of February this figure had risen to £5,600. Underwriters were as yet unable to gauge the measure of the new risk, and a general rise in their quotations threw a greatly increased business into the hands of the State. During the first two months of the submarine campaign the daily takings rose, at their highest, to £9,800, and, though underwriters' quotations gradually fell, the daily average received by the State Office from May onwards was about £3,000.

The machinery for the insurance both of hulls and cargoes, and the general principles on which the Scheme was worked, remained practically the same as in 1914. Its scope had, however, been extended to cover the sailing trade. Originally the benefits of State Insurance had been extended to the owners of sailing vessels only as regards voyages current on the outbreak of war [1]; but by December 1914 it had become evident, both that the trade was worth maintaining, and that it was practically impossible to place this class of risk on the open market. The Government accordingly agreed with a War Risks Association representing the owners of sailing tonnage, to cover any excess over £4,000 on the value of each entered vessel, or 60 per cent. of the entered value, whichever might be the smaller.[2] The cargoes were still left to be insured, if possible, on the open market; but, as the volume of sailing traffic and the dangers to which it was exposed both increased, it became necessary for the State Insurance Office to step in, and in March 1915 it under-

[1] See Vol. I, p. 183.
[2] Supplemental Agreement for New Voyages between the War Risks Association, Ltd., and the Government. *Manual of Emergency Legislation, Supplement No. 4*, pp. 280–7.

took to insure cargoes in sailing vessels at double the premium charged in respect of steamer cargoes.[1]

So far as steamers were concerned, the modifications introduced during 1915 related to points of detail only, and of these the most important was an arrangement arrived at early in the year, for increasing the insurable value of the ships. The original basis of insurance was the total first cost, less depreciation at the rate of 4 per cent. per annum, with a minimum value of 30s. per gross registered ton. Almost from the beginning of the war, however, the cost of replacement began to rise, and after September 9th, 1914, depreciation was no longer written off. For some months it was considered that this concession fairly covered the extra cost of replacement, but by March 1915 it was evident that some more substantial modification was necessary, if the shipowner were to receive adequate cover. The cost of replacement went up by leaps and bounds, owing in part to the actual cost of labour and material, in part to competition caused by the shortage of tonnage and the limited capacity of the yards for commercial work, overwhelmed as they were with Admiralty orders. For these reasons the Board of Trade agreed, as from March 10th, to permit an increase of 20 per cent. on the insurable value of the vessels, and, over and above this, the War Risks Associations were permitted to insure, for their own account, any difference between the amount insurable on a steamer under the State Scheme and her actual market value for the time being, up to a limit of £20,000.

Down to the opening of the submarine campaign, State Insurance both of hulls and cargoes had been carried on at a substantial profit. On February 18, 1915, the hull premiums received to date showed a surplus of £1,782,000 over claims paid, and the surplus on cargoes amounted to nearly another £1,000,000. From these figures, however, were excluded losses to a figure of £539,000 on vessels engaged in current voyages at the outbreak of war, and a contingent liability of £500,000 on ships interned in German ports. There were further liabilities on fishing vessels, and in respect of allowances to the dependants of officers and seamen interned in enemy countries, estimated at some £300,000 in all; but, even assuming that all these

[1] Explanatory Memorandum as to Cargo Insurance, *ibid.*, *Supplement No.* 3, pp. 449–52.

liabilities had to be met in full, there was a handsome balance in hand. It was not long, however, before the position began to be affected by the development of the submarine campaign, and by the end of May 1915 the losses on hulls had overtaken the premiums received. The cargo premiums, on the other hand, still showed a substantial surplus.

All this time the premiums remained unchanged at 1 per cent. on cargoes, and ¾ per cent. on hulls, for a single voyage, 1½ per cent. for a round voyage or a three months' time policy. These rates had been fixed in December 1914, after the destruction of the German Pacific Squadron had removed the last serious danger presented by the enemy's surface cruisers; but, in spite of the grave new perils which had arisen since that date, they were not increased. The scheme, on the Government side, was still solvent, as the surplus premiums on cargoes more than compensated for the hull deficiency, and in these circumstances the Board of Trade were unwilling to add anything to the charge on imports. The Associations were thus left to make good by calls on their members the difference between their share of the hull premiums received and the proportion of claims borne by them.

The security thus provided was quite sufficient to enable British shipowners to keep their ships running and the banks and financial houses to finance the movement of cargoes carried in British vessels. Moreover, so widely had the scheme been imitated abroad that in all the principal Allied countries, and in several of the more prominent neutral States, native shipowners and merchants could readily obtain cover for ships despatched to British ports, and the cargoes which they carried. The insurance of foreign vessels and their cargoes, on voyages between British ports and those of countries other than their own lay, generally speaking, outside the scope of these schemes; but this burden the insurance markets were well able to bear, for on such voyages the risks were not usually heavy. There was thus no financial impediment to the employment of either British or foreign shipping in the trade of the United Kingdom up to the full level of the demand, and any difficulty in obtaining space for the carriage of either import or export cargoes arose purely from the gradual diminution in the supply of tonnage.

THE COURSE OF TRADE

Throughout the summer of 1915 the drain of naval and military requirements upon the shipping resources of Great Britain had steadily increased, mainly owing to the unexpected expansion of the forces allotted to the Dardanelles campaign, and from April onwards the effect of this drain was clearly visible in the entrances of British shipping. In every month, from April to September inclusive, the British tonnage entered compared more unfavourably with the last corresponding month of peace than the average entrances for the first six months of war, and in June, July, and September the falling away was very heavy. The entrances of foreign shipping, on the other hand, somewhat increased. In the North Sea, as we have seen, the Scandinavian shipowners were very busy; and a large increase in the entrances of Spanish tonnage bore witness to the part played by native owners in the carriage of ore and fruit to the United Kingdom. Nor was the activity of neutral shipowners by any means confined to the traffic with their own countries. In spite of the strong demand arising from the withdrawal of British shipping from the routes between foreign ports, many neutral vessels were attracted by the high freights on offer into the general carrying trade of the United Kingdom. Norwegian shipowners, always enterprising in the tramp trade, were particularly active. In addition to taking the lion's share of the traffic with Norway itself and much of that with the other Scandinavian countries, they brought many cargoes from the White Sea, Spain, and North America, they replaced Dutch shipping to a considerable extent in the traffic with the Netherlands, and they found employment for a large block of tonnage in the continually expanding exports of coal from the United Kingdom to France. Dutch shipping, while it diminished on the North Sea tracks, was busy both ways in the Java trade, and developed a new interest in the traffic between the United States and British ports. The Greeks were busier than ever in the carriage of coal to Italy and Egypt. Spaniards, Greeks, and Danes alike competed eagerly for coal charters to French ports, and an appreciable proportion of the vessels which brought home the grain cargoes from the Plate and took out coal in exchange sailed under foreign flags.

Thanks to this activity on the part of neutral shipping the total tonnage entered during the second six months of the war was only about 4 per cent. less than that entered during the first half-year, and the total clearances actually showed a small increase. The comparison would have been still more favourable had not the long delays imposed by the congested condition of the ports reduced the number of voyages and the effective carrying power of the tonnage employed. On the other hand, the increase in the average weight of inward cargoes carried was fully maintained, and the volume of imports bore a much higher ratio to the tonnage entered than in normal times.

The total estimated weight of imports during the six months ending July 1915 was, in fact, almost exactly equal to that brought in during the first half-year of war. It compared even more favourably with the last corresponding period of peace, for it is during the second half of the calendar year that the heaviest imports normally arrive. The imports of foodstuffs, indeed, were a little smaller than for the first half-year of war, but both in raw materials and in manufactured articles there was a considerable increase.

So far as it was not purely seasonal, this diminution in the import of foodstuffs was due mainly to the failure of the Australian harvest and the replacement of the supplies which would normally have come from Australia during 1915, by heavy shipments brought forward from North America during the autumn and winter of 1914. During the spring and summer of 1915, when the Australian wheat should have been coming forward, the monthly imports were below the normal, but the fulfilment of all essential requirements for the 1914–15 season had already been assured. As regards feeding-stuffs, the supply of barley was restricted by the closing of the Black Sea and by poor harvests in India and Canada, but the maize shipments from the Plate were well above the normal. Maize, however, is not in itself an ideal cattle-food, as it is fattening and laxative and requires to be corrected by an admixture of other cereals. As the oats normally imported from Germany and the Black Sea were no longer available, a serious shortage of feeding-stuffs was, at one time, anticipated; but this danger was soon averted by heavy purchases in the United States.

Meat imports were still somewhat below the normal owing to the competing demand from France, but there was an increase in the actual quantities received. The

Danish supplies of bacon were well maintained, and those from North America more than doubled. We have seen, too, that the submarine campaign had failed to hold up the shipments of dairy produce and margarine from Scandinavia and Holland.

In the imports of raw materials and manufactured articles the demands of the war industries were clearly reflected.[1] The imports of iron-ore, pyrites, copper, lead, and tin were all heavier than in the first six months of war. There was a marked improvement in the figures relating to steel blooms, billets, and slabs, for the security of the Atlantic routes enabled the foundries and factories of the United States to be placed at the service of the Allies for the production of war material. Manufacturers of woollens had large contracts not only for the clothing of the British Armies, but for export, and to fulfil these demands enormous quantities of wool were imported from Australia, New Zealand, the Cape, and South America. Leather manufacturers were busily engaged in making military harness and equipment. Flax, hemp, jute, silk, and rubber were all coming forward more freely as the result either of increased demand or of the re-establishment of communications. Many miscellaneous imports showed a similar increase, but the most important factor outside the demands for war material was the return to something like settled conditions in the cotton industry, which led to immense imports from the United States and Egypt to make up the leeway of the previous months.

In August and September the same tendency was manifest. The total volume of imports as compared with peace figures, fell away, partly through a reduction of grain purchases, and partly because of the diminution in timber shipments from Russia, normally very heavy in these months; but in imports classed as "manufactured articles," the September figures approached the peace standard more nearly than in any previous month of the war.

Down to this date, the new form of attack on commerce

---

[1] It must be remembered that the Board of Trade include, under the heading of "Articles wholly or mainly Manufactured," many imports which form the raw material of British industries. Thus, while metallic ores are classed as raw materials, pig-iron, pig and sheet lead, copper regulus and precipitate, copper unwrought and part wrought, tin blocks, ingots, sheets, and slabs, crude zinc, and quicksilver appear as manufactured articles.

had proved a comparative failure. Although the submarines had already inflicted heavier direct losses than those suffered by British shipping during the period of surface attack, the indirect effect of their activities was, as yet, small. At no time had they interfered with the flow of trade to the same extent as the EMDEN, in her operations in the Bay of Bengal and off Colombo; they had sent many valuable ships and cargoes to the bottom, but they had caused no general suspension of sailings or interruption of commerce. The danger lay less in their actual achievements than in the possibilities of future developments. For the present, they had done little to diminish the stream of supplies flowing to British ports.

In view of this great volume of imports it was unfortunate that the expansion of the export trade noticed in March and April was not maintained. The May figures, indeed, were a little above those for April, but after that month there was a slight falling off, and, on the whole, the total export values were stationary during the summer of 1915. The improvement in the cotton trade lasted until July, when the exports of piece goods amounted to 538,000,000 yards, as against an average of 333,000,000 for the first six months of the war. From August onwards, exports to India and China again diminished, and, though some of the minor markets were buying freely and the new French demand persisted, they could not make up for the reduced purchases by Eastern importers. Woollen exports were still booming, mainly as a consequence of the great demand from France; but the shipments of iron and steel, machinery, and the majority of the miscellaneous exports continued to be very much restricted.

For this general restriction of the export trade no single cause can be assigned. It was the result of a complication of unfavourable factors having their origin in the general industrial and financial disturbance caused by the war. The great German market was, of course, closed to British exporters, and the purchasing power of others, notably the Indian, had been diminished by the closing of the German and Belgian markets to their own products, and the decreased demand from France and Russia. On the other hand, the great agricultural countries such as Argentina were in a position to absorb British manufactures to an increased amount had they been forthcoming, and the diminution of German and Austrian exports left many neutral markets insufficiently supplied. But British manufacturers were not in a position to take full advantage of these opportunities. Hundreds and thousands of men had been withdrawn from industrial and commercial employment to form the new armies, and although a considerable number of new workers, especially women, had been drawn into the factories and offices, the loss of so many skilled workers was not easily compensated. Of those who were left, an ever-increasing number were employed on work directly connected with the war. The continual expansion of the military demands for stores, for equipment, and above all for munitions, threw a heavy strain on the manufacturing resources of the country, and while the creation of the Ministry of Munitions and the passing of the Munitions Act in June 1915 gave good hope of an increase in the supply, this could only be, to some extent, at the expense of production for civil purposes. On September 15th the Prime Minister informed the House of Commons that since the beginning of the war not far short of 3,000,000 men had been enlisted for the Army and Navy, and more than 800,000 work-people were actually engaged in the manufacture of munitions.[1] But the demands of the war industries did not stop at munitions in the strict sense of the word. Steel machinery for naval construction, army clothing and blankets, saddlery, military buildings, and all the thousand necessities of an army and fleet at war had to be supplied in ever-increasing quantities. Both patriotism and the economic pressure of high wages and rising prices drew into industrial employment many who had never previously been so engaged, and women in particular came forward by thousands to take the places of enlisted men; but even so the diversion of labour had, necessarily, a serious effect on the productive power of the country and the surplus available for export.[2]

Even when goods for export were available there were still serious obstacles to a free flow of shipments. Out-

[1] *Hansard*, 15 September, 1915, cols. 47–8.
[2] By July 1915 the estimated proportion of men enlisted from private industry (excluding agricultural and transport) was 19.9 per cent., the net reduction in the numbers employed in industry, after allowing for all replacement whether by male or female labour, 7.9 per cent. Of the total so employed in July, 36.1 per cent. were engaged on Government work. In the metal trades the percentage engaged on Government work was 73.0; in the chemical trades, 37.8; in mining, 28.1; in the textile industries, 26.6; in the clothing trades, 23.0.

wards tonnage as a whole was fully equal to the demand, for the liner services, which distributed the bulk of the manufactured exports, were well and efficiently maintained. Nevertheless, the increase in requisitioning was not without its effect on the general export trade. Even the liner services were not free from interference, and tramps chartered to carry cargoes of heavy or bulky commodities were apt to be taken up for naval and military use after they had been fixed, with the result that the charter had to be cancelled at the last moment and a substitute procured.

A still greater difficulty was presented by the network of controls and prohibitions. The necessity of controlling exports with a view to conserving stocks and preventing the enemy countries from benefiting by the industrial activity of Great Britain could not be denied; but there were constant complaints as to delays in obtaining licences and conflicting decisions given by the authorities.

There was, no doubt, some truth in these criticisms, for in a business so vast and complicated as the control of the British export trade there was ample scope for error, and a certain amount of delay and inconsistency was inevitable while the machinery of control was getting into working order. Some of the critics, on the other hand, failed to appreciate fully the exigencies of a state of war, and the wide ramifications of Germany's indirect trade. The restrictions on the exports of tin-plate—to take a single example—bore hardly on the home manufacturer; but there is ample evidence that a large portion of the American and Scandinavian demand had its origin in the growth of the export of canned foods to Germany. It was often difficult, when the demand for a particular commodity in a neutral country expanded, to be certain whether the increased imports were simply required to replace goods of the same or a similar description usually obtained from the Central Powers, or were a part of the illicit transit trade.

Yet even when little doubt existed as to the ultimate enemy destination of British exports or re-exports, they were often allowed to pass. Down to July 1915 there were no restrictions on the re-export of tea, coffee, or cocoa, and though re-exports of coffee and cocoa were prohibited in that month, licences were freely granted. The result was that the shipments of all three to Scandinavia and Holland were enormously in excess of the normal, and there was not the slightest doubt that the bulk of the shipments ultimately reached the enemy.[1] The benefit to the enemy was undeniable, yet there were strong arguments against prohibition. It was eminently desirable to maintain the transit and entrepôt trade, and the closing of Hamburg and Antwerp as distributing centres for coffee and cocoa had given London a great opportunity. Tea and cocoa were both British colonial products, and, so long as they were not contraband, it was desirable to allow shipments from the Empire to compete with those from neutral countries. The chief source of coffee was Brazil, a friendly neutral, largely dependent on her coffee exports, and British capital to a great amount had been invested in the coffee-producing districts.[2] Tea and coffee were both, at the time, regarded as articles of luxury rather than necessity, and there was something to be said for permitting German expenditure on luxury imports, and thus forcing up the exchanges against Germany and weakening her financial position.

This exchange argument had a double edge. If it was desirable to weaken Germany's purchasing power, it was still more desirable to maintain Great Britain's. Both from Holland and Scandinavia it was necessary to procure very large supplies of foodstuffs and other essentials. It was necessary, in order to avoid heavily adverse exchanges, to maintain British exports and re-exports to those countries at the highest possible level, and this could only be done by shipping those goods for which a demand existed, whatever its origin. Further, some of our most important imports from such countries required the supply to them of raw materials—oils, seeds, and kernels to Holland for

---

[1] Estimated annual consumption of coffee in Germany   174,000 tons
Surplus imports of Holland and Scandinavia, 1915   220,000 ,,
German imports from Holland, 1915   163,000 ,,
Scandinavian imports of tea, normal (less re-exports)   863,000 lbs.
Scandinavian imports of tea, 1915 (practically all from U.K.)   6,827,000 ,,
Dutch imports of tea, normal (less re-exports)   6,060,000 ,,
Dutch imports of tea, 1915 (large quota from U.K.)   21,721,000 ,,
British exports of raw cocoa to Scandinavia and Holland:
    1913   2,599,000 lbs.
    1915 (first four months)   11,673,000 ,,
From all sources Denmark and Sweden each received over nine years' supply.

[2] Shipments of coffee from Brazil to Germany were seized in July 1915.

the manufacture of margarine, nickel and steel hardening materials to Sweden for munitions purposes. It was difficult to stop the supply of such materials from overseas, or to prohibit their export from Great Britain, without producing injurious reactions on British supplies. Yet it was impossible to secure the whole output of the finished product for the British market.

In these instances trade interests and economic considerations were allowed to override the requirements of the blockade. In other instances it is probable that the injury inflicted on British trade by the export restrictions was greater than the loss to the enemy. In truth, the factors to be considered were so complex, and often so nicely balanced, that a margin of error was inevitable; but, broadly speaking, there can be little doubt either that the restrictions imposed were justified, or that a price had to be paid for the results achieved.

As regards the bulk of traffic affected, the most important of the restrictions was that placed on the export of coal. Since the lifting of the Triple Bond after the first two or three weeks of war [1] the coal export trade had gone forward with but little administrative interference, but on May 6th, 1915, an Order in Council was issued prohibiting, as from May 13th, the exports of coal and coke to all destinations abroad other than British Possessions and Protectorates and Allied countries.[2] This proclamation had a double object. In the first place, it was necessary to secure adequate supplies for the Navy, home consumption, and the Allies, and inasmuch as naval requirements and those of the munition factories were constantly expanding, while the total production had fallen, this involved some regulation of the general exports. In the second place, the supply of coal to neutral countries who were dependent on their imports from Great Britain, formed a powerful lever in the negotiation of agreements having for their object the restriction of enemy supplies. There was, of course, no intention of enforcing the prohibition literally. All that was desired was to obtain the power to shut down any section of the export trade which appeared at the moment to be undesirable. A Board of Trade Committee, known as the Coal Exports Committee, was formed to supervise the policy with regard to exports, and

[1] Vol. I, pp. 188–90.
[2] *Manual of Emergency Legislation, Supplement No.* 4, pp. 222–3.

the War Trade Department, acting in conjunction with this Committee, issued licences freely for the export of coal to approved destinations in neutral countries.

To coal exporters, however, the proclamation was a cause of great anxiety, as they anticipated that the necessity of obtaining licences for each cargo would involve serious delays to business and render it difficult to fix contracts. In particular they objected to a stipulation requiring the steamer by which each consignment would be shipped to be named in the application for a licence. There was some uncertainty also as to the degree of restriction likely to be imposed on the continental and South American traffic. These apprehensions were shared by the tramp shipowners, who were closely interested in the volume of coal exports, and for some days after the appearance of the proclamation, business at the coal ports was almost at a standstill. This dislocation, however, lasted only for a short time. Representations made by the Chamber of Shipping and the export associations were sympathetically considered by the War Trade Department and the Coal Exports Committee, and satisfactory assurances were given against any unnecessary interference with the flow of trade. Permission was given to apply for licences by a named ship " or substitute," or, if necessary, by a ship to be named later, and arrangements were made for telegraphing the provisional decisions of the Coal Exports Committee, in order that business might go forward pending the receipt of the actual licence from the War Trade Department. These concessions, and the prompt manner in which applications were dealt with, removed at once the worst apprehensions of shippers and shipowners, and within a week or two the export trade had fully recovered its activity.

On August 3rd the nominal prohibition was extended to exports to Allied countries, but this extension had little effect on the actual volume of trade, as licences were freely granted.[1] The only object was to bring the whole trade under a certain measure of control, for the licensing system served other ends than the limitation of the total export. Thus, applications from the Midland collieries, which were able easily to dispose of their whole product at home were, in general, refused, while those received from coal-fields which enjoyed but poor facilities for

[1] *Manual of Emergency Legislation, Supplement No. 4*, pp. 252–3.

internal distribution and depended mainly on the export trade, were granted whenever possible. Again, applicants for a licence to export to Scandinavia were required to state particulars of the proposed homeward cargo, and a preference was given to shipments on vessels fixed for a return cargo of pit-props.[1]

Carefully as the restrictions were worked, the decrease in coal exports was very heavy. Tramp tonnage was scarce, the demands of the Admiralty and munitions industries were enormous, and the decrease in output was serious. Well over 200,000 miners, or 20 per cent. of the whole, had enlisted, and, after allowing for replacements, the diminution in the number employed amounted to between 14 and 15 per cent. Thanks to the energetic co-operation of the Miners' Federation in securing an increased output per man, the corresponding drop in the total output was only 10 per cent.; but even this gravely reduced the amount available for export, after fulfilling the war and domestic demands.[2] Thus the exports for the first nine months of 1915 showed a decrease of nearly 21,000,000 tons, or 40 per cent. on the 1913 figures. More than half of this decrease was accounted for by the closing of the German, Austrian, and Russian markets; but many neutral countries were also seriously affected. Differences with Sweden with regard to contraband led to the refusal of many licences for that country, and shipments to the more distant markets, such as the South American, were drastically restricted in the interests of tonnage economy. Italy also went very short. On the other hand, the exports to France increased by one-half, and both to Norway and Denmark rather more than usual was shipped, in order to make good the loss of supplies formerly received by them from Germany.[3]

To some extent the decrease in volume of exports was compensated by the increased prices obtainable, but the net decrease in the value of exported coal amounted, for the nine months, to £10,600,000, a fall of 27 per cent.

---

[1] For the whole question see *Lloyd's List*, "Coal Trade News," 8, 10, 12, 21 May, 5, 8, 9 June, 1915; *Statist*, 28 August, 18 September, 2 October, 1915; *Chamber of Shipping Annual Report*, 1915–16, pp. 13–14; *Hansard*, 19 July, 1915, cols. 1220–23 (Mr. Russel Rea).

[2] Mr. Asquith at Newcastle, *Times*, 21 April, 1915. *Hansard*, 19 July, 1915, cols. 1208–9 (Mr. Runciman).

[3] The figures quoted are exclusive of Admiralty shipments to France and Russia.

This, however, was only a small part of the all-round diminution in export values. While imports for the nine months to September were greater by over £86,000,000 than in the previous year, the value of exports was £114,000,000 less, and the problem of the trade balance began to assume grave proportions.

This problem was still more serious when considered in connection with individual countries. The chief markets which normally absorbed British exports in excess of the goods sent in return were those of India, Japan, China, and Italy. Now, the trade with India and Japan was marked by a large excess of imports, and the excess of exports to China and Italy was greatly diminished. The decline of exports to the Oriental markets, due partly to reduced productive power at home, partly to reduced purchasing power abroad, partly to shortage of tonnage and rising freights, was a very serious matter to British manufacturers, especially in the textile trades ; but the falling off in the export trade did not stop there. Exports, in fact, had diminished to every country except France, Holland, Denmark, and Norway, while the value of imports from every neutral country except Brazil and Roumania, had increased. In the Norwegian and Danish trade the ratio of exports to imports was approximately normal ; but the value of shipments to Holland, and more especially to France, was far in excess of the imports received from thence. To Russia also, Great Britain was sending more than she received. On the other hand, the excess of imports from the great food-producing countries, such as the United States, Argentina, and Australasia, was from two to four times as great as in times of peace, and the large orders for munitions and war material placed in America bade fair to increase rapidly our indebtedness to the States. The big purchases of sugar from Java, Mauritius, Cuba, and the West Indies were also only very partially paid for in goods. So far the freight earnings of British shipping had formed a valuable set-off to the apparent excess of imports, but the increasing absorption of British tonnage in war employment and the trade of the United Kingdom itself, could not but tend to cut down this, the most valuable of the invisible exports, and of the services still performed for foreigners a large proportion were for the Allies of Great Britain.

Thus the general tendency was for Great Britain to

become a heavy creditor of the Allies, who had comparatively little to send her, and to become ever more deeply indebted to her chief sources of supply. By September 7th the American exchange had already fallen five points against Great Britain, and the course of the exchanges could not be watched without anxiety. Still worse, of course, was the condition of the Allies. France had little energy to spare for industrial production, and the chief exports of Russia were blocked by the closing of the Baltic and Black Seas, yet their demand for imports both from Great Britain and elsewhere and for the services of British and neutral shipping, was great and insistent. The activity of the British Navy and the support of the State Insurance Scheme had assured to Great Britain and her Allies the uninterrupted flow of supplies; but by enabling those supplies to be maintained at a level far above that which could be paid for by goods and services, they had created a financial problem which was likely to become awkward if the war were prolonged.

CHAPTER IX

THE PROGRESS OF ECONOMIC PRESSURE DURING 1915

DESPITE the achievements of the submarines, the difficulties experienced by the Allies in maintaining their seaborne trade were still due in a greater degree to the general economic dislocation and the absorption of labour, material, and tonnage by war activities, than to the action of the enemy. The Central Powers, on the other hand, were beginning to feel the pinch of direct economic pressure. The greater part of their export trade was irretrievably lost; their supplies from overseas were grievously constricted, and for many commodities of primary war importance they could rely only on the stocks already in hand.

For this they had to thank, in large measure, the inceptors of the submarine campaign, which, by its reckless disregard of neutral interests, had permitted the British Government to disregard the legal and diplomatic considerations that had previously hampered their operations. It was the difficulty of applying to modern conditions the precedents of earlier wars, and the dependence of the Allies on neutral countries for the supply of essential foodstuffs, munitions, and raw material, that had hitherto impeded all efforts to restrict enemy trade. By rendering possible the Retaliation Order of March 11th, the submarines had presented the Allies with an opportunity of which they were quick to take advantage.

During the early months of the war the British Government concentrated its attention mainly on a few articles of special military importance, especially copper, oil, and rubber. In the stoppage of these articles they had achieved a large measure of success. Despite a good deal of smuggling of small parcels, very little rubber reached Germany after the outbreak of war, and, though large quantities of copper and petroleum were sent forward from the United States, the traffic was broken at an early stage.

It will be remembered that during October and November 1914 large quantities of copper shipped to Italian and Scandinavian ports were seized at Gibraltar or by the British patrols in Home Waters.[1] As a result of these seizures it became almost impossible to obtain insurance of consignments of copper to neutral countries which had not received the approval of the British Authorities. By November 5th, 1914, the premiums had risen to 25 per cent., less a 10 per cent. rebate on safe arrival, and by December the German agents were reporting that further shipments were impossible. But the effect of the seizures went still farther. Sweden, Denmark, Holland, and Italy prohibited the re-export of copper in order to safeguard their own supplies, and Swiss importers agreed to limit their purchases to the quantities normally required for home consumption. Best of all, the British Government was able to conclude, in December, an agreement with the American exporters themselves. The wise leniency shown by the Government in purchasing the consignments seized instead of procuring their condemnation as prize had an excellent effect on American opinion, and the exporters were now glad to agree, in return for large British contracts, to give satisfactory guarantees against exports to European neutrals other than *bona fide* purchasers for home consumption.

The importance of this achievement may be measured by the fact that, against a total consumption of 240,000 tons, the maximum German output did not exceed 35,000, and even this was not of the electrolytic type required in many branches of the war industries. A certain amount of copper and of pyrites containing copper could still be obtained from Norway, and small quantities were occasionally smuggled through the blockade; but the loss of the American supplies, amounting to 90 per cent. of the normal import, could not be made good.

For the supply of mineral oils, also, Germany was normally dependent on the United States. The consumption in 1913 amounted to 1,800,000 tons, of which 80 per cent. came from the States, and only 9 per cent. was home-produced. Practically the whole of the American supply was now cut off, for early in the war the British Government was able to conclude agreements with the American exporters and Scandinavian importers, and the Dutch and

[1] Vol. I, pp. 293-4, 363.

Scandinavian imports during 1915 were little if at all above the normal. Moreover, the Russian invasion of Galicia during the spring cut off the Galician supplies, and when, during the summer, the Russians were forced back over the frontier, they succeeded in burning stocks to the extent of some 200,000 tons previous to their retirement. It was only from Roumania that any additional supplies could be obtained, and these were insufficient to make good the deficiency from Galicia alone.

In motor-oil, unfortunately, Germany was practically self-supporting, as large quantities of benzol were obtained as a by-product of the coke industry, and enabled the stocks of petrol to be conserved for military and naval needs, especially in those of the air and submarine services. Lighting oils, on the other hand, were obtained chiefly from abroad, and by the winter of 1915 the petroleum famine was causing much suffering and discontent. In respect of lubricants the cessation of imports was still more severely felt. The normal consumption was 280,000 tons, of which 200,000 tons came from the United States and Russia, and 45,000 from Galicia and Roumania. The war requirements were probably over 350,000 tons, and those of Austria about half as great. In view of the enormous importance of lubricants in such essential branches of war activity as the air service and transport, the great reduction in the supply of lubricating oils constituted a very serious danger.

Apart from these special commodities the situation at the beginning of 1915 was far from satisfactory to the Allies. Both the import and export trade of the Central Powers was steadily reviving. The direct imports from America were comparatively small and were, of course, confined to non-contraband goods; but American exports to the neutral countries contiguous to Germany rose during the first three months of the year to nearly four times their normal value, and there was little doubt that the greater part of the increase was due to the growth of the indirect trade between Germany and the States. In addition to some cargoes shipped direct to Bremen, Germany received 300,000 bales of cotton through Holland alone, in addition to large quantities through Scandinavia, Italy, and Switzerland. Cotton was not yet contraband, and could not be interfered with, whether the shipments were direct or indirect; but even in respect of conditional contraband the activity of the patrols was to a great extent neutralised by the difficulty of securing legal proof of enemy destination.

It was in lard and meat products that the contraband trade attained perhaps its greatest volume. The American exports of lard to Scandinavia during the last three months of 1914 and the first three months of 1915 were enormous, amounting to many times the normal annual total.[1] But, during October and November, 1914, four vessels on their way to Denmark with cargoes including large consignments of lard " to order " were seized and placed in prize. Three of the ships,[2] together with the greater part of the cargoes, were subsequently condemned, and these seizures were not without effect on the traffic. Early in January the Danish Government prohibited the re-export of lard, and during the following month the Swedish and Norwegian Governments followed suit.

By this time the list of prohibited exports in each of the chief neutral countries was a long one, and the direct export of many commodities to Germany from Denmark and Norway was effectively stopped.[3] In Sweden licences to export prohibited goods were granted with greater freedom, and in addition to the Swedish exports there was a considerable leakage through that country from Denmark and even from Norway. In Holland the efficacy of the prohibitions was to a great extent neutralised by the wide extension given by the Rhine Conventions to the definition of transit trade. The gap, however, was filled by the existence of the Netherlands Overseas Trust.[4] It was a term of the agreement with the Trust that it should prevent the re-export of contraband goods or the export of contraband products derived from such goods, and to this undertaking it loyally adhered, large quantities of contraband being stored in Holland till the end of the war.

Agreements with one or two of the leading neutral steamer lines by which, in order to avoid detention, they agreed to call voluntarily for examination and to obtain guarantees against the re-export of contraband goods, were

---

[1] *Further Correspondence between His Majesty's Government and the United States Government respecting the Rights of Belligerents.* [Cd. 8234] 1916, p. 25.

[2] The *Kim, Fridland,* and *Bjornstjerne Bjornson.*

[3] After the prohibition of re-export of lard, great quantities already landed in Norway were detained and ultimately allowed to go bad, as the Norwegian market was unable to absorb them.

[4] Vol. I, p. 363.

also well kept. Nevertheless, the volume of contraband as well as of free goods reaching Germany during the opening months of 1915 was large enough to stultify in great measure the work of the patrols.

By the Order in Council of March 11th this whole situation was radically changed. That Order did not, indeed, remove all difficulties from the path. It afforded no help in determining the enemy destination of goods consigned to neutral ports nor in securing the condemnation of contraband consigned to named consignees. On the other hand, it enabled the British Authorities to detain, pending inquiry, all goods against which there was a *prima facie* evidence of enemy destination, whether contraband or no, and it enabled them, for the first time, to strike at the enemy's export trade.

The machinery for the enforcement of the Order was based, in the first place, on the interception of shipping by the Downs Boarding Flotilla in the Dover Straits and the Tenth Cruiser Squadron at the northern entrance to the North Sea. It was their business to examine or send in for examination every neutral vessel entering or leaving the North Sea, not already provided with the green war clearance or the flag of the day from Kirkwall, showing that they had already been passed by the Authorities. From the date of the Retaliation Order the number of ships voluntarily calling for examination at British ports steadily increased. The big neutral lines were naturally anxious to minimise delay to their steamers, and, in view of the increased stringency of the examination service, many of them were glad to make agreements by which they undertook to call on every voyage at Lerwick or Falmouth, and to obtain from shippers satisfactory guarantees against re-export. These agreements were equally helpful to the British Authorities. Not only did they lighten the work of the patrols and of the examination service : they added greatly to the effectiveness of the blockade, especially in the North Sea, where bad weather and low visibility made the work of interception very difficult during the winter months.

Nevertheless, the work of the patrols was heavy. During the year 1915 the Tenth Cruiser Squadron intercepted no fewer than 3,098 vessels.[1] Of these 408, or 13·2 per cent., were British or Allied ships ; 817, or 26 per cent., were

[1] Including both east-bound and west-bound ships.

fishing craft; 1,130, or 36·8 per cent., were neutral merchantmen which were allowed to pass after being boarded or identified at sea. The remaining 743 (24 per cent.), or rather more than two a day, were sent in for examination to Kirkwall or Lerwick. Of the ships whose interception was considered specially important only 8 succeeded in evading the patrols. In the Downs the volume of traffic was far greater. From 80 to 120 ships a day passed through the area, but of these about 80 per cent. were British ships only requiring route instructions. Of the remainder many were neutrals bound to British East Coast ports, on whom it was necessary only to place an armed guard, to ensure their proceeding to their destination. Others had already received the green clearance after calling voluntarily at Falmouth, or were sufficiently well authenticated to be allowed to proceed. About a dozen each day required to be searched by the naval examination service.

When a ship was sent in for examination the Customs officers, or the naval authorities in the Downs, prepared from her manifest, bills of lading, and other relevant documents a detailed analysis of her cargo, which was sent by telegram to the Admiralty, Foreign Office, and Board of Customs. If the ship was eastward bound it was sent also to the War Trade Intelligence Department. Meanwhile, the ship was searched for enemy subjects, concealed cargo not shown by her papers, or goods smuggled in passengers' luggage.

To deal with westward bound ships, the Enemy Exports Committee sat every day at the Foreign Office. This Committee was appointed on the promulgation of the Retaliation Order, and was representative of the Foreign Office, the Admiralty, and Board of Trade. Its task was comparatively simple. The temptation to run the blockade outwards was not great, for there was no such inducement as that provided by the famine prices and freights paid in Germany for goods from overseas. Hence shipowners were unwilling to risk delays, and insisted on shippers obtaining from the British consular officials certificates of origin verifying the neutral character of the shipments.[1] So widely was this system developed that very few westward bound ships had to be sent into port for discharge, and many could be allowed to proceed without their papers coming before the Committee at all. Others, calling at a

[1] Exports from Holland were verified by the Netherlands Oversea Trust.

second British port, were allowed to proceed as soon as their papers were taken off, picking them up at their port of call. The majority of west-bound ships and all liners called voluntarily for inspection, and the interception of enemy exports added comparatively little to the work of the patrols and caused little delay to neutral traffic.

East-bound ships needed and received greater attention. When the analysis of cargo reached the War Trade Intelligence Department it was necessary to prepare, from manifests previously forwarded by British Consuls, from intercepted cables, wireless messages, and letters, and from confidential information, an elaborate report on each item of the cargo. Separate files were kept for individual ships and trades, and selected members of the staff made a special study of all the facts relating to particular commodities or groups of commodities. The preparation of the report from this mass of material was an arduous task; but, as a general rule, the report on a customs cable received in the morning was ready by 3 p.m. on the same day. If the ship's manifest had been forwarded in advance, the report was ready on her arrival.

As soon as the report was ready it was sent on to the Contraband Committee, with whom rested the decision as to the treatment of the cargo. If they were satisfied of its innocence they sent at once a wire authorising the release of the ship. If, on the other hand, they were satisfied as to the enemy destination of any item of the cargo, the ship was placed in the hands of the Admiralty Marshal and ordered to a port, chosen in consultation with the Diversion of Shipping Committee, where the suspicious goods could be discharged. Having discharged the required items, she was released at once without further reference.[1]

As regards enemy exports, the operation of the Order was, from the first, completely successful. Neutral shipowners, as we have seen, refused to take the risk, and within a few months the whole overseas export trade of the Central Powers had been brought to the verge of extinction. Goods sent by parcels post were not, at first, interfered with, and certain concessions were made to

---

[1] For a general sketch of the procedure under the Order see *Report on the Administration of the Order in Council of March 11, 1915.* [Cd. 8469], 1917. For a similar sketch of the general blockade policy during 1915 see *Statement of the Measures adopted to intercept the Seaborne Commerce of Germany.* [Cd. 8145], January 1916.

neutral Powers in respect of shipments of which they were urgently in need. Further, the Allied Governments agreed to pass a certain amount of goods ordered prior to March 1st for which the neutral purchaser had already paid, or for which, under his contract, he was bound to pay even in default of delivery. The total amount exported under these concessions was, however, small, and during the last six months of 1915 the monthly figures of American imports from Germany and Austria were only from 4 to 8 per cent. of those received in 1913. By the end of the year they had almost disappeared.[1]

Further testimony to the effectiveness of the system of certificates of origin was afforded by the fact that American imports from the neutral countries contiguous to Germany showed, allowing for the rise in prices, no increase on the normal traffic. The other oversea markets of Germany were similarly cut off, and Holland, Switzerland, and Scandinavia proved quite unable to absorb the goods thus thrown back on the hands of German exporters. Indeed, the German exports to these countries were no greater, in volume, than in times of peace. It was not only that they provided a totally insufficient market for the goods which would otherwise have been sent to America : the Germans were unable to supply in sufficient quantities those commodities which they were ready and anxious to purchase. Owing to the effects of mobilisation on output, and to the demands of military transport, the exportable surplus of coal, especially from the Westphalian coal-field, had been reduced by some 75 per cent., and the majority of the larger industries, especially the textile trades, were suffering from an acute shortage of raw materials.[2]

Germany was thus unable to pay in goods even for the very restricted supplies which she was now able to obtain

---

[1] United States Imports from Germany and Austria in 1,000 dollars:

	From Germany.	From Austria.	Total.
1913	186,000	19,100	205,100
1914	194,000	15,700	209,700
1915	44,900	5,300	50,200

Of the 50,000,000 dollars imported during 1915, 28,000,000 were received in January and February. The remaining 22,000,000 include goods in transit at the date of the Retaliation Order, goods sent by parcels post, and goods specially licensed. The total amount of exports to all countries licensed up to the end of 1915 was approximately £3,000,000 [Cd. 8145].

[2] For the first six months of 1915 the German exports of coal to Holland were 1,096,541 tons, as against 4,772,291 tons in the same period of 1914.

from abroad. Except for the earnings of those companies which engaged in the Baltic trade, the services of her mercantile marine were no longer available as a means of redressing the trade balance, and in every foreign market the exchanges had fallen heavily against her.[1] Already large sales of foreign securities had become necessary in order to prevent a still further fall in the value of the Mark.

As regards the enemy's import trade the operation of the Order was less sweepingly effective. The high freights and high prices which the Germans were willing to pay formed a strong temptation to the neutral merchant and ship-owner, and the difficulty of proving enemy destination remained as great as ever. Many ingenious devices were resorted to in order to baffle the examination service. American exporters of meat products abandoned the practice of shipping large consignments in vessels specially chartered for the adventure. Instead they sent forward innumerable small parcels consigned to a host of dummy consignees located all over Scandinavia. The majority of these consignees were obscure persons, many of whom were not even regular traders, and it was practically impossible for the War Trade Intelligence Department to keep track of their activities.[2] Further to add to the difficulties of the blockade, the shipments were made, in general, by the largest neutral liners, which the British Government were most unwilling to detain except on the clearest possible proof. Brazilian coffee shippers adopted the same expedient. Another subterfuge was collusive capture. In July the *Dunsyre*, with a cargo of barley, beans, and coconut cake, was " captured " on her voyage to Stockholm and taken into Swinemünde. In October the *Eir*, with 10,000 bales of cotton for Copenhagen, evaded the British patrols and was " captured " by a German torpedo-boat in the Kattegat. Conclusive evidence was discovered that

[1] Rates on Berlin (per 100 Marks):

—	Normal.	25 September, 1915.	18 December, 1915.
Sweden (kronor)	88·88	79·20	68·75
Norway (kroner)	88·88	79·25	70·00
Denmark (kroner)	88·88	79·15	69·85
Holland (gulden)	59·26	50·65	43·60
Switzerland (francs)	123·45	108·50	—
New York ($ and cents)	38·11	33·70	30·55

[2] Cd. 8234, p. 24.

THE COTTON PROBLEM

both these cargoes were shipped by order of Karl Neumond, one of the most prominent agents of the German Government in the United States, and that their "capture" was merely a blind to avert penalties from the shipowner.

During the same month it was discovered that Neumond, whose activity was indefatigable, had resorted, for greater security, to forging the names of firms wholly innocent of enemy trade, as consignees of his shipments. Even this ingenious device brought him little success. The information at the disposal of the Contraband Committee was far-reaching in its scope, and during the autumn and winter of 1915–16 several of these disguised shipments were identified from intercepted telegrams, and placed in prize.

On the other hand, the work of the patrols and the examination service was reinforced by the effect of many agreements made with neutral shipowners and merchants. Of these perhaps the most important was that concluded in March with the American cotton exporters. The question of cotton had all along been one of the greatest difficulty. The dislocation of trade by the war, and the consequent slump in the price of cotton at the end of 1914, had hit the Southern States so hard that the declaration of cotton as contraband would have brought them to the verge of ruin.[1] In view of the dependence of the Allies on the United States for essential supplies, and the pressure brought to bear on the American Government to place an embargo on the export of arms and munitions, it had been impossible hitherto to take any effective step to stop the exports to Germany. It was now agreed that cotton sold under contracts prior to March 2nd, and shipped before April 1st, should be detained only on purchase by the British Government at contract price. Under this arrangement 250,000 bales were bought. Large quantities shipped after April 1st were also detained under the Order of March 11th without compensation; but the compromise had the effect of enabling the Allies to take effective steps for the stoppage of German supplies without disastrous results to the Southern States.

It was not till August that cotton was declared contraband. It was then placed in the absolute list; but the chief effect of the change was to enable detained cargoes to be condemned.[2] So far as the stoppage of German

[1] Vol. I, pp. 113–14, 190–1, 294–5.
[2] *Manual of Emergency Legislation*, Supplement No. iv, pp. 109–10.

imports was concerned, a more important development was the series of agreements made during the summer with neutral importers. The great difficulty in dealing with the indirect trade of Germany was that of obtaining legal proof of enemy destination. The mere fact that the imports of a contiguous neutral State were abnormal was not in itself decisive. Thus, when the Swedish imports of maize attracted the attention of the British Authorities, the Swedes were able to show that the increase was due to the failure of their own oat crop, and it was impossible to interfere with the traffic. Import statistics, however, could not, in practice, be ignored, and during March and April several large consignments of lard for Sweden were seized on statistical grounds, and placed in prize, as the Swedish Government was granting licences for the re-export of all cargoes shipped before the date of the prohibition.

Though statistical evidence was of doubtful validity in the Prize Court, it afforded a surer ground in the negotiation of agreements. The principle of regulating supplies by the amount of the normal peace import had already been applied in the agreement with Swiss copper importers, and it was now decided to attempt its application to neutral imports of cotton. This scheme was successfully carried out during the course of the summer. An agreement with the Swedish Cotton Spinners' Association providing for the restriction of imports to an agreed ration based on normal consumption, was concluded in June, and during August and September similar agreements were concluded with the Netherlands Overseas Trust, the Norwegian Cotton Spinners' Association, the Danish importers, and the Société Suisse de Surveillance Économique. In November the Danish Agreement was extended to include waste and yarn.

This series of agreements, coupled with the earlier agreement with the American exporters, closed all the more important channels by which further supplies of cotton could reach the Central Powers. Another had been stopped in August, by the addition of cotton yarn to the British list of prohibited exports. There was still a certain amount of leakage through Sweden and Switzerland, and a very few consignments from time to time evaded the patrols; but the total quantities involved were small, and practically speaking, Germany was left to rely on the stocks she had obtained during the first few months of the war.

The system of agreements was widely extended during 1915. In March the American Rubber Interests undertook to export only to Great Britain. In July the agreement with the Netherlands Overseas Trust was extended to cover all articles, whether contraband or not, manufactured from contraband material. At the same time the control of the Trust over the Dutch import trade was strengthened by a Proclamation prohibiting all exports from the United Kingdom to the Netherlands, except to the Trust, or to the person named in a licence to export restricted goods.[1] Many separate agreements were concluded with individual firms and associations in Norway; others, of great importance, were entered into with neutral shipowners. Some big neutral lines, who cared for the freedom of their regular traffic from interference far more than for the retention of the contraband trade, were willing to undertake that goods suspected to be for enemy destination should only be delivered to the neutral consignee under stringent guarantees against re-export, and in default should be returned to Great Britain for Prize Court proceedings or stored in the neutral country until the end of the war. In addition, some lines adopted the practice of submitting their cargo bookings in advance to the Contraband Committee, and refusing shipment of all consignments which, in the opinion of the Committee, were likely to lead to the detention of the vessel.[2] Such agreements lightened considerably the work of the examination service, and they were also of great advantage to the steamer companies in minimising delays. Hence they were in general faithfully and strictly observed.

In negotiating such agreements, a powerful lever lay ready to the hands of the British Government. A large proportion of the bunker depôts on the main trade routes were in British or Allied territory. Others, such as most of those in the Atlantic Islands and South America, were controlled from head offices in London, and yet others, such as those in the European neutral States, drew their supplies of coal from Great Britain, or from British territory. Only in American and Japanese waters were

[1] *Manual of Emergency Legislation, Supplement No. iv*, pp. 236-7.
[2] Cd. 8145.

the majority of the depôts wholly independent of British supplies.[1]

The result was that it was possible to exercise a large measure of control over the supply of bunkers, not only in British ports, but in many neutral ports supplied from British sources. The first suggestion for the use of this weapon as a means of restricting neutral trade in enemy interests came from Mr. W. E. Hargreaves, of Messrs. C. T. Bowring & Co., ship and insurance brokers. In June 1915 the Board of Trade consulted this gentleman with regard to the withdrawal of insurance facilities from certain steamers under neutral flags, in which German capital was beneficially interested. Mr. Hargreaves pointed out that these ships could most effectively be immobilised by persuading the bunkering firms to withhold

[1] Practically all bunker depôts in Europe outside the United Kingdom and France were dependent on British supplies. On the main trade routes the chief depôts were :

Route.	In British or Allied Territory.	Controlled from U.K.	Dependent on British Supplies.	Independent.
N. Atlantic	United Kingdom. Halifax N.S.	—	—	—
Oriental	Gibraltar, Oran, Algiers, Malta, Port Said, Aden, Perim, Colombo, Hong Kong, Fremantle	—	Padang, Batavia (dependent on India and Australia).	Newport News, etc. Nagasaki, etc.
South American	Dakar	St. Vincent, Canaries (partly), Madeira, Lisbon, Pernambuco, Rio, Buenos Aires	Valparaiso, Callao	—
South African	Dakar, Sierra Leone, Cape Town, Durban	Delagoa Bay	Loanda, Beira, Mozambique	—
Pacific	Newcastle, N.S.W., Vancouver	—	—	Nagasaki, etc., San Francisco, Hawaii

bunkers at the Atlantic islands, and the idea of a general application of this principle, for the restriction of enemy trade, was at once caught up both by the Board of Trade and the Trade Division of the Admiralty. The prohibition of coal exports provided the necessary machinery, and in July an informal committee comprising representatives of the Admiralty, Foreign Office, and Board of Trade was set up to assist the Coal Exports Committee in the supervision of the trade. The conditions now laid down for the granting of licences for the export of coal to bunker ports, were that no coal should be furnished to the enemy, to ships known to trade in enemy interests, or to ships specially notified by the British Government as objectionable, and, to prevent any evasion of the regulations, it was further stipulated that no coal should be transferred without permission, to another importer. At the same time a Black List was compiled of ships to be refused bunkers at British ports, and to be notified to foreign importers under the terms of the licensing scheme.

The right of the British Government to regulate the bunker supply in British ports, and to impose conditions on the licensing of a prohibited export, could not be disputed; but the effect of the regulations was to give them a large measure of control over neutral shipping, which depended on British coal for carrying on its trade. During the summer and autumn of 1915 several of the Dutch and Scandinavian lines concluded agreements with the British Government, by which they not only bound themselves to call voluntarily at British ports and to refuse goods of enemy origin or destination, but also to charter to the Allies a specified portion of their carrying space. To facilitate the trade of other neutral shipowners who were willing to renounce traffic in enemy interests a Ship's White List was issued in October 1915. Ships in this list were to receive bunkers freely at all depôts in British or Allied territory or under Allied control, but to obtain inclusion in the list it was necessary for the owner to sign an agreement that he would keep the British Authorities informed of the names of all vessels owned by him, and would give notice of any time-charters entered into; that he would charter no ships to the enemy, would send his ships to British ports for verification of papers, and would obtain the necessary guarantees against enemy origin or destination in respect of all goods shipped in them.

Breach of any of these conditions by one ship belonging to an owner entailed, in default of a satisfactory explanation, the black-listing of his whole fleet.

A large number of neutral owners proved willing to comply with these conditions in order to obtain for their ships equality of treatment with British and Allied vessels. Other vessels, which were neither on the White List nor covered by any specific agreement, were able to obtain bunkers, so long as there was no evidence of their being employed in enemy trade; but, when bunkered in the United Kingdom, they were usually required to bring cargo or promise to return with cargo to a British port, in return for the facilities provided.

The predominant position of London in the marine insurance market was another effective weapon in the control of neutral shipping. Lloyd's and the great marine insurance companies had already inserted a clause in their policies by which ships trading between North America and Europe were warranted not to carry goods of enemy origin or destination, and they now added a stipulation that the insurance should automatically become void fourteen days after the insured vessel was placed in the Ships' Black List.

In these ways the machinery of the blockade was reinforced by an elaborate system of agreements and regulations which supplemented most effectively the work of the patrols, and it was not long before the effect could be seen. Direct shipments to German ports ceased altogether after the issue of the Order in Council of March 11th, and American exports to the contiguous neutral countries fell away so rapidly that by September they were little above the normal.[1] It could not be said that

[1] United States Export in millions of dollars:

Monthly Average.	To Germany.	To Holland and Scandinavia.	Total: Germany, Holland, Scandinavia.
January—March 1914	28·9	12·0	40·9
April—July 1914	17·3	13·1	30·4
August 1914	—	4·7	4·7
September 1914	—	15·7	15·7
October—December 1914	0·7	28·3	29·0
January—March 1915	3·8	47·9	51·7
April—June 1915	—	25·7	25·7
July—September 1915	—	17·7	17·8

N.B.—The figures represent shipments from United States, not amounts received in the importing countries; that is to say, they include cargoes seized by the Allies.

the overseas import trade of the Central Powers had, like the export trade, been practically extinguished; but it had been reduced to a very small fraction of its normal volume.

There was, however, one branch of Germany's seaborne trade which the Allies were powerless to stop. In the lower waters of the Baltic German shipping could move freely, and towards the end of 1914 the steamers held up in Norwegian ports began to creep back to Germany, using territorial waters as much as possible. By the beginning of 1915 a brisk trade was in progress with Copenhagen and Swedish ports, and there were also a number of steamers which traded regularly to Norway, especially to the great ore port of Narvik. For the purpose of attacking the Narvik trade a number of armed trawlers were attached to the Tenth Cruiser Squadron for inshore work, and on July 8th the TENBY CASTLE, one of these trawlers, captured the *Friedrich Arp*, returning to Emden with a cargo of ore, and sank her after taking off the crew. It was only at one or two points, however, that it was ever necessary for the steamers engaged in the traffic to leave territorial waters, and though the risks incurred were too great to permit of its attaining very large dimensions, it was not wholly extinguished.

Far larger was the traffic with Swedish ports. Now that Germany was unable to obtain iron ore from Spain, the Swedish supplies were of the first importance to her munition industries. Dairy produce, timber, and woodpulp swelled the volume of traffic, and to these were added, especially during the early months of the year, many cargoes of cotton, fodder, and other commodities imported by Scandinavian merchants for re-export to Germany. With this trade it was for long impossible to interfere, for the Russian Fleet was too weak to venture into the southern waters of the Baltic; but in October 1915 the British submarines which had taken part in the defence of the Gulf of Bothnia turned their attention to the German-Swedish trade. So vigorous was their attack, assisted by one or two Russian submarines, that on October 15th it was reported that, out of some fifty steamers engaged in the metal traffic, thirty-seven were held up in Swedish ports, and the Germans were obliged to resort to night passages and convoy in order to keep any trade afoot.[1] Including one or two ships sunk by mines or

[1] *Brassey's Naval Annual*, 1916, pp. 30-1.

wrecked, the German losses in the Baltic during the last three months of 1915 amounted to about a score of steamers sunk or damaged, aggregating some 45,000 tons.[1]

Nevertheless, the German-Swedish trade continued to employ a large block of shipping both German and neutral. The German imports of iron-ore from Sweden during the war amounted to some five and a half million tons a year, and, as the ore was a purely Swedish product, and sustained operations against German shipping in the Baltic were impossible, nothing could be done by the Allies to stop the traffic.

These great imports from Sweden, added to the German output and that of the occupied districts in France, assured Germany a sufficiency of iron-ore, but great difficulty was experienced in procuring the scarcer metals used in the manufacture of special steels. All supplies of tungsten were cut off by the blockade, and an attempt to procure molybdenum from Norway for use as a substitute, was defeated by the buying up of stocks by the British Government.[2] The supply of nickel also presented great difficulties. The German production from native ores did not exceed 1,400 tons, and nearly ten times as much could have been used profitably in the war industries.[3] The sources of nickel ore were almost entirely in Allied territory in Canada and New Caledonia, and, though most of the Canadian ore was smelted in the United States, the British Government was able, by very large purchases, to secure practically complete control of the American output. In August 1915 an agreement was concluded with the Norwegian refineries which prevented Germany from receiving more than a small proportion of the Norwegian output—itself only a minor factor in the market. Some small amounts were obtained through Scandinavia, Holland, and Switzerland, and there was reason to believe

---

[1] It is hardly necessary to state that no steamer was torpedoed by a British submarine without warning, or without ample provision for the safety of the crew.

[2] Rather more than half the German import of tungsten ores before the war came from British sources, especially Burma, Australia, and New Zealand. Early in the war all Empire supplies of tungsten were requisitioned at fixed prices for the use of the Imperial Government, and a company was formed by the Sheffield steel manufacturers for the production of tungsten metal, practically the whole supply of which had hitherto been obtained from Germany.

[3] Krupp's stock at the beginning of the war was believed to be about 1,500 tons of metal, and ore containing rather more than another 1,500 tons.

GERMAN METAL SUPPLIES

that re-exports of nickel to these countries from the United Kingdom sometimes found their way to the enemy; but by the autumn of 1915 the shortage was already acute.

Of the other metals Germany obtained from Holland, early in the war, 2,000 tons of Banca tin, and the abnormal imports of the Scandinavian States gave rise to the more concern inasmuch as they were largely derived from the United Kingdom. During the latter half of the year, however, British re-exports were drastically cut down by the Licensing Committee, and agreements with American importers of British tin-plate gave a large measure of control over neutral imports.

The control of tin, as well as of tungsten (wolfram and scheelite), and nickel, was greatly facilitated by the large proportion of the raw product which came from sources within the British Empire. The supply of aluminium, on the other hand, was never effectively cut off. Bauxite could be obtained in ample quantities in Transylvania and Dalmatia, and the other essential constituent of aluminium —cryolite—could be manufactured synthetically. Moreover, the only source of natural cryolite is Ivygut in Greenland, and shipments from Greenland to Copenhagen undoubtedly found their way to the enemy. Nor could these shipments be effectively stopped, for the munition factories of the Allies, who were themselves unable to manufacture synthetic cryolite, depended on the output of the Copenhagen refinery. Large quantities of aluminium were also obtained by Germany from Switzerland.

These supplies of aluminium, and the large quantities of iron and zinc produced in Germany itself, enabled substitutes to be found, in many of their uses, for the metals such as copper which were almost wholly cut off by the blockade; but this use of substitutes led inevitably to raising the price and reducing the stocks of the substituted metals themselves. So early as December 1914 the German Government found it necessary to fix maximum prices for copper, aluminium, nickel, antimony, and tin, and to take power to requisition stocks on this basis. In May 1915 all manufacturers of these metals or of lead were required to notify their stocks to the Berlin War Office, and all sales for industrial purposes were forbidden except under licence. In July these restrictions were extended not only to all stocks in private hands, but to all manufactured articles, such as ordinary domestic utensils (with a few exceptions) containing copper, brass, or nickel. At the same time an appeal was made to patriotic citizens to deliver up all such articles to the Authorities, either as a free gift or at a low fixed price, and it was intimated that, should the response to this appeal prove inadequate, compulsory requisitioning would follow. Meanwhile, the occupied territories were systematically and ruthlessly ransacked.

Still clearer evidence of the success of the blockade in cutting off the supplies of nickel was given by the withdrawal of the 5-pfennig nickel coinage from circulation, and its replacement by iron coins, in order that the nickel might be melted down for military use. The use of iron weights was also authorised, as those of brass, copper, or nickel were required for smelting.

By these means the essential requirements of the munition factories continued to be met; but there was little or no surplus for the fulfilment of civilian requirements, and the manufacturers depended almost entirely on army contracts to keep their works running. In the textile industries the position was much the same. Imports of cotton had now been cut off. Those of jute had been stopped by the outbreak of war, as India was the sole source of supply. Wool was imported in time of peace mainly from the British Empire, and little had been received from abroad even in the early days of the blockade. The home production both of wool and flax was much below the normal consumption. Nearly all the stocks of textile materials had been requisitioned for army purposes, and those available for civilian consumption were both insufficient and enormously costly, while amongst the textile workers there was considerable unemployment and distress.

The food supply, too, gave cause for anxiety. Although imports from overseas had represented but a small percentage of the normal consumption, the effect of the blockade was out of all proportion to the actual reduction in available supplies.[1] In the first place, there was a

[1] Consumption and import of foodstuffs in billion calories, 1912–13:

	Consumption.	Import.
Vegetable products	50·8	2·3
Meat	5·3	0·3
Other animal foods	8·1	0·6
Fats (animal and vegetable)	13·7	3·7

The total dependence of Germany on imported foods for human con-

real shortage in fats, the imports of which had borne a larger proportion to the total consumption than those of any other class of foodstuffs. Increased imports of dairy produce from Holland and Scandinavia did much to make good this deficiency, and during the earlier stages of the war they were supplemented by large re-exports of oil and oil seeds from the United Kingdom to Holland. These re-exports were explained in large measure by the importance to Great Britain of the Dutch margarine factories, for it was not till much later in the war that British factories were able to supply the requirements of the population, though the business of crushing palm-kernels from the West Coast of Africa was taken up by British companies early in 1915.[1] It was necessary, therefore, to keep Holland supplied with materials, but the quantities re-exported were obviously greater than were required for the normal Dutch production, and during March and April linseed-oil, cotton-seeds, and palm-kernels were added to the list of prohibited exports. Even after that date large exports continued to be licensed; but, as the result of the agreement with the Netherlands Oversea Trust relating to non-contraband products, the export of vegetable oils from Holland to the enemy fell away, from July 1915, to less than the normal figures.[2]

Apart from the question of fats, the chief difficulty, at this period, was the fact that the incidence of the deficit was very unevenly distributed. The very fact that the bulk of the food supply was home-produced and could not, like imports, be controlled in bulk from the source, rendered the work of the Food Control extraordinarily difficult. While there was as yet no appreciable general shortage, there were many local and temporary shortages of particular kinds of food, especially in the large towns, and the task of remedying these shortages was complicated not only by the military demands on transport, but by inter-State jealousies, and by the fact that the

sumption was less than 10 per cent. of the normal consumption; but, if imported manures and feeding-stuffs are taken into consideration, the proportion of imports to total consumption rises to about 15 per cent.—*Report on Food Conditions in Germany* [Cmd. 280], 1919.

[1] *Statist*, 24 April, 1915. Annual Report of Elder Dempster Line.
[2] Exports of vegetable oils from Holland to Germany in metric tons:

August 1914	4,500
June 1915	39,000
August 1915	4,500
September 1915	3,000

initial measures of price regulation had antagonised the agricultural interests. Thus, while the available food supplies were sufficient as a whole, there was a certain amount of individual hardship among the urban poor, and the machinery of regulation and control, which became continually more and more complex and extensive, was a perpetual source of friction and irritation.

This irritation was increased by the depressing effect of the famine in lighting oils, the reduction in the supply of textile and other manufactures for civilian use, and the shortage of soap. This shortage, arising from the necessity of using all available oils and fats for food purposes, led during the autumn to the extensive substitution of paper for linen in collars, cuffs, napkins, and handkerchiefs, with a view to economy in washing; but it had not yet become a serious menace to public health.

It was, however, the future rather than the present which was the real cause of anxiety. Germany's dependence was not so much on imported foods as on imported fodder and fertilisers, and it was in respect of these that the blockade assumed its most threatening aspect. The lack of concentrated feeding-stuffs was the more serious inasmuch as German cattle were mainly stall-fed, even during the summer months, and the problem of maintaining live-stock was already serious. In the early months of the war pigs were slaughtered in large numbers in order to set free potatoes and mill offals for human consumption; but the effect of this measure was to threaten the already depleted supply of fats. On the other hand, the stocks of cattle were carefully maintained, but their utility for the supply of meat and milk was threatened by the difficulty of procuring sufficient feeding-stuffs to keep them in good condition. In the event of a prolonged war actual shortage both of meat and milk was inevitable.

Equally serious, in a long war, was the prospect of diminished cereal production, due to the cutting off of imported fertilisers. Without a free use of manures the poor and sandy soil of Germany would not yield anything approaching the normal harvests. The total annual consumption of artificial manures was 1,591,000 tons, of which 536,000 tons consisted of potash, 782,000 tons of phosphoric acid, and 273,000 tons of pure nitrogen. Ample potash for all requirements was produced at home, but at least 50 per cent. of the nitrogen and a still larger proportion of the materials for phosphoric acid was imported, and practically the whole of these imports were cut off from the very outbreak of war.[1] Some low-grade phosphate was obtained from the occupied territories, but the rich phosphate rock of which Germany had imported some 900,000 tons a year from Florida, Curaçoa, and Tunis was entirely lost, and the manufacture of sulphuric acid for the treatment of rock phosphate was hampered by the loss of almost all the imported pyrites. The supplies of iron ore, too, were reduced, despite the imports from Sweden, and this had its effect on the output of basic slag. Even more serious was the effect of the blockade in depriving Germany of the annual imports of Chile nitrate, amounting to 750,000 tons, of which 500,000 tons were used in the supply of fertilisers.[2] The scanty stocks remaining were mostly required for munitions, and, though there was already a considerable home production of artificial nitrates and some further supplies were obtained from Norway, this did not go far to redress the balance.

This shortage of fertilisers had a very serious effect on the production of cereals both for direct human consumption and for use as fodder. Further, the shortage of concentrated feeding-stuffs and the heavy slaughtering of pigs involved a great diminution in the supply of animal manure, and a vicious circle was set up which affected alike the supply of animal and of vegetable food. By extending the area under wheat at the expense of other grains and of sugar-beet, a wheat crop was procured in 1915 large enough to make good the loss of imports; but the effect of the reduction in available fertilisers was already seen in the diminished yield per hectare of the principal crops, and the total harvest, both of cereals and of roots, was a long way below the normal. If the war were prolonged, it was apparent that the impoverishment of the soil by deprivation of its accustomed nourishment must inevitably be cumulative in its effects.

In Austria-Hungary conditions were much the same. Exports had practically ceased, and the exchanges ran still more strongly against Vienna than against Berlin. There

[1] Cmd. 280, p. 23.
[2] Nitrate was not declared contraband till 4 October, 1915, but all shipments destined for Germany had been stopped since 11 March, and even before that date there were very few shipments, as the Chilean nitrate industry was largely controlled by Allied capital. German sailing vessels carrying about 20,000 tons of nitrate were captured during 1914.

was an acute shortage of raw materials, and, though the Empire should have been practically self-sufficing as regards foodstuffs, the food supply gave continual trouble. The Food Control was less efficient than in Germany, and defective transport, aggravated by provincial jealousies and friction between Austria and Hungary, led to grave difficulties in the feeding of the larger towns. The price of essential foodstuffs rose to fantastic heights, and in Vienna especially, where the cost of living was always high, gave rise to much suffering and discontent.

Towards the end of the year the blockade machinery received another turn of the screw. The "rationing" principle, by which neutral imports were limited to the normal annual import of various commodities, was extended by the conclusion of several important agreements. In Switzerland the Société Suisse de Surveillance Économique performed a function similar to that of the Netherlands Overseas Trust, and the agreement concluded with that body in September was framed on a rationing basis. In November a rationing agreement covering oils, maize, wool, and other commodities was concluded with the Netherlands Overseas Trust itself, and during the same month an agreement was made with the Danish Merchants' Guild and Chamber of Manufacturers, which provided not only for guarantees against re-exports, but for the acceptance in principle of the rationing system on a basis to be worked out.[1]

There was thus every indication that the effect of economic pressure would steadily increase. More and more the Central Powers were forced back upon their own resources, and those resources themselves were being slowly but steadily diminished by the diminution of productive power.

[1] The term "rationing" was officially adopted in the *Statement of the Measures adopted to intercept the Seaborne Commerce of Germany*, presented to Parliament in January, 1916 [Cd. 8145].

CHAPTER X

THE INCREASE OF REQUISITIONING IN THE SUMMER AND AUTUMN OF 1915

If the war at sea in its economic aspects be considered as a whole, the advantage in the summer of 1915 lay decidedly with the Allies. Destructive as the German submarines had proved, they had failed to reduce appreciably the volume of British trade, while the Allies, on the other hand, had been able greatly to strengthen their control of neutral traffic, and to increase the severity of economic pressure on the Central Powers. Nevertheless, the situation contained elements of danger which only required time to become more clearly manifest. The progress of events in France and Flanders pointed to a long war, and, though economic pressure might gradually wear down the enemy's power of resistance, the process of exhaustion was not likely to be rapid. The chief hope of ending the war at a blow lay in the Gallipoli Expedition, and by September 1915 the hope of a speedy success in that quarter was already fading.

In a long war the strain on the resources of Great Britain was bound to be very great, and nowhere greater than in the demands upon merchant shipping. Hitherto the available carrying power had sufficed to maintain the essential imports at a level which enabled all demands of the fighting services to be fulfilled without imposing any grave hardship on the civil population. But the rise in freight and prices was already serious, and any further reduction in the available tonnage must inevitably force them up still further, and might even threaten actual shortage in the necessaries of life and the raw materials of industry.

Thanks to the great number of enemy ships captured, seized, or detained, the total tonnage available was even now greater than at the outbreak of war. It was, however, a steadily diminishing total. The merchant tonnage launched, which amounted to 416,000 for the last quarter of 1914, fell in the quarter ending March 1915 to 267,000, and in the June and September quarters it was only 148,000 and 146,000 respectively.

As to the cause of this progressive diminution in output there was at the time much controversy. It was alleged by a section of the employers that the rise in wages since the outbreak of war had produced a tendency to work short time, and that both Admiralty and mercantile construction were seriously delayed through heavy drinking. These charges were emphatically denied by the Unions, who attributed the decline rather to the fact that a large number of the strongest and most skilful workers had enlisted, thus reducing the average efficiency of the men employed, and to the exhaustion and overstrain consequent on continuous overtime during the early months of the war.

The great obstacle to mercantile construction was, undoubtedly, the diversion of labour and material to war purposes. From the outbreak of war the Admiralty had controlled the whole shipbuilding facilities of the country, but it was not till the beginning of 1915 that all berths, as they became vacant, were filled with warships and auxiliaries. The requirements of the anti-submarine campaign and the construction of monitors for coastal service gave an immense impetus to naval construction, and the demands of the Admiralty on berths, material, and labour left few facilities available for commercial work. The men themselves undoubtedly preferred Admiralty work, for not only was it better paid, but they could more readily understand its national importance in time of war; but the difficulty of obtaining material was at least as great as the difficulty of obtaining labour. Prior to the war much of the material used in the shipyards and marine engineering shops had been imported, and of the imports the greater part came from Germany.[1] The cutting off of these imports was severely felt, and the competition of the munitions industries for iron and steel added to the difficulty of providing sufficient material to supply both the naval and the mercantile demand.

---

[1] In 1913 about 30 per cent. of the castings and 40 per cent. of the forgings used for ships and marine engines were imported. See *Reports of the Departmental Committee on Shipping and Shipbuilding* [Cd. 9092], especially Appendix A, Second Report.

DECLINE IN SHIPBUILDING

Not only was it exceedingly difficult to place orders for new construction; it was almost equally difficult for shipowners to obtain delivery of ships on the stocks or even of those already launched and well advanced towards completion.

In June 1915 the President of the Board of Trade appointed a small Committee to report, after personal inspection, on the number of vessels under construction, and the time which would be necessary, under normal conditions, to complete them. The report of this Committee showed that about forty vessels were within a few weeks of completion, but were held up through lack of labour and material owing to the prior claims of the Admiralty.

By this time the rate of construction was far smaller than the rate of sinking, and by the end of September the total losses from all causes—war and marine—were already slightly greater than the total output since the outbreak of war.[1] There was, however, the big margin in hand provided by prize and detained vessels, and, unless the average rate of sinkings should be considerably increased, it would be a long time before this margin was exhausted. But it was not the destruction of merchant shipping by the mine and submarine which was, at this time, the most serious factor in reducing the tonnage available for the carriage of imports. Heavy as was the total of losses, it was far smaller than the total of tonnage withdrawn from commercial employment for naval and military purposes.

The Fourth Sea Lord's Conference in January had suggested some possible economies in the use of requisitioned tonnage, but held out little hope of a substantial reduction of the total.[2] For the whole period from the beginning of the war to January 1915 the average proportion of British ocean-going tonnage under requisition for all purposes was estimated at about 20 per cent.

Unfortunately, even this figure was by no means final. By the early months of 1915 it had become clear that Great Britain was committed to maintaining in France and Flanders an army on the continental scale, and as fast as new divisions could be trained and equipped they were poured across the Channel. Not only did this involve the

---

[1] Total losses from all causes, August 1914—September 1915 . . . . 1,294,000 tons
Total new construction . . . . . 1,233,000 ,,
Enemy tonnage, captured or detained . . . 682,000 ,,

[2] See p. 47, *supra*.

employment of a large body of troop transports, but with every division that was added to the strength, the demand for shipping to carry drafts, munitions, and stores was permanently increased. Down to September 20th, 1914, the transport of the Expeditionary Force had involved a daily average of thirteen voyages, representing over 52,000 gross tons of shipping a day. With the completion of the original force, the volume of military cross-Channel traffic somewhat diminished, in spite of the constant stream of reinforcements, and from September 21st, 1914, to April 18th, 1915, the average daily despatch was ten ships of 31,000 tons. By April, however, the New Armies were pouring across in increasing numbers, and for the period from April 19th to September 26th the daily sailings averaged between fifteen and sixteen ships with an aggregate tonnage of 40,000.

Still more serious was the effect of the Gallipoli Expedition. By the beginning of 1915 the Imperial Concentration in its first stage was complete. The outlying garrisons had been brought in and replaced by Territorials from home; the Indian Expeditionary Force and the first Canadian Contingent had arrived in Europe; the Australian and New Zealand troops in Egypt. Drafts and reinforcements for the Indian and Dominions troops, and for the forces engaged in Mesopotamia and the various minor oversea campaigns, would necessarily absorb a certain amount of tonnage, but the worst strain of long-distance transport appeared to be over. But, with the inception of the Dardanelles operations, any such hope at once disappeared. The transport of the first three divisions during March and April involved the use of forty-seven ocean-going steamers, and by April 11th, when only the first two divisions had arrived, the number of ships in the Mediterranean on military service, including storeships and the transports which had brought the Indian Contingent to Marseilles, was already ninety-six. In May and June the 52nd Division was despatched, and during June and July five more divisions followed.

The work thus thrown on the Transport Department was very heavy, and was rendered heavier by the circumstances in which the Gallipoli Expedition was conceived. Great as were the results anticipated from the forcing of the Dardanelles, military opinion was divided as to the wisdom of diverting effort from the Western Front, and the Government themselves were not unanimous.[1] Every decision to send a new division to Gallipoli represented a struggle in the Council Chamber, and the natural result was that no definite programme of transport could be mapped out. When a decision was finally taken the despatch of the troops had become urgent, and the notice received by the Transport Department from the War Office allowed little time to secure and fit out the necessary tonnage. Again and again the Department protested that with a month's definite notice of requirements they could meet every demand, but that the actual notice received was never sufficient in point of time, and that, even when it was received, subsequent alterations were frequently made as regards the numbers to be moved and the port of embarkation. In these circumstances it was impossible for them to meet the Mediterranean requirements with ships released from other service, and it became necessary to requisition ships at short notice and at the cost of serious dislocation of trade.

Nor was this their only trouble. Once ships were despatched to the Mediterranean with troops or stores, it was very difficult to get them back. The advance base at Mudros was deplorably ill-equipped. There were neither piers, nor quays, nor warehouses for sorting and storing cargoes, and ships were detained for weeks at a time with part cargoes on board to act as floating warehouses for munitions and supplies. Owing to the short notice given to the Transport Department of the War Office requirements, it was frequently impossible to secure good stowage at the home ports. The contractors rushed goods forward before the ships were ready to receive them, the ports were congested, and the ships were loaded hastily and sometimes unsuitably in order to clear the quays and make their due sailing date. In the early days of the campaign several ships were unloaded at Alexandria and re-stowed in order to facilitate discharge at the advance base; but, when the German submarines began to make their presence felt, Admiral de Robeck, commanding in the Eastern Mediterranean, urged strongly that the voyage should be curtailed by sending the transports direct to Mudros, and, after the sinking of the *Royal Edward* on August 11th, this course was definitely approved. While decreasing the risk of loss from submarine attack, the

[1] See Corbett, *Naval Operations*, vol. ii, *passim*.

new policy aggravated the congestion at Mudros. Even when the best practicable stowage had been given to the ships, it was impossible to stow cargoes in such a way as to ensure discharge in order of priority of the military demands, which fluctuated with the changing circumstances of the campaign, and, owing to the lack of proper sorting and stowage facilities ashore, large portions of a cargo had often to be discharged and reloaded in order to get at a particular consignment which was urgently required. The actual work of discharge was frequently delayed by heavy weather, and at the best was very slow. The lighters and tugs available were insufficient in number, and the lighters themselves were frequently laid up for days when full, owing to inability to take discharge ashore. Labour had to some extent to be provided by military fatigue parties, and this involved some measure of military interference with the essentially naval operation of unloading ships. In the absence of any definite system of control or centralisation of responsibility, it was impossible for even such facilities as were available to be used with the maximum economy and efficiency.

Undoubtedly the most serious difficulty was the lack of piers and storage accommodation, but the Naval Transport Officer on the spot was unable to get anything done in the way of improving the equipment of the port. General Headquarters were optimistic as to the result of the campaign. A big advance was almost daily expected, and would involve the shifting of the base to the peninsula. Mudros was regarded as a temporary rather than a permanent base, and no time or labour could be spared for improving its resources. Had it proved possible to force the Straits by a *coup de main*, the chief transport difficulties would never have arisen; had a prolonged campaign been foreseen from the beginning most of them might have been avoided. In the events which happened it was impossible to work out a definite programme either at home or in the Mediterranean. The continual changes in policy at home and the fluctuations of the campaign in the peninsula involved frequent eleventh-hour decisions, and troops and stores were rushed forward from Great Britain to the Mediterranean and from Alexandria to Mudros in irregular batches and without ascertaining that they could be dealt with on arrival. With the hope of an immediate advance always before them, the Military Authorities were naturally anxious to have all the resources at their disposal on the spot; but the accumulation of deeply laden transports in Mudros Harbour only added to the difficulty of dealing with the ships.

Nor was it only laden vessels which were thus detained. Provision had to be made for the contingency of an evacuation, in the event of defeat, or a change of objective, and this involved keeping a reserve of empty ships in the Eastern Mediterranean. Moreover, the heavy casualties incurred overtaxed the supply of hospital ships available, and in July twenty-five transports were taken over to serve temporarily for this purpose. As these were not under the Red Cross flag, the fastest steamers had to be chosen, in order to secure immunity from submarine attack. Further, there was a tendency to use large steamers as depôts and staff headquarters to supplement the meagre accommodation at Mudros.

This was not all. The naval forces co-operating with the army had been largely increased and required supply-ships, ammunition ships, and colliers. Here, too, the disadvantages of Mudros as a base were severely felt. In particular, the lack of piers or hulks rendered it impossible to accumulate a stock of coal on the spot and necessitated the retention of colliers until their cargoes were exhausted. In January 1915 there were forty-one colliers on the Mediterranean station; by October the number had risen to ninety-eight.

But the Gallipoli Expedition was now no longer the only drain on tonnage in the Mediterranean. During August and September the attitude of Bulgaria had become definitely hostile, and on October 3rd Allied troops landed at Salonika. Six days later Bulgarian troops crossed the frontier, and on October 15th a state of war with Bulgaria was proclaimed. With this new commitment on our hands the number of military transports and store-ships actually in the Mediterranean rose to 150, and the drain appeared likely to increase rather than to diminish.

Amidst all these difficulties the Transport Department strove hard to meet the military demands with the minimum of dislocation to trade. Their greatest difficulty lay in the impossibility of obtaining in advance definite decisions which would enable them to adjust the resources already under their control to the demands made upon them. They succeeded, however, in making some use of the ships which had brought the Australian and New Zealand troops to Egypt, and by urgent representations they were at times able to procure the return for further service, of empty transports detained in the Mediterranean. But, both in refitting such vessels for a new voyage and in fitting out newly requisitioned ships, they were grievously hampered by the congestion of the ports and the shortage of labour in the shipyards. In the early days of the war a ship could be delivered for service about a week from the date of requisition; by the autumn of 1915 at least three weeks were required.

As the demands increased and the shortage of tonnage grew more acute, the Department became very anxious to minimise the number of transports required, by using the largest and fastest passenger liners for the carriage of troops. Such ships were in many ways unsuitable for the purpose, as they were specially exposed to submarine attack owing to their inability to enter closed harbours, and were not easy to handle with the available facilities. On the other hand, they represented a great economy of carrying power, as they could carry large numbers of troops and make twice as many voyages in a given time as the ordinary transport. Further, the largest passenger liners had become white elephants to their owners owing to the decrease in the passenger trade and the heavy cost of insurance against marine risks, and such vessels as the great Cunarder *Aquitania* and the White Star Liner *Olympic* were in fact laid up for want of employment. While peculiarly adapted for the carriage of troops, they were ill suited to ordinary cargo traffic and could be requisitioned with little or no addition to the strain on the mercantile marine. For some time the proposal was resisted by the Admiralty on account of the submarine risk, but both the above-named vessels, together with the *Mauretania*, were eventually used for Mediterranean trooping.

It was, of course, outside the scope of the Transport Department to question the necessity or wisdom of the War Office requirements. Their task was confined to fulfilling those requirements with the minimum of dislocation. Nevertheless, the cordial relations existing between the Department and the Director of Movements enabled them to suggest, and at times to press, economies. Thus, in the expectation of an early advance, the troops originally despatched to Gallipoli were accompanied by a great quantity of heavy motor transport and by horses for the 3rd Mounted Division. Neither could be used in the peninsula, but they were intended to be landed on the quays at Constantinople. The horses were finally landed at Alexandria, but the motor transport remained on board ship, totally immobilising the tonnage employed. On this subject the Department made strong representations, and on their persuasion the War Office refrained from sending horses or motor transport with the later divisions. The Department were also able to prevent the use of further ships as depôts for staffs and ordnance, though they were unable to procure the release of the *Aragon* (9,588 tons) and *Minnetonka* (13,528 tons), which were thus employed, or the substitution of less valuable vessels. Efforts were also made, though with little success, to prevent the despatch of stores before they could be dealt with. In view of the haste with which ships were loaded at home ports and the extreme difficulty of giving quick discharge at Mudros, the Department strongly urged that the transports could be sent direct to Alexandria, where the stores should be landed, sorted, and forwarded in smaller vessels to Mudros as and when required. This suggestion, however, was not adopted, mainly through reluctance to expose the cargoes to a double submarine risk.

But, while it was in the Mediterranean that the Transport Department encountered the greatest difficulty in securing economical use of requisitioned tonnage, their troubles were by no means confined to that sea. Persistent pressure by the Department had good results in avoiding delays to the cross-Channel troop-ships, but the running of store-ships employed in the supply of the British Armies was far from satisfactory. Here, too, there was a tendency to rush stores to the port of shipment without regard to whether ships were ready to receive them, and the consequent congestion of the quays and sheds delayed the loading of the vessels when they arrived. Far more serious were the delays on the other side. Owing partly to insufficient facilities—especially in respect of railway trucks—and partly to the inexperience of the officers who found themselves in charge of highly technical operations, the discharge of cargoes at the Northern French ports, and their distribution from those ports to the advance bases and depôts was frequently very slow. The transit-sheds provided for the purpose of sorting cargoes and facilitating their quick distribution were used for storage purposes, and the enormous accumulations of reserve stores at the ports, blocked the unloading of newly arrived ships. Long delays in port were common, and when the effect was felt in delayed delivery of urgently required material the common result was a request for more ships to be sent, with the inevitable consequence of further congestion and further delays.

Such conditions, whether in the Mediterranean or in France, involved, of course, an even greater increase in the number of ships allotted to the various services than was necessitated by the actual growth in military requirements. On the naval side some economies had been effected as a result of the January Conference, which cut down the number of vessels employed as colliers and supply-ships in Home Waters, and since the disappearance of the German surface cruisers from the Trade Routes, it had been possible to effect a very considerable reduction in the number of colliers on foreign stations. Those reductions, however, were more than offset by the increase in Mediterranean requirements and the needs of the patrol organisation created in response to the mine and submarine menace.[1] Moreover, the work of the blockade called for an increasing number of boarding and examination steamers which had to be provided from the merchant service.

The demands of the Allies had also to be met. Coal for the French and Egyptian State Railways, coal and munitions for the White Sea employed a considerable body of requisitioned tonnage provided by the Naval Branch of the Transport Department, who were responsible also for bringing home the purchases of the Royal Sugar Commission. In all, the number of ships under requisition on September 1st, 1915, amounted to 1,304, with an aggregate

[1] Colliers arrived, *en route*, or allocated on October 1st, 1914, and October 1st, 1915.

Home Waters :	1 Oct., 1914.	1 Oct., 1915.
(a) Home Fleet Colliers	163	126
(b) Dockyards, Transport, and Trawler Bases	9	48
Allocated to (a) and (b)	9	22
Mediterranean Fleet and Transports	22	83
Other Stations :	72	43
Allocated to Mediterranean and Foreign Stations	14	10
Yard purpose coal (including allocated)	—	7
Colliers to be allocated	36	26
Total colliers allocated to Fleet Service	325	365

tonnage of 5,050,694, and by the end of the following month it had risen to 1,450, with a tonnage of over 5,500,000. These figures are exclusive of yachts and prizes, but include a number of railway steamers, paddle steamers, and other small vessels employed in the cross-Channel traffic and other special services.[1] The great bulk of the requisitioned tonnage, however, consisted of ocean-going steamers, and the proportion of British ocean-going tonnage under requisition had risen to some 25 per cent.

It must not be overlooked that some vessels included in the list of requisitioned steamers still carried commercial cargoes. Such were the ships employed in the coal supply of the Allies, and those, some 50 to 60 in number, which were bringing sugar at Blue Book rates for the Royal Sugar Commission. A few ships had also been allocated from time to time to carry nitrate and other cargoes for the War Office and the Ministry of Munitions, when any special difficulty was experienced in obtaining space. Apart from sugar, however, the number of import cargoes carried under requisition was very small, and represented a much less important factor than the system of temporary releases, which had now been highly developed. From April to September inclusive over 200,000 tons of iron ore and 87,000 tons of pyrites were brought home in colliers returning from Mediterranean service, and it was only on rare occasions that the refusal of the owners to comply with the conditions of release obliged the Transport Department to undertake the voyage on their own account.

But against the commercial services performed by vessels under requisition or temporarily released must be placed the fact that over 230 British vessels were under charter to France and Russia. These ships were chartered at market rates and were, in practice, exempted from requisition as a concession to the requirements of the Allies; but the majority of them were withdrawn altogether from the British import service. Moreover, it was impossible to exercise any supervision over the way in which they were handled or to ensure economical use of their carrying power.

The tonnage situation was, in fact, becoming very grave. Although space for all essential imports had hitherto been

[1] The figures quoted include tank steamers employed as naval oilers. The number of prizes employed on naval and military service on 1 October was 57, with an aggregate tonnage of 240,000.

obtained, the monthly decrease in the total entrances of British tonnage showed a perceptible upward curve, and in September 1915 it was heavier than for any previous month of the war. Neutral shipping as yet showed no sign of being driven away from British ports by fear of the submarine, but, in view of the increasing withdrawal of British shipping from the general carrying trade, the demands of the Allies, and the requirements of neutral countries themselves, the supply of neutral tonnage was likely to diminish rather than to expand.

The liner services were still adequately maintained, but trades dependent on tramp tonnage were heavily hit. Despite the aid given by temporarily released transports, the munitions industries had great difficulty in fulfilling their requirements for ore, and timber importers were equally unable to satisfy their demands for space. Coal exports, too, suffered severely. An additional blow to the coal export trade was the action of the Greek Government, which, as a result of the friction arising out of the Salonika landing, requisitioned the greater part of the tonnage under the Greek flag. This was a serious matter, as Greek ships played an important part in the carriage of coal to Italian and Egyptian ports; but the coal trade had for a long time been suffering from a shortage of tonnage both for export and for coastal distribution, arising from the large proportion of colliers requisitioned for Admiralty use. So bad was the situation in October that there was serious fear of the exporting coal-fields being obliged to reduce output through inability to charter.

In these circumstances the Advisory Committee put forward a strong plea for reconsideration of the tonnage position as a whole. While recognising the paramount importance of meeting naval and military demands based on strategical requirements, they urged that the attention of the Admiralty and War Office should be drawn to the gravity of the situation, and that steps should be taken to co-ordinate departmental demands and minimise the drain of carrying power. A week later the Director of Transports presented to the Board of Admiralty a full report on the tonnage in naval and military service. In the report the employment of such vessels was carefully analysed and the attention of the Board was drawn in detail to the various factors making against economical use of requisitioned tonnage, especially in the Mediterranean.

AN INQUIRY ORDERED

After describing the conditions in that sea, the Director reported that in such conditions the provision of additional ships would increase rather than diminish the difficulties of transport and that some improvement in the handling of requisitioned tonnage was as important for the efficiency of the transport work as for the relief of the tonnage situation in general. He suggested, therefore, that a Flag Officer should be sent out to be responsible for the economic use of all transports in the Mediterranean, and should be accompanied by a first-class shipping expert to advise him in technical matters.

This report made a profound impression on the Board, who were at the same time receiving from high Naval Authorities alarming accounts of the chaos in the Ægean. They recognised, however, that any action taken, to be effective, must be taken in conjunction with the War Office, and they accordingly suggested to the Army Council that a small Commission consisting of one Flag Officer, one General Officer, and a leading shipping expert should be sent to the Mediterranean to report and advise on the whole position. To this proposal the Army Council agreed, and on October 28th the Mediterranean Transport Commission was formally appointed by the Prime Minister. It consisted of Rear-Admiral F. G. Eyre, Brigadier-General A. B. Hamilton, C.B., and Mr. Thomas Royden, and the terms of reference instructed the Commissioners to proceed to the Eastern Mediterranean to ensure release of redundant tonnage. For this purpose they were to place themselves in communication with the military headquarters and the Admiral commanding; but their functions were not restricted to the tendering of advice, as they were empowered to give direct orders to Naval Transport Officers in that area, subject only to the provision that such orders were not to interfere with operations actually in progress or impending.

CHAPTER XI

THE STATE INTERVENES
NOVEMBER 1915

By this time the Board of Trade had become seriously alarmed as to the effects of shortage of tonnage on the wheat supply of the country. The decrease in imports during the first half of the year was accounted for, as we have seen, by the heavy shipments from North America during the autumn and winter of 1914; but with the approach of the 1915–16 season, greatly increased arrivals would normally have been expected. All through the summer of 1915, however, the imports of wheat and flour showed a progressive decline from the normal level, and the total for the nine months ending September 30th was only 3,885,000 tons, as against 4,507,000 tons in the previous year, and 4,723,000 in 1913.[1]

The position was the more serious inasmuch as only one source of supply was now open. Australia would have nothing to export before 1916, and, though a few cargoes were on their way from Archangel, it was impossible to ship through the White Sea port more than a very small proportion of the Russian crops. The Argentine surplus, part of which had been bought by the British Government, had been hurried forward during the spring and early summer, and was now exhausted; the Indian exports, under the control of the Viceregal Government, had all been received by the end of September. Prospects for the 1915–16 season were good in all countries, but it was only from North America that the immediate requirements of the United Kingdom could be met, and neither from Canada nor the States were supplies coming forward at a rate commensurate with those requirements.

Both in Canada and the States ample stocks were avail-

[1] Flour converted into its equivalent in wheat at the rate of 7 tons flour = 10 tons wheat.

DECLINE IN WHEAT IMPORTS

able. Early in the war the Canadian Cabinet had appointed a special Committee to supervise the wheat exports of the Dominion, and this Committee reported in September that the Western provinces had responded enthusiastically to the demands of the Allies, and that some 200,000,000 bushels were ready to be shipped if tonnage could be obtained to lift them. Nearly the whole ocean-going shipping on the Dominion Register had, however, been requisitioned for the carriage of troops to Europe, and owing to the effect of requisitioning in Great Britain, the arrivals at Canadian ports had greatly diminished. In these circumstances the Committee proposed to the British Government that the Admiralty should either release sufficient ships to lift the whole Canadian wheat surplus or charter substitutes for this purpose at Blue Book rates.

This request was passed on to the Transport Department, who were, of course, quite unable to release so large a block of tonnage at a time when their commitments were rapidly increasing. To the alternative course of requisitioning further tonnage for the purpose, the Advisory Committee demurred. They were still opposed on principle to the carriage of commercial cargoes at Blue Book rates, as tending to destroy the normal incentive to economical and efficient use of tonnage, and the Canadian proposal was particularly objectionable to them as involving the use of requisitioned tonnage for a portion only of the wheat imports. If Canadian wheat were brought at Blue Book rates, while imports from the United States, and from other sources when they became available, were left to take their chance of the freight markets, the effect must be either that imports from all other sources would be discouraged, or that the price of Canadian wheat would be raised to the same level as that of wheat carried at the market rates. Thus, while a big advantage would be given to the Canadian exporter, no ultimate benefit would accrue to the consumer in Great Britain. Nor was this the only objection. Although there was some immediate shortage, plentiful supplies were in prospect in the near future, and it was unnecessary to accumulate a larger reserve than could conveniently be handled. The storage capacity of the granaries in the United Kingdom was limited, and to provide requisitioned tonnage for the whole Canadian surplus would lead almost inevitably to a rush of imports, which must increase to a disastrous extent the congestion at British ports.

These arguments proved decisive, and the action of the Transport Department was ultimately confined to the allocation of three prize steamers for the carriage of Canadian wheat, and the release of a single transport for the same purpose; but in the meantime the Board of Trade had turned their attention to the whole question of wheat tonnage in the North Atlantic, and the means whereby the supply of shipping might be increased with a minimum of dislocation to the ordinary machinery of commerce. For this purpose they communicated with the Chamber of Shipping and the Liverpool Steam Ship Owners' Association, calling their attention to the decline of wheat imports from North America, and inviting their views as to the best means of attracting tonnage into the trade.

In their reply to the Board of Trade, both the Chamber of Shipping and the Liverpool Steamship Owners denied that either shortage of tonnage or the advance in freights had been the chief factor restricting imports. The Liverpool Association, in particular, contended that down to the middle of September the amount of wheat actually on offer at American and Canadian ports had been well within the capacity of the available tonnage, and that, as the rise in freights amounted to only about a quarter of the rise in prices, it could not have been sufficient to keep wheat out of the country.[1] In their view the lack of demand for wheat tonnage was due mainly to commercial and financial considerations. The experts of the *Corn Trade News* had estimated the world's import requirements at 52,000,000 quarters, to meet which surpluses amounting to 100,000,000 quarters were available. Acting on

---

[1] For the first year of war the average price of wheat was 48*s*. 2*d*. per quarter, as against 32*s*. in the twelve months ending July 1914, an advance of 16*s*. 2*d*. The average advance in freights for the same period was from 2*s*. 4*d*. to 6*s*. 9*d*. per quarter; that is to say, of the 16*s*. 2*d*. rise in price, freight accounted for 4*s*. 5*d*. War Risk Insurance at the average State Rate accounted for a further 9*d*., making the total rise due to freight and insurance 5*s*. 2*d*. Taking import values as the basis of comparison, the average import value of North American wheat in August 1915 was 52*s*. 9*d*. as compared with 35*s*. 3*d*. in August 1914, an advance of 17*s*. 6*d*. The advance in North Atlantic freights was from 1*s*. 8½*d*. to 6*s*. 10*d*.; or 5*s*. 1½*d*. In September the freight advanced to 9*s*. 1¼*d*., but the import values fell to 49*s*. 8*d*.—*Liverpool Steam Ship Owners' Association*, Annual Report for 1916, Appendix III, and Secretary's *Report on the Shipping employed in Ocean Oversea Trade and the Effect of the War thereon*, October 1915.

CAUSES OF DECLINE

this assumption the market had put the price for future deliveries substantially below the price for immediate shipments, and buyers had accordingly deferred placing orders, in the expectation of a fall in prices. This disinclination to place orders was increased by difficulties in relation to the American exchange, which was now going against Great Britain, and by the general uncertainty as to the wheat position. The large Government purchases of Indian wheat had tended to discourage private operators, and the possibility of a further extension of Government activity in purchase or transport rendered the placing of large forward contracts unduly speculative. Apart from State action, there was still a possibility that the forcing of the Dardanelles, or an early termination of the war, might bring about a sudden fall in prices involving heavy loss to importers whose contracts were already placed. Thus, everything in the market conditions tended to increase the reluctance of importers to undertake large commitments. Meanwhile many contracts already placed had been cancelled, owing to the unsatisfactory character of the winter crop in the United States, and there was no great eagerness to replace the cancelled purchases by later deliveries.

To whatever cause the stagnation of the market might be attributed, there was admittedly a leeway to be made good, and it was in respect of this leeway that the real tonnage difficulty arose. So far as ordinary trade requirements were concerned, there was no reason to anticipate that the tonnage available for future shipments would be insufficient. The import of North American wheat was, in the main, a liner trade, tramp shipping being employed only on a comparatively small scale to supplement the liner services. Out of 73 vessels normally employed by lines in the Liverpool Association on the North Atlantic routes, 43 had been requisitioned by the Transport Department, but 32 other steamers had been chartered by the lines as substitutes or transferred from other services in order to make good the deficiency, and including new tonnage 65 vessels were now running. For the carriage of the normal imports this should suffice, but, having regard to the small shipments during July, August, and September, there might be some difficulty in making up the leeway unless tramp tonnage could be attracted into the trade or further ships were chartered by the lines.

The owners of tramp steamers were, however, generally averse from engaging in the North Atlantic trade, partly because of the special submarine risk, but mainly because vessels in this trade, being frequently in British ports owing to the comparatively short voyage, were especially liable to requisition. For these reasons it would be necessary for the lines to pay high rates for any additional tonnage chartered, and such rates could not well be paid so long as the attitude of buyers and of the Government remained uncertain.

In a further communication the Association suggested that, with a view to attracting outside tonnage into the trade, all vessels employed between the American and Canadian grain ports and the United Kingdom should, up to the middle of December, be exempted from requisition on the voyage out and home, and for a period of six weeks from completion of discharge. With this inducement they believed that the accumulations of wheat could speedily be cleared off by tramp shipping, and that the regular lines would then be able to maintain supplies at the normal rate. Should this step fail to produce the results anticipated, they suggested that the State should bring over in requisitioned ships the whole of the wheat required to make up the leeway. But to place requisitioned tonnage at the disposal of private importers would probably result either in locking up tonnage at the port of shipment to await the convenience of shippers, or in a rush of shipments which would lead to hopeless congestion of the receiving ports. Moreover, the carriage of specified private cargoes at Blue Book rates would render all outside trade impossible, and it would become necessary for the Government to provide tonnage for the whole wheat imports of the country. If, therefore, it became necessary to provide requisitioned tonnage for any part of the North American wheat accumulations, the Association urged that such wheat should be purchased as well as transported by the Government, who would then be able to fix the selling price in such a manner as not to interfere with the normal course of imports.[1]

The Board of Trade had now passed from a consideration of the tonnage available for North Atlantic wheat to a wider survey of the whole tonnage situation; but, as a

[1] The arguments and suggestions contained in these Memoranda are summarised in the Association's Report for 1915, pp. 22-4.

temporary alleviation of the more restricted problem, they announced during October that ships bringing wheat from North America would receive a measure of exemption from requisition on the lines of the Liverpool proposals. It proved impossible, however, to maintain this concession in face of the continued pressure of military demands, and the privilege was withdrawn within a few days of its announcement. In the meantime a considerable amount of outside tonnage had been attracted into the trade. Further ships were also diverted by the lines into the North Atlantic service, but the rate of import showed no sign of increase and was, indeed, steadily diminishing. The rapid increase in requisitioned tonnage during the autumn of 1915 was accompanied by an all-round rise in freights, and some vessels attracted into the North Atlantic trade were unable to obtain cargoes, as shippers were holding back in the hope of a fall.[1] This, however, was only one factor in the situation, and not the most important. Apart from the considerations set forth by the Liverpool Steam Ship Owners' Association in their memoranda to the Board of Trade, a determining influence on the course of the market was the financial position of the agricultural countries. In 1914 the financial pressure on these countries had compelled early shipments, but by the autumn of 1915 they had established themselves in so strong a position as the result of war demands for their produce, that they were able to hold out for higher prices than importers were yet willing to pay.[2]

The wheat situation, however, formed a part only of the general tonnage and freight problem which the Board of Trade were now investigating, and the solution of that problem was rendered more difficult by the general tone of press and Parliamentary criticism. The problem of freights and the problem of supplies was in fact one and indivisible, but it was to the freight aspect that public attention was almost exclusively directed. It must be remembered that there was as yet no widespread apprehension of a real shortage of essential supplies. Although the entrances at British ports during the first twelve months of war were nearly 30 per cent. below those of the

---

[1] By October the North Atlantic grain freights were 9s. 6d. per quarter and by November 13s. 4½d. The average import values for these months were 50s. 1d. and 52s. respectively.

[2] *Statist*, 13 November, 1915, p. 504.

last corresponding period of peace, the average cargoes carried were so much heavier that the total decrease in the volume of imports was under 13 per cent., and the war had as yet produced no substantial alteration in the habits of life of the people or their consumption of imported commodities. But, as we have already seen, the pressure of this unrestricted demand on a continually diminishing supply of available shipping had forced up freights to an unprecedented level, and to this increase in freights the greater part of the rise in prices which had been so marked since the beginning of 1915 was popularly attributed. By September 1915 the *Statist* Index Number of wholesale prices stood at 107·8, an increase of nearly 33 per cent. on the figure for June 1914, and the Board of Trade Index of retail prices showed a still greater advance.[1] It was in foodstuffs, as a class, that the increase was greatest, and it was the rise in the price of foodstuffs that bore most hardly on the working classes and produced the greatest discontent. It was, too, in grain freights that the increased cost of transport was most notorious, and in every parliamentary discussion on the cost of living the rise in grain freights was made the target of hostile criticism.

The part played by freights in producing this increase in prices was, no doubt, grossly exaggerated. Now, as during the earlier months of the war, the curve of freights and the curve of prices neither synchronised in point of time nor corresponded in the extent of the increase recorded. Other influences—the effect of the war on the demand for particular commodities, the closing of sources of supply, the fluctuations of the export trade, and the fall of the exchanges—had a greater effect than the advance in freights. The import values of such important materials as cotton, tin, and wool remained constant or showed only a small increase, although all these commodities had to bear their share of the freight burden, because the diminution of the continental demand threw on the market a larger surplus than British consumers could absorb. On the other hand, the cost of meat and sugar, which enjoyed

[1] *Statist* Index Number. Average 1867–77 = 100 :

	Food.	Materials.	Total.
June 1914	74·8	85·7	81·2
September 1915	105·2	109·6	107·8
Increase per cent.	40·6	27·9	32·8

the advantage of carriage at Blue Book rates, continually increased.[1]

Even the rise in grain freights, great as it was, represented only one factor in the retail price of bread, but it was a factor which tended to increase in importance, and it bulked large in the public eye.[2] The publication of figures showing that certain shipping firms and companies—especially owners of tramp tonnage—had made very large profits, excited widespread comment, and there was a strong demand that something should be done to reduce the cost of maritime transport.

The application of the Excess Profits Duty to the shipping industry by the Finance Act (Number 2) of 1915 did something to satisfy public opinion with regard to ship-owners' profits, but the Excess Profits Duty, while it diverted a large sum of money from the owners to the Exchequer, did nothing to reduce freights or add to the supply of tonnage. That problem had to be met by other measures, and, in their attempt to solve it, the Government were faced with the difficulty that one-third of the total imports brought into the country were carried in foreign, and chiefly in neutral vessels. The freights

[1] Average import values for the six months ending:

		July 1914.		Jan. 1915.		July 1915.		Jan. 1916.	
		s.	d.	s.	d.	s.	d.	s.	d.
Cotton	per cental	64	2	45	10	45	10	61	5
Tin ore	per ton	1,895	5	1,725	11	1,720	4	1,622	7
Tin	,, ,,	3,207	9	2,873	9	3,335	8	3,129	11
Wool	per lb.	0	10	0	11	0	11	0	11
Beef, chilled	per cwt.	39	7	54	0	60	1	65	3
Beef, frozen	,, ,,	35	7	51	10	57	11	61	8
Mutton, frozen	,, ,,	41	10	48	7	57	6	64	1
Sugar, refined	,, ,,	12	11	24	7	23	6	26	1
Sugar, unrefined	,, ,,	10	0	20	4	20	2	18	8

[2] Wheat in the quartern loaf. Increase on August 1914:

	Freights New York— Liverpool.	Import values.	Retail price.
	d.	d.	d.
December 1914	·39	1·01	·50
March 1915	·69	2·57	2·25
June 1915	·66	2·61	2·75
September 1915	·80	1·56	2·25
October 1915	1·20	1·61	2·00

charged by neutral shipowners could not be fixed by the British Government, and if freights on British vessels were fixed at rates substantially below those ruling in the world's freight markets, shipments in neutral vessels would become commercially impossible, and a third of the available carrying space would be lost.

It was necessary, therefore, for the Board of Trade to narrow the scope of their inquiry, and there were two points in particular to which their attention was turned: the North Atlantic grain freights and the employment of British shipping to carry cargoes between foreign ports. The position occupied by bread among the staple foodstuffs in this country made the question of grain freights one of special importance, and the continued employment of British ships outside the trade of the United Kingdom was continually put forward as a grievance by critics of the shipowners and of the Government.

On both these points the Board of Trade consulted the Chamber of Shipping and the Liverpool Steam Ship Owners' Association, and special meetings of these important bodies were held to discuss the situation, following on which a conference between their representatives and the President of the Board of Trade was held on October 15th. In the course of the discussion which preceded and followed this conference both the Chamber of Shipping and the Liverpool Association emphasised the fact that the high level of freights was due to the preponderance of the demand for shipping over the supply, and that no substantial relief could be expected unless the supply of tonnage was increased. They urged, therefore, that the first object should be to increase the available carrying power by pressing on the completion of vessels under construction, by enforcing economical use of requisitioned tonnage and by dealing with the congestion of the ports in such a way as to ensure a quicker turn-round and a greater number of voyages within a given period.

To meet the immediate emergency the President of the Chamber of Shipping (Sir Kenneth S. Anderson, K.C.M.G.) suggested that a Committee of Shipowners, with a Chairman appointed by the Government, should be empowered to requisition tonnage for the carriage of essential supplies, and that the employment of British shipping between neutral ports should be regulated by licence, with the object of diverting a portion of this tonnage into British trade.[1]

The Liverpool Steam Ship Owners' Association put forward a more drastic proposal. In their view the real problem was one not of freight but of supplies. It was increasingly evident that neither the available tonnage nor the distributive facilities of the ports could deal adequately with imports on a peace basis. In order to ensure a sufficiency of carrying power for essential supplies and to relieve the pressure on the ports, it was necessary that consumption should be cut down and the balance between demands and resources restored by the exclusion of non-essentials. If this were done, not only would the supply of essentials be secured, but the restoration of an equilibrium between the demand for tonnage and the supply would automatically be followed by a fall in freights. They suggested, therefore, that, as the only alternative to leaving unnecessary cargoes to be excluded by the continuous rise in freights, the Government should themselves exclude by prohibition or taxation those imports which were not regarded as essential under war conditions.

Strong as these arguments were, the Board of Trade shrank from the responsibility of so drastic a measure. It was no easy task to decide on the articles to be excluded, and where some portion, but not the whole, of a particular commodity could be regarded as essential, there were considerable administrative difficulties in adjusting the incidence of partial prohibition among the various importers. To be effective the total reduction must be substantial, and any substantial reduction in the volume of imports must inevitably cause grave dislocation of trade, and lead to serious unemployment in the industries affected. It involved, moreover, the possibility of serious friction with the producing countries, Allies, friendly neutrals, and the British Oversea Dominions. The Board preferred, therefore, to confine their action to the two specific problems of the North Atlantic grain freights and shipping in the inter-foreign trade.

The result of their decision was seen in two Orders in Council issued on November 10th. By the first of these the Board of Trade were empowered to requisition ships for the carriage of foodstuffs and of other articles of

[1] Chamber of Shipping, Report of 39th Annual Meeting, 3 March, 1916, pp. 8–9.

commerce. By the second all British steamships of 500 tons gross and over were prohibited from carrying cargoes between foreign ports except under licence to be obtained from a Committee appointed by the President of the Board.[1]

For the purpose of giving effect to the first of these orders a Committee known as the Requisitioning (Carriage of Foodstuffs) Committee, was appointed. Apart from the Chairman, the Rt. Hon. J. H. Whitley, M.P., the members were all shipowners, Mr. F. C. Gardiner, Mr. Ernest W. Glover, and Mr. R. D. Holt. Mr. Glover and Mr. Holt were original members of the Advisory Committee to the Admiralty Transport Department, and Mr. Gardiner had been added to that Committee in October 1915. It was hoped in this way to prevent any clashing of interests or policy between the new Requisitioning Committee and the Transport Department, and for the same purpose Mr. J. A. Salter of the Transport Department was appointed joint secretary of the new Committee, with Mr. F. P. Robinson of the Board of Trade.

Although the Order gave wide powers to requisition shipping for the carriage of any article of commerce, it was not intended that its action should extend, for the time being, beyond the provision of tonnage for North American wheat, nor was the shipping for this purpose to be requisitioned at Blue Book rates. The objections to employing fully requisitioned ships for the carriage of private cargoes were fully appreciated by the Board, and the instructions to the Committee were framed on this basis. They were directed not to act until set in motion by the Board of Trade on behalf of the Food Supplies Committee of the Cabinet, who would inform them as to the level of imports considered necessary. On receipt of this information they were to ascertain how far these imports could be carried by the tonnage available in the normal course of business, and divert into the service a sufficient number of ships to carry the balance.

Ships so diverted were to be left free to obtain the ordinary market rates and to fix charters in the ordinary course of business. In fact, requisitioning by the Committee implied no more than the issue of instructions to shipping to proceed to a particular source of supply and

[1] A "foreign port" was defined in the Order as "any port outside His Majesty's Dominions," and did not include Empire ports overseas.

lift a particular kind of cargo; but it was intended that the supply should be kept a little in excess of the demand, and a gradual fall in freights was expected to follow. In order to minimise the dislocation of business, the Food Supplies Committee promised to give the longest possible notice of their requirements, and in order to avoid port congestion, the recently created Port and Transit Executive Committee [1] were instructed to furnish periodical statements of the position at the wheat-receiving ports.

The Ship Licensing Committee set up under the second Order in Council of November 10th consisted of four members—Messrs. R. Burton Chadwick, F. W. Lewis, T. P. Purdie, and Arthur Scholefield—nominated by the Chamber of Shipping, and two representatives of the Liverpool Steamship Owners' Association—Messrs. H. F. Fernie and Harold A. Sanderson.[2] As Chairman of the Committee the President of the Board of Trade nominated Mr. Maurice Hill, K.C., a specialist in shipping law, who had drafted the agreements under the State Insurance Scheme. Mr. Thomas Lodge of the Board of Trade was appointed Secretary.

Very full and careful instructions were provided by the Board of Trade for the guidance of the Committee. In these instructions the object of the Order in Council was defined as being " to increase the amount of tonnage available for trade to or from British ports " in such a way as " to do as little permanent harm as possible to British trade." This proviso was, of course, an important one. The withdrawal of further British shipping from the inter-foreign trade must in any event have an unfavourable effect on British trade by diminishing the invisible exports and thus further weighting the exchanges against Great Britain. This temporary sacrifice might be faced, if the object of the Order in Council could thereby be achieved; but, with a view to economic recovery after the war, it was essential to avoid so far as possible the break-up of old established trade connections and the permanent replacement of British by foreign services.

By the Order in Council the Committee were empowered to grant either general licences in respect of classes of ships engaged in particular classes of voyages, or special licences to specified ships for specified single voyages.

[1] See Chapter XII, *post*.
[2] Mr. W. H. Tregoning was subsequently added.

They were further instructed by the Board that the terms of the Order might be construed as authorising the grant of contingent licences for a stated period to individual steamers, for trade within certain prescribed limits.

In granting licences, whether general or particular, it would of course be necessary for the Committee to consider each application on its merits; but certain broad principles were laid down for their guidance. Ships trading from or to British ports, carrying goods between foreign ports of call as an incident of their voyage should, in general, receive a licence for this purpose without difficulty. In like manner, favourable consideration would be given to applications from ships desirous of carrying cargo from one foreign port to another in order to secure, at the port of arrival, a cargo for the United Kingdom. Ships whose trade between foreign ports was auxiliary to British trade fell within the same category, as, for instance, those which collected or distributed the cargoes of the big liners. Special consideration was also to be given to regular services between foreign ports established prior to the outbreak of war, and to ships time-chartered to neutral firms or running under a continuing contract for trade between foreign ports, which was binding upon the shipowner. So much was necessary in order to avoid friction with neutral Governments and the possible arrest for breach of contract of British ships arriving in neutral ports to load cargoes for the United Kingdom. So far as possible, however, the Committee were to secure that where licences were granted for voyages between foreign ports they should be for cargoes to be delivered to regular and reliable consignees on the various White Lists in the possession of the Government Departments, and not for the benefit of black-listed firms.

Voyages for the benefit of Allied countries, though falling within the scope of the Order, would, of course, enjoy a degree of preference.

Finally, the Committee were instructed to take into consideration the danger of driving away neutral ships engaged in British trade. The mere replacement of neutral by British tonnage would be of little or no advantage, and the Committee were, accordingly, to conduct the withdrawal of British ships from the inter-foreign trade carefully and gradually, so as to avoid a sudden rise of freights on the inter-foreign routes.

CHAPTER XII

THE PORT AND TRANSIT COMMITTEE
OCTOBER—DECEMBER 1915

A FEW days before the appointment of the Ship Licensing and Carriage of Foodstuffs Committees, a most important step was taken in connection with the problem of port congestion. That problem, in spite of all the efforts of the Board of Trade Committee and the Committee for the Diversion of Shipping, had become more and more pressing all through the summer, and by the autumn it had arrived at such proportions as to render immediate action imperatively necessary.

It was at Liverpool that conditions were worst in the spring of 1915, and at that port some advance towards a proper adjustment of the traffic and other demands on its facilities, was made quite early in the year. The great difficulty at this, as at other ports, was to reconcile the demands of the Navy, Army, and Transport Department with the maintenance of the flow of traffic which was itself of vital national importance, comprising as it did munitions and war material, food for a thickly populated industrial area, and raw material for the greatest of British industries. The experience of the first nine months of war showed that the demands of the various importing Departments and of the various branches of the fighting services tended to come into conflict not only with commercial interests but with each other, and in May 1915, as the result of strong representations by the Liverpool Steam Ship Owners' Association, the Government agreed to the creation of a small Committee representative of the chief interests concerned, and empowered to supervise the general working of the port and decide between competing demands on its facilities. This body, known as the Liverpool Co-ordination Committee, was appointed jointly by the Admiralty, War Office, and Board of Trade, and the Admiralty, the War Office, the Shipowners, and the Port Authority were all represented upon it. From the first also it worked in close co-operation with the Mersey Docks and Harbour Board, the Liverpool Steam Ship Owners' Association, and the Government Departments concerned.[1]

One of the first questions raised by the Co-ordination Committee was the use of the port for Armed Merchant Cruisers of the Northern Patrol. Two or three of these large vessels were usually in port at a time, and were of course entitled to an absolute priority in the use of berths, tips, and trucks. The Committee suggested, therefore, that in view of the fact that five or six merchantmen were usually waiting for free berths in order to discharge, the possibilities of an alternative base should be carefully investigated. These arguments were undoubtedly strong, and the proposal had in fact already been made in Major Hawkins' report to the Diversion of Shipping Committee; but, while recognising and regretting the inevitable interference with the flow of traffic, the Admiralty were unable to agree to any change. The facilities for rapid coaling and repairs were so much greater at Liverpool than at any alternative port to which the vessels could be sent that it was necessary, in this instance, to override commercial considerations.

In other directions the Committee were able to take effective action. They succeeded in effecting an adjustment of the various conflicting demands to the capacity of the port, and by strictly limiting the number of quays set aside for the discharge of particular commodities, they were able to some extent to regulate the imports and prevent any essential commodity being crowded out by an undue proportion of other traffic.

Similar committees were subsequently set up at Glasgow and Bristol, and though the local conditions and the organisation of the interests using those ports rendered it impossible to create so strong or representative a body as at Liverpool, good work was done. To London the scheme was altogether inapplicable. The Port Authority itself

[1] Composition of the Committee: Mr. A. A. Booth (Chairman of the Liverpool Steam Ship Owners' Association), Chairman; Admiral Stileman (Senior Naval Officer at Liverpool); Captain J. D. Daintree (Divisional Naval Transport Officer); Lt.-Col. F. K. Essell (Deputy Assistant of Railway Transport), military representative; Sir Helenus Robertson (Chairman, Mersey Docks and Harbour Board); Mr. L. A. P. Warner (Mersey Docks and Harbour Board), Secretary.

controlled only a small part of the labour employed, and none of the craft into which the greater proportion of the cargoes were discharged, and the interests using the port were too numerous and too loosely organised for an effective committee to be formed.

What was wanted, however, was not merely local but national organisation. By the beginning of August the anxiety of the Diversion Committee had become acute. Their immediate task of finding berths for ships sent in under the Retaliation Order was proceeding smoothly, although 154 ships had now been sent in since March 11th; but, as the blockade became more and more stringent, the number of contraband cargoes discharged in this country was bound to increase, and meanwhile the general position of the ports was going from bad to worse. In spite of the efforts of the Co-ordination Committee, Liverpool was fuller than ever, and heavy shipments of cotton were shortly expected. London was choked with wool which only went forward very slowly to Bradford. As soon as the North American grain began to move freely very large arrivals were to be expected in order to make up the summer leeway. The Argentine maize harvest had begun to arrive. The Ministry of Munitions was initiating a very large programme. Thus, the immediate demands upon the ports were certain to increase rather than diminish, and on August 6th the Committee reported to the Admiralty that, unless prompt action was taken, the congestion of the ports was likely to become worse than anything yet experienced, with disastrous results to the effective supply of essential commodities.

This resolution was communicated to the President of the Board of Trade, who passed it on to Lord Inchcape's Committee, at the same time requesting the Diversion Committee to supply certain detailed evidence in support of their contentions. This was supplied, but in the meantime the Resolution had come to the cognisance of the Man Power Board, of which Mr. Austen Chamberlain was Chairman. This Board had received through the Board of Trade particulars as to the conditions at some of the ports which appeared to conflict with the statements of the Diversion Committee. The discrepancy probably arose through the anxiety of the Port Authorities to secure traffic in competition with each other; but, whatever its cause, it attracted the attention of Mr. Chamberlain, who referred the matter to the President of the Board of Trade. It was obvious that the question was of the first importance, and Mr. Runciman accordingly appointed a small Joint Committee, consisting of three members each from the Diversion and Inchcape Committees, to go thoroughly into the whole matter.[1]

This Joint Committee met for the first time on October 7th, and from the first its members were in complete agreement as to the seriousness of the situation. They were particularly anxious as to the effect of Lord Derby's Recruiting Scheme on the supply of labour, as dock labour was not covered under any of the lists of reserved occupations; but hardly less anxiety was felt with regard to the supply of railway trucks, the congestion of the transit sheds, and the effect of naval and military demands on the accommodation of the ports. In response to the urgent representations of the Government, the North Atlantic Liner Companies were now putting extra ships into the trade with a view to an increase in the imports of North American wheat; but so badly were the West Coast ports blocked, and so slow was the distribution, that this seemed likely to increase the congestion of the ports without, in practice, adding to the effective supply.

On all these points the Committee made recommendations to the Government, but its powers were advisory only, and so many different Departments, services, and interests were affected by every phase of the port problem that there appeared little prospect of obtaining prompt and effective action on any proposal unless some Central Authority were created for all the ports. Accordingly the members of the Committee decided, at an early stage in their deliberations, to ask for executive powers.

In order that they might carry with them in their decisions the chief Departments concerned, they asked that the new Central Authority should be appointed jointly by the Admiralty, War Office, and Board of Trade. Its work would thus be placed under the ægis of all three Departments, and its hands would be greatly strengthened

---

[1] Composition of the Joint Committee :
Board of Trade Committee: Lord Inchcape, G.C.M.G., K.C.S.I., Chairman ; Mr. J. G. Broodbank ; Sir Sam Fay.
Diversion Committee: Sir Frederic Bolton ; Sir A. Norman Hill ; Sir Edward Hain.
Sir Frederick G. Dumayne (Secretary, Board of Trade Committee) ; Major T. H. Hawkins, R.M.L.I. (Secretary, Diversion Committee), Joint Secretaries.

in deciding between competing claims on port facilities or accommodation.

In this proposal the Joint Committee were warmly supported by the Admiralty, and after some discussion it was concurred in both by the Board of Trade and by the War Office. Joint representations to the Prime Minister were accordingly made by the three Departments, and on November 3rd Mr. Asquith signed a Minute establishing the Port and Transit Executive Committee, " To inquire into the difficulties and congestion arising from time to time at harbours, ports, and docks (including the docksheds and warehouses " in the United Kingdom ; to regulate the " work and traffic thereat ; to co-ordinate the requirements of all interests concerned so as to avoid so far as possible interference with the normal flow of trade and to decide all questions relating to the difficulties and congestion aforesaid that may be referred to them, and to give direction to all Executive Bodies at the harbours, ports, and docks, for carrying their decision into effect."

Into this Committee both the Admiralty Committee on the Diversion of Shipping, and the Board of Trade Committee on Congestion in Docks were absorbed. The personnel was very strong, comprising representatives of the Admiralty, War Office, and Board of Trade, of the principal Shipowners' Associations, the Port Authorities, and the Railway Executive Committee. The Chairman, Lord Inchcape, and the Secretary, Sir Frederick Dumayne, had acted in the same capacities on the Board of Trade Committee, and most of the members had served either on that or the Diversion Committee, while the presence of Sir Frederic Bolton and Major Hawkins ensured full advantage being taken of the investigations carried out before the war.[1]

---

[1] Composition of Port and Transit Executive Committee :
   (a) The Lord Inchcape, G.C.M.G., K.C.S.I., K.C.I.E., Chairman.
       Mr. Graeme Thompson (Director of Transports) ⎫ Representing
   (b) Major T. H. Hawkins, R.M.L.I. (Trade Division) ⎭ the Admiralty.
       Brigadier-General Hon. A. R. M. Stuart Wortley, C.B., D.S.O., representing the War Office.
   (b) Sir Frederic Bolton, Lloyd's.
   (a) Mr. J. G. Broodbank, Port of London Authority.
   (a) Sir Sam Fay, General Manager, Great Central Railway, Member of Railway Executive Committee.
   (b) Sir Edward Hain, London Group of War Risks Associations.
   (b) Sir A. Norman Hill, Liverpool and London War Risks Insurance Association, Liverpool Steam Ship Owners' Association.
   (a) Sir Frederick G. Dumayne, Board of Trade, Secretary.

Those marked (a) had served on the Board of Trade Committee on Congestion in Docks, those marked (b) on the Admiralty Committee for the Diversion of Shipping.

From the date of their appointment the members of the Port and Transit Committee started on their work with the greatest energy. The Committee itself met weekly, but a Standing Sub-Committee consisting of Lord Inchcape, Sir Frederic Bolton, Major Hawkins, and Sir Norman Hill met every day to deal with urgent current business. The policy of the Committee was to minimise as much as possible interference with the interests using the ports, or the work of the Port Authorities, but to work with and through these bodies, acting as a clearing-house for information as to the facilities of the ports and the demands upon them, and securing the co-operation of all the different interests in maintaining the regular flow of traffic. Their coercive powers were held so far as possible in reserve, and when employed were exercised through the agency of the Port Authorities themselves. In this way the Committee was able to perform its work with a minimum of friction and dislocation and at a trifling cost.[1] At the same time the representative character of the Committee enabled it to bring effective pressure on the various Departments, and its executive powers were sufficient to ensure compliance with its directions on the part of local interests.

For the purpose of its work the Committee obtained daily returns from all the principal ports in Great Britain (forty-three in number) showing the state of the port as regards berths, rate of discharge, warehouse and cold storage accommodation, transit sheds, labour, barges and craft, trucks and sheets, railway movements, and cartage, and a weekly return showing the import of the more important commodities. It also obtained from the various Government Departments weekly returns showing the position as regards expected arrivals of wheat, iron ore, munitions, and other commodities on Government account or for war purposes, and it was in constant touch with the Shipowners' Associations, Chambers of Commerce, and private firms of importers and exporters from whom information could be obtained as to the flow of traffic. From this information the Committee prepared and circulated a weekly summary of the information relating to the twelve principal ports, a weekly summary showing the labour conditions in the smaller ports, a weekly comparative survey of the wheat position, a weekly summary showing

---

[1] The total expenditure of the Committee to 31 March, 1919, was £4,057 16s. 1d.

the rate of discharge of iron ore, and a monthly summary showing the total weight of imports and the total tonnage, British and Foreign, by which such imports were brought.

These summaries were of the utmost value in adjusting the demands of the various services to the capacity of the ports, and though the Committee had, of course, no power to limit the volume of imports, it was able, when necessary, to make representations backed by ample and detailed evidence as to the probable effect of any increase of traffic. It was, however, the actual utilisation of the port facilities which fell more especially within its province. From the first the Committee did its utmost to impress both on the Port Authorities and on the interests using the ports that rapid distribution was the essential element of the problem, and that the quays, transit sheds, and grain elevators must not be used for storage purposes, but must be kept free for the regular flow of traffic through the ports.

The first and most urgent question with which the Committee had to deal was the safeguarding of the labour supply. Lord Derby's Recruiting Scheme had just been launched, and it was imperative, if the flow of traffic was to be maintained, that the depleted labour staffs of the ports should not be further reduced by indiscriminate recruiting. Lord Derby and the President of the Board of Trade had issued a joint statement pointing out that officers and men of the Mercantile Marine would be serving their country as truly by remaining in their customary employment as by enlisting in the Army, but the carrying power of the ships could not be used effectively if the time spent at sea was reduced by long delays in port, and it became vital to apply the same principle to the essential work of distribution.

The points aimed at by the Port and Transit Committee in this connection were two—to obtain the inclusion of all transport workers in the list of reserved occupations, and to secure that the Tribunals by whom appeals were decided should be bodies acquainted with the needs of the ports. The effect of putting men into the list of reserved occupations was that such men might be attested and placed in a Reserve Group; but Recruiting Officers were instructed that they should not actually be called up for service so long as their services in their normal occupation were indispensable. Of this question the Local Tribunals were the judges, and it was therefore of the utmost importance that the Tribunals should possess full knowledge of the essential requirements of the ports. For this reason the Port and Transit Committee proposed that the Co-ordination Committees at Liverpool, Bristol, and Glasgow should be accepted as Tribunals for those ports, and that in respect of all other ports the Port and Transit Committee itself should constitute the final Court of Appeal.

In respect of the list of Reserved Occupations the Committee carried its point. On November 12th Lord Derby agreed that transport workers indispensably required in the ports should not be accepted for immediate service, and at the beginning of December a long list of categories embracing practically all classes employed on transport work at the ports was added to the list of Reserved Occupations. Many dockers, carters, and lightermen had been enlisted in the meantime, but the concession came in time to stop any wholesale further depletion of port labour.

With regard to the Tribunals, great difficulties were experienced. Lord Derby agreed at the outset that the Port of London Authority should act as the Tribunal for London Transport Workers, and at Liverpool he arranged for all transport workers' appeals to be dealt with by the Co-ordination Committee. He was further willing to agree to give similar powers to the Co-ordination Committees at Bristol and Glasgow, and to the Port and Transit Committee acting as a Central Tribunal for transport workers at the other ports. To this, however, the Local Government Board objected, on the ground that it constituted too great an interference with the general scheme of Tribunals. They agreed, however, that the Port Authorities should be represented on the Local Advisory Committees by whom the Recruiting Officers were assisted, and that both the Port Authorities and other employers should have the right to appear before the Local Tribunal. In the event of an appeal to the Central Tribunal, the Port and Transit Committee itself had the right to attend and be heard.

In this way a large measure of protection was obtained for the labour supply of the ports, and in return, the Committee took steps to impress on the Port Authorities the necessity of releasing for immediate active service all men who were not indispensable to the work of the ports or for whom substitutes could be obtained. These, however, were comparatively few, and even after the conclusion of the arrangements outlined above, the drain of men from the ports continued to cause anxiety. This drain was due, in large measure, to the patriotism of the workers themselves, many of whom offered themselves for immediate service, and were frequently accepted by the Recruiting Officers without reference to the Port Authority. For the purpose of preventing this drain the Committee revived the suggestion of a special badge for transport workers; but the suggestion was not adopted, and many workers continued to feel uneasy in the performance of duties the direct war importance of which they did not wholly perceive. It was not only through enlistment in the Army that men were lost. The Labour Exchanges were busily recruiting for the Ministry of Munitions, and during November and December it became necessary for the Committee to protest strongly against the taking of skilled dock workers for munition work. The engineering departments, in particular, suffered severely. The Mersey Docks and Harbour Board reported during December that they had not a single fitter left in their service, and there was grave danger of a breakdown in the dock gates machinery. The Tyne Commissioners reported that men on their permanent staff had received letters from a Labour Exchange, urging them to volunteer for the munition factories on the ground that their employment was not " war work." Strong representations were made on this subject, both to the Ministry of Munitions and the Board of Trade, for it was obvious that the munition work itself must come to a stop unless the supply of materials could be adequately handled in the ports.

The labour problem was, however, only one among many with which the members of the Committee had to deal. Early in November they began to press for the pooling of railway trucks, already suggested by the shipowners in their Memorandum of January 22nd, and by the Diversion Committee, and from this time onward they were in constant communication with the Board of Trade and the Railway Executive Committee on this subject.

Among other matters which engaged the early attention of the Committee was the clearing of the quays and transit sheds. There was, as we have seen, a tendency on the part of consignees to leave goods on the quays or in the sheds till sold, rather than pay the expenses of removal and warehousing away from the ports. The effect was, of course, to block the flow of traffic and hamper the work of discharge, and the Committee strongly urged the Port Authorities to expedite, if necessary by the enforcement of penal rents, the removal of goods.

It was not, however, the import traffic only which engaged the Committee's attention. The export trade was, at this period, seriously hampered by the conditions as to pre-entry imposed by the War Trade Department on shipments under licence of prohibited goods. The object of these conditions was to put obstacles in the way of trade by enemy subjects resident in neutral countries; but it had become a question whether the danger of a small leakage was not more than counterbalanced by the injury to the export trade and the congestion caused by the accumulation in the ports of goods awaiting licence. The Committee accordingly took up the matter with the War Trade Department. In respect of goods for which pre-entry was required no modification of the restrictions could be obtained; but considerable relief was afforded by an arrangement proposed by the Customs Authorities, by which goods not requiring pre-entry could be put on board ship immediately on their arrival at the docks, provided shipping notes giving full particulars were sent to the ship's agent at the docks, simultaneously with the arrival of the goods.

All these questions fell directly within the scope of the Committee's original terms of reference, but towards the end of November its responsibilities were considerably enlarged. The Admiralty Transport Department were at this time beset by constant demands for the use of requisitioned tonnage for the carriage of commercial cargoes, such as wheat, ore, and nitrate, in which Government Departments were interested, and the Advisory Committee felt themselves insufficiently acquainted with the requirements of the country to advise definitely on these questions. The President of the Board of Trade suggested, therefore, that, in order to avoid setting up a new committee, the Port and Transit Committee should take over the duty of advising in such matters. The Prime Minister accordingly directed, on December 10th, that the Committee should " be requested to advise in the light of existing commitments of shipping tonnage for Government purposes and of the state of the transport arrangements in the United Kingdom, as to the practicability of proposals of the Civil Departments of State to call for shipping services from the tonnage under requisition or to be requisitioned for the purpose."

On the same day the Prime Minister appointed Mr. Harry Gosling, President of the Transport Workers' Federation, to be a member of the Committee, as representative of Labour. In view of the very large part played in port problems by questions of labour supply and organisation, this was an appointment of the greatest value, and materially strengthened the hands of the Committee.

The first question with which the Committee had to deal under their new terms of reference was that of the carriage of pyrites from Spain. Pyrites was required in large quantities for the manufacture of sulphuric acid for explosives, but there was great difficulty in obtaining tonnage for its transportation. The Spanish ships usually employed in the trade had gone off into other employment, and freights had risen by 5s. to 7s. 6d. a ton. In these circumstances the Ministry of Munitions was anxious to obtain the use of requisitioned shipping, and the Committee agreed to recommend the allocation of requisitioned tonnage for all pyrites intended for Government stores, or imported by traders whose whole output of acid was requisitioned by the Government. They considered, however, that such traders, being commercially interested in the by-products, should be charged by the Transport Department a freight sufficient to cover the cost of the voyage. Subsequently, in January 1916, the Committee concurred in the provision of requisitioned tonnage for the import of 600,000 tons of pyrites during the year 1916, in order to cover all possible requirements of the Ministry of Munitions, but subject to the full market rate of freight being charged on cargoes used for other purposes than the manufacture of explosives.

Nitrate cargoes required for munitions purposes were dealt with in a similar way, but the question of using requisitioned tonnage for the carriage of iron ore raised larger and more difficult issues. If requisitioned tonnage were provided at Blue Book rates for a substantial part of the ore, there was a danger of driving out of the trade all non-requisitioned tonnage, British or foreign; and so much of the ore was carried in neutral vessels that this risk could not lightly be taken. The Committee suggested, therefore, that, before coming to a final decision, further inquiry should be made as to the exact amount of anticipated requirements, the capacity of the ports and railways to deal with those requirements, the steps taken to supply the amount required, and the existing contracts for supply. At the same time they emphasised the large part played by difficulties in discharge at, and distribution from, the ports, in creating a shortage of ore at the blast furnaces and steel works.

So far as American wheat was concerned, the Committee were, of course, relieved of all responsibility by the existence of the Requisitioning (Carriage of Foodstuffs) Committee; but towards the end of the year they were asked to advise on a request by the Commonwealth Government that shipping should be made available for lifting the Australian crops. Against this proposal they strongly protested. The length of the Australian voyage was such that the forty to fifty ocean-going steamers asked for by the Commonwealth Government could bring into this country three times as much wheat if employed in the North Atlantic trade as they could bring in the same period from Australian ports. In view of the shortage of tonnage it was obviously of the first importance that the available carrying power should be used to its utmost capacity, and the diversion of so large a block of tonnage from a shorter to a longer route would be wholly uneconomic.

It will be seen that the new terms of reference had added greatly to the responsibilities of the Committee; but these new responsibilities were not long left upon their shoulders. Throughout the winter of 1915–16 the tonnage problem was continually increasing in urgency and complexity, and shortly after the opening of the new year it became necessary to make fresh arrangements with regard to the allocation of shipping.

CHAPTER XIII

THE ALLIES DEMAND FURTHER ASSISTANCE FOR 1916

SINCE the middle of September the activity of the German submarines had been confined almost entirely to the Mediterranean. Here, as we have seen, the problem of defending merchant shipping against submarine attack was particularly difficult. To provide patrols on the scale adopted in Home Waters was beyond the resources of the Allies, and the strain thrown on the Allied Fleets by the necessity of providing escort for transports and supply-ships, left no force to spare for escorting merchantmen. In short, the merchant steamer in the Mediterranean had to rely chiefly on her own speed and manœuvring powers, or on such armament as could be given her.

Down to the spring of 1915 the only ships carrying a defensive armament were those liners, mostly in the South American and Australasian trade, which had been so equipped before the war. Then, as a reply to the submarine campaign, came the order to equip a number of coasters and Admiralty colliers with one 12-pr. gun each, and the arrangement whereby outward-bound liners in the eastern trade unshipped their guns at Gibraltar to be remounted in homeward-bound vessels about to enter the danger zone. Several liners in the South American and New Zealand trade received for the first time a permanent armament, and by July some 250 merchantmen had been permanently armed, or fitted to receive a transferable armament. Of these fifty-two were transports on Mediterranean service, fifty-nine liners in the meat-importing trade, and the remainder mostly coasters, colliers, or vessels employed as military store-ships.

In arming merchant vessels it was, of course, necessary to preserve carefully their non-belligerent status, especially in respect of ships requiring to enter neutral ports. All guns were accordingly mounted right aft, and definite instructions were issued, forbidding defensively armed ships to open fire unless actually attacked, or pursued by a submarine in such a fashion as to leave no room for doubt that an attack was intended. Even under these conditions the United States refused for a long while to admit defensively armed ships to their ports. Their attitude was somewhat modified after the sinking of the *Lusitania*, but so late as September 1915 the *Waimana*, a $13\frac{1}{2}$-knot Shaw, Saville and Albion Liner, was held up by the United States Authorities, and finally compelled to land her gun before she was allowed to leave. On September 19th the American Government issued new rules permitting the reception of slow ships having a gun mounted aft, but their interpretation of the rules was still a little uncertain. Holland went still further in the refusal to admit defensively armed merchantmen to her ports; but the majority of neutral States raised no objections, or, at most, stipulated that on the arrival of the vessel a formal declaration should be made by the master or by the British Consul that the armament was carried for defensive purposes only, and that nothing had been or would be done to forfeit her commercial status.

It was shortage of guns rather than the attitude of neutrals which stood in the way of arming a much larger number of vessels, but the device of transferable armament enabled this difficulty to be partly overcome. On the appearance of submarines in the Mediterranean the scope of the scheme was extended. East-bound liners retained their guns as far as Port Said, where they were transferred to homeward-bound vessels entering the Mediterranean from the Red Sea. For vessels following the Cape route, outwards or homewards, the port of transfer was the French base at Dakar in Senegambia. In this way the limited supply of guns was made to do double duty, and by September the number of ships fitted for transferable armament had risen to over 150. During the autumn and winter the work went on apace, and by the end of December some 750 vessels of various classes had been fitted to receive guns, but of this number about 170 were temporarily disarmed. The supply of guns was still very short. In addition to the demands of the Army, Navy, and Auxiliary Patrol, the increasing frequency of Zeppelin raids had led to a great increase in the allocation of guns to the anti-aircraft defences of London and other towns, and the resources of the armament factories were severely strained. The number of weapons allocated to the arming of merchantmen was insufficient to equip the ships fitted to receive them, and it became necessary to take guns from the armed coasters and from some of the colliers in order to equip more important vessels. Of the defensively armed ships a large proportion were on naval or military service as transports, colliers, oilers, or store-ships. The ocean-going vessels on the list which were still engaged in ordinary commerce, numbered about 200, and of these the majority were liners with transferable armament on the eastern routes. The usual armament for these ships was one 4·7-in. gun; but, owing to the shortage of guns, some of them had to be content with smaller weapons. A large proportion of the armed transports and colliers were also on Mediterranean service, and the number of ships in that sea possessing some means of self-defence continually increased.

The value of such armament was soon proved, for during October, November, and December several ships attacked in the Mediterranean, beat off by gunfire their submarine assailant. But even now the defensively armed merchantmen formed but a small proportion of the whole, and though a dozen or more ships succeeded in shaking off their pursuers, or were rescued by British warships, the tale of losses during the last quarter of 1915 was all too long. In October ten ships were sunk in the Mediterranean, in November twenty-three, in December eleven. Among these was the big P. & O. liner *Persia*, torpedoed without warning on December 30th with a loss of 334 lives. On the same day the *Clan Macfarlane* met a like fate, and in her, 52 lives were lost. Both these ships carried a defensive armament, but neither had an opportunity to use it before the torpedo struck home.

More than a score of French and Italian ships, two Japanese liners, and a few neutrals were also sunk in the Mediterranean during the December quarter. Among them was the Italian liner *Ancona*, which was torpedoed off Cape Carbonara on November 7th, after having been shelled by the submarine. She was crowded with passengers, and some 300 persons perished. Among them were 20 American citizens, and a strong note of protest came from the United States, demanding disavowal of the action of the submarine commander, his punishment, and the payment of reparation. To these demands the Austrian Government replied by a refusal to admit responsibility; but they agreed to payment of an indemnity, and stated that the commander of the submarine would be punished for his failure "to take into sufficient consideration the panic which occurred amongst the passengers, rendering the embarkation more difficult, and the spirit of the regulation that Imperial and Royal Naval officers should not refuse help to anyone in distress, not even to the enemy."

Such losses as occurred in Home Waters during the period were due almost entirely to the activities of the mine-laying submarines based on Zeebrugge and Ostend. Travelling so far as possible submerged, and laying their mines at night, these craft rendered the navigation of the eastern entrance to the Channel and the approaches to the Thames very dangerous, and almost every week two or three ships, British or neutral, were sunk or damaged in the neighbourhood of Folkestone, Dungeness, or such sea-marks as the Tongue and Longsand light vessels. Several of these casualties were attended with loss of life, and on November 17th there was a particularly sad disaster when the Hospital Ship *Anglia*, returning with wounded from France, was blown up off Folkestone and 25 lives were lost.

These occasional losses from mines were, however, a very different matter from the wholesale destruction wrought by submarines in the South-Western Approach during the summer months, and during October and November no British merchantman was sunk by gunfire or torpedo in Home Waters. It was not till December 20th that this form of attack reappeared. On that day two small steamers were torpedoed without warning off Boulogne, and during the next few days three other ships were captured and sunk by submarines at the entrance of the Bristol Channel or off the south coast of Ireland.

In all areas, 70 British merchantmen were sunk by mine or submarine during October, November, and December, as against 96 in the previous three months; but, as a result of the concentration of the submarine attack on the Mediterranean routes, the average size of the vessels sunk was rather greater than in the summer, and the total tonnage lost amounted to 228,000 gross against 303,000, giving an average of 74,000 as against 100,000 a month. This was a substantial decrease, but the total was still too large to be viewed with complacency, and the continuance of the submarine campaign in the Mediterranean threatened especially the larger classes of ocean-going steamers. Moreover, the Allies of Great Britain were suffering far more heavily than they had done hitherto. French and Italian shipping had been but little affected by the operations of submarines in British Home Waters, but with the transference of the attack to the Mediterranean, this comparative immunity came to an end. The losses of Allied shipping during the three months amounted to over 100,000 tons, and, as shipbuilding in France and Italy had come practically to a standstill, and the available tonnage under the French and Italian flags was already quite insufficient for the fulfilment of national requirements, any further depletion of the total could only increase the dependence of the Allies on British assistance.

To neutrals, on the other hand, the change in the incidence of the attack brought a welcome respite. During the three months the total losses of all neutral shipping aggregated only 35,000 tons, and the Norwegian losses, the most important of all from the point of view of British trade, were only one-half what they had been in the previous quarter. Thus, so far as concerned shipping directly engaged in the trade of the United Kingdom, there was an appreciable diminution in the ratio of destruction.

On the other hand, the diversion of tonnage from commercial to naval and military employment was increasing rather than diminishing. It is true that the despatch of troops to Gallipoli had ceased after the failure of the final attempt to break the Turkish lines in August. During December the positions at Suvla and Anzac were evacuated, and by January 8th, 1916, the evacuation of the peninsula was complete. But no relief was thus given to the Transport Department, for they had now the Salonika expedition on their hands, involving large movements of French as well as British troops, and necessitating the accumulation of large quantities of stores in the Eastern Mediterranean. Thus, for the present at least, there could be no appreciable reduction in the tonnage allocated to Mediterranean services.

Meanwhile, the Mediterranean Transport Commission had completed their investigations and returned to England. While in the Mediterranean they had been able to arrange with the Naval Transport Officers and Admirals de Robeck and Wemyss several minor economies in the use of tonnage. They had also been in constant communication with the Admiralty, and, as a result of their representations and of the painful experience which had by this time been gained, a considerable improvement was effected in the organisation of transport arrangements within the Straits. The transport staff at Alexandria was strengthened, and both on the naval and military side the control was tightened. Urgent representations as to the necessity of economising tonnage were addressed by the Admiralty and War Office to the officers commanding on the spot, and arrangements were made by the Admiralty to increase the stocks of coal at the shore depôts, especially at Malta, with the object of avoiding detention of colliers.

On January 1st, 1916, the Commissioners presented their report, which was accompanied by a supplementary memorandum by Mr. Royden on various points of detail. In these documents the conditions already described were set forth with abundant confirmatory detail, and special stress was laid on the lack of co-ordination, the delays caused by forwarding stores faster than they could be handled at the base, and the effect of the lack of piers or hulks at Mudros. The Commissioners recognised that this lack of piers was due, in the main, to the expectation of an immediate advance, and that the work of transport was inevitably conditioned by military exigencies; but they considered that much waste of tonnage might have been avoided had expert advice on questions of stowage, unloading, and handling of requisitioned tonnage been obtainable and employed.

By this time the whole situation had changed. The evacuation of the peninsula was already in progress, and, with the change of base to Salonika, the discharge and turn-round of transports became much easier. The report was, however, forwarded by the Admiralty to the War Office in April with a letter concurring generally in its conclusions and emphasising the importance of leaving the whole work of loading, unloading, and general conduct of transport operations to the responsibility and direction of the Admiralty. In this the Army Council fully concurred, and they were able to point to a considerable improvement in the turn-round of Mediterranean transports as a result of the steps which had already been taken to improve the organisation.

Nevertheless, whatever economies might be effected, the

supply and reinforcement of the Salonika force remained a serious drain on the tonnage resources of Great Britain ; nor was it only in the Eastern Mediterranean that shipping had to be provided for military operations outside the main theatre of war. The conquest of the Cameroons was completed by the end of February 1916, but in German East Africa the enemy's resistance was stubborn, and necessitated the employment and supply of a very considerable force, while the blockading squadron had to be supplied with coal from Durban and Delagoa Bay.[1] The Mesopotamian Expedition, too, had grown into a big undertaking, and a large fleet of transports and colliers was tied to the Persian Gulf. For the bulk of both these services tonnage was found by the Government of India ; but whether on British or Indian requisition, the ships were equally removed from commercial employment.[2] Indeed, the fact that the majority of the steamers serving the Mesopotamian force lay outside the immediate jurisdiction of the Transport Department, was an impediment to economy of tonnage, as it interfered with the centralisation of responsibility and interchangeability of services at which the Department aimed.

It was not, however, the demands of the Admiralty and War Office alone which tended to withdraw an ever-increasing proportion of British tonnage from the service of British commerce. A new and alarming feature in the situation was the growing urgency of the requests received from the Allies. Down to the winter of 1915 the chief commitments undertaken by the Transport Department on behalf of the Allies, were the supply of coal for the French State Railways, and of coal and munitions for Russia. These obligations had been amply fulfilled. Over a million and a half tons of coal, coke, and patent fuel had been shipped to France at Blue Book rates for the use of the State Railways. Of this amount some 350,000 tons was delivered at Channel ports by the smaller colliers taken from the coasting and short sea trades ; but the bulk of the supplies were for St. Nazaire, La Rochelle, and other ports on the Bay of Biscay, and required the use

[1] To economise tonnage, large stocks of coal, brought by the railways from the interior or by large colliers from the Bristol Channel, were accumulated at the South African ports, and distributed by smaller colliers specially allocated to the African services.

[2] Many of the ships on Indian requisition were ships on the Register of the United Kingdom.

of ocean-going colliers. Over 100,000 tons was sent to the Mediterranean in colliers of the largest class. In all, no fewer than 536 separate voyages were involved, and by the end of the year the service was estimated to be equivalent to the permanent allocation of some forty to fifty vessels.[1] In addition, 300,000 tons purchased by the Nord and Est Railways had been shipped in requisitioned tonnage.

To Russia some forty requisitioned colliers had been allocated. The total shipments from the United Kingdom and France to the White Sea during the 1915 season amounted to nearly 700,000 tons of coal and some 500,000 tons of general cargo, the greater part of which consisted of munitions and war material—motor-cars, army boots and blankets, and the like—on Russian Government account, though there were also some shipments of private cargo, such as agricultural machinery, the import of which had been licensed by the Russian Government. Of the total, amounting to some 1,200,000 tons, about one-half was carried in British ships, and nearly all the coal so carried, as well as much of the general cargo, was shipped in requisitioned vessels.

Now that the White Sea was frozen, the whole of the British tonnage employed should have been available for other work; but, unfortunately, there had been a grave miscalculation on the part of the Russian Authorities consulted by the Transport Department, as to the date to which Archangel would be open. On their estimate the return passage could be undertaken up to the middle or even the end of December; but by the beginning of that month the Dwina was already frozen, and ships could only be got in or out by the use of ice-breakers. The winter proved to be the most severe experienced for over a quarter of a century, and by the

[1]

	Voyages.	Total cargoes.	Average size of cargo.
		Tons.	Tons.
Channel ports	168	355,900	1,100
Bay ports	337	1,062,512	3,150
Mediterranean ports	31	121,409	3,900
Total	536	1,539,821	

middle of December the entrance to Archangel was closed, despite the employment of ice-breakers, to all but the most powerful ships. The result was that some sixty or seventy steamers were frozen in for the winter, among them eleven requisitioned colliers and many British steamers on charter to the Russian Government. The loss of three colliers sunk by war risks on passage could be borne with patience as an ordinary incident of war; but the waste of tonnage involved in the enforced idleness of so many ships till the ice dispersed in May was a disappointment the more bitter in that it was due to miscalculation.

Apart from the services undertaken by the Transport Department and the Admiralty, the Board of Trade, as will be remembered, had undertaken the purchase and carriage of meat for the French armies. On the entry of Italy into the war, the Italian Government also applied for assistance in the transport of purchases made by them in South America, and the Board accordingly arranged for certain insulated ships hitherto trading between the Plate and New York, to be diverted to Italian ports. The Board of Trade, however, were strongly opposed to competition between the Allies in the meat market, and, as the result of negotiations with the Commission Internationale de Ravitaillement and the Italian Government, an agreement was arrived at in September 1916 by which the Italians undertook to make all contracts through, or under the supervision of, Sir Thomas Robinson, while the Board of Trade guaranteed to them for six months, from October 1st, a minimum monthly supply of 5,000 tons of frozen meat, which might be increased to 7,000 tons for any one month on due notice being given.

It was a condition of the agreement that any Italian steamers fitted, or to be fitted, for the carriage of frozen meat were to be placed at the disposal of the Board of Trade. In return, the Board agreed to allow British firms to undertake the equipment with insulated space of a number of Italian steamers. About the same time the French undertook to equip ships for the carriage of frozen meat, and here, too, the Board gave a permit for the export of the necessary plant and machinery.

Under these arrangements France received, during 1915, 242,000 tons of frozen meat and Italy 15,000. With the exception of a few cargoes shipped to Italy prior to the September agreement, and some small supplies drawn by the French from their own colonies and from Venezuela, the whole of this meat was supplied through the Board of Trade, and by far the greater proportion was carried in British ships. In estimating the value of the assistance thus given to the Allies it must be remembered that the quarter of a million tons of imported meat consumed by the French and Italian armies represented an absolutely new factor in the meat trade of the world. It was necessary to contract for an increase of 25 per cent. in the output of Argentine and Uruguay, and to develop minor sources of supply wherever they could be found. Although many insulated ships had been sunk by the enemy or requisitioned for naval or military service, it was necessary to lift half as much meat again as in 1913.[1] Moreover, many of the meat ships had to be routed to new ports. It was necessary to arrange regular services to France and Italy. For the supply of the British and Allied Armies in the Eastern Mediterranean, cargoes amounting to 30,000 tons were delivered in Egypt direct, besides 5,000 tons sent out from Great Britain. That all commitments on behalf of the Allies should have been fulfilled, and the large meat ration of the British Army maintained, without serious hardship to the civilian population in the United Kingdom, is a remarkable tribute to the energy and capacity of Sir Thomas Robinson, the Board of Trade officials, and the committees of shipowners who supervised the running of the services. That so great an increase in demand could be met without prohibitive cost, was due to the monopoly of carrying power acquired by the Board in the spring of 1915.

To the services performed for the Allies by British

[1] The estimated world output of refrigerated meat in 1913 was 720,000 tons, practically the whole of which came to the United Kingdom. The production and imports in 1915 were as follows :

Output.	Tons.	Shipments.	Tons.
Argentina and Uruguay	545,000	British Army	280,000
Australia	197,000	British Civilians	410,000
New Zealand	158,000	French Army	242,000
United States	72,000	Italian Army	15,000
Brazil, Venezuela, China, Madagascar	32,000	U.S. Civilians	50,000
		U.S. Government, Hawaii and Philippines	7,000
	1,004,000		1,004,000

The only meat ship lost on the homeward voyage during 1915, was the *Tokomaru*, with about 2,000 tons of meat on private account:—

requisitioned tonnage, and the direct assistance given in various ways by the British Government, there must, of course, be added the services of the long list of British ships chartered to the Allied Governments or to private firms in France or Italy. These ships were wholly under Allied control, and were trading in Allied interests. Some of them, running between British and Allied ports, brought return cargoes to the United Kingdom; but for the most part they represented not only an effective contribution to the fulfilment of Allied needs, but a dead loss of carrying capacity to British trade.

Taking together the services rendered by requisitioned tonnage, the ships on Allied charter, and the cargoes carried by British ships to Allied ports in the course of their ordinary commercial employment, the assistance rendered to the Allies by British shipping during 1915 was very substantial, and constituted no light strain on the shipping resources of Great Britain. For 1916, however, still greater demands were put forward. Towards the end of 1915 both the French and Italian Governments made strong representations that unless British requisitioned tonnage could be allocated to their service on a large scale, the maintenance of supplies essential to their military efficiency would be seriously endangered. France requested tonnage for the carriage of further supplies of coal, wheat, oats and maize, horses and mules, hay, munitions, steel, and timber. Italy put forward during December a claim for no fewer than 150 steamers of an average deadweight capacity of 5,000 tons, to be requisitioned or chartered by the British Admiralty for Italian service, in addition to all those already engaged in Italian trade. According to the statement of the Italian Government, every ocean-going Italian steamer was already under requisition or engaged in the import of essential materials, and all suitable prizes had been brought into service [1]; but, unless the carrying power of Italian shipping and of British and neutral shipping in Italian service was supplemented by this big further allocation, there would be a deficiency during 1916

---

[1] Eleven Austrian steamers at Venice had been dismantled and four others were employed as barrack ships, etc. The German ships in Italian ports had now been brought into service except eight (including some large liners) "found not suitable for transport of materials." Those at Massowah had not yet arrived at Genoa.

equivalent to 4,000,000 tons of imports, principally cereals and coal.

In addition to the demands of France and Italy the claims of the Belgian Relief Commission had to be considered. When all these demands were reviewed in the light of the continuous pressure of naval and military requirements on the shipping resources of Great Britain, it became evident that, great as those resources were, the point must soon be reached at which the equation of demand and supply would become impossible without making dangerous inroads on the carrying power available for British trade.

CHAPTER XIV

LICENSING AND DIRECTION OF SHIPPING, NOVEMBER 1915 TO FEBRUARY 1916—APPOINTMENT OF THE SHIPPING CONTROL COMMITTEE

HITHERTO, the gaps made by requisitioning in the tonnage employed in the trade of the United Kingdom, had been made good mainly by the withdrawal of tonnage from the inter-foreign trade, by direct substitution, by rearrangement of services, or through the pull of the freight markets. By the appointment of the Ship Licensing Committee this process had been systematised and accelerated, but a report presented by the Committee on January 4th, 1916, made it clear that any further relief to be expected from this source was limited and uncertain. From the date of its appointment in November 1915 the Committee had scrutinised most carefully every application received for a licence to carry goods between foreign ports. Their work was in the highest degree exacting, for it was of the utmost importance that the machinery of trade should not be dislocated by delays in the fixing of vessels, due to the difficulty of obtaining licences. The Committee sat every day, and by unremitting attention to business they were able to boast that no ship had ever been kept waiting a day for their decisions except when the application gave insufficient particulars on which to frame a judgment. The liner trades could easily be dealt with by the issue of general licences specifying by name the ships owned by the lines and the ports between which they were permitted to carry cargoes. No such method was possible in dealing with tramp steamers, and every tramp fixture for a voyage between foreign ports was separately scrutinised and decided on its merits. The one object which the Committee kept before them in this task was to increase the tonnage available for the trade of the United Kingdom without creating such a vacuum in any of the inter-foreign trades as would inevitably draw neutral shipping away from British ports. The nature of the cargo, so long as it was not contraband, and the freight at which the ship was chartered, did not concern the Committee; but they took into consideration the condition of the foreign ports; since if ships were allowed to accept charters for seriously congested ports they were liable to delays which would not only remove them for a longer period from the possibility of requisition, but would increase the world shortage of carrying power. Thus, during December 1915, the Committee decided to refuse all licences for cargoes to Genoa until the existing accumulation of imports had been cleared off, and the turn-round improved. This prohibition was enforced for about a month, and had the effect of relieving very materially the congestion of the port.[1]

By January 4th, 1916, the Committee had granted licences in respect of a total of 1,355 steamers; but of these 698 were liners trading to and from the United Kingdom, which carried cargo between foreign ports only as an incident of their voyage.[2] Tramps to the number of forty-four were also licensed for the carriage of goods between foreign ports as part of a voyage in the trade of the United Kingdom, or for the purpose of getting into a position to load a cargo for a British port. Thus the number of steamers of 1,600 tons gross and upwards, wholly engaged in trade between foreign countries, had been cut down to 613, considerably less than half the number normally so employed. Even from this figure it was necessary to make large deductions in order to arrive at any estimate of the relief which might be obtained from a more drastic refusal of licences. Of the liners, 65 were employed in regular services to French, Russian, or Italian ports, and could not well be withdrawn without grave injury to the interests of the Allies. There were, indeed, 203 liners trading wholly between neutral ports, but of these a little over one-half belonged to the two big lines engaged in the coasting trade of the China Seas, and were mostly unsuitable for general ocean traffic, while their present employ-

[1] On November 20th, 1915, the goods in the warehouses, on the quays, or in ships awaiting discharge amounted to 749,000 tons, and 102 ships were discharging or awaiting berths, 46 of them in the outer harbour. By the end of January 1916 the amount of goods in the port had fallen to 356,000 tons; and 34 ships only were discharging or awaiting berths.

[2] This figure includes a small number of steamers running between foreign ports on services ancillary to British trade; that is to say, steamers collecting and distributing the cargoes of the big liners.

ment was of great importance both to the foreign exchanges and to British trade connections in the Far East. The remainder comprised vessels of the Khedivial Mail, trading in Egyptian interests, the Pacific Steam Navigation's Coastal Service, and various lines plying between South America and the United States. The withdrawal of the South American service would be absolutely disastrous to the neutral countries concerned, in which a great amount of British capital was invested. The steamers trading between North and South America were performing valuable services to the exchanges, and carried many cargoes of nitrate from Chile to be turned into munitions for the Allies.

Setting aside 55 oil tankers which were not available for general trade, the visible pool of available tonnage consisted of about 300 tramps, whose employment would come up for review on the completion of their current voyage. But the demands now put forward by the Allied Governments were estimated by the Licensing Committee to require the employment of over 370 steamers, so that these demands alone would more than swallow up the available supply. Further, some 250 of the tramps in question were actually fixed or under option for Allied ports; while the new demands were for tonnage additional to all ships already employed in Allied trade. If the Allied demands were to be met in full, the pool resolved itself at once into a deficit.

In the meantime the action of the Committee had forced a certain amount of additional tonnage into the trade of the United Kingdom; but ships were still being requisitioned at the rate of 100 per month, and it was evident that the demands of the Transport Department and the import requirements of the United Kingdom were sufficient to absorb every ship which could be obtained, irrespective of the needs of the Allies. The application of the licensing system served merely to arrest the depletion of the tonnage available for commercial purposes, not to provide a surplus.

The first effect of this diversion of shipping from inter-foreign to British trade was to check, to some extent, the rise in freights which had so alarmed the Government during the earlier months of 1915. Owing, however, to the continued increase in requisitioning, the supply of tonnage was still inadequate to the demand. The improvement brought about by the action of the Ship Licensing Committee proved to be only temporary, and towards the end of December there was an all-round advance in freights which took them to heights much above any yet recorded during the course of the war. Nor was this increase confined to voyages to British ports, for grain freights from North America to France and Italy showed a still greater advance.

It was, as will be remembered, the special function of the Requisitioning (Carriage of Foodstuffs) Committee to direct further tonnage into the North Atlantic grain trade, with the object of forcing down freights, as well as of lifting the accumulations of North American wheat. At the time of their appointment in November 1915, their instructions from the Board of Trade were that the Cabinet Committee on Food Supplies desired to increase the imports from all sources to an average of 800,000 quarters (about 170,000 tons) per week. For the time being, practically the whole of this must come from North America, and it was to North American ports that all diverted tonnage was sent. But it was useless, even had it been possible, to provide tonnage for so large a quantity as 800,000 quarters weekly, unless it was certain that importers were prepared to buy to this extent. The first thing the Committee had to do was, therefore, to ascertain, as accurately as possible, the extent of the market requirements, on the assumption that ample tonnage to meet those requirements would be forthcoming. In addition, however, they had to take into consideration the decision arrived at by the Government in November 1915 to resume the purchase of wheat on Government account, with the object of building up a reserve of grain in this country, over and above the normal imports for immediate consumption. As to the amount of Government purchases there was no difficulty; the Committee were simply informed of the purchases effected and instructed to provide tonnage accordingly; but the market requirements had to be estimated week by week, and tonnage directed into the trade in accordance with the fluctuations of the demand.

For their estimate of market requirements the Committee were mainly dependent on reports and information obtained from the trade itself. In estimating the tonnage already available to meet the demand they were greatly assisted by the fact that a large proportion of North Atlantic wheat was carried by the regular lines. As the result of a Conference with representatives of the Liner Companies, it was agreed, on December 15th, that the lines would undertake to load wheat and flour up to 50 per cent. of the deadweight capacity of their fleets, and this figure, being a constant, gave a basis on which the total supply of carrying-power could be estimated with very fair accuracy. But, after taking into account both the liner space and the tramp tonnage fixed or on offer for the North Atlantic trade, there was still a deficiency which the Committee had to supply. In calculating this deficiency, however, they allowed some margin for tramp steamers which might be fixed in the ordinary course of business, in addition to those already reported, and for the arrival of sailing vessels with wheat cargoes from the Pacific coast. The effect of this was that the Committee were, in reality, requisitioning a little under the market requirements; but they believed that the actual margin of shortage was small, and that the assistance thus provided would be sufficient to lift all purchases made and to bring down freights by restoring the equilibrium between demand and supply.

The provision of tonnage for British grain imports was not, however, the whole of their task. The demands of the Allies for assistance in the carriage of grain were too urgent to be ignored. In Italy the 1915 harvest had been disappointing, stocks were low, and consumption had increased through the higher standard of living necessary for the armies, the stoppage of emigration, the annexation of new territory, and the high cost of other foods. Although tonnage had been diverted into the cereal trade at serious cost to the textile industries, which were unable to procure space for their raw materials, Italian shipping could carry less than half of the estimated requirements of 325,000 tons per month during the importing season, and the Government were apprehensive of bread riots arising from the scarcity and prohibitive cost of the staple foodstuffs.

France was little better off than Italy in the matter of grain supplies, though a larger proportion of her requirements could normally be met from home production. Increased consumption by the armies, and the reduction in the harvest due to the German invasion, compelled her largely to increase her imports, and she too turned to Great Britain for assistance. Tonnage for imports intended for civilian consumption was provided by the Hudson Bay Company as chartering agents for the Ministry of Commerce, and many British steamers on French charter were already engaged in this service; but for the grain programme of the French Ministry of War further assistance was required.

In December 1915 an International Joint Committee was entrusted with the purchase of the wheat required for the Government reserve in the United Kingdom, and of all wheat, flour, and maize required by the French War Ministry and the Italian Government. At the same time, Messrs. Ross T. Smythe, who acted as agents for the British Government, were instructed to arrange for the lifting of such purchases. Freight for all shipments from Australia, whether for Great Britain or the Allies, was provided by the Australian Government, and some purchases in other markets were effected on c.i.f. terms, under which the shippers chartered the necessary tonnage. The great bulk of the Committee's purchases were, however, f.o.b., and for these tonnage had to be found.

Of the Italian ships under requisition a considerable number had already been allocated to the carriage of wheat, but these were not all available to lift the purchases of the Joint Committee. Prior to the arrangement for joint purchase, the Italian Government had bought in Canada a large block of wheat requisitioned by the Canadian Government. To lift this the Canadian Government had itself chartered a number of vessels, but for the carriage of the greater part Italian requisitioned tonnage was employed. The remainder of the requisitioned ships, together with a few vessels time-chartered to the Italian Government, were now placed at the disposal of the Committee. Even so, there was a considerable surplus for which tonnage had to be provided, and for almost the whole of the purchases made on account of the French War Ministry it was necessary to charter.

Messrs. Ross T. Smythe were now acting as chartering agents for the French and Italian as well as for the British Government, and this centralisation of chartering was in itself a gain in respect of both freight and tonnage economy. Freights, however, were high and tonnage scarce; the needs of the Allies, especially those of Italy, were urgent; and in January 1916 the Board of Trade instructed the Carriage of Foodstuffs Committee to direct tramps to load cargoes for both France and Italy as well as for the United Kingdom. To relieve the immediate crisis half a dozen steamers already under orders for the United Kingdom were diverted to French or Italian ports.[1]

From November 15th, 1915, when the Carriage of Foodstuffs Committee was appointed, to February 15th, 1916, it issued loading instructions to 111 tramps, in addition to the liners affected by the 50 per cent. agreement. In order to avoid clashing with the work of the Transport Department, the instructions were given through that Department itself, and the possibility of immediate requisition at Blue Book rates was sufficient sanction, if any were needed, to ensure faithful compliance with the instructions given. Of the 111 tramps, 5 were ordered to France and 24 to Italy, to assist the operations of the Joint Purchasing Committee. The remaining 82, less 1 lost on passage, eventually delivered their cargoes at British ports.

By the middle of February, however, it had become evident that the action of the Committee was not producing the results anticipated, either as regards imports or freights. The market was, indeed, buying more freely, for prices in America had fallen, and in view of the short shipments during the summer months, importers could no longer hold back orders in the expectation of a further fall. Their readiness to buy was increased by the fact that all immediate prospect of the re-opening of the Dardanelles had practically disappeared. In January and February, however, a sharp recovery in f.o.b. prices somewhat checked the expansion of business,[2] and uncertainty as to the future extent of Government operations acted as a further check. The imports for November, December, and January, showed a great advance on those

[1] Five to Italy, one to France.
[2] Wheat prices per quarter in United States and Canada:

		Winnipeg. No. 2. Northern		Chicago. No. 2. Hard Winter	
		s.	d.	s.	d.
1915	July	45	4	45	8
	August	41	4	39	2
	September	30	7	36	5
	October	33	5	38	7
	November	32	9	35	1
	December	35	5	37	2
1916	January	37	5	41	0
	February	40	4	42	9

of the previous months,[1] but the total fell far short of that desired by the Cabinet Food Supplies Committee. In fact, the average weekly imports attained as a result of the Committee's action, did not exceed 510,000 quarters, as against the suggested maximum of 800,000.

Even the shipments effected, imposed a strain on the ports which, in the existing conditions, they were ill able to bear. From the first the Transport Advisory Committee and the Port and Transit Executive Committee had protested against the suggestion of a weekly import of 800,000 quarters, as certain to increase the congestion of the ports, and the justice of their view was shown by the fact that, with a much smaller import, no less than eighteen grain ships, with cargoes amounting in the aggregate to 90,000 tons, were, on December 30th, awaiting berths at London and other ports.

As to the North Atlantic freights, far from falling, they were higher than ever. In October the average rate had been 9s. 6½d. per quarter; by December it was 13s. 5d., and by February 16s. 8d. The advance in import values was still greater, owing to the increased f.o.b. prices in America, and by February the retail price of the quartern loaf had risen from 7¾d. in October to 8¾d.

It was evident that, if freights were to be reduced, more drastic action was necessary, and the Committee accordingly abandoned their policy of requisitioning under the market requirements, and, as from the middle of February, began to direct tonnage into the trade in excess of the estimated deficiency. They represented, however, to the President of the Board of Trade that the figure of 800,000 quarters per week was, in their view, impossible of attainment, and, in response to their representations, it was reduced to 700,000.

Meanwhile, the competing demands of the United Kingdom for wheat and general imports, of the naval and military authorities, and of the Allies, continued to claim the attention of the Government. The report of the Ship Licensing Committee showed that the visible supply

[1] Imports of wheat and flour (taking 7 tons of flour as equal to 10 tons of wheat):

		In thousands of tons.
1915	October	313
	November	488
	December	497
1916	January	521
	February	379

of tonnage was inadequate to meet these requirements, yet neither the demands of the Allies nor the claims of British importers could be lightly disregarded. Throughout the first eighteen months of the war, British shipping had met effectively, if with increasing difficulty, all the demands upon it. All tonnage required for transport had been found; all essential supplies had been brought in. It was only the continual rise in freights which bore witness to the progressive depletion of carrying power, and the reflection of this rise in the increased cost of living had tended to concentrate attention upon the symptom rather than the disease. By the beginning of 1916, however, the increasing requirements of the Departments and of the Allies had crystallised the situation, and compelled attention to the necessity of maintaining some equilibrium between the supply of tonnage and the demands upon it.

In December 1915, about a month before the Report of the Ship Licensing Committee was presented, the Port and Transit Executive Committee had sounded the first clear note of warning in a Memorandum on the condition of the ports addressed to the Prime Minister. The conditions disclosed were sufficiently serious, especially with regard to the shortage of labour and railway trucks; but the Committee felt it their duty to go beyond this, their more immediate province, and deal with the problem of ocean transport, as well as internal distribution. Their analysis of the shipping entrances and the employment of ships entered in the War Risks Association showed that some 80 per cent. of the ocean-going tonnage of the United Kingdom was already in Government service. In trade between the British Overseas Dominions and foreign countries, and in trade wholly between foreign countries, some 21 per cent. was employed, as compared with 48 per cent. before the war, leaving available for the trade of the United Kingdom only 49 per cent. as against the normal proportion of 57. But the entrances of foreign shipping had decreased by nearly 86 per cent. during the first twelve months of war, and were not likely to increase, even if they did not further diminish as a result of the continued withdrawal of British vessels from the inter-foreign trade. Thus, the loss of carrying power was still greater than the figures given would suggest, and every additional ton requisitioned involved the shutting out of imports. During the first twelve months of war the volume of imports had diminished by less than 13 per cent.; but since July 1915 the available shipping had been decreased by requisitioning to the extent of 700,000 tons net, and the annual carrying power of this tonnage amounted to some 10 per cent. of the imports carried in the year ending July 31st.

In view of this deficiency, the increasing demands on the transport services, and the proved inability of the ports to handle with reasonable despatch even a diminished volume of imports, the Committee urged strongly that it had become necessary either to abstain from all interference with freights and prices, and leave the rates to rise to a point at which particular trades would become unprofitable, and would cease to compete for carrying power, or to exclude by prohibition or taxation all imports not essential to national existence under war conditions. In a subsequent Memorandum prepared in reply to inquiries by the President of the Board of Trade, they indicated as articles the importation of which might be cut down, tobacco, grain and sugar for brewing and distilling, wood-pulp, paper and paper-making materials, and timber. For this purpose they proposed that the use of maize and rice in breweries and distilleries for other than war or industrial use should be prohibited, and that the use of paper in bill-posters, trade catalogues, and advertisements should be checked by taxation or postal rates. They further suggested that the consumption of wheat and flour might be checked by prohibiting the use of wheatmeal for fancy bread, cakes, and confectionery, that expert advice should be taken as to the metal and ore imports necessary for war purposes, and that the imports of manufactured articles should be reviewed, with the object of prohibiting the import of luxuries.

In January 1916 came the Report of the Ship Licensing Committee, with its revelation of the total inadequacy of the available tonnage to meet in full the demands of the Allies and at the same time maintain British imports at the level of 1915. In forwarding their Report to the Board of Trade, the Committee emphasised the importance of endeavouring to restore the balance by relieving the congestion at the ports, ensuring the maximum economy in the use of requisitioned tonnage, and pressing on the completion of ships already plated and launched, which amounted to over 500,000 tons gross. They, too, urged the policy of restriction of imports as the only measure which could ensure permanent and effective relief.

This was followed on January 14th by a joint Memorandum prepared by the Ship Licensing Committee and the Requisitioning (Carriage of Foodstuffs) Committee. In this Memorandum also, a variety of remedial measures were advocated, such as longer notice of requisition, the purchase of Government stores from the nearest source of supply, and their carriage direct to their destination in France or elsewhere, thus avoiding transhipment in the United Kingdom. But once more drastic restriction of imports was urged as the only remedy which, in view of the world shortage of tonnage, could be regarded as adequate.

It was, indeed, evident that whether or no imports were restricted by legislation, their volume must inevitably be cut down through sheer inability to procure space. But to leave the equilibrium between demand and supply to be restored by allowing freights to rise to the point at which the carriage of certain articles became unprofitable, involved the danger of essential commodities being driven out by the competition of non-essentials. It was impossible, as the Liverpool Steam Ship Owners' Association had already urged, for the shipowners to apply any other criterion of urgency than the rough and ready test of the freights which importers of competing commodities were willing to pay; for they did not, and could not, possess the data on which judgment could be formed. In normal times the freight test was reasonably accurate, for whatever profit the manufacturer might derive from the luxury trades, it was the big cargoes of foodstuffs and essential raw materials which provided the shipowner with the greater part of his earnings. But in the conditions which now existed, it was necessary to discriminate not only between luxuries and necessities, but between the competing claims of imports normally regarded as essential. This could only be done by the Government itself, for no one else was in a position to estimate and weigh all the factors that had to be taken into consideration—the demands of the Army and Navy for equipment and munitions, the food supply of the troops and the people, the provision of employment for those still engaged in civil industries, and the provision of raw materials for the export trades by which the foreign exchanges were maintained.

So clear was the danger that the Board of Trade, though still shrinking from wholesale prohibition of imports on account of the administrative and political difficulties, and dislocation of trade involved, were convinced of the necessity for some measure of restriction. On January 27th Mr. Runciman announced in the House of Commons that the Government had decided to prohibit a great part of the normal import of paper and paper-making materials, amounting to over 1,600,000 tons a year, and that they contemplated the exclusion of other articles and materials of a bulky nature, including raw tobacco, many building materials, furniture woods and veneers, and some fruits. The question of grain imported solely for brewing and distilling purposes was also under consideration.

At the same time an important step was taken towards the co-ordination of naval, military, Allied, and commercial demands. The Transport Department, as we have seen, had no power to question the necessity or wisdom of the demands made upon it. Its function was restricted to supplying, with as little commercial dislocation as possible, the tonnage indented for by the Departments, and while it was at times able to make effective representations, it could exercise no general supervision over shipping policy. In reducing dislocation to a minimum, and in tendering advice as to the tonnage situation, it had been greatly assisted by the Advisory Committee; but the powers of that Committee were advisory only. Moreover, the whole shipping position had developed rapidly since its appointment. The demands for requisitioned tonnage were far more numerous and more varied, the shortage of shipping was far more serious in January 1916 than in January 1915. In these circumstances the members of the Advisory Committee felt strongly that they had not sufficient knowledge of the competing claims of the Government services, the Allies, and the import and export trades, to enable them to advise effectively as to the effects of further requisitioning or the allocation of tonnage, even if they could be sure that the advice tendered would be accepted. They urged, therefore, that some central authority should be appointed to review all claims for the allocation of tonnage in relation to the available supply, and should be furnished with sufficient material to enable it to decide the broad lines of shipping policy.

For a short time, as we have seen, the responsibility of

advising on tonnage allocation was exercised by the Port and Transit Executive Committee; but the members of that Committee were already heavily burdened with their own special task, nor had the Committee itself, strong as it was for its own purposes, the weight and representative character which would ensure acceptance of its rulings on broad questions of policy involving Departmental and Allied interests of the first importance. Some new and authoritative body was required, and on January 27th, 1916, the Shipping Control Committee was appointed by the Prime Minister.

The terms of reference of this Committee were to decide on the allocation of British ships to essential requirements of the Allies; to decide similarly on the allocation of British ships to essential requirements of the United Kingdom; and to make representations to the Cabinet with regard to the tonnage required for naval and military purposes. The members of the Committee were: Lord Curzon, Chairman; Lord Faringdon (Chairman of the Great Central Railway Company); Mr. Thomas Royden (Deputy Chairman of the Cunard SS. Co.); and Mr. F. W. Lewis (Deputy Chairman of Furness, Withy & Co.); with Captain Clement Jones (a Director of the Booth Line) as Secretary.

The terms of reference, as will be seen, were very wide, and invested the Committee with a large measure of executive power. Inasmuch as no administrative staff was provided, the actual work of giving effect to its decisions and of supervising in detail the employment of the shipping allocated to the various services, was left to the Transport Department, assisted by the Advisory Committee; but this limitation was in full accordance with the views expressed by the members of the Committee themselves, who considered that their work would be more effective if confined to the decision of broad lines of policy, and were anxious to avoid the possibilities of friction and duplication of effort inherent in a dual organisation. In practice the final responsibility for decisions affecting important Allied or service interests necessarily rested with the Government, but the presence, as Chairman, of Lord Curzon, a member of the Cabinet, not only ensured close and constant touch between the Committee and the Government, but practically ensured confirmation of its decisions, and gave even to its recommendations a weight which they might otherwise have lacked. Through its members, too, the Committee was closely connected with the chief executive authorities exercising control over shipping, for Mr. Royden was a member both of the Requisitioning (Carriage of Foodstuffs) Committee and the Advisory Committee to the Transport Department, and Mr. Lewis was a member of the Ship Licensing Committee. The new authority was thus admirably framed to secure a wide co-ordination both of knowledge and policy, and a better informed and more balanced view of the tonnage situation as a whole than had yet been possible.

CHAPTER XV

THE TONNAGE DEFICIT AT THE BEGINNING OF 1916—ASSISTANCE GIVEN TO THE ALLIES

THE problem by which the Shipping Control Committee was confronted on its appointment, was both difficult and delicate. The terms of reference appeared to assume the existence of a margin of available tonnage to be allocated; the actual situation was that a deficiency had to be made good. It was the task of the Committee to devise some means of making good this deficiency, and should this prove impossible, to decide in what proportion the deficit should be borne by the various competing services.

The demands of the Allies, as put forward in December 1915 and January 1916, were estimated by the Committee as involving the allocation of 1,428,000 gross tons of shipping over and above all ships already requisitioned for Allied services or running on Allied charter. From whence this additional tonnage could be drawn it was not easy to see. British shipping in the inter-foreign trade had already been combed out by the Ship Licensing Committee, and from the report presented by that Committee it was clear that the vessels remaining in employment between foreign ports and capable of withdrawal without serious prejudice to British or Allied interests, were wholly insufficient to meet the new demands. If these demands were to be met it would be necessary to draw upon shipping engaged in the trade of the United Kingdom, and that shipping was already barely equal to the carriage of import requirements.

During the first twelve months of war the estimated weight of imports was about 48,750,000 tons, as compared with 56,000,000 tons in 1913-14. The tonnage entrances for the six months ending January 31st, 1916, were less by over 300,000 tons than those for the preceding half-year; but the weight of cargoes per 100 tons of shipping entered was still on the increase, and the total weight of imports for the six months was nearly 25,000,000 tons. Space for these imports was, it is true, only procurable at very high and continually increasing freights, but space had so far been procured. Whatever discontent might be aroused by the cost of transport, each successive half-year of war had seen an actual increase in the volume of traffic. It was obvious, however, that so great a volume of imports could no longer be maintained.

Tonnage under requisition had gone up, during the latter part of the six months in question, by leaps and bounds. The total, which had risen from 1,804 ships of 5,050,000 tons gross on September 1st, 1915, to 1,450 of 5,540,000 tons on November 1st, had again risen by February 1st, 1916, to 1,766 ships of 6,519,000 tons. Some of these ships were still in fact engaged in the import service of the United Kingdom, whether as temporarily released ships or as vessels bringing sugar, nitrate, pyrites, and other Government cargoes at Blue Book rates, but the great majority were withdrawn from commercial employment, for Naval and Military purposes or for the service of the Allies, and in the near future the effects of this progressive increase in the tonnage under requisition would certainly become apparent in the import trade.

Thus, apart from the demands of the Allies, or any further requirements put forward by the Admiralty or War Office, there was the prospect of a considerable tonnage deficiency in the trade of the United Kingdom itself, and this could no longer be made good, as when the strain of requisitioning first began to be felt, by diverting or attracting ships from the routes between foreign ports. Yet no other source of additional carrying power was readily available. Owing to the prior claims on labour and material of the Admiralty and Ministry of Munitions, commercial shipbuilding was practically at a standstill, except for the construction of oil-tankers and frozen meat ships, and the total output for the last quarter of 1915 had sunk to 93,000 tons, little more than was required to make good the war losses of a single month.[1]

---

[1] Thanks to the comparatively satisfactory output of the first quarter, the total for the year was 648,000 tons, but this was only one-third of the figure for 1913. As compared with the average of the three years prior to the war, the figures of mercantile and Admiralty construction were as follows :

	Average, 1911-13.	1915.
Merchant vessels, gross tons	1,808,000	648,000
War and auxiliary vessels : (1 ton displacement = 2 tons gross)	388,000	873,000
Total gross tons	2,196,000	1,521,000

AN ALARMING ESTIMATE

From British shipping, therefore, there was little to be hoped; but the system of bunker pressure, devised for the prevention of neutral trade with the enemy countries, was already being applied to the purpose of driving neutral shipping into British trade, and especially of compelling vessels bunkering in the United Kingdom for a voyage in neutral interests, to return with cargo to a British port.[1] By this means the tendency towards withdrawal observed in the autumn of 1915 appeared to have been checked, and the foreign entrances for the six months ending January 31st, 1916, were, in fact, slightly higher than for the previous half-year, the decrease already noticed being accounted for wholly by the falling off in British shipping. Bunker pressure, however, was a weapon which needed caution in its employment. There were already signs that, if indiscriminately applied, it might end by driving neutral shipping altogether away from British ports, and in any event the relief to be expected from its use was comparatively small, as most of the additional tonnage obtained would probably be required either on the North Sea routes, where comparatively little British tonnage was normally employed, or in the service of the Allies. At most, it could not go far to make up the deficit in the trade of the United Kingdom.

On the assumption that the demands of the Allies were to be granted in full, the Shipping Control Committee estimated this deficit as 8,260,000 tons, representing a deficiency of 13,000,000 tons weight of imports in the year, or over 25 per cent. of the total volume of imports during the first twelve months of war. So desperate did the situation appear that the Committee proposed, in order to avoid the delay consequent on a lengthy analysis of imports for the purposes of restriction, that for a period of three months from March 31st, the import of *all* commodities other than those comprised in certain clearly defined categories, should be totally prohibited. This course would have reduced imports for the three months in question to a rate of about 36,000,000 tons a year, but the Committee anticipated so great an improvement in the condition of the ports as a result of the opportunity provided for clearing congested storage space, as to permit a fuller flow of traffic at the end of the three months. During the period of prohibition the Committee believed

[1] See Chapter IX, *supra*.

that the majority of the trades affected would be able to live on their accumulated stocks.

Serious as the situation was, the Government were unwilling to resort to such heroic measures which, even if applied as the Shipping Control Committee suggested, with a large degree of elasticity, must have involved very grave dislocation of trade. They decided, however, to proceed with the restriction of the articles mentioned by Mr. Runciman in his statement of January 27th, up to a total of 4,000,000 tons, beyond which figure the Board of Trade considered it impossible to go. This decision was embodied in an Order in Council, dated February 15th, 1916, by which the import of paper and paper-making materials, tobacco, furniture woods, and stones was prohibited except under licence.[1]

It was still, however, the advance in freights, rather than any serious anxiety as to shortage of supplies, which occupied the chief attention of the Government. It will be remembered that, to this date, the action of the Requisitioning (Carriage of Foodstuffs) Committee had neither had the effect of bringing up the total wheat imports to anything like the figure proposed by the Cabinet Committee on Food Supplies, nor of preventing a still further rise in North Atlantic grain freights. So seriously were the Committee alarmed by this continued rise in freights, that they considered it their duty to urge upon the Government the necessity of considering whether it was practicable to provide requisitioned tonnage for the carriage of *all* wheat at a fixed freight, and if so, whether this course would involve State purchase and distribution of the wheat, as well as State transport. On this question of State ownership the Committee felt themselves unable to advise; but it was probably the decisive factor in inducing the Government to reject the scheme. There were grave doubts as to whether the benefit of restricted freights could be effectively passed on to the consumer, so long as the wheat itself continued to be imported on private account, and the Government were not yet ready to assume sole responsibility for the wheat supply of the country. In the meantime, as we have seen, the Committee had changed its policy with regard to the direction of shipping into the North Atlantic trade, and was now requisitioning in excess of the market requirements,

[1] *London Gazette*, 15 February, 1916.

instead of leaving a margin to be supplied by casual fixtures.

From February 16th to April 30th no fewer than 88 tramps were directed to load for the United Kingdom, in addition to 14 for France and 27 for Italy. Of those directed to the United Kingdom 6 were from the Plate—for the Plate voyage had now been brought within the scope of the Committee. The remainder were from North America. Of the 88 vessels, only one was lost on passage.

The full effect of the new policy was not, of course, immediately felt; but even during the period under review, the average weekly imports of wheat went up from 510,000 to 564,000 quarters, and at the end of April they were still rising. Still more strongly marked was the effect on North Atlantic grain freights. At the end of February they stood at 18s. 3d. per quarter. By the end of April they had dropped to 12s. 6d. Wheat prices in North America were still rising, and the average import values were maintained, or even a little increased, but with larger supplies on the market, the price of the quartern loaf, which rose to 9d. in March, fell back in April to 8$\frac{3}{4}d$., the February level. Thus, while the action of the Committee had not, in fact, reduced the cost of living, it appeared to have had an appreciable effect in checking the advance. Freights, at any rate, had been reduced, and for the time being, the question of extending State Control over the purchase and distribution of wheat lapsed into abeyance.

Wheat freights, however, formed only one part of the problem, and during the first two or three months of 1916 various schemes were under consideration for centralising control over the whole Mercantile Marine, and fixing freight rates on all imports. These schemes mostly broke down on the same points, the lack of any organisation capable of controlling effectively the vast and complex organisation of British shipping, the impossibility of controlling neutral tonnage, and the actual disproportion between the demand for tonnage and the supply. Even if the difficulty of creating an efficient centralised Board of Management for the whole British Mercantile Marine were overcome, it would be impossible to fix the freights to British ports appreciably below the general market level, without driving away the neutral tonnage which still played so large and essential a part in the import trade. And whatever might be accomplished in the control of shipping, the problem of supplies could never be effectively solved so long as the import demands of the United Kingdom continued to exceed the total available carrying power.

As a first step towards restoring the balance between demand and supply, it was obvious that the output of the shipyards must if possible be increased, and with this object it was suggested that some portion of the shipowners' profits should be compulsorily applied to new construction. The great difficulty, however, lay not in the unwillingness of shipowners to place orders, but in the impossibility of getting those orders fulfilled. Until slips, labour, and material could be rendered more freely available for commercial work, there was little hope of any substantial increase in output.

Nevertheless, the financial factor was by no means negligible. The cost of labour and material had been rising steadily ever since the beginning of the war, and builders who had contracted for new tonnage before the rise, found it almost impossible to carry out their contracts on the original terms. Further, in face of the difficulties caused by the Admiralty demands for labour and material, it was impossible to complete any ship by or near the contract date without incurring additional expenses. In the aggregate these additional and " acceleration " costs constituted a heavy addition to the purchase price, and though the market rates of freight were so high that an owner could easily recoup himself for his expenditure if he were able to take advantage of them, he had no guarantee that his ship would not be requisitioned at Blue Book rates as soon as completed. Whenever possible the Board of Trade acted as intermediary between owners and builders, and arranged for both parties to make sacrifices in order to expedite delivery; but as the proportion of ships under requisition increased, such arrangements became more and more difficult. The Shipping Control Committee accordingly suggested, on February 1st, that when owners would agree to pay acceleration costs, they should be guaranteed a short period of immunity from requisition. This suggestion was adopted by the Transport Department, and a certain number of free voyages were allowed, the profit on which would, it was estimated, cover the additional expenditure incurred.

There remained the obstacle presented by lack of

labour and material, and, in the hope of overcoming this' the Board of Trade sought and obtained power to certify certain merchant ships as " munition work," thus entitling them to priority in respect of material, and bringing the labour employed on them under the provisions of the Munitions Acts. On February 18th Mr. Runciman announced in the House of Commons that 140 vessels, which were already well advanced towards completion, had been so certified, and he indicated that the Government contemplated an early extension of this priority to all commercial shipbuilding.

Meanwhile the Shipping Control Committee were doing what they could to increase the effective carrying power of the available tonnage. For this purpose they strongly supported the Port and Transit Committee's recommendations with regard to pooling of railway trucks, prohibition of the use of quays and transit sheds for storage purposes, and supply of labour. With a view to reducing the tonnage employed in the carriage of timber, they supported also the proposals of the Home-Grown Timber Committee for felling British timber for home requirements, and they played an important part in the arrangements made with the War Office for procuring locally a part of the stone and timber required by the armies in France. By this measure alone they calculated that the equivalent of some 40,000 tons of shipping a month would be saved in the cross-Channel traffic.

From the first the Committee worked in close touch with the Transport Department, the Ship Licensing Committee, and the Committee for the Carriage of Foodstuffs. This was indeed necessary, both to provide them with information on which to base their decisions, and to enable them to exercise an effective supervision over the employment of British shipping. The Transport Department itself would have been glad for them to go further. Its responsibilities were continually increasing, and shortly after the appointment of the Shipping Control Committee the representatives of the Department suggested that the Committee should provide themselves with a statistical and administrative staff, and should take over the direct control of temporarily released tonnage, and of vessels not on full requisition, which had been directed into particular trades. This, however, the Committee refused. They had declined from the first to undertake the details of administration, and preferred to work with and through the existing authorities. Thus, while they agreed to accept general responsibility for the employment of temporarily released and directed shipping, the actual work continued, as before, to be performed by the Transport Department and the Advisory Committee. The Shipping Control Committee arranged, however, that, as from March 3rd, two of their number, Mr. Royden and Mr. Lewis, should be in daily attendance, in order to deal with a wider range of questions than could be disposed of at their regular meetings. At the same time they arranged to strengthen the hands of the Transport Department by putting pressure on the buying Departments of the Government not to arrange purchases abroad without first consulting the Director of Transports as to shipping facilities, thus eliminating to some extent an element of competition and uncertainty in the demand for tonnage.

The organisation of the Transport Department itself had been considerably extended and improved during the last few months of 1915. Down to the winter of that year, each of the two Executive Branches—Military and Naval—had requisitioned on its own account the tonnage required for those services for which it was responsible, except that ships required by the Collier Section of Naval Branch were taken up by Messrs. Mathwins, the Admiralty coal agents, on behalf of the Section. Notice of all ships requisitioned or released was sent to the Advisory Committee, in order that they might be in a position to advise in the application of the system of Proportionate Requisitioning; but as the work of the Department increased it became evident that the application of that system was hampered by the existence of three independent requisitioning authorities, however closely related. There were also, in these arrangements, possibilities of friction and over-lapping, which became serious as the proportion of tonnage under requisition increased; but it was some time before any adequate system of centralisation could be worked out.

An essential preliminary to any such centralisation was the possession of complete and up-to-date information with regard to the available tonnage, and in April 1915, following a conference between the Transport Department, the Advisory Committee, and Messrs. Mathwins on March

IMPROVED ORGANISATION

23rd, a circular was sent out to all shipowners other than liner companies in the passenger trade, publishing a regular programme of sailings, asking them to render a detailed statement of the type, present employment and position, and future engagements of their vessels, with a view to equalising the incidence of requisition. By July 1915 replies had been received from nearly all the owners, and the information thus obtained was arranged and classified by a separate Intelligence Section under Mr. Saunders, formed within the Collier Section. In September, the shipowners were again circularised and requested to render regular monthly statements, and in the following month it was decided to form a new Branch to centralise the whole business of shipping intelligence and classification. Mr. J. A. Salter, who had previously been Superintendent of Finance Branch, was now placed at the head of the new Branch, the scope and functions of which followed the lines of a memorandum submitted by him on October 20th.

The first duty of Information Branch, as it was originally called, was to form from the shipowners' monthly returns and such other information as could be collected, a complete card index of all British shipping, which would show at a glance the position and employment of all available vessels. All inquiries as to shipping were to be made by the new Branch, and all offers of ships to be received by it and passed on to the Executive Branches. When either of these needed additional tonnage its requirements were to be stated to Information Branch, which would make out a list of all free vessels of suitable size and type, available for requisition by the specified date. The papers would then be returned, through the Naval Assistant, who would select the actual ship or ships to be taken up, to the Executive Branch concerned, by whom the process of requisition would be carried out. All papers relating to Proportionate Requisitioning would be kept by Information Branch, which would also be responsible for securing co-ordination with Messrs. Mathwins in the matter of collier requisition. It was further suggested that the formal letter of requisition for colliers should go out from the Admiralty direct at the request of Messrs. Mathwins, a step which, in the interests of centralisation, the Advisory Committee greatly desired.

By December 1915, the new Branch was in working

order, and sufficient experience had been gained to suggest an extension of its functions. It was now decided that, on receiving notice of requirements from an Executive Branch, Requisitioning Branch, as it was now called, should make a definite recommendation as to the ship or ships to be taken up, and, if the Executive Branch concurred, should, in general, send out the requisitioning telegram. The formal letter of requisition, together with instructions as to delivery, would be subsequently sent out by the Executive Branch. In order to minimise, so far as possible, dislocation of trade, the Executive Branches were instructed to give the longest possible notice of requirements, so as to permit of requisitioning in advance, without interference with current voyages.

All exchanges of vessels between the different services run by the Executive Branches were ordered to be made through Requisitioning Branch, and this Branch was also made responsible for meeting the requirements of the Carriage of Foodstuffs Committee. Further, the allocation of requisitioned tonnage to the Allies, or to the service of Government Departments other than the Admiralty and War Office, was carried out by Requisitioning Branch in co-operation with the Port and Transit Committee or, after January 1916, the Shipping Control Committee. As regards colliers, it was decided that as from January 3rd, 1916, no further requisitions should be made by Messrs. Mathwins direct. Each week a statement of the collier tonnage required during the next four weeks was furnished to Requisitioning Branch, by whom the vessels were obtained and requisitioned in co-operation with Collier Section.

In this way the new Branch became a clearing house for all information relating either to requisitioned tonnage or tonnage available for service, while the actual process of requisitioning was centralised to a much greater extent than ever before. As the basis of its work, a card index of ships, classified under the owners' names, had by this time been prepared, and was kept up to date from the monthly returns, supplemented by other information. This index Mr. Salter proposed to extend so as to cover the present employment, not only of all ships available for requisition, but of all ships running on requisitioned service. For this purpose the index was to be rearranged under ship names in alphabetical order, and arrange-

THE SHIPPING INDEX

ments were being made to supplement the shipowners' returns by information obtained from Lloyds, the Customs, the Ship Licensing Committee, and other sources. The Indian and Dominions Governments were applied to for the fullest particulars of all United Kingdom registered vessels in their service, and the Commission Internationale de Ravitaillement for details of all ships in the service of the Allies, whether requisitioned or chartered. The whole of this information was to be kept constantly up to date, and was to serve as the basis of all such periodical returns as might be desirable, either for administrative purposes or for arriving at decisions on questions of policy.

This, however, was not the only new Branch added to the organisation of the Transport Department at the end of 1915. All through the year the work of the Department had been steadily expanding in directions which lay altogether outside its original functions of providing ships for direct Naval and Military Service. When the Government agreed to supply coal for the French State Railways, and subsequently for Russia, in requisitioned vessels, the work was undertaken without much difficulty by Collier Section, and that section undertook also the provision of tonnage for the purchases of the Royal Sugar Commission, for a great part of which returning or disengaged colliers could readily be used. Such tonnage, however, required to be supplemented by the carriage of liner parcels from Java, Mauritius, the West Indies, and South America. There were also many Government purchases, especially of munitions from North America, which were either insufficient in bulk to provide a tramp steamer with a full cargo or unsuitable for shipment in tramp tonnage. Hence, almost from the beginning of the war it had become the practice of the Transport Department to arrange for space in liners for such shipments on terms approximating to the Blue Book rates, and as the demands of the Ministry of Munitions expanded, this system of " Requisitioned Space " grew steadily in importance.

Still more onerous was the work entailed on the Department by the system of " temporary release " which had been so highly developed under the guidance of the Advisory Committee. Under this system the Department became responsible for directing ships returning from the completion of a voyage on Government service to lift essential cargoes such as ore or pyrites on their homeward voyage, and when release on these conditions was refused by the shipowners, for fixing the vessel themselves for an inwards voyage in the essential trades. Ore and pyrites from the Mediterranean, flax and timber from the White Sea, were the cargoes most commonly lifted, but it was the business of the Advisory Committee to keep in the closest possible touch with commercial requirements, so that tonnage might be directed into any essential trade in which there was a shortage of carrying power. By the end of 1915 this business had become very extensive, and over a hundred temporarily released vessels were normally engaged in the import trade.

The majority of these ships were on Naval Service, and their voyages were arranged through Collier Section. Vessels on Military Service were, as a rule, kept by the War Office on full requisition, and a few such ships had been used by Military Branch during the year, to bring cargoes of nitrate from Chile, on War Office account. Towards the end of the year the Port and Transit Committee decided that all military nitrate should be imported in requisitioned tonnage, and a regular nitrate service was established by Military Branch. The same principle was extended, as we have seen, to pyrites for munitions purposes, and the use of requisitioned instead of temporarily released tonnage for iron ore was under consideration.

For some time past the Advisory Committee had come to the conclusion that effective supervision of all these commercial services, in addition to the task of securing economy and equality in the requisitioning of shipping for Naval and Military purposes, was beyond their powers. They had cordially co-operated in the establishment of Requisitioning Branch as an important step towards effective control of requisitioned tonnage; but they considered that the organisation of the Department required to be supplemented by the creation of a special branch to deal with the various commercial services for which it had become responsible. By December 1915 this Commercial Branch was in process of formation, and by the early months of 1916 it was firmly established. Mr. F. C. Gardiner of the Advisory Committee was at first placed at its head, with a permanent Civil Servant, Mr. Cyril Hurcomb (transferred from the Post Office), as second in command, but Mr. Gardiner soon found the double work too much for one man to undertake, and as he preferred to confine himself to the work of the Advisory Committee, he was replaced on March 15th by Sir Percy Bates, Bart., a Director of the Cunard and Anchor Lines.

The duties of Commercial Branch were to arrange, in concert with Requisitioning Branch, for the tonnage or space required for the carriage of Government imports, such as sugar and munitions material, to supervise the running of ships so employed, to arrange with the Advisory Committee as to the trades to be worked by temporarily released ships and direct or fix them accordingly, and to advise the Naval and Military Branches on commercial practice and market rates. For these purposes it was equipped with a staff comprising men of shipping and commercial experience, who could relieve the Advisory Committee of much of the detail work with which they had previously been obliged to struggle, and under whose supervision the service members of the staff speedily learned the routine of shipping business.

Wheat ships chartered by Messrs. Ross T. Smythe, or loading under direction of the Carriage of Foodstuffs Committee, lay outside the scope of the Branch, as they were not, in fact, requisitioned vessels, and tonnage required for the carriage of coal for the Allies continued to be provided by the Collier Section of Naval Branch. The Board of Trade, too, continued to be responsible for all shipments of frozen meat, whether on British or Allied account. With these exceptions practically all vessels carrying commercial cargoes under the control of the British Government, either for Great Britain or for the Allies, came within the jurisdiction of Commercial Branch.

As organised in March 1916, the Branch had three sections. The Sugar Section was responsible for lifting the purchases of the Royal Sugar Commission, and Mr. H. D. Bell was transferred from the Collier Section of the Naval Branch to manage this part of the work. The Ore Section, under Mr. W. A. Stewart, controlled the shipment of iron ore, pyrites, and similar cargoes, whether in requisitioned vessels or ships temporarily released. Mr. Connop Guthrie, at the head of the General Section, was responsible for the transport of nitrates imported for munitions purposes, hitherto undertaken by the Military Branch, and for various miscellaneous services.

In this way—by the creation of Requisitioning and Commercial Branches, and the development of the shipping intelligence system—the organisation of the Transport Department was rendered at once more centralised and more flexible. Thanks to this improvement in organisation and to the representations made by the Department itself, by the Mediterranean Transport Commission, and by the Shipping Control Committee, a considerable measure of economy was attained in the use of requisitioned shipping; but owing to the increasing demands of the Departments and the Allies, the number of ships on requisition continued to rise, and it was still vitally necessary to ensure the utilisation of all vessels remaining in commercial employment, to the utmost of their capacity and in the most profitable manner. The objection which had proved fatal to all schemes for the direct centralised control of merchant shipping did not apply to the system of ship licensing, and with the object of securing the maximum tonnage for the essential trades, the Shipping Control Committee and the Board of Trade concurred in recommending that the powers of the Ship Licensing Committee should be extended. Accordingly, by an Order in Council, dated February 15th, 1916, it was provided that no British steamship exceeding 500 tons gross and registered in the United Kingdom should proceed on any voyage whatsoever, other than voyages in the coasting trade, without a licence from the Committee, whose powers were thus extended from voyages with cargo in the inter-foreign trade, to all ocean voyages, whether with cargo or in ballast. In communicating the Order to the Committee, the Board of Trade instructed them that laden voyages to or from the United Kingdom should as a general rule be licensed as a matter of course, and that licences for voyages to or from a British Possession or an Allied country should not be refused without some specific reason, such as congestion at the proposed port of arrival. Ballast voyages were as far as possible to be discouraged, especially in the trade of the United Kingdom and Allied countries, but no licences were to be refused on account of the nature of the proposed cargo, except on the direct instructions of the Board.

Although these instructions restricted considerably the new powers given to the Committee, the right to refuse or recommend the refusal of licences in respect of all voyages,

EXTENSION OF LICENSING

was an instrument for the control of shipping which was not necessarily ineffective because its full exercise was kept for the moment in abeyance. In two respects, in particular, the immediate extension of the Committee's activities produced valuable results—the restriction of ballast voyages and of voyages to congested ports. As a general rule, the shipowner himself was averse from a ballast voyage, but such voyages might be directly in the interest of a time charterer. Thus, when a vessel was chartered to take coal to Italy, the Italians were generally anxious to send her back in ballast, so as to minimise the time occupied in turn round, and secure the maximum number of coal cargoes within a given period. But such ballast voyages, on a wider view, were a waste of carrying power, and the Licensing Committee were now able to stipulate, before granting a licence, that the ship should call at a Spanish port on her way back, to load ore for the United Kingdom. In the same way, licences for voyages with coal to French ports were made conditional on lifting a return cargo of pitwood from the south of France, or ore from Spain. Equally important was the power to refuse licences for voyages to congested ports. The refusal of licences for ships from foreign ports to Genoa during December, had enabled the accumulations at that port to be, to a great extent, cleared off, and the result was a permanent improvement in the condition of the port, and a consequent economy of carrying power. The same principle was now applied to all voyages from the United Kingdom to French and Italian ports. Regular reports as to local conditions were obtained by the Committee, and licences were frequently refused for voyages to ports at which ships were subject to long delays. It was in the French coal trade that the delays were the most numerous and the most serious, and in their efforts to reduce these, the Committee received valuable assistance from the Coal Exports Committee, who controlled all shipments of coal from the United Kingdom. The two Committees worked closely together. No cargoes for France or Italy were licensed by the Exports Committee in excess of the licensed tonnage; no tonnage was licensed unless a licence had previously been obtained for the cargo. In deciding the allocation of both coal and tonnage, regard was paid to the receiving capacity of the ports. Frequent remonstrances were received from France as to the refusal of licences, but the

Committee held that when a port was unable to take delivery of the cargoes despatched to it, with reasonable speed, the licensing of any further shipments would only increase the congestion, causing further delays to British shipping and consequent waste of carrying power, without increasing the effective supply of coal to the French consumer.

As regards cargoes, the Committee's instructions gave them no general power of discrimination. They were, however, frequently able to bring informal pressure to bear on the shipowner for the substitution, for instance, of ore for fruit on a homeward voyage from Spain.

It will be observed that the instructions to the Licensing Committee placed no general restriction on Allied chartering of British tonnage; but during the first three months of 1916 the whole question of Allied services, whether performed by requisitioned or chartered shipping, continued to engage the attention of the Transport Department, the Shipping Control Committee, and the Cabinet. It was obvious that, in view of the tonnage situation as disclosed in the Reports of the Licensing and Shipping Control Committees, it was impossible to give the Allies a blank cheque on the tonnage resources of Great Britain; it was equally impossible to ignore their claims to assistance in maintaining essential supplies, and it became necessary to scrutinise and weigh with the utmost care each request received.

The principal demands of the Allies were for the transport of grain, coal, and munitions. There could be no question of the urgency of these demands; but in view of the tonnage situation, it was necessary to restrict the assistance given to the essential minimum. Accordingly, in December 1915, the Transport Department requested the Commission Internationale de Ravitaillement to centralise and sift as much as possible all Allied demands for tonnage, with the object of enabling a more accurate judgment to be formed as to the necessity of each service.

The original demands of Italy were for 100 additional vessels for the transport of cereals, and 50 for coal. So far as wheat was concerned, the demand was met, not by the allocation of fully requisitioned tonnage, but by the instructions given during January to the Carriage of Foodstuffs Committee to direct ships to load for Italy and France. The full programme, as it stood in March

GRAIN AND COAL FOR ALLIES

1916, contemplated the direction of 78 voyages to France and 88 to Italy during the importing season, December–July, representing a total cargo capacity of nearly 900,000 tons.[1] Even so, the Italian demands were not fully satisfied; but there appeared to be little doubt that their most urgent needs would be met, and the Shipping Control Committee declined to sanction the allocation of further ships.

No less insistent were the demands of the Italians for collier tonnage. Their plight was, indeed, serious, having regard to their absolute dependence on imported fuel. Shipments from Great Britain had fallen from 9,647,000 tons in 1913 to 5,788,000 in 1915, and though large purchases had been made in North America, they were insufficient to make good the deficit. Moreover, the import of coal from North America instead of from Great Britain was a distinct waste of carrying power.

So bad was the situation at the beginning of 1916 that the Italian Government reported serious danger of important steel works closing down for lack of fuel. To allocate fifty additional ships for continuous employment in this service was, however, impossible. Already supplies in Egypt were running short, and the South Wales Railways were congested by the blocking back of traffic, through insufficiency of tonnage to lift the accumulations at the ports. Many British steamers were already engaged in the Italian coal trade, and there was not sufficient collier tonnage available to warrant any great increase in the number. As in respect of the French State Railways, however, it was decided to undertake the provision of a guaranteed supply at fixed rates for the essential services, and on February 1st the Shipping Control Committee agreed to the allocation of requisitioned tonnage for the carriage of 45,000 tons of coal, to be supplied by the Admiralty to the Italian Government. This arrangement was subsequently extended to cover a fixed shipment of 50,000 tons a month on Admiralty account.[2]

To France further assistance had already been given. Hitherto colliers had been supplied by the Admiralty only for the French railways. The French Navy had shipped its supplies from Wales in French or chartered tonnage. In view, however, of the increasing shortage both of sup-

[1] Inclusive of British ships chartered by Ross T. Smythe.
[2] In addition, large quantities carried in Italian or chartered shipping, were purchased through the medium of the Admiralty.

plies and shipping, the French Government requested the Admiralty, as from the beginning of 1916, to undertake the transport of 70,000 tons a month for the French Marine, and to this request the Admiralty agreed.

This, however, was not all. Both France and Italy required large quantities of munitions material from America, especially shell steel, and large shipments of oats and maize for use as military fodder.[1] As the combination of weight and measurement cargo made for economical stowage, these requirements were dealt with by a single service. For this service six requisitioned vessels, carrying 21,000 tons of oats, were fixed during the first two months of 1916, and by March the combined steel and oat service was in full swing. The final arrangement was for a monthly quota to average 140,000 tons of steel and oats or maize, to be apportioned between France and Italy by the Commission Internationale de Ravitaillement, in accordance with current needs. A few cargoes for Belgium were also arranged. Responsibility for the whole service was assumed by the General Section of Commercial Branch.

Meanwhile the meat supply of the Allies had again come under consideration, and on March 31st a new agreement was signed with France which, however, did not greatly extend the obligations already undertaken. By this agreement the British Government guaranteed, subject to sufficient tonnage being available, the continuance of the monthly quota of 20,000 tons of frozen meat to be conveyed in British ships. They further agreed to supply on similar terms a quantity of frozen meat equivalent to the fresh meat of French origin consumed by British troops in France, and to allow British liners to carry the French supplies from Madagascar and Venezuela. The export of refrigerating machinery and plant for the equipment of French steamers under construction was to be permitted, provided that the building of British vessels was not thereby impeded. In return the French Government agreed that all contracts for meat to be imported in French ships, built or to be built, should be placed through Sir Thomas Robinson, and that not more than 70,000 tons a year should be bought under such contracts except after consultation with the British Government. Finally all meat supplied for the French or British forces was to be

---

[1] The French production of oats, as of wheat, was reduced by about 25 per cent. through the invasion and other effects of the war.

considered as for the common service of both Allies, and the Board of Trade were empowered to divert meat steamers accordingly, whether the meat in the ships was on British or French contracts, so long as the guaranteed average supplies were maintained.

The Italian meat agreement was also renewed in March for a further period of six months. As before, the guarantee was for 5,000 to 7,000 tons a month, and no new provision of tonnage was necessary.

In addition to these main services, the Transport Department requisitioned tonnage provided for the carriage of some 80,000 tons of shell steel monthly from Great Britain to France, and allocated requisitioned ships or requisitioned space to various minor services, such as the carriage of war stores ordered by the Commission Internationale de Ravitaillement, shipments of wool from Australia, jute from India, and timber from Canada. To supplement the ships thus allocated, a number of neutral vessels, chartered for the Board of Trade, were made over to the Allies.

Both France and Italy were themselves large charterers of neutral tonnage; but towards the end of 1915 the supply of this tonnage had become very short, and freights and time-charter rates correspondingly high. There was as yet no organisation for centralising Inter-Allied chartering, but in January 1916 the Board of Trade instructed Messrs. Furness, Withy & Co., whose position and experience rendered them exceptionally well-equipped for the work, to charter neutral steamers for the Board's account. The original intention was that the firm should charge the ordinary brokerage commission, but this they absolutely refused, and from the first the work was carried out by Messrs. Furness, Withy & Co. without remuneration of any kind. Nearly the whole of the tonnage thus secured was made over to France and Italy, who thus obtained the ships on much more favourable terms than if they had been fixed, in competition with each other, by the Allied Governments.

Thus, in one way and another, very heavy commitments on account of the Allies were accepted by the British Government and the Transport Department during the first three months of 1916, and it must not be forgotten that these new commitments were in addition to, not in substitution for, the assistance given to the Allies by the great block of British tonnage already in their employment. The allocation of requisitioned tonnage had, however, one very important advantage over the employment of ships on Allied charter. Little or no effective control could be exercised by the British authorities over the employment of vessels chartered to Allied Governments or firms and exempted on that account from Admiralty requisition; but the requisitioned ships now allocated to Allied services remained under the direct control of the Transport Department, who were thus able to ensure their being used to the best possible advantage, and to bring effective pressure to bear for the purpose of avoiding undue delays in port or other interference with their economical employment.

Important as were the new services undertaken for the Allies, and greatly as they added both to the work of the Transport Department and the strain on British shipping, they fell short of the assistance originally asked for by France and Italy. Nevertheless, it soon became evident that they represented as much as could safely be granted. Even while the negotiations were in progress the available tonnage was reduced by further losses, and though the ratio of loss was still much below that reached in the black month of August 1915, the latest developments of the war at sea gave reason to anticipate an increase rather than a further diminution in the effectiveness of the submarine attack.

CHAPTER XVI

SUBMARINES, MINES, AND RAIDERS
JANUARY AND FEBRUARY 1916

DURING the first two months of 1916, attacks on merchantmen by enemy submarines were almost entirely confined to the Mediterranean. In that sea eleven British steamers were sunk, and the increasing boldness of the attack was shown by the fact that whereas casualties had hitherto been confined to the eastern half of the sea, or to the coasts of Tunis and Algeria, three vessels were sunk during February within a radius of some sixty miles from Marseilles. Although the transport routes were frequently varied and steamers on commercial voyages were ordered to practise the widest possible dispersal, it was evident that no part of the Mediterranean could be considered safe, and it was reasonable to suppose that, with the coming of summer, the intensity of the attack would be increased. On the other hand, the value of defensive armament was again conclusively proved, for on no fewer than ten occasions the assailant was driven off by gunfire. One vessel was rescued and six others owed their escape to speed. The losses of French, Italian, and neutral shipping were comparatively unimportant.

In British Home Waters the mine-laying submarines were very active. During February alone the loss of British tonnage due to mines amounted to 36,000 tons, a loss more than twice as great as had been suffered through this cause in any previous month of the war. Altogether seventeen British ships were sunk and four damaged during the two months, the most important victim being the P. & O. Liner *Maloja* of 12,431 tons, which was blown up off Dover on February 27th, with the loss of 122 lives. Several neutral vessels were also sunk or damaged, including the Dutch ss. *Rijndam*, of 12,527 tons, which struck a mine on January 18th, but succeeded in reaching Gravesend for repairs.

These mines, laid by mine-laying submarines, constituted a far more difficult problem than the original minefields in the North Sea. Moored in small groups off prominent seamarks and continually renewed, they imposed on the mine-sweeping service the necessity for incessant vigilance, in order to keep a clear passage along the southern and eastern coasts. It was evident that submarine minelayers were penetrating the barrage in the Straits of Dover, for ships were sunk not only off Dover, Folkestone, and Boulogne, but as far west as the Needles. The greatest number of casualties, however, was still reported from the Straits themselves and the approaches to the Thames, where shipping was thickly crowded and confined to narrow and clearly defined channels.

Four attacks by hostile aircraft were also recorded during the two months. On three occasions the bombs missed, but on February 1st the *Franz Fischer*, a detained German steamer employed in the coasting trade, was hit by bombs from a Zeppelin, and sunk off the Kentish Knock, with the loss of thirteen lives. This was the only success scored by hostile aircraft, out of nineteen attacks on British merchantmen, down to the end of February 1916, and the inhumanity of this form of attack was thrown into strong relief by its absolute ineffectiveness in the prevention of commerce.

Taking together ships sunk by submarines, mines, and aircraft, the loss of tonnage during January and February was much smaller than it had been in any two consecutive months since April 1915; but though this fact was in itself satisfactory, it afforded no great reason for complacency. The mine peril was evidently on the increase, and with the return of summer an intensification of the submarine campaign might be looked for in the Mediterranean, accompanied in all probability by a renewed outbreak off the British coasts. Moreover, disquieting intelligence had come in which showed that the immunity so long enjoyed by British shipping in more distant waters was liable to be roughly disturbed.

Since the internment of the KRONPRINZ WILHELM and PRINZ EITEL FRIEDRICH in April 1915, British shipping on the ocean trade routes had been free from attack. The danger area was confined to the waters round the British Isles and, in recent months, the Mediterranean. Once outside these areas, ships were immune from molestation.

There was, of course, always the possibility that some new raider might break out from the North Sea, or that one of the German steamers sheltering in neutral ports might succeed in putting to sea and obtaining an armament, and the Admiralty saw no reason to relax the precautions hitherto enforced, even on the most distant trade routes. In August 1915 the instructions to merchantmen underwent further revision, and in the new instructions the necessity for avoiding the normal tracks in mid-Atlantic, or in more distant seas, was emphasised as strongly as the precautions to be taken in Home Waters against submarine attack. So far as was known, however, no surface raider had put to sea for the purpose of an attack on the trade routes, since the internment of the KRONPRINZ WILHELM in April 1915.

The work of the British squadrons in distant waters was thus practically confined to the interception of contraband and the watch on German steamers in neutral ports. In these circumstances the Admiralty were able to bring back many of the cruisers on foreign stations for the purpose of reinforcing the Home and Mediterranean Fleets, but about a score of cruisers with a dozen armed merchant cruisers were in the Atlantic, in Eastern Seas, or on the West Coast of South America, keeping watch on the chief focal points, and the neutral ports in which enemy steamers were sheltering. The French still had a couple of cruisers in the West Indies, co-operating with the West Indies squadron, and a division of light cruisers and armed liners on the Moroccan Coast, while the Japanese Fleet undertook the patrol of the Pacific and the Far Eastern seas.

Throughout the latter part of 1915 the work of these squadrons was singularly uneventful. The German steamers abroad attempted no movement of importance, and the only sign of enemy activity was in the Far East, where the British and Japanese cruisers in Indian waters were busy from July onwards in the prevention of gun-running to Indian and Malay ports, as part of a German attempt to foment local insurrections.

So matters went on until February 1st, 1916, when the accustomed tale of submarine activities was diversified by news of a return to the old order, and it became known that a German surface raider was once more at large in the Atlantic. On that day the *Appam*, of the Elder Dempster Line put into Norfolk, U.S.A., under the German flag, and within a few hours it was disclosed that she had on board the crews of five British steamers, which had been captured and sunk on the Atlantic tracks, and that two other vessels had also been sunk or captured by the same raider.

From information given by the Master of the *Appam*, it appeared that the raider was a vessel of merchant type, heavily armed, but with her guns cleverly concealed, so that she could pass as a neutral merchantman when approaching her quarry or if sighted by a British cruiser. The details given were sufficient to enable the Admiralty to identify her as the *Pungo*, a 14½ knot steamer of 4,500 tons, built in 1914. It appeared, however, that the name MOEWE was borne on the capbands of some of the crew.

This news was at once sent out by the Admiralty to all officers concerned, and the British cruisers in the Atlantic were everywhere on the alert, but nothing more was heard of the raider until February 22nd, when the ss. *Westburn* put into Teneriffe with a prize crew on board, and landed the crews of seven more ships, including two previously reported by the *Appam*. From the masters and officers of these ships very full information was obtained, and as it appeared that the raider was now on her way back to Germany, the cruiser squadrons holding the entrance to the North Sea were keenly on the alert. On February 29th their vigilance was rewarded, but not by the capture of the MOEWE. Their prey was another disguised raider, the GREIF, which was endeavouring to break out into the Atlantic for a cruise against Allied commerce.[1] Of the MOEWE, nothing was seen, and it was subsequently ascertained that she had arrived at Wilhelmshaven on March 4th with the crews of two additional prizes on board.

Her cruise had been a profitable one.[2] Under the command of Commander Burggraf Graf Nikolaus zu Dohna-Schlodien, she put out towards the end of December 1915, when the rough weather and long nights gave special facilities for running the blockade, and passing North-about laid a minefield off the western entrance to the Pentland Firth, by which the battleship KING EDWARD VII and two merchant vessels were sunk.

[1] Another similar vessel was reported to have come out with the GREIF, but to have sighted British cruisers and turned back.
[2] The principal published authority for the MOEWE is, *The Two Cruises of the Raider "Möwe,"* by Korvetten-Kapitän Burggraf Graf Nikolaus zu Dohna-Schlodien, Gotha, 1916 and 1917.

She then ran for the Bay of Biscay, and under cover of night, laid another minefield off the mouth of the Gironde. This field also claimed its victims, three steamers, two French and one Spanish, and three or four French fishing craft being sunk during February and March.

After laying the Bay of Biscay minefield, the MOEWE passed into the Atlantic, keeping wide out from the coast, and from January 11th to 15th inclusive captured seven steamers, the last of which was the *Appam*, captured 135 miles E½N. from Madeira. Most of the prizes were homeward bound with valuable cargoes from Spain, Africa or South America, but two were outward bound colliers, and one of these the *Corbridge* was sent off to a rendezvous on the Brazilian coast. The other prizes with the exception of the *Appam* were sunk out of hand after removal of their crews. On January 16th the *Clan Mactavish*, homeward bound from New Zealand, was encountered. She was a defensively armed ship, and though she had nothing better than a single six-pounder given her for the purpose of resisting submarine attack, she pluckily opened fire. The contest, however, was too unequal, and she was speedily overpowered. After her crew had been removed, she too was sunk. Her loss during the engagement was seventeen killed, all of whom were Lascars.

Next day the *Appam* was sent off to Norfolk with the crews of all the sunken ships, except the *Clan Mactavish*, and the MOEWE went off to rejoin the *Corbridge*. On her way she captured and sank the *Edinburgh*, a sailing vessel homeward bound from Rangoon, but no other prizes were made until the rendezvous at the mouth of the Amazon was reached.

As Count zu Dohna-Schlodien intended to return before the close of winter increased the difficulties of eluding the patrols, he had no time to waste, and only 1,000 tons out of 4,000 or 5,000 in the *Corbridge* were transhipped before the collier was sunk and the MOEWE set out on her homeward voyage. As she came up the Atlantic tracks she captured three British steamers and one Belgian in the neighbourhood of Fernando Noronha and the St. Paul Rocks (February 6th–9th), but had a somewhat narrow escape from the GLASGOW, which was now hunting for her. All these prizes were sunk except the *Westburn*, which was sent off to Tenerife with the prisoners, including the crew of the *Clan Mactavish*. The master and two gunners of the Clan liner were, however, detained, together with the master and second officer of the *Westburn*.

A barren period succeeded to this batch of successes, for, to quote Graf zu Dohna-Schlodien, "the British system of warning and reporting works most admirably," and as the MOEWE came up the tracks west of the Cape Verdes and Canaries, she found them completely deserted. It was not till she was making a wide cast round the British Isles for the purpose of running the Northern blockade that two further prizes were made—the French steamer *Maroni* on February 22nd and the *Saxon Prince* on February 25th. As there was no further opportunity to send off prisoners, the crews of these vessels were taken to Germany in the raider. The passage through the North Sea cordon was an anxious one, but the MOEWE's luck held good, and, as already related, she reached Wilhelmshaven in safety at the beginning of March.

Including the *Westburn*, which was sunk by a boiler explosion on the day after she arrived at Tenerife, the MOEWE had accounted for fourteen steamers and one sailing vessel, with an aggregate tonnage of over 50,000. In addition, the *Appam* of 7,781 tons was interned at Norfolk. It was an aggravation of her success that all her prizes carried cargoes, many of them of great value, and on the whole she could claim fully to have equalled the exploits of the earlier Atlantic raiders. It is pleasant to add that her prisoners were, in general, well-treated, though the people in the *Westburn* came in for rather rough treatment at the hands of the commander of the prize crew. It was some consolation, too, that no fault could be found with the behaviour of the British masters. In no one instance were the confidential Admiralty instructions captured, and most of the prizes were made at a distance from the normal tracks which showed that those instructions were being faithfully observed. The fight put up by the *Clan Mactavish* was in every way creditable to her officers and crew, and plucky efforts to escape or to summon assistance by wireless were made by several of the other ships.

One result of the MOEWE's cruise was to call attention to the danger of other surface raiders passing into the Atlantic, and during February the Admiralty were busy working out a scheme for the use of colliers fitted with wireless, as decoy ships attached to groups of cruisers and armed merchant cruisers. The shortage of tonnage precluded extensive adoption of this system, and it never got beyond the experimental stage; but this was of the less importance as for many months no attempt was made to repeat the MOEWE's exploits, except by the ill-fated GREIF. Rich as the reward of success was seen to be—for the MOEWE had done as much damage during her two months' cruise, as all the German submarines in the Mediterranean had accomplished during the same period—the Germans preferred for the time being to concentrate everything on the submarine attack.

They had indeed, considerable reason to be satisfied with the results of the submarine campaign. Although the losses inflicted during the winter of 1915-6 were smaller than those which had been suffered by British shipping in the previous summer, they were far too heavy to be regarded with indifference at a time when large new demands were being made on a supply of tonnage already manifestly insufficient. But this was not all. The effect of the Mediterranean losses went beyond the actual destruction of tonnage, and for the first time in the war British shipping was about to abandon, partially, one of the leading trade routes, as a result of hostile operations.

The concentration of the attack in the Mediterranean since September 1915 had, indeed, afforded a welcome respite to shipping on the Atlantic tracks; but against this must be placed the fact that the Mediterranean losses fell entirely on ocean-going steamers. Down to the end of February 1916 the total number of British merchantmen sunk by submarines within the Straits was 63, and the average size of these vessels was 4,164 tons, as against an average of 3,042 tons for 179 vessels sunk by submarines in other areas since the beginning of the war. Of those 179 vessels, 125 were steamers of 1,600 tons gross and above, the remaining 54—nearly one-third—were smaller steamers and sailing vessels. The Mediterranean victims were all steamers of the larger class.

Moreover, it must be remembered that, while the losses in the South Western Approach and English Channel were distributed among the shipping of all the ocean routes, those in the Mediterranean fell, apart from a few ships in the service of the Admiralty or War Office, exclusively on the traffic of the Mediterranean itself and the Oriental Route. Thus, while the total losses of British shipping diminished, the ratio of loss in the trades immediately concerned was high, and the difficulty of trade defence in the Mediterranean was so great that the Admiralty saw no hope of keeping the attack permanently in check. It was impossible to spare direct escort except for transports, oil-tankers, and other vessels of special naval or military importance, and the local conditions prevented the adoption of other methods of defence.

In these circumstances the Admiralty decided that the target exposed to attack in the Mediterranean must be reduced. British shipping engaged in the traffic of the Mediterranean itself could not be greatly reduced, for most of it served essential Allied interests. Coal and grain to Italy and the South of France, coal to the Mediterranean depôts, cotton from Egypt, ore from Algeria and Spanish ports within the Straits, must go forward whatever the risks. But part at least of the through traffic could be diverted to the route round the Cape of Good Hope, and on March 7th instructions were sent to the War Risks Associations that until further notice, no vessel trading between ports in the United Kingdom or Atlantic ports in Europe or America and ports east of 100° E. should, on a voyage begun on or after March 15th, enter the Mediterranean, unless such vessel should be sailing in an established service having regular ports of loading or discharge in the Mediterranean itself. For the purpose of these instructions a voyage was deemed to be begun at the time when the loading of cargo commenced.

The effect of these instructions was to divert to the Cape Route practically the whole of the traffic to and from Australia and the Far East, including the sugar ships from Java. The Indian trade was still allowed to sail viâ Suez, partly because the loss of carrying power consequent on diversion would have been relatively greater than on the longer voyages, and partly because it was doubtful whether the coaling stations on the Cape Route were sufficiently well stocked to coal the Indian traffic in addition to the Far Eastern and Australian. The War Risks Associations were warned, however, that further diversion might become necessary, and that the coaling stations were being developed with a view to this possibility.

The target exposed to attack in the Mediterranean was thus reduced, but with an appreciable loss of carrying power, for the new route added considerably to the length of the voyage for ships engaged in the Australian and Far Eastern Trades. Necessary as the step had become, it added another factor to those producing the tonnage deficit by which the Shipping Control Committee were faced in their task of allocation.

CHAPTER XVII

EFFORTS TO ADJUST THE BALANCE, APRIL–MAY 1916—
RESTRICTION OF SUBMARINE WARFARE

AGAINST the heavy losses suffered during the opening months of 1916 there was little to be put, for the tonnage output for the March quarter showed no improvement on that for the preceding three months, and the great majority of the neutrals chartered by Furness, Withy & Co. had been assigned to the Allies. Moreover, the full effect of the great increase in requisitioning during the autumn and winter months was now making itself felt. During the three months January to March inclusive the entrances of British ships with cargoes fell short by 1,038,000 tons of the total for the corresponding period of 1915, a reduction of nearly 18 per cent. As compared with the last corresponding period of peace the percentage decrease was over 35.

While the tonnage available for the carriage of British imports was thus diminishing, the demands for some of the most essential imports were increased, owing to the great expansion in the requirements of the war industries. At the beginning of March the Ministry of Munitions presented to the Shipping Control Committee a programme of their requirements for the three months April, May, June. In this programme the Ministry estimated their demand for iron ore from Spain, the Mediterranean, and Scandinavia at not less than 600,000 tons a month, a figure exceeding the entire average monthly import of the three years before the war. Of shell steel, shells, and component parts, principally from the United States, they required 163,000 tons a month; of copper, small arms ammunition, spelter, lead, etc., 12,000 tons. From Spain they required 75,000 tons of pyrites monthly; from Chile about 27,000 tons of nitrate. For the production of glycerine and other explosive materials they required oil seeds, palm kernels, and palm oil from West Africa, soya beans from Korea, copra from the Pacific, linseed from India and South

America, to a total of 50,000 tons a month. The whole programme gave a monthly total of nearly 1,000,000 tons.

In the import of iron ore, neutral shipping and steamers on commercial charter played an important part, as well as temporarily released vessels. For most of the other items of the programme, requisitioned tonnage or requisitioned space had to be provided. Already 20 per cent. of the space in the Atlantic liners was under requisition for munitions purposes, and in some ships as much as 30 per cent. had been taken. As, under the agreement with the Requisitioning (Carriage of Foodstuffs) Committee, an average of 50 per cent. of the deadweight capacity of these liners was allocated to wheat, only 20 to 30 per cent. remained available for the carriage of general cargo; but even so, it had become a question whether it was not necessary to impose still further restrictions. The exports of manufactured goods from the United States to the United Kingdom had been steadily rising since the first set-back administered by the outbreak of war, and included large quantities of goods which could not possibly be described as essential in time of war. In particular, the Ministry of Munitions called attention to the heavy imports of automobile parts for private use. These were specially objectionable, since the assembly of the cars diverted skilled labour from munitions work.

The effects of this great volume of non-essential imports was two-fold. It occupied space which might be filled by essential imports such as munitions and machine tools for the equipment of munitions factories. In conjunction with the munitions traffic it caused serious congestion of the North American ports and railways. At New York 20,000 tons of munitions had accumulated, at Philadelphia 7,000, and at Boston, Baltimore, and other ports there were similar accumulations. Owing to the inability of the Ministry's agents to ship goods on their arrival, the railways were refusing to accept delivery from the manufacturers, and the whole traffic was becoming disorganised.

For these reasons the Ministry urged the prohibition of non-essential imports, and in this suggestion the Shipping Control Committee fully concurred. It was, indeed, one which they had already put forward; but since they made the proposal the tonnage situation had changed for the worse, and during March they decided that, whatever were done with regard to import restriction, a definite limit must be placed on the assistance given to the Allies. The obligations already undertaken were sufficiently heavy. For the steel and oat service it had been necessary to set aside permanently some 50 to 60 ocean-going vessels, in addition to which 15 others were to perform single voyages. The average allocation of wheat ships to Italy alone was 17 or 18 voyages a month, equivalent to the continuous employment of 35 steamers. The new coal commitments to France and Italy called for the despatch of some 24 colliers monthly, in addition to those already allocated for the supply of the French State railways. Moreover, the export season to the White Sea would soon begin, and it was evident that some provision for the necessities of Russia would have to be made.

All these considerations were reviewed by the Shipping Control Committee in a Report to the Prime Minister dated March 19th. From figures supplied by the Intelligence Section of the Transport Department, it appeared that out of 1,574 ocean-going steamers available for the trade of the United Kingdom on January 29th,[1] 261 had since been withdrawn by war losses or requisitioning, and the Department had been warned that further vessels for Naval and Military service would be required in the near future.

Even assuming that no further tonnage was allocated to the Allies, the Committee calculated the tonnage deficiency on the basis of the 1915 imports at 2,700,000 tons gross, representing about 100 steamers in continuous employment. About half this deficit, however, would be wiped out if the decision to reduce imports by 4,000,000 tons were rigidly adhered to.

In these circumstances the Committee again urged that, for the purpose of preventing a further rise in freights, and still more, of preventing the crowding out of essential by non-essential cargoes, the Government should prohibit at least temporarily the import of all non-essential goods. Not only would this measure at once increase the space available for essential imports, but by allowing the ports and warehouses to be cleared both at home and in America,

[1] Including requisitioned and directed vessels carrying wheat and sugar, but excluding oilers, ships temporarily released, and ships trading abroad under licence.

it would enable the flow of traffic to resume its normal carrying power.

In the meantime the Committee considered that, in view of the serious deficit already existing, the French and Italian Governments should be informed that no further British tonnage could be allotted to them, and that they must fulfil their requirements with the tonnage already in their service, their own shipping, and any neutral vessels that could be chartered for them in the open market.

The demands of Russia stood on a different footing. The requirements of the Russian Armies could not possibly be met by the employment of Russian shipping, and the White Sea voyage was so unfavourably regarded by shipowners that an adequate supply of neutral tonnage would be difficult to procure.

The Russian programme for 1916 contemplated an import of about 8,000,000 tons of coal, munitions, and Government stores from Great Britain, France, and the United States, and of this the Shipping Control Committee calculated that the Russian Government, who stated that they were requisitioning their entire mercantile marine, could lift about one third. For the remainder the Committee were instructed by the Government to provide tonnage. The Russian Government had undertaken the transport of all material shipped from the United States by the Vladivostok route; but the greater part of the cargoes to the White Sea from North American Atlantic ports, as well as from France and the United Kingdom, had still to be arranged.

For the French exports, the Hudson Bay Co. had again arranged a White Sea service with ships chartered from Russian, French, British, and neutral owners. These ships were, as before, to carry war material from France to Archangel and return to France with cargoes of wheat and wood-alcohol, used in the manufacture of munitions, on French Government account. The service required, however, to be supplemented by British requisitioned vessels, and the whole of the coal and war material shipped from the United Kingdom had also to be provided for by requisitioned shipping or by chartered neutrals, with the exception of such portion as the Russians themselves could lift. For munitions from the United States to Archangel further British tonnage was required to supplement available Russian and neutral shipping.

In order to centralise the freight arrangements it was agreed that all neutral tonnage required should be chartered by the Board of Trade through Messrs. Furness, Withy & Co.; but the relief to be obtained in this way was comparatively small. After making all allowance for the employment of Russian, French, and neutral shipping, the greater part of the White Sea programme had still to be carried out by British vessels. Having fully considered the available resources, the Shipping Control Committee accordingly decided to allocate about 100 steamers to the service of the Russian Government, and this decision they communicated to the Prime Minister on March 31st. At the same time they stated definitely that no further tonnage could be spared for the service of either France or Italy, a decision in which they were confirmed by the Ship Licensing Committee who had the employment of British shipping constantly under review.

Even on this basis the Shipping Control Committee estimated that there would be a shortage of about 400 ocean-going steamers, after allowing for the restriction of imports by 4,000,000 tons. They urged, therefore, that 200 steamers should be withdrawn from Naval and Military Service, and that imports should be further restricted to the extent of 8,400,000 tons, the equivalent of another 200 vessels.

All these recommendations were taken into consideration during April by the British Government. On the question of restriction of imports they consulted the Board of Trade, who reported that, for the present, no further step in this direction was possible without undue dislocation of trade and the possibility of friction with the Oversea Dominions and the Governments of Allied and neutral States whence the imports it was proposed to restrict were drawn. On the other hand, the Government definitely approved the recommendation for the withdrawal of 200 steamers from naval and military employment, and instructed the Admiralty and War Office to make arrangements, so far as possible, for carrying out this programme. This, in its entirety, proved to be impracticable. The pressure of strategical requirements, especially those arising from the Salonika Expedition and the presence of a large fleet in the Mediterranean, was too great to permit of such a sweeping reduction. Nevertheless, considerable economies were effected. The increase in requisitioning of which the

Shipping Control Committee had been warned was stopped; some ships were released or replaced by others of smaller size, and by one means or another the tonnage in naval and military employment was gradually but appreciably reduced. What was even more important, the decision to restrict the allocation of tonnage to the Allies to ships already in their service, was confirmed by the Government and communicated by them to France and Italy.

So far as requisitioned tonnage was concerned, the responsibility for giving effect to this decision rested on the Transport Department, but as regards vessels chartered either by the Allied Governments or by private importers in France or Italy, the machinery of control was in the hands of the Ship Licensing Committee. Accordingly, as the result of an interview with the President of the Board of Trade, the Committee wrote to the Commission Internationale de Ravitaillement, stating that no new licences for voyages to France or Italy could be granted except in substitution for existing licences. The Committee suggested, therefore, that the French and Italian Governments should themselves decide what cargoes were most urgently needed, so that the tonnage available for Allied service might be utilised to the best advantage. If this were done, the Committee were ready to agree that no licence for a voyage charter to a French or Italian port should in future be granted, unless the application were supported by a representative of the Government concerned.

The datum line adopted was the tonnage actually in the service of France and Italy on May 1st, and within two or three weeks of that date the necessary arrangements for giving effect to the decision were fully worked out between the British and Allied Governments. In France the applications for licences were centralised in the Comité Maritime des Transports, through their representative in London, M. de Berlhe. In order to facilitate the task of the Comité Maritime, the Licensing Committee agreed to furnish M. de Berlhe month by month with a list of the British ships which were expected to complete licensed voyages to France during that month, thus giving the number of new licences which could be granted. They also agreed to furnish him immediately with particulars of every application received; to refuse all licences which he considered unnecessary; and, in the absence of any preponderating reason to the contrary, such as grave congestion of the discharging port, to comply with all applications approved by him up to the limit of the number of licences which could be granted during the month in question.

As between Great Britain and France no question of importance arose during the course of the negotiations; but the Italian Government were seriously alarmed at the idea of any restriction being placed on coal tonnage, and strove hard to obtain the exclusion of colliers from the new arrangements. The position of Italy with regard to fuel was, indeed, deserving of the most sympathetic consideration. Producing practically no fuel herself, she was absolutely dependent on imports for the means of maintaining her transport services and industries. But the assistance which Great Britain could give in the supply of fuel was limited by the shipping resources available. To exclude coal, the bulkiest export, from the decision as to tonnage would be to defeat the whole object of that decision, and, however reluctantly, the request had to be refused. The Licensing Committee readily undertook, however, to give every possible consideration to the representations of the Italian Government as to the allocation of the licences it was possible to grant, and to give a general priority to ships whose regular business it was to take out coal to Italy and return with ore from Spain.

While showing every possible consideration for Allied interests in carrying out the Government's decision, the Licensing Committee were unable to hold out any prospect of that decision being reversed or modified. What had already been granted was more than could well be spared if British imports were to be maintained at or near the level of 1915.

Excluding oilers and prizes, the total number of British steamers of 1,600 tons gross and over, as shown by a Transport Department Return of May 25th, was 3,572: with an aggregate gross tonnage of 15,779,000.[1] Of these, 1,253 were on full requisition for the service of the Navy, Army, Dominions, and Allies, or under notice for such service. Those " black-listed " for the Allies or Dominions— that is to say, exempted from requisition at the request of Allied or Dominion Governments—numbered 828. To

[1] The Transport Department Returns included some vessels on Colonial Register.

these must be added about eighty ships carrying wheat to Allied ports on Ross T. Smythe charters or by direction of the Carriage of Foodstuffs Committee.¹ In all, about 1,660 ships aggregating 7,460,000 tons gross were definitely withdrawn from the trade of the United Kingdom. To the Allies alone, about 12 per cent. of British ocean-going tonnage had been allocated, and the commitments undertaken went even beyond this figure, since loading for the Russian summer programme was only just beginning.²

Of the remaining ships about 400 were trading under licence between foreign ports, many of them in the interests of the Allies. There were thus available for the import services of the United Kingdom just over 1,500 steamers. Of these, 60 were requisitioned ships carrying sugar for the Sugar Commission, 174 were temporarily released vessels, and 98 were carrying wheat to the United Kingdom under direction of the Foodstuffs Committee. The remainder were "free" ships, trading to and from the United Kingdom under supervision of the Licensing Committee. In all, the tonnage available for the trade of the United Kingdom was about 7,000,000 gross, or 44 per cent. of the whole, as against over 9,000,000 tons normally employed in that trade.³

It was of the utmost importance that, if possible, the tonnage employed in the trade of the United Kingdom should be increased, and towards the end of March the Admiralty put forward a proposal for withdrawing all ships still employed on voyages between neutral ports. This proposal was rejected by the Shipping Control Committee, who were supported in their refusal by the Director of Transports. The number of ships affected was comparatively small, and many of them were running on long time-charters which could not be broken without some friction, especially with the United States. Moreover, several of the ships were engaged in trades, such as the carriage of nitrate from Chile to the United States for use in the manufacture of munitions, which were directly

---

¹ Of these 80 ships 50 were directed by the Carriage of Foodstuffs Committee. The other 30 were mostly on Ross T. Smythe charter, with French or Italian options, but some of them may have brought their cargoes to the United Kingdom.

² There were also about 80 steamers *under* 1,600 tons gross black-listed for the Allies.

³ A few of the ships shown as on naval or military employment were carrying nitrate or other Government cargoes on their return voyage.

serviceable to the Allies. Apart from this, any general withdrawal of these vessels would almost certainly lead to their replacement by neutral tonnage at present in Allied service, and important trade and exchange interests would thus be sacrificed without obtaining any equivalent advantage. The Transport Department were endeavouring to obtain a few ships whose charters were approaching expiration, but no considerable addition to the available tonnage could be looked for from this source.

But this was not the worst. The available tonnage was still being reduced, week by week, through war losses. The Germans had now a greater number of ocean-going submarines available, and the coastal submarines and submarine mine-layers of the Flanders Flotilla were growing in boldness and efficiency. With the coming of the spring, the attack was no longer confined to the Mediterranean. Out of 26 vessels torpedoed or captured and destroyed during March, 3 only were sunk in that sea; the remainder were attacked in British Home Waters. The greatest number of casualties occurred in the South Western Approach, where 9 vessels were sunk out of 16 attacked, but two ships were destroyed off the west coast of Ireland, and both submarine mine-layers and ordinary submarines penetrated the English Channel and the approaches to the Thames. The total destruction of British shipping by mine and submarine amounted to 99,000 tons, nor did either Allied or neutral shipping escape without heavy loss. Among the neutral losses by far the most important was the great Dutch liner *Tubantia*, which was torpedoed in the North Sea on March 16th, while outward bound from Amsterdam for Buenos Aires. A nearly new steamer of 13,911 tons belonging to the Royal Holland Lloyd, she was the largest neutral ship which fell a victim to the submarine during the whole course of the war. Two days later the *Palembang*, a Rotterdam Lloyd liner of 6,674 tons, outward bound for Java viâ London, was torpedoed off the Galloper Buoy, and the sinking of these two big vessels brought up the total destruction of neutral tonnage during March to 43,000 tons, the highest point as yet reached.

Heavy as were the losses of British shipping in March, they were heavier still in April, and the Shipping Control Committee saw, with alarm, that the deficit on which they had calculated was being daily increased. From March 19th, when they presented their Memorandum to the

Prime Minister, to April 11th 30 ocean-going British steamers, to say nothing of smaller vessels, had been sunk by war causes; and in view of the approach of finer weather and the greater radius of the latest German submarines, they saw no reason to hope for any reduction in the rates of destruction. In these circumstances they again urged strongly the necessity of accelerating merchant shipbuilding. They pointed out that in addition to the vessels under construction a large number were already contracted for but not yet laid down, and still further orders were waiting to be placed as soon as slips became vacant. It was not a paucity of orders that was delaying additions to the mercantile marine, but the lack of labour, material, and facilities. They proposed, therefore, that a certain number of those shipbuilding yards and marine engineering works best suited for mercantile and least suited for Admiralty construction, should be definitely set apart for the building of merchantmen, and that steps should be taken to provide such yards with the necessary labour and material.

All through April the tale of losses continued. Shipping in the English Channel was comparatively immune, but there were several casualties, both by mine and torpedo, in the North Sea and the Thames Approaches, 9 ships were sunk in the Mediterranean, and about a score in the South Western Approach. The defensive measures in that area prevented the enemy from operating successfully close inland or from penetrating the St. George's Channel and Irish Sea, but the new German submarines were able to carry on their work of destruction far out into the Atlantic, and the radius of the danger area extended from 100 to 150 miles from the Fastnet on the north and Ushant on the south.

In all, 37 British ships were sunk by submarines during the month of April, and 6 by mines. The total tonnage destroyed amounted to over 140,000, and the loss of life to 131. No such loss of tonnage had been suffered since August 1915, and the record of that month was very closely approached. Allied shipping escaped more lightly, but neutral losses were again heavy, and the tonnage under all flags sunk by mine and submarine amounted to over 190,000 tons, the heaviest reduction of the world's mercantile shipping which had yet taken place during any month of the war.

The zeal of the German submarine commanders had,

however, carried them too far. Among the ships attacked during this phase of the campaign was the French cross-channel steamer *Sussex*, torpedoed without warning on March 24th. Although the *Sussex* did not sink, and ultimately succeeded in reaching Boulogne, the loss of life was heavy, and among those who perished were a number of American citizens. The result was a renewed outburst of indignation in the United States, which found vent in a strong note despatched to the German Government on April 18th, protesting against the inhumanity of the submarine campaign, and especially against the destruction without warning of passenger vessels. The American Government went so far as to threaten to break off diplomatic relations with Germany should their protest be disregarded, and, though naval and military opinion in Germany was strongly opposed to any restriction on the submarine campaign, the German Government were too conscious of the possible consequences of American belligerency to take the risk. They accordingly issued orders that the submarine attack on commerce was to be conducted henceforth in strict conformity with the Prize Court rules, which entailed visit and search and the removal of passengers and crew as a preliminary to the destruction of the ship.

The effect of these instructions was greatly to reduce the effective activity of the German submarines in Home Waters. It is true that, in opposition to the British contention, they interpreted the obligation to provide for the safety of the crew as fulfilled by allowing time for them to leave in their own boats; but, even so, an attack on commerce conducted under Prize Court rules involved spending too much time on the surface to be safely undertaken in waters constantly searched by the British patrols. Even during March and April many vessels encountered far out from land had been captured before destruction; but the effectiveness of the attack depended on the ability of the submarine to use a torpedo without warning, if the vicinity of a patrol vessel was suspected. In these circumstances Admiral Scheer considered that a continuance of the attack in British waters would involve heavy risks for no corresponding gain. He accordingly recalled all submarines operating in those seas, leaving the attack to be continued only in the Mediterranean, where the risk was appreciably less.

During the first few days of May a few ships were sunk in the Atlantic or at the western entrance to the Channel by submarines which had not yet received their notice of recall; but with this exception the submarine campaign during the summer of 1916 was practically confined to the Mediterranean. In that sea Allied shipping suffered heavily, but a large proportion of the victims were Italian sailing vessels, mostly of small size, whose loss could be more easily borne than that of steam tonnage. The destruction of British shipping was more serious, inasmuch as the losses fell mainly on steamers of some size; but the submarine attack in the Mediterranean was kept in check by the progress which had now been made in the armament of merchantmen. Out of 9 defensively armed vessels attacked during May in the Bay of Biscay and Mediterranean, 8 escaped, 7 of them by gunfire. In the following month 11 were attacked, all in the Mediterranean, and again only 1 was sunk.

Thus, thanks in part to the intervention of the United States, and in part to the progress made in the provision of defensive armament, the submarine campaign had, for the moment, received a decided check. The total loss of British tonnage in May was rather over 64,000 tons, less than half the April total, and in June it dwindled to 37,000 tons, the lowest figure recorded since August 1915.

Even so, the cumulative effect of the long-continued havoc was sufficiently serious. Since January 1st, 1916, nearly half a million tons of British shipping had been destroyed, two and a half times the shipbuilding output for the same period. Coupled with the drain of requisitioning for naval and military purposes or the service of the Allies, this was no light matter, and the effect of the double strain was clearly reflected in the trade returns. Month by month the entrances of British shipping showed a heavy decrease, not only on the normal volume of peace time traffic, but on the figures for 1915. If the volume of imports had not been correspondingly reduced it was mainly because the entrances under foreign flags were comparatively well maintained.

CHAPTER XVIII

NEUTRAL SHIPPING IN BRITISH TRADE TO THE SUMMER OF 1916

DURING the first eighteen months of the war nearly one-third of the tonnage entered with cargoes at British ports flew a foreign flag. In tonnage cleared the proportion was equally high, and though British ships carried, on the average, rather heavier cargoes, it may safely be assumed that between one quarter and one-third of the whole foreign trade of the United Kingdom was carried in foreign ships.

Of this foreign shipping the greater part belonged to neutral shipowners. From Allied shipping little assistance was received, except in the carriage of British exports to the Allied countries themselves. Many French and Italian steamers came to British ports to load coal or other cargoes, but the majority of these ships arrived in ballast, partly in order to secure a quicker turn-round, and partly because there was no equivalent volume of imports to be brought from those countries, and the shortage of tonnage was too great to allow the ships to be used for intermediate voyages in the general trade. Many Belgian steamers were now running from British ports,[1] and many of such Russian steamers as were not shut up in the Baltic and Black Sea carried cargoes in the general trade to and from the United Kingdom during the months when the White Sea was closed by ice; but neither Belgian nor the available Russian shipping was of sufficient extent to give much assistance to British trade. Japanese shipowners, too, found profitable employment for the greater part of their tonnage in the trade of the Pacific and Far East, and only the big liners running direct between Great Britain and Japan, participated in the carriage of British imports and exports. French, Italian, Belgian, Russian, and Japanese shipping together accounted for only 16 per cent. of the

[1] The others were employed for France or Italy or for the Belgian Relief Commission.

foreign tonnage entered, and 20 per cent. of the foreign tonnage cleared at British ports during the calendar year 1915.

Far more important were the services of neutral shipping, but the character of the service rendered varied greatly as between the various neutral flags. American shipping took practically no part in the trade of the United Kingdom except in the direct traffic between Great Britain and the United States, and even there, provided in 1915, less than 6 per cent. of the tonnage employed. Spanish tonnage, too, was mainly confined to the direct trade between Great Britain and Spain, though it gave some little assistance in the carriage of coal to France and Italy, and a few ships brought cargoes from the United States and Argentina, or carried British exports to South and Central America. Dutch shipping was somewhat less confined in its operations. Well over half the tonnage entered and cleared during 1915 was engaged in the direct traffic between Great Britain and the Netherlands, but the big liners running to North America and the Dutch East Indies were of considerable service to British trade, and there was a certain amount of Dutch tonnage on the Plate tracks, taking out coal and returning with wheat or maize.

It was, however, only the Greek and Scandinavian shipowners who had any large block of tramp tonnage to place on the freight markets for general service. Greek shipping was almost entirely of this class, and responded readily to the pull of freights on any route, since only a small proportion of the whole could find employment in Greek commerce. Steamers under the Greek flag carried British imports and exports from and to many countries in 1915; but it was in the maintenance of the Italian coal supply that they were most prominent, and nearly a quarter of the tonnage cleared for Italy was Greek. It was this, above all, which rendered the partial withdrawal of Greek shipping at the beginning of 1916 so serious a matter.

Still more important were the services of Scandinavian, especially of Norwegian, shipping. In view of the valuable supplies of foodstuffs and raw material drawn from Scandinavia, it was no small matter that the bulk of the traffic on the North Sea tracks was carried in Scandinavian bottoms; but the shipowners of the three countries were far from restricting their activities to this trade. Both the Swedish and Danish flags were to be found on many routes, and Danish ships in particular were active in the trade with France, Spain, Portugal, and the Mediterranean, especially in the export of coal. The assistance derived from Norwegian tonnage was, however, on a much larger scale, for Norway had a greater amount of tramp tonnage to place on the freight markets than any other country except Great Britain herself.

In almost every important branch of British commerce, except that with Australia and the East, Norwegian shipping took an active part; but it was in the French coal trade that the greatest number of ships found employment. The urgent needs of France for coal, and the requisitioning of so many British colliers for naval service, combined to attract into this trade a large proportion of the Norwegian shipping thrown out of employment by the diminution of the general continental traffic. So great was the demand, and so ready were the Norwegian shipowners to meet it, that the tonnage under the Norwegian flag cleared with cargoes for French ports went up from 740,000 tons net in 1913 to 2,577,000 in 1915—a quarter of the whole tonnage cleared for France.

It was mainly due to the prominence of Scandinavian shipping in the French coal trade,[1] and to the heavy coal shipments to the Scandinavian countries themselves, that Norwegian, Danish, and Swedish ships accounted together for no less than 25 per cent. of the total tonnage cleared at British ports in the course of the year. In the import traffic Swedish vessels were less active, except in the carriage of cargoes from their own country; but more than half the Danish and Norwegian tonnage entered came from other countries. In all, 18 per cent. of the total entrances from all countries were under the Scandinavian flags.

Thus, both in the import trade of the United Kingdom and in the carriage of British exports, especially to the Allies, neutral tonnage played an invaluable part. As British shipping was more and more depleted by losses or requisitioning, this dependence on neutral shipping increased, and it became a matter of the utmost importance to increase the neutral tonnage available for the service of Great Britain and her Allies, or at least to prevent that

---

[1] The total Scandinavian clearances to France amounted to 3,050,000 tons—30 per cent. of the whole.

tonnage from being attracted into other trades by the rise in freights due to the withdrawal of British steamers from traffic between foreign ports. This could, of course, be done by out-bidding all competitors; but, as freights rose higher and higher, this simple solution of the difficulty became exceedingly costly, while, as the risks of navigation increased in the waters round the British Isles, many neutrals came to have a preference for other trades, which it required no small inducement to overcome.

One way of meeting the difficulty was found in the system of centralised chartering for Allied services through Messrs. Furness, Withy & Co., adopted at the beginning of 1916; but, in order to secure the requisite tonnage, pressure was at times necessary, as well as inducement. We have already seen that, so early as the summer of 1915, the Bunker Regulations were used as a lever to obtain agreements with neutral lines, providing not only for their abstention from enemy trade, but for the allocation of a definite proportion of the cargo space on their vessels to the service of the Allies, and that from the first it was a general principle that neutral vessels not on the White List should be required to bring cargo, or promise to return with cargo to a British or Allied port as a condition of receiving bunkers in the United Kingdom. Even Black-Listed vessels could sometimes obtain bunkers in the United Kingdom by bringing a cargo of some essential commodity, and it was possible for a Black-Listed owner to obtain bunkers and repair facilities for his vessels by time-chartering them to British or approved neutral firms to be run in approved trades, or by signing the bunker conditions and agreeing to run the whole of his fleet in approved trades—by which was meant, of course, the carriage of cargoes in the interests of Great Britain or her Allies.

As tonnage became scarcer, and the demands for coal by the Allies, the Admiralty, and the British war industries more and more insistent, it became a question how far bunkers could be supplied, even to White List vessels, except in return for some direct service to Allied trade, and during December 1915 licences for the bunkering of White List ships were occasionally made subject to a stipulation that the ship should, if possible, carry cargo both ways. This regulation was not, however, generally applied to White List vessels. At the end of the month the Port and Transit Executive Committee advised that caution should be used in forcing ships to return with cargoes, partly on account of the existing congestion at British and Allied ports, and partly for fear of driving neutrals away from British ports altogether. There were, indeed, many protests from White List owners during January 1916 that they were not receiving the promised equality of treatment with British ships, and with the object of removing any legitimate ground of complaint, British shipowners were circularised on January 28th to use every possible care to avoid ballast voyages.

From stipulating for a return voyage with cargo to a British or Allied port, it was only a step to stipulating for a return with cargo of a particular nature, and, as regards non-White List vessels, this step also was taken during December 1915. The supply of pit-props from the South of France, Spain, and Portugal was of great importance in view of the cutting off of the Russian exports; but the trade was exceedingly unpopular with shipowners, and tonnage was difficult to obtain. It was accordingly stipulated that all non-White List vessels receiving bunkers for a voyage with coal to French Bay, North Spanish, or Portuguese ports must return with cargoes from thence unless good cause could be shown to the contrary.

Although primarily intended to provide tonnage for the import of pit-props, it was hoped that this regulation would have some effect also on the Spanish ore trade, for which tonnage was exceedingly short. During the first six months of the war the demand for iron ore fell away very considerably, owing to the diminution in the exports of iron and steel; but this slackening in the commercial demand was speedily replaced by the requirements of the munition factories, and during the latter part of 1915 the imports rose very nearly to the normal level.

The ore trade, however, was not popular with shipowners. The freights, though high, were less than could be earned elsewhere, and the conditions of the trade were unsatisfactory. Congestion at the ore ports, especially Glasgow and Barrow, led to serious detention of vessels, and during the winter months the delays at the loading ports were still worse. Many of the Northern Spanish and Mediterranean ports were of the most primitive character, ill-equipped and providing very insufficient shelter. In heavy weather, loading could be carried on only for a few days at a time, and the risk to ships was appreciable. Under ordinary conditions many of the Spanish and North African ports were avoided by shipping during the winter months, but it so happened that the mines served by some of those ports produced special qualities of ore having an exceptionally high value for munitions purposes, and it was of the utmost importance that a regular supply should be obtainable. We have already seen that, from an early date, the system of temporary release was applied by the Advisory Committee to drive British tonnage into the ore trade, and that the Ship Licensing Committee also co-operated for this purpose. Nevertheless, the shortage of tonnage in the ore trade had become acute by the beginning of 1916. Tonnage for some of the worst loading ports was practically unprocurable except under pressure by the Transport Department, and there was a grave danger of important munition works in Lancashire and Scotland being obliged to close down a number of their furnaces for lack of the necessary supplies.

The position was complicated by the increasing congestion of the ore ports at home. In order to avoid expensive delays to temporarily released transports, the Admiralty introduced a new form of charter which allowed a shorter time for discharge and imposed heavy demurrage rates on the consignee in the event of detention. The result was that importers, who were quite unable in the existing condition of the ports to take delivery in the stipulated time, were put to heavy expenses and restricted their chartering in consequence. This difficulty was partially met by the exertions of the Port and Transmit Committee, who, in February 1916, persuaded the Scottish railway companies to agree to the pooling of railway trucks, and secured both at Glasgow and Barrow the diversion of certain other traffic which had been impeding the discharge of ore. The new arrangements, however, did not immediately come into effect, and throughout the first three or four months of 1916 discharge continued to be very slow.

So grave was the shortage of ore that the question of bringing the whole supply in requisitioned tonnage was raised; but, as we have seen, the Port and Transit Committee advised caution with regard to this step, and neither the Transport Department nor the Ministry of Munitions were desirous that it should be taken. The neutral tonnage employed in the trade, chiefly Spanish and Scandinavian, was sufficiently important to cause hesitation in adopting any measure which might tend to drive it away, and it was doubtful, moreover, whether any great advantage would be gained by forcing a large amount of additional tonnage into the trade so long as the ports were unable to take delivery and send the cargoes forward to the munition works with reasonable despatch.

It was, nevertheless, essential that the tonnage in the trade should be at least maintained, and it was hoped that the return cargo regulations and the inclusion of the coal and ore traffic in the list of " approved trades " for the purpose of releasing Black List and bunkering non-White List steamers would give some assistance in this direction. But meanwhile it became evident that the return cargo regulations were not working altogether well as regarded pit-props. The outward coal freights were so high, and the delays at the French pit-prop ports so lengthy, that Scandinavian shipowners found it more profitable for their ships to return in ballast in order to lift as many coal cargoes as possible in a given time. They accordingly resisted or evaded the regulations to the best of their power. Difficulties also arose with the Norwegian State Insurance Office, and the situation became decidedly delicate. The regulations were not wholly withdrawn; but, in order to render them more palatable, steps were taken to minimise the delays, by confining their application to ships loading coal at South Wales ports (the chief ports importing French props), and ensuring that only prompt cargoes should be lifted from the pit-prop ports.

Meanwhile, the Ministry of Munitions had become seriously alarmed as to the rise in ore freights. Under the financial system adopted in controlled establishments, every addition to freights reacted disproportionately on the actual cost of production, and in the endeavour to keep down costs the Ministry were driven to guarantee transport at a fixed rate of 17*s*. per ton. In accordance with this arrangement all c.i.f. ore contracts were converted into f.o.b., and the Ministry, in March 1916, appointed an Official Ore-broker—Mr. T. Woodward Owen —to fix the tonnage required. As any difference between the " parity rate," as it was called, of 17*s*., and the actual cost of transport fell on the Ministry, they were exceedingly anxious to keep down the freights which stood, at that time, as high as 26s. for the voyage from Bilbao to Middlesbrough.

The substitution of centralised chartering for independent competitive chartering by a large number of importing firms was expected to give good results in this direction; but a sudden fall in rates was in itself a danger. The ore trade was already sufficiently unpopular, and, with the addition of falling freights to its other disadvantages, there was a serious danger of ships being driven away into other employments. So far as British shipping was concerned, this could be met. Onerous as were the conditions of the ore trade, many owners were still willing to accept them for temporarily released ships, and when they refused, it was always in the power of the Transport Department to continue the vessel on requisition and fix her themselves with the Official Ore-broker; but neutrals presented a more delicate problem. Spanish tonnage was an important element in the trade, and Scandinavian entrances had increased appreciably during the last quarter of 1915, as a result of bunker pressure and rising freights.[1] The effect of any considerable withdrawal of neutral tonnage would be very serious, and it was necessary that, if freights were depressed, some measure should be adopted to keep neutrals in the trade. Accordingly, the appointment of the Official Ore-broker was accompanied by a regulation that all neutrals, even those on the White List, loading coal to South French or Bay ports, should return with approved cargo—that is to say, ore or pit-props.

Meanwhile, a new problem had arisen in the North Sea. On the Scandinavian tracks ballast voyages were a usual feature of the trade, for the exports to the Scandinavian countries consisted largely of coal, and considerably exceeded in volume the homeward cargoes. In 1913 over 45 per cent. of the tonnage entered from Norway, Sweden, and Denmark was in ballast, and in 1915, though the majority of imports from Scandinavia were well maintained, the proportion rose to 51 per cent. During the first three months of 1916 an actual shortage of tonnage for homewards cargo was experienced which forced up the freights

---

[1] The increase occurred prior to the return cargo regulations, but may have been influenced by the release, on conditions, of Black Listed vessels. Some Scandinavian vessels probably came in voluntarily to replace Greek and Italian steamers withdrawn from the trade.

on Narvik ore, timber, and other essential Scandinavian products to a very high level. It was accordingly decided that, as from April 1st, all ships, British, Allied, or neutral, loading a coal cargo for Norway, Sweden, Denmark, Iceland, or the Faroe Islands, should be required to return with cargo or produce a certificate from the Board of Trade that no return cargo was available. Owners of good standing on the White List were at first allowed to give an undertaking to return with cargo; other firms had to produce actual evidence of the fixture.

Against this regulation the Danish shipowners protested. Danish colliers were specially built for the coal trade, and were accustomed to run in that trade without regard to any other freight market. Moreover, the bacon and dairy produce which were Denmark's principal contribution to the supply of the United Kingdom were carried by the regular liners, and could not, in any event, be brought by returning colliers. Thus, the effect of the regulation was to impose on the Danish shipowner the obligation of going in ballast to a Swedish or Norwegian port, where bulk cargoes such as timber, ore, or wood-pulp could be obtained.

The force of these arguments could not be denied, but the Bunker Committee were unwilling to abandon the principle of enforcing service in return for bunkers or coal cargoes, and an alternative to the return voyage from Scandinavia was found in the French coal traffic. It was only for the most essential national services that British requisitioned tonnage could be spared to carry coal to France, and a limit had been set to the employment of both requisitioned and licensed tonnage by the Shipping Control Committee's decision of March 1916. French shipping itself could do little, for it was not strong in the tramp class, and the French tonnage available had been reduced both by losses and by the demand for tonnage in other essential services. Thus a great part of the work fell on neutral shipping, and it was of the utmost importance to keep as much neutral tonnage as possible in the trade. A number of Danish vessels clearing with coal for Denmark were accordingly allowed, from May 1916 onwards, to perform a voyage in the French coal trade, in substitution for the undertaking to return with cargo from Scandinavia, and of this alternative they eagerly availed themselves.

A further regulation having for its object to increase the tonnage available for the export of coal was made in the same month. Many Dutch and Scandinavian vessels were in the habit of proceeding in ballast to North America during the summer months, in order to return with grain cargoes, and on these vessels was now imposed the obligation of performing, in return for bunkers for the ballast voyage, an intermediate voyage with coal to Italy, French Bay, or Mediterranean ports, or to the Allied coal depôts at Gibraltar or Dakar.

It was not, however, only in the ore and coal trades that the Bunker Regulations were now being used to force neutral tonnage into the service of the Allies. Hitherto it was only at ports in the United Kingdom that the obligation to return with cargoes had been enforced; but in the existing conditions of coal and tonnage shortage, it was felt to be only fair that the grant of bunker facilities should be conditional upon the performance of some reciprocal service, and during April it was decided that non-White List vessels requiring bunkers at any port in the British Overseas Dominions, or at any bunker depôt under British control, should be required to make a voyage with cargo in one of the approved trades.

Thus, by the summer of 1916 the Bunker Regulations, originally introduced as a blockade measure, had developed into an elaborate system of restrictions and concessions, having for its primary object the increase of neutral tonnage in Allied service. These restrictions could hardly be popular with neutrals, and had, at first sight, the appearance of an arbitrary and high-handed attempt to control the employment of neutral tonnage. On the other hand, there could be no question of the right of the British Government to regulate, and if necessary to prohibit, the export of an article so essential to the conduct of the war as coal, and from this followed naturally the right to impose conditions in return for the issue of bunker and export licences. The restrictions were, nevertheless, strongly resented in some neutral countries, and in May 1916 the Swedish Government went so far as to bring in a bill (which became law in July), enabling the King to prohibit the time-chartering of Swedish vessels to foreigners, or the performance of voyages between foreign ports. This, however, did not prevent many Swedish shipowners from complying, formally or informally, with the Bunker Regulations. With Norwegian shipowners there was little trouble. The majority of them had no objection to complying with the White List conditions, and the Christiania Coal Importers' Association co-operated cordially in seeing that those conditions were observed. In fact, the Norwegian owners would have found it difficult to obtain employment for their great block of surplus tramp tonnage outside British and Allied trade, and had little reason to complain of the conditions imposed.

CHAPTER XIX

CLEARING THE PORTS, JANUARY–JULY, 1916

WHATEVER might be done to increase the amount either of British or of foreign tonnage available for the trade of the United Kingdom, the maximum carrying power of such tonnage could be developed only if ships were turned round promptly in the ports, and the shortage of tonnage during the first six months of 1916 would have been much more severely felt had not the port conditions been considerably improved by the activities of the Port and Transit Executive Committee. The work of this Committee was exceedingly laborious, for it was necessary for them to keep in constant touch with all the various Port Authorities, with the Government Departments and services requiring the use of port accommodation or facilities, with the shipowners, and with the importing interests, to watch carefully fluctuations of traffic, and to be ready to advise or decide at a moment's notice on innumerable questions affecting the loading, discharge, or distribution of goods. Among the problems presented to them there were, however, three of primary importance: the supply of labour, the supply of trucks, and the congestion of the quays and transit sheds.

As regards the supply of labour, a large measure of security had been attained by the inclusion of transport workers in the list of reserved occupations under the Derby scheme. These immunities continued to be granted under the First and Second Military Service Acts which came into operation respectively on February 10th and May 25th, 1916; but there were still frequent complaints that men essential to the transport services were being recruited, and strong protests on the subject were, from time to time, made by the Committee. At the same time they were careful to impress on the Port Authorities, and other employers of labour, that protection for essential workers could be justified only so long as every possible effort was made to release for military service men who could be spared, or for whom an adequate substitute could be found.

In May 1916 the Board of Trade established at the principal ports Port Labour Committees for dealing with the exemption of dock workers, in place of the Local Tribunals. This step showed an appreciation of the importance of dock labour, but the Committee strongly pressed on the Government their view that the onus of claiming exemption should not be placed on individual workers, but that active measures should be taken to impress on the men officially that they would serve their country better by remaining in their accustomed employment than by quitting it for the Army.

It was for this purpose that the Diversion of Shipping Committee had, early in 1915, proposed the issue of a badge to transport workers. But, whatever was done to retain men in their employment, the congestion of particular ports, at particular times, owing to the re-routing of trade and the fluctuations in traffic due to war conditions, could only be overcome by the creation of a mobile, centralised reserve of labour. This measure also had been proposed by the Diversion Committee, but not adopted. In Liverpool a Dockers' Battalion had been raised by Lord Derby during the autumn of 1915, and had done good work, but it was not by such means that the problem could be solved. What was wanted was a mobile reserve or pool of labour from which men could be directed to any port where temporary difficulties had arisen, and such a pool could not be provided from whole-time workers without keeping back an unduly large number of men from the armies, nor could a whole-time force be effectively employed without grave risk of friction with civilian labour.

For these reasons Colonel Hawkins had proposed to the Diversion Committee that a Transport Workers' Battalion should be formed of men enlisted for Home Defence only; that such men should continue their military training, and should be in all respects under military discipline; but that they should be liable to be called upon for work in any port where there was a proved deficiency of civilian labour, and should receive civilian rates of pay while so employed. The advantage of this scheme was twofold. On the one hand, it provided the necessary labour reserve without taking any men from those enlisted for service abroad, or permanently withdrawing men enlisted for home defence. On the other hand, it provided a pool of labour which could be used in any port, and since the men of the Battalion were to be employed in dock labour only when and so long as civilian labour was demonstrably insufficient, and were to receive civilian pay while so employed, it gave no grounds for suspicion on the part of the workers that it represented an attack on Trade Union rates or an attempt to introduce industrial conscription.

From the date of its appointment in November 1915, the Port and Transit Committee placed the creation of such a force in the forefront of its programme; but the War Office were, at first, unwilling to allow men under military training to be employed in commercial work, and it was not until the beginning of March 1916 that, as the result of long negotiations and continuous pressure from the Committee, the Army Council authorised the establishment of the first Transport Workers' Battalion, with its headquarters at Colsterdale, and appointed Colonel W. R. J. McLean to the command. An inland site was purposely chosen for headquarters, partly as providing a more central position with regard to the ports, partly in order to emphasise the fact that the men of the Battalion were primarily soldiers, and were only to be used as dock workers in an emergency.

The establishment of the Battalion, designated the 16th York and Lancaster Regiment, was fixed at 647 of all ranks. It was essential, in order to avoid the appearance of industrial conscription, that it should be recruited only from men who had volunteered for the service; but the Army Council issued instructions that men in Home Defence battalions, especially those with previous experience of transport work, should be encouraged to volunteer, and that all necessary steps should be taken for bringing the Transport Workers' Battalion up to strength.

Concurrently with the negotiations leading up to the formation of the Transport Workers' Battalion the Port and Transit Committee made strong representations to the Railway Executive Committee, and the Prime Minister, as to the necessity for the pooling of railway wagons. Those negotiations also took time, as the arrangements were complicated and the companies were, at first, averse from losing control over their own empties. In January 1916, however, the Great Northern, Great Central, and Great

Eastern Railways agreed to the pooling of their trucks, and in the following month their example was followed by the Scottish companies. Two months later a similar agreement was concluded with the London and North-Western, Great Western, Midland, North-Eastern, and South-Western lines. It was some months before these arrangements became fully effective, and the agreements were limited, at first, to certain classes of trucks; but some measure of relief was almost immediate, and by the summer of 1916 the majority of the ports were able to report a great improvement in the supply of wagons.

It was not sufficient, however, to improve the facilities for distribution of goods from the ports unless the receivers of goods could be induced or compelled to take full advantage of those facilities. The use of quays and transit sheds for purposes of storage had, all along, been one of the chief causes of port congestion, and was not entirely due to the difficulties of traffic. We have already seen that the Port and Transit Committee had, almost immediately on its appointment, pressed the Port Authorities to impose penalty rents on goods not removed within a reasonable time, but the powers possessed by the Authorities varied greatly, and it became clear that some machinery for more drastic action was required. Accordingly the Committee sought power for itself to order the imposition of penalty rents both on Government and private cargoes, and at the beginning of February such powers were conferred upon it.

Thus, by the spring of 1916 the Port and Transit Executive Committee had made some progress in dealing with all the three chief problems presented to it : labour, trucks, and removal of goods from the quays and sheds. It had dealt also with many other matters : the supply of tugs, the lighting restrictions in the Port of London, the diversion of traffic to slack ports, and a great number of questions relating to the equipment of particular ports and the handling of particular classes of traffic.

There were still, however, great difficulties to be overcome. The formation of the Transport Workers' Battalion went forward very slowly. In spite of the instructions issued by the Army Council, little was done to encourage men to volunteer, and there was a tendency to regard the Battalion as, at most, a convenient dumping-ground for physically unfit men whom their commanding officers were not anxious to retain. On May 2nd the Battalion at Colsterdale consisted of only 177 of all ranks, and even this number included a large proportion of men who had no previous experience of transport work, or were physically incapable of performing it. Very strong representations were made by the Committee as to the absolute necessity of bringing this indispensable central labour reserve at least up to its modest authorised strength, and of supplying it only with men physically fit for the arduous work required. Nevertheless, it was not till the end of July that the Battalion was brought up to strength, and, though the formation of four additional companies was authorised on July 29th, these too were very slowly raised, and the quality of recruits continued to be unsatisfactory.

At the outset there appeared to be some risk of the whole scheme being jeopardised by friction with civilian labour. The Transport Workers' Federation were of opinion that there was no actual shortage of dock labour and that the apparent shortage at many of the ports arose from the bad organisation of employment. In this contention there was some truth, and the Port and Transit Committee were able to effect considerable improvements in the methods of engaging labour at several of the ports; but there was unquestionably a real and serious shortage of labour at particular ports in times of stress, and the Committee were able to make the facts sufficiently clear to enlist the co-operation of the Federation. In this they were greatly assisted by the presence of Mr. Harry Gosling on the Committee.

The chief difficulty, however, arose from the occasional use of military labour—other than men of the Transport Workers' Battalion—for work in the docks. Such use of soldiers as transport workers, without any of the guarantees for civilian labour contained in the Colsterdale Scheme, inevitably aroused the suspicions of the Federation. To this danger the Port and Transit Committee were fully alive. In several instances they procured the withdrawal of soldiers from civilian work, and in others prevented their employment on such work when it was in contemplation. For the same reason they protested strongly and successfully against schemes which were put forward for the formation of a full-time Dockers' Battalion in the Port of London, and for the recruiting of coloured labour to work in the docks. At the same time they made it clear that the men of the Transport Workers' Battalion itself were only to be employed in the ports when, and so long as, local civilian labour was demonstrably incapable of meeting the requirements of traffic.

The decision as to when it was necessary to call on the Transport Workers' Battalion for assistance was left in each port to a Local Committee to which the Admiralty, the War Office, the Port Authority, and the Labour organisations each nominated a member. No employer of labour sat on any of the Local Committees, but any employer was at liberty to appear before it and apply for a certificate that there was a deficiency of civilian labour in the port. If such certificate were granted he could then lodge a written application stating the number of men required, the number of days for which they would probably be employed, and the nature of the work to be performed. He had also to guarantee the observance of the conditions of employment laid down in the scheme, including the payment of full current civilian rates to the non-commissioned officers and men employed.[1] In order to discourage unnecessary demands, no application could be made unless the employer could guarantee at least five days' work to the number of men applied for, and, should further civilian labour prove to be available after the arrival of a draft, a corresponding number of men were at once returned to Headquarters.

Thanks to the careful lines on which the scheme had been laid and the strong stand taken by the Port and Transit Committee on the question of employing outside military labour, it was not long before the hearty co-operation of the Transport Workers' Federation was obtained, and from the first there was a complete absence of friction between the men of the Battalion and the civilian labour with whom they worked side by side in the docks. Small as was the number of men available, the value of the scheme was quickly proved. In June the average number daily employed was 200. In July it rose to double that number, and in August to nearly 600. The actual work performed by such a handful was, of course, negligible in proportion to the

---

[1] Payment was made by the employer to the officer in charge of the party, who himself saw to payment of the men, no payment of any kind being made direct to the men by the civil employer. No charge was made to the employer in respect of the services of officers. The employer assumed responsibility for death or disablement allowance within the provisions of the Workmen's Compensation Act.

total volume of traffic; but, as they were employed only in ports where heavy arrivals or other circumstances had produced acute difficulties, the value of their work in preventing temporary congestion from becoming cumulative and permanent was out of all proportion to the tonnage handled. Moreover, the moral effect of the Colsterdale scheme was excellent, and went far beyond the actual work performed. The knowledge that military assistance could only be obtained after every reasonable effort to secure civilian labour had been exhausted was a strong inducement to employers to improve the organisation of port labour, while it did much to remove the supicions of the Unions as to the possibility of military labour being used for the purpose of strike-breaking or an attack on the Union organisation. At the same time, the knowledge that the Transport Workers' Battalion would be called in should serious congestion arise, and that the men would be taken away from their military training for the purpose, was an effective stimulus to the utmost possible exertion on the part of the civilian workers. For this reason the Committee were anxious to emphasise the military aspect of the battalion, and in this they were ably seconded by Colonel McLean. A surprise inspection of the battalion in June by the Officer Commanding No. 5 District brought forth a most favourable report on its soldier-like appearance, and the Committee were constantly, though vainly, pressing for the issue of arms, in order that the military training of the men might be completed.

It was recognised, of course, that refusal on the part of civilian labour to work, resulting in a stoppage of traffic, must necessarily be treated as a " deficiency of labour," since the one object of the scheme was to maintain the flow of traffic through the ports. The number of men in the battalion was, however, far too small to render it effective for the purpose of strike-breaking in any big dispute, and practically no friction on this score arose. Before any men of the battalion could be employed a certificate had to be obtained from the Local Committee, on which Labour was represented, and in practice it seldom if ever became necessary to call in men of the battalion as a result of industrial disputes. When such disputes arose, the invariable practice of the Committee was to preserve a rigid neutrality, but to bring pressure to bear on both sides to settle the matter by negotiation or arbitration, and to continue working in the meantime. In these efforts they received the utmost assistance not only from the presence of Mr. Gosling, Chairman of the Transport Workers' Federation, on the Committee, but also from the co-operation of Mr. Robert Williams, the Secretary, and the other officials of the Federation. The result of their efforts was encouraging. By bringing home both to the employers and the workers the vital national importance of a quick turn-round in the docks, they were able to secure important modifications of existing customs and organisations, which had an appreciable effect on the rate of loading and discharge. In the South Wales ports, where trouble had arisen over the question of week-end work, Mr. Williams succeeded, on behalf of the Committee, in arranging a settlement which saved much time to vessels in the French coal trade, and in many of the ports the Local Committees were able to arrange with the employers improved systems for the engagement of civilian labour, tending to greater regularity of employment.

Among other questions dealt with by the Committee during the spring and summer of 1916 were the establishment of definite rules for priority in the discharge of vessels, according to the nature of their cargo, and the quicker forwarding of imported wool to Bradford, in order to clear the receiving ports, London and Liverpool. In dealing with both these questions they had the support of the Shipping Control Committee, who went so far during May as to request shipowners in the Indian trade to ship no further wool until the accumulations at Liverpool had been removed.

Excellent results too were obtained from the imposition of penalty rents on goods not promptly removed from the quays and transit-sheds. In order to facilitate early removal, arrangements were made for envelopes marked as containing " Shipping Documents " to receive priority of examination in the Postal Censors' Department, thus minimising delays and enabling the goods to be dealt with immediately on their arrival in the docks. The free movement of imports was thus greatly facilitated, but the outward trade was equally an object of the Committee's attention, and on their representations, the War Trade Department consented to modify the formalities required by the export regulations, so as to remove certain obstacles to the flow of traffic.

A SUBSTANTIAL IMPROVEMENT

Working in close touch with all the Government Departments, the Committee were able to arrange for Government cargoes, including those in which the Allied Governments were interested, to be dealt with at the ports possessing the greatest margin of facilities. In making these arrangements they were greatly assisted by receiving advance notice of the principal requirements; thus, so early as the beginning of June they were inquiring as to the capacity of the ports to deal, during the autumn, with timber brought from Archangel, by ships allocated to the fulfilment of the Russian programme.

Despite all hindrances and difficulties, the Committee were able to report in July, in answer to inquiries from the Board of Trade, that the situation at the ports showed a substantial improvement on that existing at their appointment in November 1915. The number of ships awaiting berths had been greatly reduced, the quays and sheds were generally speaking free from congestion, the supply of railway trucks was much more satisfactory, and thanks in large measure to the assistance rendered by the Transport Workers' Federation, the effective supply of labour had been greatly increased. Above all, a large measure of co-ordination had been achieved between the various Government Departments and commercial interests using the ports.

The conditions, however, were still far from normal, and special anxiety was caused by the necessity of dealing with imports of grain and flour, which had again become exceptionally heavy.

It was during May and June that the full results of the change of policy adopted by the Carriage of Foodstuffs Committee in February became manifest. During those months the average weekly imports rose to 665,000 quarters, a figure little below the 700,000 which the Cabinet Committee had accepted as the revised maximum. Since the tonnage directed into the trade was in excess of the market requirements, this great increase in imports was accompanied by a steady fall in freights. By the end of June they were down to 8s., and during July the average price of the quartern loaf was reduced to $8\frac{1}{4}d.$, the lowest figure at which it had stood since January.

These results were not, however, achieved without involving some corresponding disadvantages. North American exporters were still inclined to hold out for higher prices than buyers were willing to pay, and, as tramps were being directed into the trade in advance of the demand, ships were frequently held up in port to await cargo, while negotiations were concluded. This was, in itself, matter for regret, since it involved a waste of carrying power; but a still more serious matter was the inability of the receiving ports in the United Kingdom to deal with the volume of imports. An overwhelming proportion of the whole supply was still coming from North America. The length of the Australian voyage forbade the direction of tonnage by the Carriage of Foodstuffs Committee to Australian ports, and though the Committee were instructed during April to provide tonnage from India, it was not until July that they began to direct tramps to Karachi in any considerable numbers, and during the first six months of 1916 the total imports from India were negligible. Rather more came from Argentina; but the total imports from all sources other than the United States and Canada amounted to less than 10 per cent. of the whole. The result was to throw the strain almost entirely on the larger West Coast ports, and it was severely felt. They might, perhaps, have dealt with the market demands without serious inconvenience; but the Government, as we have seen, were also buying for reserve, and these reserves were not kept at disposal in America but hurried across the Atlantic to be passed into stock, in fear of a temporary interruption of the routes.

It was at Liverpool that the strain was heaviest. Under ordinary conditions the wheat imports at that port averaged about 100,000 quarters a week, but for the ten weeks ending April 29th, 1916, the average was nearly 60 per cent. above this figure. At the same time very heavy demands were being made upon the port for the handling of munitions and other essential cargoes. The port facilities, under war conditions, were unable to cope with the pressure, and the result was serious delay to grain ships and consequent waste of carrying power. In response to the representations of the Port and Transit Committee, Messrs. Ross T. Smythe, as agents for the Government, made arrangements to stow the reserve stocks as far as possible in the East Coast ports or inland, in order to keep the West Coast ports clear for the reception of the ordinary supplies; but while this afforded considerable relief, the congestion was still serious. The Port and Transit Committee accordingly suggested that the policy of forcing tonnage into the trade should be reviewed in the light of the existing wheat situation, and the Shipping Control Committee supported them to the extent of requesting the Government to authorise a reduction in the number of vessels allocated to this service. The Cabinet Committee on Food Supplies were strongly opposed to any material reduction in the existing stocks, which they considered no more than sufficient to provide against the risk of interruption of supplies; but the Shipping Control Committee continued to urge that the rate of import was excessive in view of the existing tonnage situation as well as the position of the ports, and on June 7th the Carriage of Foodstuffs Committee were instructed that the rate of import might be reduced to about 400,000 quarters a week.

The results of this decision were important. In the first place, it enabled the Carriage of Foodstuffs Committee to reduce the agreed proportion of space devoted by the North American Liner Companies to wheat and flour from 50 to 33 per cent., as from July 1st, thus setting space free for the carriage of other essential cargoes. In the second place, it appreciably relieved, for the time being, the strain on the West Coast ports.

It was not, however, British ports alone to which attention was at this time directed. The condition of the Northern French ports in use by the British Army had long been a source of grave anxiety owing to the continual delays to colliers and store-ships. These delays inevitably entailed the employment of a greater amount of shipping in the cross-Channel service than was warranted by the volume of traffic. By the summer of 1916 the situation had become so bad that the Shipping Control Committee considered it necessary to initiate a special inquiry into the causes of congestion. Their decision was approved by the Government, and on June 10th Mr. Thomas Royden proceeded to France to carry out the investigation. He was accompanied by two expert advisers, Lieutenant-Commander Underwood, R.N.V.R., of the Great Central Railway, and Mr. L. A. P. Warner, Assistant Manager of the Mersey Docks and Harbour Board. The ports visited were Havre, Rouen, Dieppe, St. Valery-sur-Somme, Boulogne, Calais, and Dunkirk. By arrangement with the Inspector-General of Communications, the advanced bases and railway regulating sidings at Abancourt and elsewhere were also inspected.

The conditions disclosed by this inspection were extremely unsatisfactory. The average rate of discharge was little more than half the normal minimum, and ships were continually held up either at their ports of departure or at the French ports themselves, owing to the impossibility of clearing berths as fast as they were required. The principal causes to which the congestion was attributed were the shortage of equipment and railway trucks, the slowness with which empties were returned by the French Authorities, the forwarding of winter material too late for immediate use, the use of transit sheds as stores or depôts, the exceedingly close and elaborate method of checking in vogue, and the lack of expert knowledge in handling the labour on the quays. In respect of all these points recommendations were made which subsequently bore good fruit, but to deal with so complex a problem drastic action on a large scale was necessary, and it was some time before any great improvement could be effected.

CHAPTER XX

BRITISH AND GERMAN TRADE IN THE SUMMER OF 1916

DESPITE all that had been done to improve the tonnage position, the entrances with cargoes at British ports for the six months ending July 31st, 1916 showed a decline of 10 per cent. on the preceding six months. British entrances were down by nearly 1,400,000, and foreign by 370,000, tons.

The chief cause of this decline, even more than the continued heavy losses suffered by British shipping, was the great extension of requisitioning during the winter months of 1915–16, the full effect of which was now apparent. Another contributory factor of importance was the White Sea programme, which withdrew a large number of British ships from the trade of the United Kingdom during the summer months. But for the firmness of the Shipping Control Committee in refusing the allocation of further ships to France and Italy, the reduction would have been still greater, and might have led to serious consequences.

So far as foreign shipping was concerned, no great part of the falling off in entrances can be traced to the operations of the German submarines. The losses of French and Italian shipping had been considerable; but few of these had fallen on the comparatively small proportion of Allied vessels which brought cargo to British ports. Neutral losses had been little above the level of the previous year, and shipbuilding in Holland and Scandinavia had hitherto kept abreast of the rate of destruction; nor had neutral shipowners as a whole showed any marked disposition to shrink from the risk of voyages to the United Kingdom.

In the main the decreased entrances of foreign shipping were due to other causes. The withdrawal of British shipping from the inter-foreign trade, though most carefully worked by the Ship Licensing Committee, could not but produce a vacuum on many of the routes, into which neutral shipping was attracted by the pull of freight markets, supplemented by the attractions of a safer voyage. Further, as British exports decreased in volume owing to the increasing absorption of labour and material by the fighting services and the war industries, other countries, especially the United States and Japan, stepped into the place hitherto held by Great Britain as a source of supply to neutral markets, and this redirection of trade diverted a large number of ships from British ports. It must be remembered, too, that the action of the Carriage of Foodstuffs Committee, while it increased the total tonnage in the North Atlantic grain trade, had the effect of driving out of that trade such neutral tonnage as had hitherto been employed in it.

The requirements of the Allies constituted another important factor in the situation. Various demands, arising subsequent to the decision to limit the number of British ships in French and Italian service, had been met by the allocation of neutrals time-chartered by Messrs. Furness, Withy & Co., and of 65 ships so chartered which had been definitely allocated down to June 5th, no fewer than 30 were in French and 26 in Italian employment.[1] The bunker regulations were also being used, as we have seen, to obtain tonnage for the Allies. Many of the ships thus diverted into Allied employment brought back cargoes of ore or pit-props to the United Kingdom; but the return cargo regulations did not apply to the French Northern ports, where little cargo was available, nor could they be universally enforced in the Bay and Mediterranean trades. Hence the increase in neutral tonnage cleared to France and Italy involved, of necessity, an increase in the proportion of neutral ships entered in ballast at British ports. Even in the Spanish trade there was no increase in the total neutral tonnage entered with cargoes. The entrances of Scandinavian ships from Spain rose considerably towards the end of 1915, but this was balanced during the early months of 1916, by a decrease in the entrances of Spanish tonnage, to which the bunker regulations could not be strictly applied. The increased employment of Scandinavian ships in the trade was, however, important, as it was easier to insist on their bringing essential cargoes, such as

---

[1] Five others were allocated to the Egyptian Government.

ore and pit-props, than to impose similar restrictions on the lading of Spanish vessels.

These heavy reductions in shipping entrances naturally involved a falling off in the volume of imports; but the weight of imports per 100 net tons entered again rose, and the comparison with the previous year was less unfavourable as regards goods than as regards shipping. The total estimated weight of recorded imports was only 7 per cent. less than in the preceding six months, and only 6 per cent. less than in the six months ending July 31st, 1915. Indeed, the comparison was better than these figures would suggest, as the proportion of Government cargoes not appearing in the trade returns was on the increase.

In two respects the import figures were specially satisfactory. In the first place, the heavy arrivals of wheat from North America had made good the short shipments during the latter part of 1915 and enabled the Government to build up their reserve stocks. In the second place, the imports of iron ore both from Spain and the Mediterranean and from Scandinavia were well above the figures for 1915. Indeed, they were considerably larger than in times of peace. Even so, they hardly met the full requirements of the munitions industries.

The most alarming feature in the situation was the huge adverse trade balance. In 1913 the excess of imports over exports and re-exports was £180,000,000. For the year 1915 it was £370,000,000, and for the first six months of 1916 £179,000,000. Nor did these figures fully disclose the danger of the position, for the value of Government imports not included in the trade returns was continually increasing, and greatly exceeded that of export shipments on Government account. Moreover, the earnings of British shipping formed a less valuable set-off now that so large a proportion of the ships were running at Blue Book rates or in trades where the freights were artificially restricted, and so many vessels had been withdrawn from the inter-foreign trade.

Further, the redistribution of the export trade, so strongly marked in 1915, became more and more accentuated, and a large proportion of the exports represented, in effect, loans made to the Allies of Great Britain. On the other hand, the proportion of imports drawn from the United States steadily increased, and many of the purchases made by the Allies in that country were financed or guaranteed by the British Treasury. Despite heavy shipments of gold, the New York exchange showed, during the latter months of 1915, a discount against Great Britain varying from 3 to 5 per cent. This addition to the cost of all imports from the States was in itself a serious matter; but the main problem was to prevent a still further fall in the exchanges. There could be no hope of increasing exports to an extent which would redress the balance, and there was a limit both to the amount of gold which could be transferred without serious financial risks, and to the amount which America could readily absorb. It was necessary to fall back on the plan of financing imports by the sale of American securities held by British investors, and during the latter months of 1915 the Treasury took active measures to this end. A partial census was made of American securities held in Great Britain, and considerable purchases were made by the Treasury for resale in America. On December 13th the Chancellor of the Exchequer outlined in the House of Commons a definite plan for the "mobilisation of securities," by which holders of selected stocks and bonds on which interest was payable in dollars, were invited to sell or lend them to the Treasury for the purpose either of resale in America or of being used as collateral security for loans raised in the States. During the first half of 1916 this scheme was widely extended, especially for the purpose of providing collateral, and it was announced on May 2nd that there would be a penal tax of 10 per cent. on income derived from securities coming under the mobilisation scheme but not surrendered to the Government. The success of this scheme in securing its immediate purpose was very pronounced. Its initiation was promptly followed by a rise in the American exchange, and by the beginning of February 1916 the discount against Great Britain was only 2 per cent., at which figure it was maintained throughout the year.

The main factor restricting the export trade was not, even now, shortage of tonnage. Collier tonnage, indeed, was short, and, even had a larger surplus of coal been available for export, it would have been impossible to maintain at their normal level shipments to the more distant markets, such as South America. The liner services on the other hand, had been much less seriously depleted by requisitioning than tramp shipping. On the inward voyages of the liners, a large part of their space was devoted to Government cargo at Blue Book rates; but on their outward voyages they were capable of dealing with a larger volume of manufactured goods than was actually available for export. It was the diversion of labour, plant, and material to war uses which was the governing factor.

The total number of persons employed in industry was slightly greater in July 1916 than in July 1915, for though the proportion of enlisted males had risen to nearly 30 per cent., there had been a large influx of replacement workers. On the other hand, the percentage employed on Government work had risen from 36·1 to 44·9, and in the metal industries it was as high as 81·6. After the demands of the Ministry of Munitions were satisfied, little of the output of those industries remained for export. The textile industries were less heavily hit, as the proportion of workers engaged on Government work was under 25 per cent., but the cotton trade, though amply supplied with raw material, was still faced by a serious reduction of demand in its principal markets. The price of the raw material fluctuated violently owing to speculation in the States, based partly on the effect of heavy rains on the crop and partly on the circulation of peace rumours. Manufacturing costs and freight were both much higher than before the war, and the result on the price of the manufactured article led to very restricted purchases on the part of both India and China. Political unrest in China added to the depression. On the other hand, the French demand, though smaller than in 1915, was still several times the normal, and some of the other minor markets were also buying more freely. Thus the total export during the first half of 1916, though still much smaller than before the war, was better than in the corresponding period of 1915.

In the woollen trade conditions were more favourable. There was a strong demand not only from the Empire markets, South America, and the Far East, but from France and Scandinavia, and fortunately British manufacturers were in a position to respond to it and to take advantage of the gap created by the shutting down of German and Belgian exports. Although all supplies of raw material, including the home clip, were strictly controlled, it was found possible to release large stocks for industrial use. Indeed, every effort was made to give export orders a priority only second to army contracts, and all through the first half of 1916 the export of woollen tissues, which had risen well above the peace level in 1916, was steadily rising. The export of tops and yarns was subject to many restrictions, and army orders occupied the attention of a large proportion of the worsted mills; but the woollen export trade as a whole was in a very satisfactory condition.

Export figures as a whole naturally reflected the rise in values which had so swollen the figures of the import trade, but the diminution in the volume of shipments was so great that it was not until May that the total money value of exports and re-exports reached the peace level. In May, June, and July, however, the figures were substantially higher than for the last corresponding month of peace, and making all due allowance for inflation of values, this sudden spurt did represent an appreciable increase in the activity of the export trade.

During the same months the efforts of the various bodies which had been at work on shipping problems throughout the winter and spring began to bear fruit in a distinct amelioration of the tonnage position. The beginning which had been made in restriction of imports was not much; indeed, it was already evident from the freedom with which licences were granted to import prohibited cargoes, that the saving was not likely to amount to more than about half the 4,000,000 tons originally indicated by the Board of Trade; but even this did something to relieve the pressure on the available tonnage. Meanwhile, the carrying power of that tonnage had been increased through the improvement of port conditions obtained by the Port and Transit Committee, and in addition there was, despite losses, actually more tonnage available. Thanks to the efforts of the Shipping Control Committee and the improved organisation of the Transport Department, the increase of requisitioning had been checked, and an appreciable number of vessels had been released from naval and military service for commercial employment. Moreover, the arrest of requisitioning had an indirect effect, hardly less important, in avoiding dislocation of sailings and services, and restoring confidence in shipping circles.

Thus, while there were still many grave problems to be faced, the state of British seaborne trade in the summer of 1916 was, on the whole, distinctly better than at the beginning of the year. Despite the heavy losses sustained

THE MINISTRY OF BLOCKADE 301

and the increased pressure of Allied demands, the volume of essential imports had been maintained with little diminution; there were signs of a limited but welcome increase in the volume of exports; much had been done to clear the congested ports; much had been done to secure greater economy in the use of the available tonnage.

Very different was the situation of the Central Powers. The gradual tightening of the blockade during 1915 had been continued during the first half of 1916. Great as were their resources, the enemy were beginning to feel the pinch. They were still far from collapse, but the foundations of their economic strength were being slowly but surely undermined.

So well did the system of " Certificates of Origin " work that the overseas export trade of Germany and Austria had practically ceased to exist. Such as it was, it was confined almost entirely to shipments permitted by the Allies in consideration for the essential requirements of neutral States, and the total volume of this licensed traffic was now very small.[1] But, serious as was the complete loss of her oversea markets to Germany's financial position, the stoppage of her export trade was a less vital matter than the increasing restriction of her supplies.

In January 1916 the machinery of economic pressure was strengthened and co-ordinated by the creation of a Ministry of Blockade. Lord Robert Cecil, Under-Secretary for Foreign Affairs, was appointed Minister, with a seat in the Cabinet, to hold his new office in conjunction with the Under-Secretaryship, and the Contraband Department of the Foreign Office was transferred to the new Ministry, to supply his staff.

From the first the Ministry of Blockade adopted the rationing principle as the basis of its policy, and during the first few months of 1916 several important agreements were concluded in which this principle was applied. The first of these was made in February with the Danish Merchants Guild, in accordance with the previous agreement of November 1915, and covered all the main Danish imports except fodder and fertilisers, on which no restriction was placed, as their re-export was prohibited and it

---

[1] U.S. Imports from Germany, 1916 . . $5,800,000
U.S. Imports from Austria, 1916 . . 600,000
The imports from Germany represent a little over 3 per cent. of the 1913 values, from Austria about 0·3 per cent.

was considered desirable to encourage Danish agricultural production in view of the supplies obtained from Denmark by the United Kingdom.

In March an agreement was concluded with the Norwegian importers of margarine materials, and many similar agreements were made with other Norwegian Associations and firms. Although no central body existed in Norway corresponding to the Netherlands Overseas Trust, the Danish Merchants Guild, or the Société Suisse de Surveillance Économique, the separate Norwegian agreements were so numerous that, for all practical purposes, the ground was completely covered. With regard to Swedish imports no such arrangements were possible, as a Swedish War Trade Law prohibited agreements between Swedish firms and foreign Governments imposing any limitation on Swedish imports. The only Swedish agreements, therefore, were those relating to cotton and oil, which had been entered into before the passing of the law, and during the spring the Ministry of Blockade found it necessary to place embargoes on consignments of various commodities which were being shipped to Sweden in quantities greatly in excess of the normal consumption.

Among these commodities were coffee and cocoa. The food value of cocoa was so great that the policy hitherto adopted of permitting indirect shipments to Germany, out of consideration for British Colonial interests, could no longer be justified now that the blockade was being developed into a really effective weapon. By the agreement with the Société Suisse de Surveillance Économique, Swiss exports to Germany were limited to the average exports before the war. This was the most that could be effected, having regard to the large British imports of chocolate from Switzerland; but cocoa was strictly rationed under the February agreement with the Danish Merchants Guild, and in March a rationing agreement was concluded with the Netherlands Overseas Trust, based on an estimate of the amounts required for domestic consumption and the continuance of the Dutch exports of chocolate and cocoa preparations to Great Britain. With Norway and Sweden no agreements existed, and in April the Ministry of Blockade decided to place an embargo on all shipments to those countries, since the quantities they had already received amounted to many times the normal import.

This embargo was extended also to shipments of coffee.

Although the food value of coffee was much less than that of cocoa, it was among the most prized rations of the German troops, and no valid reason could be found for continued abstention from interference. It was accordingly decided to refuse all export licences for coffee, as well as cocoa, to countries contiguous to Germany with whom no agreements had been concluded, and to detain all shipments from overseas. As a result of these measures Norway and Sweden prohibited all re-exports of coffee, and rationing agreements were concluded with the Norwegian Grocers' Association and the Netherlands Overseas Trust. Denmark and Switzerland were covered by the agreements previously concluded. Tea was not seriously interfered with till July, when it was placed on the list of exports prohibited from the United Kingdom, and steps were taken to prevent excessive imports into neutral countries.[1] The delay in dealing drastically with this commodity was due to the policy of encouraging the enemy's expenditure on unnecessary luxuries, and very large amounts of tea reshipped from the United Kingdom had undoubtedly reached the enemy. Now that his supplies of coffee were cut off it was important to prevent him, if possible, from using tea as a substitute[2]; but so large were the supplies already obtained that ample stocks existed in Germany for many months' consumption.

A still more important development was an agreement concluded in April with the American meat-packers, which finally solved the problem of the shipments of meat products, which had given so much trouble during 1915. This, like the cotton agreement, was based on the purchase by the British Government of a large quantity of consignments detained in prize; but the concession was fully warranted by the results achieved, for the exporters agreed to submit all shipments for approval in advance, and to restrict the total exports to neutral countries to the amounts required for the normal consumption of such countries themselves. In view of the great difficulty

[1] Tea was first placed on the prohibited list in August 1914, but was deleted a few days later. In November 1914 export was restricted as a result of the loss of the *City of Winchester* and *Diplomat*, but the restrictions were removed in the following month. In June 1915 supplies to the enemy through Holland were restricted by making tea consignable to the Netherlands Overseas Trust, but till July 1916 there was no restriction on the Scandinavian trade.

[2] In the winter of 1915 coffee ran short in Austria, and "five-o'clock tea" became a recognised institution.

which had been experienced in obtaining proof of enemy destination of the innumerable small parcels in which meat products had latterly been forwarded, this was a great achievement. The agreement was well kept and from this date the German import of meat products, already greatly reduced, was entirely stopped.

What was even more important, the system of advance bookings, already adopted by some of the chief neutral lines, was, during the spring of 1916, extended, at the request of the American exporters themselves, to the whole Scandinavian trade. The inconvenience and loss arising from detention of ships and cargoes under the Order in Council of March 11th, 1915, outweighed the profits to be derived from the contraband trade, and it gradually became a regular principle for all proposed shipments to be submitted in advance to the Trade Department of the British Embassy in Washington, who obtained by cable the opinion of the Contraband Committee as to whether the shipment was likely to lead to difficulties. In giving its decision the Contraband Committee was guided by the information collected by the War Trade Intelligence Department and the War Trade Statistical Department, and the application of the rationing system to all exports from the United States to Scandinavia became comparatively easy. The " Navicert System," as it was called, from the code word employed, became, in fact, one of the chief instruments in the prevention of enemy trade, and during the course of the war it was extended to United States exports to Holland, and in a modified form, to many shipments from South America and Spain.

It was not only in these ways that German trade was hampered. The position of London as the greatest financial and insurance centre in the world provided a powerful weapon, the use of which was greatly developed during the early months of 1916. Prior to the war London had financed German trade to the extent of some £70,000,000 a year, and, though all direct transactions with Germany were stopped by the outbreak of war, the complex ramifications of international commerce and finance rendered it very difficult to ensure that the facilities of the London money market were not used to finance indirect shipments to Germany from neutral countries. Such information as was available with regard to the enemy connections of neutral firms was concentrated in

THE STATUTORY BLACK LIST

the hands of the Government, and was not generally available to bankers and traders. It was accordingly necessary to take steps to prohibit transactions which might assist the enemy either in obtaining supplies or in maintaining his financial position, and by virtue of the Trading with the Enemy (Extension of Powers) Act [1] which received the Royal Assent on December 23rd, 1915, a Statutory Black List of firms in neutral countries with whom all commercial transactions were forbidden was issued in February 1916. This list included both firms of enemy nationality, domiciled in neutral countries, and neutral firms who were known to be engaging in enemy trade. In May a Financial Section was added to the organisation of the Ministry of Blockade, and on May 10th a Regulation was issued under the Defence of the Realm Acts prohibiting all banking and financial transactions with firms on the Statutory List.[2] In the same month marine insurance was added to the list of prohibited transactions.

The effect of these measures was to prevent black-listed firms from exporting to or importing from the United Kingdom, from shipping goods in British ships, and from receiving credit or settling balances through British banks. Further, they were gravely hampered in obtaining goods, markets, tonnage, or credit facilities in neutral countries, since neutral shipowners feared that the carriage of goods for black-listed firms would result in the denial of bunker facilities to their ships, and neutral merchants and banks were anxious to avoid any transactions which might lead to their being themselves placed on the Statutory Black List.

Against this policy the United States strongly protested, on the ground that it constituted an unwarrantable interference with neutral rights; but the British Government strongly maintained their attitude, pointing out that the Trading with the Enemy (Extension of Powers) Act was a piece of purely municipal legislation, and that there was an inherent right in sovereignty and national independence for a State to prohibit transactions by any of its citizens which were contrary to the public interest and safety.[3]

[1] 5 and 6 Geo. V, c. 98.
[2] Defence of the Realm Regulation 41b, *Defence of the Realm Manual* (4th Enlarged Edition), 1917, pp. 132-3.
[3] There was also a certain amount of friction with the United States as to the treatment of neutral mails, which it had been found necessary to examine owing to the smuggling of securities and articles of relatively small bulk and high value, such as rubber.

The Statutory Black List was therefore maintained, and from time to time banks and traders were confidentially informed as to the status of firms not on the published list, with whom it was undesirable to do business. During the summer the system of embargoes was extended to many other articles besides coffee and cocoa, which were being shipped to Sweden in abnormal quantities, and which there was reason to believe were reaching the enemy. These embargoes were reinforced by a request to the banks to refuse financial facilities for specified commodities, and this request was loyally observed. Of the general success of the Statutory Black List as an instrument of the blockade there could be no doubt. The business of black-listed firms in South America and elsewhere showed an extraordinary decline, and not only were the Central Powers hampered in obtaining the very restricted supplies now available to them, but a severe blow was struck at many of the enemy agents abroad who had distinguished themselves by their endeavours to foment trouble between the British and neutral Governments, and to destroy by arson or otherwise factories and ships employed in the interests of the Allies.[1]

By this time the Allied Governments had come to the conclusion that the application to warfare, under modern conditions, of the rules laid down in the Declaration of London could no longer be upheld. The modifications in practice introduced by the Orders in Council of August 20th [2] and October 29th, 1914,[3] had already been widely extended. An Order in Council of October 20th, 1915, abrogated Article 57 of the Declaration, providing that the neutral or enemy character of a ship should be determined by the flag she was entitled to fly [4]; an Order of March 30th, 1916, provided that contraband, whether absolute or conditional, having an ulterior enemy destination might be captured, although the carriage of the goods to their destination entailed transhipment or subsequent

---

[1] *Correspondence with the United States Ambassador respecting the Trading with the Enemy (Extension of Powers) Act*, 1915. [Cd. 8225], 1916. *Further Correspondence* [Cd. 8353], 1916.
[2] Vol. I, p. 73. [3] *Ibid.*, pp. 297–8.
[4] The object of this Order was to enable the Allies to deal with German-owned ships registered at a neutral port. The *Presidente Mitre*, a ship owned by the Hamburg-Amerika Line, but registered at Buenos Aires and flying the Argentine flag, was captured by the ORAMA in November, 1915, but was subsequently released.

transport by land [1]; that enemy destination might be presumed if the goods were consigned to or for a person who had previously forwarded imported contraband goods to the enemy; and that, contrary to Article 19 of the Declaration, neither a vessel nor her cargo should be immune from capture for the breach of blockade on the sole ground that she was, at the time of capture, on her way to a non-blockaded port.

So numerous and so far-reaching were the modifications now in force that little was left of the original rules, and for the purpose of avoiding friction and misconstruction it appeared better to lay the Declaration on one side and rely only on the application of principles underlying the historic and admitted rules of International Law. An Order in Council was accordingly issued on July 7th repealing the Declaration of London Order in Council of August 20th, 1914, and the subsequent Orders of October 29th, 1914, October 20th, 1915, and March 30th, 1916, and defining the rules which the Allies regarded as applicable under International Law to the changed conditions of commerce. The most important of these were as follows:

" (a) The hostile destination required for the condemnation of contraband articles shall be presumed to exist, until the contrary is shown, if the goods are consigned to or for an enemy authority, or an agent of the enemy State, or to or for a person who, during the present hostilities, has forwarded contraband goods to an enemy authority, or an agent of the enemy State, or to or for a person in territory belonging to or occupied by the enemy, or if the goods are consigned ' to order,' or if the ship's papers do not show who is the real consignee of the goods.

" (b) The principle of continuous voyage or ultimate destination shall be applicable both in cases of contraband and of blockade."[2]

[1] This clause embodied a principle already applied in practice, and was intended to remove possible ambiguities in the wording of the Order in Council of 24 October, 1914.
[2] *Note addressed by His Majesty's Government to Neutral Representatives in London respecting the withdrawal of the Declaration of London Orders in Council* [Cd. 8293], 1916.

The object of the first of these rules was to dispose of the difficulty in procuring condemnation of contraband which had arisen under the Order of October 29th, 1914. The second gave formal recognition to the principle already applied in the interception of non-contraband goods destined for the enemy and consigned to neutral ports.

So tightly was the cordon now drawn round the Central Powers that the only sources from which any considerable volume of supplies could be procured were the neutral countries within the ring of the blockade. Of these supplies the most important were grain and oil from Roumania, iron ore from Sweden, fish and dairy produce from the Scandinavian countries and Holland.

The recovery of Galicia in the summer of 1915 had enabled the enemy to procure oil once more from the Galician wells, and, despite some damage done by the Russians, the output for 1916 was not far short of that in the year preceding the war. This, however, was totally insufficient for the requirements of Germany and Austria, and, now that the American supplies were cut off, Roumania was the only source whence additional imports could be obtained. Even this did not go far towards making up the shortage, but in the desperate need of the Central Powers for lighting oils and lubricants, the Roumanian supplies assumed a disproportionate importance. Still greater was the value of the Roumanian grain exports. Negotiations for the purchase of supplies had taken place during 1915, but difficulties with regard to payment and transport hampered delivery, and not much food was actually obtained. As a result of the comparative failure of the German harvest it became necessary to acquire cereals on almost any terms, and to make great efforts to facilitate transport of the purchases. Accordingly the Central Powers, in December 1915, made a contract with the Roumanian Central Export Company for 500,000 tons of grain and pulse, and despite initial delays due to transport difficulties, delivery of the whole of this contract was completed by the beginning of April. In March a second contract was concluded for 1,000,000 tons of maize and 400,000 tons of other kinds of grain, of which Germany was to receive 60 and Austria 40 per cent. Of this quantity about half may have been delivered when, on August 27th, the Roumanian Government finally threw off the mask and declared war against Austria. A certain amount of grain, flour, and other food products was also acquired either by private purchase or by an Austro-German Government Syndicate, and the exports of cattle, meat, and fat from Roumania to Austria-Hungary were so large as to cause scarcity in Roumania itself.

The supplies thus received during the spring and early summer of 1916 were of the utmost value to the enemy. Owing to the poverty of the 1915 harvest, the months immediately preceding the gathering of the 1916 crops were a time of great difficulty, and had not the Roumanian supplies helped to bridge the gap, the sufferings of the civil population in Germany must have been severe.

Imports of fish and dairy produce from Scandinavia and Holland were of less importance than the Roumanian grain supplies; but they were considerable in themselves, and did something to make good one of the weakest points in the German food supply—the deficiency in oils and fats. The Norwegian herring catch had, as we have seen, been purchased *en bloc*, and the total imports of fish during 1915 and 1916 were probably larger than in time of peace. The imports of meat and dairy produce bore a smaller proportion to the requirements of the German people, but since the beginning of 1915 those imports had been steadily increasing. So high were the prices the Germans were prepared to pay that they succeeded to a great extent in ousting British purchasers from the Danish, Swedish, and Dutch markets. While the exports to the United Kingdom steadily diminished, those to Germany as steadily increased. During the first six months of 1916 Germany was receiving 66 per cent. of the Dutch exports of meat and from 82 to 96 per cent. of the exports of potato-flour, cheese, eggs, and butter. Swedish exports of butter to the United Kingdom had almost entirely ceased, owing to the absorption by Germany of the exportable surplus, and though Great Britain was still the most important customer of Denmark for butter, bacon, and pork, large quantities of these products were going to the enemy; Germany had replaced the United Kingdom as the largest buyer of Danish eggs, and German imports of meat and live cattle from Denmark, for which Great Britain did not seriously compete, were twice as great as before the war.

In comparison with the total food requirements of Germany, the sum of these imports was not great. During the first quarter of 1916 the total food imports from all contiguous neutral countries—Scandinavia, Holland, and Switzerland—amounted, in terms of calories, to just under 4 per cent. of the normal quarterly consumption; in the second quarter they were a little over 8 per cent. Nevertheless they had, as has been said, a special value, owing to the German shortage of the principal commodities which they comprised.

The flow of these supplies could not be stopped by direct means, for it was impossible for the Allies to deny the right of neutrals to trade across the frontiers in their own products. The only feasible course was to come to an agreement with the exporting interests, and the trade connections of the States concerned with the United Kingdom held out some prospect of success along these lines. After long negotiations an agreement was concluded in June 1916 with the Dutch Agricultural Association, which secured for Great Britain and the Allies, though at high cost, one half the exportable surplus of meat, bacon, potatoes, and potato-flour, three-quarters of the condensed milk and milk-powder, and one-third of the butter and cheese to be exported from the Netherlands. Owing to difficulties with regard to official recognition of the Association, the full effect of the agreement was not felt for some months; but from the first it produced a marked restriction of the supplies available for the Central Powers.

At or about the same time very successful efforts were made to restrict the enemy's future supplies of fish. The activity of the Dutch fishermen in German trade had brought them within the scope of the Retaliation Order, and during the summer of 1916 no fewer than 150 Dutch fishing craft were brought in by the patrols. During August, as the result of agreements reached with the trawling and herring fishing industries, these vessels were released, and their cargoes purchased by the British Government, and by the terms of the agreements an option was secured over the greater portion of the Dutch catch. In the meantime very large purchases of herrings and fish products had been made in Norway, with the object of forestalling any attempt of the Germans to repeat their bargain of the previous year. These purchases were, naturally, extremely expensive, and it became doubtful how far the policy could be continued; but during July the Government secured an option, on more reasonable terms, over 85 per cent. of the entire Norwegian exports of fish, fish-oil, and other fish products, as from August 18th. This agreement was exceedingly important. Very large quantities of highly nutritious foodstuffs were diverted from Germany to the United Kingdom, or to approved neutral markets,[1] and this result was attained without injury or offence to the sea-going population of Norway—a point of great importance in view of the character of the Norwegian coast-line, and the services rendered to the Allies by the Norwegian mercantile marine.

Another avenue of fish supplies to Germany had already been blocked. The main Icelandic products—fish, wool, sheepskins, and fish-oils—were all of particular value to the enemy. So high were the prices procurable that, in addition to a certain amount of indirect trade through Scandinavia, an attempt was made in April 1916 to run a cargo of wool and sheepskins to Germany direct. Fortunately, the vessel employed, the Norwegian steamer *Gustaf E. Falck*, was intercepted by the patrols, and ship and cargo were condemned. Shortly afterwards an agreement was concluded by the Board of Trade with the Icelandic Government, by which the Board acquired an option over the whole exportable surplus of Icelandic products which would normally have been shipped to Scandinavia or Holland, and for which no market could be found in Allied or in approved neutral countries. The export of essential supplies from the United Kingdom to Iceland was also guaranteed. This agreement, too, could be regarded with peculiar satisfaction, since by no other means could the enemy have been deprived of the valuable supplies in question without inflicting ruin on an innocent and defenceless population.

The total effect of these measures in restricting the enemy's food supplies was formidable, but it was some time before that effect could be fully felt. The food situation in Germany was, however, already becoming serious. Down to Easter 1916 the supplies available for the population as a whole had been not greatly inferior to those available before the war. At Easter it became necessary to reduce the meat ration; but the guaranteed rations of all foods were still reasonably sufficient when

---

[1] Although the option extended over 85 per cent. of the catch, it was not exercised in respect of fish exported to a neutral market whence re-export to the enemy was impossible.

supplemented by the available unrationed food, such as fruit, vegetables, fish, and polished barley.[1] By the end of the summer, however, the stocks were running low, and gloomy forecasts with regard to the new harvest, coupled with the loss of the Roumanian supplies, threatened further reductions which would bring the ration below the minimum required for maintaining health.

Meanwhile, inequalities in distribution, and the shortage of particular kinds of food, especially fats, continued to give rise to much discontent. Despite the most strenuous efforts of the Authorities, it was impossible to bring all available food supplies into the common stock. Producers continued to consume their own products at, or little below, the normal rate, and despite rationing and price fixing, they succeeded in disposing of large quantities by illicit trade, at prices which only the well-to-do could afford. Constant recriminations between the different States and districts of the Empire added to the prevailing irritation. The West charged the East with withholding potatoes. The North charged the South with withholding meat and dairy produce. The general attitude was summed up in March, 1916, by the comic paper *Ulk* in the comment: " Oh, yes ! There is butter enough in Bavaria, but the English won't let it come through."

Among the poorer classes in the large towns, especially in Northern Germany, there was a great deal of real privation. Meat, butter, milk, and eggs were all very short, and apart from the actual reduction in the amount of food available, the restricted and often unpalatable nature of the diet was a serious evil.

Nor was it only in respect of foodstuffs that the enemy's position was growing worse. By June, the shortage of materials for civilian purposes had become so acute that it was necessary for the German Government to issue regulations restricting purchases of clothing to about 20 per cent. of normal requirements. The loss of the jute supplies produced a serious shortage of sacks. Efforts to produce synthetic rubber had given but poor results, and army requirements were only fulfilled by requisitioning bicycle-tyres, and other articles, and even restricting the sale of rubber teats. The requisitioning of metals was proceeding vigorously both in Germany and Austria, and in Austria even the church-bells were being taken. Iron ore was still

[1] Cmd. 280, p. 2.

procured from Sweden in large quantities, and though several German steamers were sunk or captured in the Baltic during the summer months, any effective attack on the ore trade was prevented by the attitude of the Swedish Government, which, in marked contradiction to its closing of the Kogrund Passage to British ships,[1] did everything possible to secure the safe passage of German steamers, within territorial waters, to and from the great iron port of Lulea. Sufficient iron ore was thus procured for the use of the war industries, but production for civilian use was greatly restricted, and little iron or steel was available for export to the contiguous neutral States. The stocks of nickel, copper, and tin were running very low.

One important consignment of nickel was, indeed, brought direct to a German port. On July 15th the commercial submarine *Deutschland* arrived at Norfolk, Virginia, with a cargo of dyestuffs, having successfully eluded the British patrols. On August 23rd she set out on her homeward voyage with 325 tons of nickel, surreptitiously procured through intermediaries, and a little tin and rubber. Favoured by fog and mist, she again succeeded in running the blockade, and her arrival in Germany gave rise to exaggerated hopes of the establishment of a regular submarine traffic with America. Nothing, perhaps, gives clearer proof of the reality and efficiency of the blockade at this time than the excitement created by the arrival of this small cargo, so insignificant in comparison with the volume of British and Allied trade.

[1] See pp. 335–6, *infra*.

CHAPTER XXI

ALLIED SERVICES DURING THE SUMMER OF 1916—THE RUSSIAN SUMMER PROGRAMME—THE ITALIAN COAL CRISIS

THROUGHOUT the summer of 1916 the Shipping Control Committee adhered to their decision limiting the tonnage in the service of France and Italy to that actually in such employment on May 1st. The number of ships running on the various Allied services fluctuated from month to month, according to circumstances; but substantially the position remained unchanged. No fresh commitments were undertaken by the Transport Department; no licences were granted by the Ship Licensing Committee, except in exchange for those which had expired.

The Shipping Control Committee had, however, agreed to the allocation of about a hundred steamers for the execution of the Russian Summer Programme, and from May onwards the number of ships on Russian service continually increased. In addition to their original commitments, the British Government made themselves responsible during the summer for an important addition to the Russian food supplies. In 1914 the United Kingdom had exported herrings to Russia to the value of £700,000, and Russia had felt the cessation of these shipments. By the purchase of the Norwegian catch it became possible to fill the gap. At the same time the sale of the herrings provided the British Government with funds, in roubles, at Archangel, which could be applied to defray the local disbursements of the Transport Department.

There were also certain shipments for the Roumanian Government to be arranged. Although it was not till August 1916 that Roumania entered the war, the Roumanian Government had begun, some months earlier, to purchase stores and munitions with a view to the possible outbreak of hostilities, and, with the Dardanelles in Turkish hands, these could only be imported through Archangel.

For these shipments Roumanian steamers were employed, but the Board of Trade agreed to undertake the insurance of such ships and their cargoes against war risks, at the current rate of premium for British vessels.[1]

The volume of traffic now converging on Archangel was very great. From the United Kingdom there was a continual stream of vessels carrying coal and munitions or other war material together with a comparatively small amount of private imports licensed by the Russian Government. Practically the whole of the munitions and three-quarters of the coal was carried in British requisitioned ships, which brought back cargoes of timber and flax either under requisition or on temporary release. Nearly a quarter of the coal was carried by Russian colliers, which, in order that the greatest amount of work might be got out of them, returned in ballast, thus enabling them to make two, or even three voyages within the season. The balance of the coal, together with a proportion of the private cargoes, was shipped in neutral steamers chartered by Messrs. Furness, Withy & Co.

Munitions and general cargo from the United States were shipped mostly in Russian and neutral vessels, though these had to be supplemented by requisitioned British tonnage; but nearly two-thirds of the French munition shipments were carried in British ships. The Norwegian herrings, though nearly half of them were landed in and shipped from Great Britain, were carried mainly by neutrals.

By July the number of requisitioned vessels in Russian service had risen to over 100, irrespective of homeward bound steamers, and irrespective also of nearly forty vessels on Russian charter. The strain, however, could be the more easily supported inasmuch as the wheat requirements both of the United Kingdom and of France and Italy were, at this period, considerably reduced.

It was not to be supposed that the German submarines would lose sight of the opportunity afforded by this great body of traffic, so vital to the military operations of the Allies, and, as we have seen, they penetrated even into the Arctic Ocean in search of their prey. The Norwegians, however, were on the alert to prevent the establishment of submarine bases among the islands by which their coast is fringed; the British Admiralty were careful to indicate

[1] *Government War Insurance Schemes* [Cmd. 98], 1919.

courses providing the maximum of safety, and British patrols were at work in the danger areas. The White Sea Minefield, which had given so much trouble in the previous year, had been swept clear, and the Germans were unable to renew it. Thus the losses were, altogether, extraordinarily small in proportion to the volume of traffic, and the chief effect of the submarine attack was the necessary prolongation of the voyages by deviation to avoid dangerous areas.

This necessity, which frequently added 50 per cent. or more to the length of the voyage, was one reason for the large amount of tonnage which had to be set aside for the service. Another and perhaps still more important reason was the length of time taken to turn round at Archangel. The equipment and communications of the port, though better than in 1915, were still inadequate, and the labour supply was short in quantity and poor in quality. The discharge of munition ships, which was in the hands of Messrs. R. Martens & Co., agents for the Admiralty, was fairly satisfactory; but the discharge of coal, which was entirely in Russian hands, was very slow. Further, while the majority of the ships were bunkered for the round voyage in the United Kingdom, many colliers required bunkering at Archangel for the return passage, and this was a lengthy process, the rate seldom exceeding 40 to 50 tons a day.

Matters would have been still worse had not the Russian Government consented, at the beginning of the season, to the appointment of Captain G. P. Bevan, R.N., as Principal Naval Transport Officer. The presence of this officer was of great assistance in enabling the Transport Department to impress on the Russians the necessity of improvement in equipment and organisation; but, even so, the White Sea service, essential as it was, continued to be extremely uneconomical as regards the use of tonnage.

Meanwhile, Italy was again pressing earnestly for further assistance. The Italian grain problem had been practically solved by the middle of the summer; but the coal shortage had become still more acute.

Even with the assistance of the requisitioned ships allocated at the beginning of the year and of neutral steamers chartered by Messrs. Furness, Withy & Co., and handed over to Italy, the exports from the United Kingdom were, each month, far below the normal level. On the other hand, the consumption was increased by the demands of the Italian armies and by the diversion to the railways of the traffic usually carried by coasters in the Adriatic. Steps had been taken by the Italian Government to regulate consumption, and many industrial establishments—notably glass-works—had been compelled to close down owing to the cutting-off of their supply of fuel. There remained, however, the essential requirements of the armies, the munition factories, and the railways by which they were supplied. These could not be cut down, nor was it possible entirely to prohibit civilian consumption.

During the first six months of 1916 the imports had averaged roughly 600,000 tons a month, of which about 100,000 tons had been drawn from North America and the rest from Great Britain. The consumption, however, had been somewhat in excess of the imports, and the deficiency had been made good by drawing on stocks, which were dangerously depleted. In the circumstances the Italian Government desired to increase the monthly import from 600,000 to 1,000,000 tons, and at the beginning of June they made urgent representations that assistance should be given them to this end.

The necessity of ensuring to Italy adequate supplies of fuel for her essential services was unquestionable, for without these supplies she could no longer continue her war effort. At the same time the problem was by no means a simple one. The total surplus available for export was limited by the reduction in output and the immense demands of the Admiralty and the war industries. Of the available surplus a large proportion was allocated to France and Russia. For the remainder, the exports to neutral Powers formed an invaluable lever in negotiating agreements relating to the blockade or to tonnage. It was the more important that this lever should not be thrown away, since the German output provided a considerable surplus for exportation, and should British exports to a continental neutral fall below the essential minimum, the German surplus would undoubtedly be used as a means of bargaining for food supplies.

Moreover, the amount which could be exported was governed by the tonnage available, and the provision of tonnage was at least as difficult as the provision of coal. Only about 330 tramps were now free from requisition, and of these 130 were trading abroad, while 70 were already carrying coal, under licence, to France and Italy.

Notwithstanding these difficulties it was decided, after a Conference held at the office of the Coal Exports Committee, that an attempt must be made to satisfy the Italian requirements. In view of the many claims on both supplies and tonnage, the Admiralty were unable to undertake any permanent commitments beyond the 50,000 tons a month already arranged; but, in order to meet the immediate emergency, they agreed to provide 500,000 tons as soon as tonnage could be arranged. The question of tonnage was referred to the Shipping Control Committee, who were of opinion that the requisite shipping could be secured without violating their previous decision. The Italian coal shortage had been caused in large measure by the diversion of tonnage from coal to wheat, and as the wheat crisis was now over, the Committee suggested that 85 steamers, the equivalent of the wheat allocation, should be assigned to coal, the balance being made good by neutrals chartered through Messrs. Furness, Withy & Co., and a few licensed vessels.

The negotiations lasted all through June and July, and the final arrangements were not made till August, but in the meantime some little assistance was given to Italy by the Ship Licensing Committee. At the request of the Italian Government, this Committee agreed in June to permit the larger British ships licensed for coal voyages to Italy to return in ballast. Neutral ships under charter to the Italian Government or Italian firms were usually sent back empty in order to secure the maximum number of coal voyages within a given time; but in pursuance of their general policy of discouraging ballast voyages, the Committee had hitherto stipulated that British colliers should load ore from Spain, or other approved cargo, on the homeward voyage. The concession now made, while helpful to Italy, did not in substance infringe this policy, for in return the Italians agreed to bring from the Mediterranean, in tonnage owned or controlled by them, 25,000 tons of ore a month, using vessels of less importance to their own import trade than the big British colliers.

This was not the only way in which the Ship Licensing Committee were able to show consideration for Italian interests. The number of licensed ships in Italian service on the date selected as the basis of the arrangement was thirty-four on time and thirty on voyage charter, and it had been intimated to the Italian Government that losses could not be replaced. Since that date, however, several of the steamers on voyage charter had been replaced by larger time-chartered ships, and not only was the actual tonnage in Italian service thus increased, but some of the smaller vessels so displaced were allowed to continue in the Italian coal trade, either because they were specially suited to trade within the Mediterranean or because they were wanted to bring back ore. Indeed, vessels applying for a licence to take coal to Italy were frequently allowed to do so irrespective of the number of ships in Italian service at the time, provided they were fixed for an ore cargo on the homeward voyage. In such instances the application was considered as granted in British interests; but Italy got the benefit of the coal.

To France, Admiralty coal continued to be supplied under the agreements previously made. The undertaking with regard to the supply of the French Marine would have expired on August 15th, but during July the Admiralty and Shipping Control Committee agreed to extend the period covered by the undertaking for three months at the original rate of 70,000 tons a month, and for a further period of three months at 50,000 tons a month. No new demand, however, was made for requisitioned tonnage. On the other hand, a very important modification was introduced into the regulations governing the ordinary commercial export.

Hitherto the commercial export of coal to France had been subject only to the necessity of obtaining licences for the shipments from the Coal Exports Committee, and for tonnage from the Ship Licensing Committee, and such licences had been granted without regard either to prices or freights. Both prices and freights, however, had been rising continually since the beginning of the war, and the French, whose dependence on imported fuel had been greatly increased by the loss of the northern coalfields, viewed with grave apprehension the prospects of a still further advance. Supplies at reasonable rates had been secured for the Navy and State Railways by agreement with the British Admiralty, but the cost of the ordinary coal imports had a serious effect on the financial position of France, and it was also politically undesirable that Great Britain should bear the odium of extorting huge profits out of the necessities of an Ally. The Board of Trade accordingly took the matter in hand and determined, if possible, to fix both freights and prices, with the object of preventing any further advance. During the spring of 1916 meetings of coal-owners and shipowners were held at the offices of the Board, as a result of which the coal-owners agreed to sell and the shipowners to carry the coal at fixed rates. Administrative machinery was brought into being in Great Britain for regulating the export, and in France for regulating the distribution of the coal, and on June 1st, 1916, the Coal Freights Limitation Scheme came into operation.

The scope of this scheme covered all exports of coal and coke from the United Kingdom to French ports on the Channel and Bay of Biscay. Shipments to the Mediterranean were, for the time being, excluded from its operations as regards freights, though they were subject to the scale of maximum prices as regards f.o.b. values.

For the purpose of working the scheme on the British side, Local Committees, composed of coal-owners, exporters, and shipowners, in equal numbers, were formed at the principal coal-exporting centres, Swansea, Cardiff, Hull, Newcastle, Liverpool, and Glasgow, each exercising jurisdiction over a defined area. A Central Executive Committee in London, composed of delegates from the Local Committees, exercised a general supervision over the working of the scheme, acted as a Court of Appeal, and decided questions of principle.

On the French side a Bureau des Charbons, with branches in the principal import centres, was formed to centralise all applications for imports, and supervise the distribution of the coal. No shipments were permitted except on the written authorisation of the Bureau.

Orders thus authorised by the Bureau des Charbons were submitted to the Local Committees, whose duty it was to distribute them among the British exporters in their districts. In the execution of this duty they were guided mainly by the ratio of *ante-bellum* exports and by the preferences expressed by buyers, for it was the object of the scheme to interfere as little as possible with the normal machinery of trade. They were, however, entrusted with a wide discretion. In order to avoid delays and minimise the work to be done, the export licences granted were general licences for periods of from one to three months.

When the orders had been allocated, tonnage for transport of the coal was fixed in the usual way between the

COAL FREIGHTS LIMITATION

exporter and the shipowner; but the Local Committees exercised a strict supervision over the chartering. Brokers having tonnage on offer were required to seek the instructions of the Local Committee as to the exporters to whom it should be offered, and no vessel could be definitely fixed without a permit from the Committee. A licence from the Ship Licensing Committee had, of course, to be obtained in the usual way.

It was a further function of the Local Committees to determine, in accordance with information received from the Bureau des Charbons, the priority in which orders should be executed. In the event of congestion at the intended port of discharge, they were empowered to divert the vessel to such other port as the Bureau might direct. Their powers of supervision were thus very definite, and extended to every branch of export and shipment.

For every class of coal a maximum f.o.b. price was fixed, and all c.i.f. contracts were prohibited. These prices were maximum only, and transactions under the schedule prices were permitted; but the Local Committees were instructed to prevent undercutting or undue preferences as between one exporter and another. Selling prices to the consumer in France were fixed by the Bureau des Charbons. Maximum freights were fixed to each French Northern or Bay Port from the main coal exporting centres, with special allowances in respect of certain small ports. These freights varied according to the size of the ship and applied equally to British, Allied, and neutral vessels. Definite provision was also made for brokerage, agency, discharging, and demurrage charges. Rates for sailing vessels and steamers under 800 tons gross were not included in the original schedules; but such vessels came under the general control of the Local Committees, and rates in respect of them were subsequently agreed. Liners carrying coal as part cargo were also brought under the scheme.

The maximum freights originally fixed by the Conferences at the Board of Trade were based on the current market rates. As the scheme depended on agreement with the shipowners, and as, moreover, it was to be applied to the neutrals who provided some 60 per cent. of the tonnage in the trade, it was not considered feasible to fix them below this level. The object of the scheme was to prevent a further advance. But between the date when the rates were fixed and the coming of the scheme into operation, the market rates rose still further, and by June 1st the Limitation Rates represented not only a prohibition of further increase, but an appreciable actual saving on the then current rates.[1]

It was not only in the French coal trade that the burden of rising freights and the threat to essential supplies arising from shortage of tonnage gave grave concern to the Allied nations. Proposals were already under consideration for the creation of an Inter-Allied organisation to control not only the allocation of Allied tonnage but the chartering of neutral vessels for Allied services, with a view to eliminating competition and bringing down freights. At an Allied Conference held in Paris during April a resolution was passed that—

" The Conference decides (a) to continue the organisation begun in London of a central bureau of freights (b) to take common action with the shortest possible delay with a view to discovering the practical methods to be employed for equitably distributing between the Allied nations the burdens arising from maritime transport, and for putting a stop to the rise in freights."

This resolution, which appears to have originated in a misconception of the function and powers of the Shipping Control Committee, was received by that Committee with dismay. In their view there could be no question of placing under the jurisdiction of an Inter-Allied Committed the British tonnage which formed four-fifths of the whole body of Allied shipping. They were further of opinion that the allocation of British ships to Allied services could be

---

[1] The date taken as a basis was 8 March, 1916. As finally fixed the basic rates from the Tyne to Channel ports and Brest varied from 25s. 6d., to 28s. 6d., to Bay ports from 35s. to 43s. 6d. The extent to which freights had risen may be gauged by comparing the Limitation Rates for typical ports with those prevailing before the war:

	July 1916.		Average 1915.		Average 1914.		Average 1913.	
	s.	d.	s.	d.	s.	d.	s.	d.
Havre	25	6	17	11¼	5	11¼	4	8¼
Rouen	27	6	18	9	6	8	5	3¼
Rochefort	35	0	24	0	6	4	5	9
Bordeaux	40	0	24	2¼	7	2½	5	8

accomplished with less risk of friction by direct agreement with the several Allied countries than by handing over the agreed proportion of tonnage *en bloc* for allocation by an Inter-Allied Committee. They accordingly urged on the Board of Trade and Foreign Office that the resolution should be rescinded, pointing out at the same time that British shipping was already, in fact, used for the benefit of the Allies as a whole.

France was equally determined to keep the management of French tonnage entirely in her own hands, and in these circumstances the proposals contained in the April resolution were allowed to drop. The idea of centralised chartering was, however, at work in many minds. Messrs. Furness, Withy & Co., as agents of the Board of Trade in chartering neutral tonnage for the benefit of the Allies, were frequently met by the competition of French and Italian Government Departments, and early in 1916, Mr. O. G. Holmden, of Messrs. H. Clarkson & Co., a firm of brokers with a wide experience of Scandinavian chartering, suggested to the Board that some machinery should be created to eliminate such competition by centralising the chartering of all non-national tonnage required by any of the Allied Governments. The Trade Division of the Admiralty held similar views, and during July a scheme was worked out in the Division, for establishing a chartering branch of the Commission Internationale de Ravitaillement to centralise all direct chartering for Allied Governments, and creating central chartering Committees for each of the three great trades—grain, coal and ore— to charter tonnage, fix rates, and allocate the ships as between individual merchants. These Committees were to be backed by a general system of licensing for every ship, British, Allied, or Neutral, loading or discharging cargo in a British or Allied port, and the power to grant or withhold licences was to be used to direct ships into particular trades where freights were abnormally high. This scheme also came to nothing. The Advisory Committee were of opinion that the necessity of making all purchases f.o.b. and fixing freights for all descriptions of cargo on all routes presented insuperable difficulties, and the proposals were never actively pushed. Nevertheless, the problem of Inter-Allied chartering of neutral tonnage continued throughout the summer to occupy the attention both of the Admiralty and of the Board of Trade.

In the meantime the question of the assistance to be given to Italy in the matter of her coal supply was definitely solved. Mr. Runciman, who had been in bad health throughout the year, was now in Italy, where he was convalescing, and it was arranged that he should meet the Italian Ministers for the purpose of coming to a definite agreement. The Conference took place at Pallanza on August 9th-14th. Mr. Runciman was accompanied by Sir Rennell Rodd, the British Ambassador, Sir E. Wyldbore Smith, Director of the Executive Staff of the Commission Internationale de Ravitaillement, Captain Clement Jones, Secretary of the Shipping Control Committee, and other expert advisers. The Italians present were Signor Errico Arlotta, Minister of Marine and Railway Transports, and Signor Gieuseppede Nava, Minister of Commerce, Industry, and Labour, together with their expert assistants.

At this conference the Italian representatives announced that an organisation was being created in Italy to centralise all imports of coal and distribute them at cost price to the consumers, and they requested that the Coal Freights Limitation Scheme should now be extended to Italian purchases.[1] To this request Mr. Runciman acceded, and promised to convoke a meeting of coal producers and shipowners on his return to Great Britain, for the purpose of initiating the extension. With regard to the guaranteed quantities, the British representatives were obliged to make it clear that the Admiralty could not make themselves responsible for anything beyond the monthly 50,000 tons, and the emergency shipment of 500,000, which was to be delivered during August and September. They announced, however, that the British Government would do its utmost to continue to furnish 250,000 tons of additional coal monthly up to the end of the year, and to procure tonnage for its transport; but neither as to coal nor tonnage could any formal pledge be given. In return for the assistance provided, the Italian Ministers agreed to minimise so far as possible their purchases of coal in America, so as to avoid the employment of large colliers in the long Atlantic voyage, and to bring all indispensable imports from that source under the control of the new organisation which was being created.

[1] By July 1916 coal freights from the Tyne to Genoa and Savona had risen to 70s. per ton, as against 37s. 8d. in 1915, 9s. 10d. in 1914, and 11s. 9d. in 1912.

Among other matters dealt with at the conference was the licensing of a certain amount of shipbuilding material for export to Italy; but the most important development, apart from the arrangements with regard to coal, was a request by the Italian delegates that the system of centralising the chartering of neutral vessels through the medium of the British Government should be strengthened and extended, and that the ships so chartered should be divided between the Allies in proportion to their necessities; and further that, in view of the high level of neutral freights, the British Government should assist in equalising the proportion of Allied and neutral ships in the service of each of the Allies. To this the British delegates assented, not as a hard-and-fast rule, but as a general principle. The immediate effects were small, for the complexity of the problem and the difficulty of establishing the necessary organisation forbade rapid progress; but the principle of Inter-Allied Chartering and proportionate distribution received a distinct impetus.

Another important result of the Conference was an undertaking by the Italian Ministers to do everything possible to accelerate discharge in their ports, and to observe, as an invariable rule, the order of arrival as regulating priority of discharge. The importance of this lay in the fact that neutral shipping was so much more costly than British, especially requisitioned British tonnage, that there was a strong tendency to give neutral vessels a preference, irrespective of the order of arrivals. Serious delays to British steamers had thus been caused, and the Shipping Control Committee had strongly impressed on the Government the necessity of the stipulation now agreed to.

Tonnage for the carriage of the emergency 500,000 tons was promptly arranged. If the Italians were anxious for delivery of the coal, the Shipping Control Committee were no less anxious to get the full amount shipped before the autumn months brought the usual seasonal rush in the import trade. In lieu of diverting British steamers on wheat service, the Italians agreed to supply tonnage under the national flag, set free by the slackening in wheat imports. The Shipping Control Committee, for their part, agreed to allocate thirty steamers from among the neutrals chartered or to be chartered by Messrs. Furness, Withy & Co., and to make good the balance by

British ships specially licensed or temporarily released from requisition for this purpose. With the owners of these ships Messrs. Furness, Withy & Co. were instructed to make the best possible arrangements as to freight, and, while the terms arranged were above Blue Book rates, they were decidedly below those ruling on the open market.

The part played by neutral tonnage in this transaction was a good illustration of the importance of the step taken by the Board of Trade in authorising Messrs. Furness, Withy & Co. to charter on their behalf. Down to September 5th, 103 charters had been reported to the Shipping Control Committee, the average size of the ships being 5,000 to 6,000 tons dead-weight. Of these fifty had been allocated to Italian, and forty to French services. Apart from these ships many neutral steamers had been chartered by Messrs. Furness, Withy & Co. for the Russian Government, and were running in the White Sea and Vladivostok services.

There were, however, some drawbacks to the system. It was difficult to exercise any control over the employment of time-chartered vessels which had been allocated to the Allies. The Shipping Control Committee complained, for instance, that ships allocated to France in response to requests for assistance in the transport of timber from Canada were used in less essential services, such as the import of wood-pulp. Moreover, while Messrs. Furness, Withy & Co. watched the market very carefully, and made the best possible arrangements as to freight, they were exposed, as has been said, to the competition of Departments of the French and Italian Governments, other than those in whose interests they were chartering. Such Departments frequently paid very high rates for neutral tonnage; on the other hand, tonnage offered through Messrs. Furness, Withy & Co. on the best terms procurable was as frequently rejected, so long as the smallest hope could be entertained of obtaining British ships at Blue Book rates. Useful as the measure had been in supplementing the tonnage at the disposal of the Allies, it was a very imperfect substitute for an effective general scheme of centralised chartering. Meanwhile, the use of bunker pressure for forcing neutral tonnage into the employment of the Allies had been, to some extent, neutralised by the application of maximum freights to the French coal trade.

So far as British shipping was concerned, the Freight Limitation Scheme had little effect on the supply of tonnage. The majority of the shipowners were fully prepared to co-operate in working the scheme, and even had they not been so, the powers of the Ship Licensing Committee and the threat of requisition were quite sufficient to prevent any considerable withdrawals from the trade. Over neutrals there was no such hold. The return cargo regulations for Bay colliers had already produced much discontent among neutral shipowners, and the announcement of the Freight Limitation Scheme was immediately followed by the withdrawal of many neutral steamers from the French coal trade. Efforts were made to retain them by refusing to accept any other voyage as an "approved trade" for the purpose of obtaining bunkers, in respect of vessels hitherto employed in the carriage of coal to France; but this was a measure which could not be generally applied to White List vessels without the risk of serious friction. The problem was complicated by the fact that the French, while anxious to obtain the advantage of the Limitation Rates, were by no means whole-hearted in enforcing the return cargo regulations, since more coal could be delivered in a given time by a ship returning in ballast to British ports.

On the other hand, there was, during the summer months, a considerable influx into the French coal trade of Scandinavian shipping from the North Sea. The Return Cargo Regulations in the North Sea trade had at first worked well, as regards both freights and supplies. The imports of iron ore from Narvik increased, and so early as May 6th the leading papers in the Norwegian timber trade reported that North Sea freights were weakening as a result of the negotiations; by the end of June they were reported to have fallen 20 per cent. By July and August, however, the difficulty of obtaining approved cargo from Scandinavian ports was acutely felt. The import restrictions on timber and wood-pulp placed a definite limit on the supply of two of the main bulk cargoes, and the shipments of iron ore from Narvik were affected by the increasing premiums demanded for insurance against war risks. The entrances from Scandinavia continued to bear a higher ratio to the clearances than in the previous year, though they showed no absolute advance; but from July onwards an increasing number of Norwegian and Swedish as well as Danish vessels seeking bunkers for a voyage to Scandinavia, applied for a licence to carry coal to France, as an alternative to the return voyage from their home ports.

This influx from the North Sea counterbalanced to some extent the withdrawals from the French coal trade due to the Freight Limitation Scheme; but at an early date it was found that the strict application of this scheme to neutral shipping was likely to be too dearly purchased by the loss of carrying power. An agreement was accordingly made with the Norwegian Shipowners' Association by which they received time-charter rates intermediate between the limitation rates and the market rates which they superseded. Thanks to this elasticity in the working of the scheme and to the effect of the alternative voyage provisions under the North Sea Regulations, the clearances of Scandinavian shipping to French ports, which had fallen heavily during June and July, rose again in August and September to a satisfactory level.

CHAPTER XXII

THE WHEAT SITUATION IN THE AUTUMN OF 1916

No sooner were the French and Italian coal problems solved for the time being than the Authorities controlling British shipping were called upon to face a much more serious crisis. The improvement in the general tonnage situation during the summer months was due in part to reduced monthly losses, in part to the more careful adjustment of requirements to resources brought about by the efforts of the Shipping Control Committee, the Transport Department, and the Port and Transport Executive Committee. During the late summer and early autumn the balance was again upset by heavy losses and by the development of a grave crisis in the wheat supply of the Allies.

From July onwards the activity of the German submarines increased. Their success had been somewhat checked by the progress of defensive armament and by the limitations imposed as a result of the American protest against the sinking of the *Sussex*. On the other hand, Admiral von Capelle, who had succeeded Admiral von Tirpitz as Minister of Marine, had been urging forward the construction of under-water craft, and by shifting the point of impact of the attack it was found possible to employ effectively the increasing force available without coming into conflict with the United States.

In British Home Waters the submarines were still bound by their new instructions, and during July and August only two British ships were torpedoed without warning outside the Mediterranean. For the most part, the enemy confined their attention to neutrals and fishing craft. Since August 1915 the losses of British fishing craft had been comparatively small, but during July the North Sea fisheries were systematically harried, and no fewer than 36 boats were captured and destroyed, ranging from little craft of 5 or 6 tons up to big steam trawlers of 150 to 250 tons. In August, a dozen more were lost. Of the neutrals destroyed in the North Sea a large proportion were small sailing vessels with pit-prop cargoes from Scandinavia.

Several ships, British and neutral, were also sunk by mines, but the most notable development of the campaign in the North Sea was that, during July, three British steamers were successfully carried into port by German submarines or surface patrols. This development had, indeed, been foreshadowed during the last week of June, by the loss of the *Brussells*, whose capture was rendered notorious by the fate of her gallant master, Captain Fryatt; but the British patrols were too active for many such captures to be effected.

It was still, however, in the Mediterranean that the German submarines were busiest. The target presented to them was of vast extent. It was estimated by the Transport Department in August that, including transports, there were in the Mediterranean at one time no fewer than 350 British steamers of 1,600 tons gross and over. Of these a considerable proportion were armed. By the middle of August nearly 40 per cent. of the ocean-going steamers under the British flag, other than those permanently trading in distant waters, had been fitted for guns of some kind. The majority of the permanently armed ships were on Government service, and many of these were in the Mediterranean, while practically all the liners which still used the Suez route were fitted for transferable armament. There were still, however, many ships engaged in private trade in the Mediterranean which had no guns, and in addition, there was a great body of defenceless tonnage under Allied flags and a constant stream of neutral shipping in Allied service.

In July, 18 British steamers were attacked in the Mediterranean, mostly off the Algerian coast, and 10 of them were sunk, 2 without warning. In August the impact of the attack shifted to the neighbourhood of Marseilles, Majorca, and the Spanish and Italian coasts. Again 10 British steamers were sunk, while 9 escaped, mostly by making good use of their guns; but it was on Allied shipping that the attack fell most heavily. Sailing vessels under the Italian flag suffered terribly; on one day alone 14 were sunk and during the whole month 40 were destroyed. In addition over a dozen French and Italian steamers were lost, including the *Stampalia*, of 9,000 tons, one of the largest liners under the Italian flag. Two Japanese steamers swelled the list of casualties, and Greek, Spanish, Danish, and Norwegian shipping also suffered, the losses including half a dozen neutral colliers bound for Genoa or Savona.

Altogether August was a black month for Allied and neutral shipping. British losses from all causes fell from 82,000 tons in July to 43,000, owing to the smaller average size of the ships destroyed, but Allied losses rose from 24,000 tons to 83,000, and neutral from 8,500 to 35,000. Only once before, in April 1916, had neutral losses been so heavy, and those of the Allies were far greater than in any previous month of the war.

Encouraged by their success, the German submarines redoubled their activity in September. In the Mediterranean 38 British steamers were attacked, but of these 20 escaped. Several beat off the attacking submarine by superior gunfire, others were rescued by patrols, yet others succeeded in dodging the torpedo or shaking off their pursuer. Of the 18 sunk, 6 were torpedoed without warning, for the Germans were now putting forward a claim to treat defensively armed merchantmen as warships, and in the Mediterranean there was less risk of endangering American lives. Allied and neutral losses were also heavy. The Norwegian *Elizabeth IV* of 7,895 tons, with sugar from Java for Marseilles, was sunk by an Austrian submarine, and several neutral colliers were captured and destroyed on their way to Italian ports.

But the havoc was not confined to the Mediterranean. During August a German submarine had succeeded in penetrating the English Channel and sinking a dozen vessels, mostly small French sailing vessels, off Portland Bill, Cape Antifer, and the Isle of Wight. Others now followed, and in September the losses in the Channel were serious, including the Dutch liner *Antwerpen*, of 7,955 tons, on her way from New York to London. In the North Sea several neutral merchantmen and thirty-eight British fishing craft were destroyed. Submarines penetrated into the Arctic Ocean to attack the Archangel trade; they were active off the entrance to the Channel in the neighbourhood of Ushant; they lay in wait off Cape Finisterre for the Mediterranean traffic. In all these areas they were still hampered by the new instructions, but even under those limitations they were able to do terribly effective work. Including ships sunk by mines and the packet-boat *Colchester*, captured by torpedo-boats in the North Sea, British losses during the month amounted to 105,000 tons, Allied to 45,000, and neutral to 76,000.

It was the neutral losses which were, perhaps, the most significant. Greater by 50 per cent. than in any previous month, they showed how far the Germans were prepared to go in the effort to terrorise neutral shipping. Norway alone lost 45,000 tons, and apart from the actual reduction of carrying power, so sharp a rise in the curve of destruction could hardly be without effect on the operations of neutral shipowners.

Yet the British losses were sufficiently serious. For the three months they amounted to 93 vessels, of 230,000 tons, and 60 out of the 93 were steamers of 1,600 tons or over. So heavy was the monetary loss that for the first time since December 1914 it became necessary to increase the insurance premiums under the Government War Risks Scheme. On September 20th the premium on hulls was raised from $\frac{3}{4}$ to 1 per cent. for a single voyage, and from $1\frac{1}{2}$ to 2 per cent. for a round voyage or a 91 days' time policy. No change, however, was made in the cargo rate: the reserve of premium income accumulated in the earlier days of the war was sufficient as yet to ensure the solvency of the scheme, and cargoes in British ships could still be insured at 1 per cent.[1]

The most encouraging feature of the campaign was the stout resistance made by defensively armed ships. From January 1st to September 7th, 228 British ships were attacked by submarines. Of these 90 carried guns, and only 19 of them were sunk. Of the 138 unarmed vessels only 22 escaped. Thus the ratio of sinkings to attacks was 84 per cent. for unarmed but only 21 per cent. for armed vessels. There were, indeed, signs that the progress of defensive armament might lead to a relaxation of the restrictions under which, for the most part, the submarines had acted since the American note; but the value of defensive armament had been clearly established, and the work of armament was pushed on as fast as guns became available. During August the Transport Department arranged to give Trade Division the earliest possible notice of all ships going to the Mediterranean, in order that their equipment might

[1] *Government War Insurance Schemes* [Cmd. 98], 1919.

ARMAMENT AND REPLACEMENT

be put in hand before the commencement of their Mediterranean voyage. The prior demands of the Army and Navy, and the great development of anti-aircraft defences, still continued to restrict the supply of weapons, but by September 18th, the total number of ships on all services fitted for guns had risen to 1,749, and in the Mediterranean the proportion of armed vessels rose so rapidly that by October it was estimated by the Transport Department as 5 in 7, as compared with 1 in 7 a few months before. During the summer of 1916, too, a beginning had been made in the issue of smoke-producing apparatus to ships whose armament consisted of guns lighter than the 12-pounder.

In the replacement of losses by new construction some progress had been made; but, though mercantile shipbuilding had recovered from the complete stagnation of the spring and early summer, the position was still unsatisfactory. The danger arising from the continued depletion of tonnage was not unrecognised; but orders for commercial construction had still to take second place to the demands of the Navy.

As a result of the Memorandum on Merchant Shipbuilding presented by the Shipping Control Committee in April, a Conference was held at the Admiralty on May 18th at which the Committee was represented by its Chairman, Lord Curzon. Mr. Runciman, President of the Board of Trade, was also present. At this Conference the Admiralty agreed that eight shipyards should be released for commercial work as soon as the Admiralty work then in progress was completed, and should receive no further Admiralty orders. They agreed also that a number of marine engineering works should be released at the same time in order to provide machinery for the additional merchant vessels to be laid down.

The estimated capacity of these yards was about a quarter of a million tons, but it was, of course, a matter of months before the effect of their release could be felt in delivery of new tonnage. Meanwhile, the steps taken earlier in the year to adjust the difficulties arising from additional and acceleration costs had met with a large measure of success. From 80,000 gross in the March quarter of 1916 the tonnage launched in the June quarter rose to 156,000, and in the September quarter to 192,000. Moreover, the vessels laid down during the three months ending September 30th amounted to 320,000 tons gross, as against 103,000 in the first three months of the year. There was, therefore, some reason to hope that the improvement in output would be maintained or extended in the future. The two principal obstacles were the shortage of labour, especially in the marine engineering shops, and the enormous demands of the Ministry of Munitions for steel, which threatened to leave insufficient material available to meet the joint requirements of naval and mercantile construction.

Even if the improvement in output were maintained there was a serious leeway to be made up. The total tonnage launched from October 1st, 1914, to September 30th, 1916, was 1,499,000. Against this there had been lost by enemy action since the outbreak of war 1,837,000 tons of shipping on the Register of the United Kingdom, and by ordinary marine risks 374,000. The deficiency had been made good in part by the acquisition of prizes and interned vessels; but even with this help, the additions to the Register had failed to keep pace with the losses. Of steamers of 1,600 tons and over, there were in July 1914, 3,888, with a gross tonnage of 16,840,000 tons. By September 18th, 1916, the total had sunk to 3,642 of 16,255,000 tons, a decrease of 246 ships and 585,000 tons.

Nor were the whole of these ships available for the purposes of war or trade, for the total included steamers locked up in the Baltic and Black Seas. The number of such ships had, however, been reduced during the summer of 1916.

Since the outbreak of war in August 1914 no fewer than ninety-two British steamers had been laid up in Russian and Swedish Baltic ports. It was not, of course, the perils of the North Sea passage which had kept them immobilised. Such perils were daily faced both by British and neutral vessels with an unconcern which deprived the German submarine campaign of appreciable effect as a deterrent, however serious might be the actual losses inflicted. The real crux of the problem lay in the German command of the entrance to the Baltic by the Skagerrak and Kattegat, and this had appeared to impose an insuperable obstacle to escape.

During the spring of 1916, however, the high freights obtainable by free tonnage led the owners of these immobilised vessels to consider whether it was, after all, absolutely impracticable to bring them out, and an Anglo-Swedish Syndicate was formed to attempt the task. Recognising the value of any addition to the available shipping resources of the country, the Admiralty readily agreed that all steamers escaping from the Baltic should be exempt from requisition, and, with lucrative employment thus assured to their vessels, the owners were able and willing to pay heavily for the services of the Syndicate in organising their escape. During the temporary immobilisation of the German High Seas Fleet after the Battle of Jutland, the first ships slipped through, and by the middle of July about a dozen had arrived safely at British ports.

The plans of the Syndicate were carefully laid. Collecting at Soderhamn or Gefle in the Gulf of Bothnia, the steamers kept within Swedish territorial waters as far as Cape Falsterbö, where they passed through the inshore Kogrund Passage, and continued their voyage in territorial waters as far as Frederikshald or Christiania in Norway. From one or other of these ports they put out across the North Sea as opportunity offered.

Even with the precautions taken the voyage was perilous, for German cruisers were never scrupulous as regards the invasion of territorial waters. The measure of the risk was reflected in underwriters' quotations of 25 per cent. for the whole voyage, or 23 per cent. as far as a Norwegian port and 2 per cent. for the North Sea passage. Nevertheless, by taking advantage of the movements of Swedish warships on the coast, ship after ship passed out in safety. By the end of July twenty-nine had escaped from the Baltic, and sixteen others had crossed from Russian to Swedish ports in preparation for the voyage. High hopes were entertained that all would be clear before the winter; but at this point some forty of the remaining steamers were requisitioned by the Russian Government until the middle of August. The Shipping Control Committee at once urged the Admiralty to do everything possible to procure the release of the vessels in time for them to get clear before the freezing of the Baltic, but in the meanwhile the whole scheme had been fatally wrecked for the time being by the action of the Swedish Government.

Friction between Sweden and the United Kingdom, arising out of the bunker restrictions and blockade policy, was at this time at its height, and yielding to German pressure, the Swedish Government, at the end of July, laid a minefield in the Kogrund Passage and closed the channel through the minefield to any but Swedish ships.[1] Despite strong protests by the British Foreign Office, the Swedes refused to modify their attitude, and for the time being it was necessary to abandon the project, since the risk of rounding Cape Falsterbö outside territorial waters was too great to be undertaken. Still, the addition of even twenty-nine steamers to the available shipping resources of the country was, at such a time, an appreciable gain.

Excluding prizes, oilers, and ships locked up in the Baltic and Black Seas or otherwise unavailable, the total number of ocean-going steamers included in the Transport Department's Return of Employment for September 30th was 3,536, with a gross tonnage of 15,580,000. As compared with the position in May this showed a decrease of 36 ships and 200,000 tons; but thanks to the constant pressure exercised by the Shipping Control Committee, backed up by the Transport Department itself, the tonnage available for commercial purposes was appreciably larger than in the earlier month. Although the decision limiting the allocation of tonnage to France and Italy had been closely adhered to, the total tonnage on Allied service had increased by about 100 vessels, owing to the Russian White Sea programme, which was now in full swing. On the other hand, great economies had been effected by the Admiralty, especially in the employment of colliers, and though the War Office had been obliged to put forward considerably increased demands in connection with the Salonika Expedition, these had been fulfilled, thanks to economies in other services, without adding appreciably to the number of ships in military employment. The full reduction of 200 vessels proposed by the Shipping Control Committee in April, and approved by the War Committee, had not been effected; but from a total of about 1,000 vessels, the number in the service of the Army and the Navy, including Indian and Dominion transports, had been reduced to 867, and this saving more than counterbalanced the increase in requisitioning caused by the Russian programme.

Including ships in the service of the Navy, Army, Allies, and Dominions, and ships under notice of requisi-

[1] *Correspondence* re *Mining of the Kogrund Passage* [Cd. 8478], 1917.

tion, but not yet allocated to a particular service, the total number in war employment was 1,547, as compared with 1,660 in May. Requisitioned and directed vessels carrying commercial cargoes for the United Kingdom were practically unchanged—335 as compared with 332—but those free to trade without further restrictions than were imposed by the Ship Licensing Committee had risen from 1,579 to 1,654. In all, 1,989 ships of 8,929,000 tons were available for the import service of the United Kingdom and for general trade. Of these about 400 were trading, under licence, between foreign ports, mostly in the interests of the Allies and Dominions; but the total connage available for the carriage of British imports was roughly 7,580,000 tons, an increase of 1,000,000 tons.[1]

[1] The following figures show the comparative position. Owing to hanges in the methods of classification, some of the figures are estimated.

	25 May, 1916.		30 September, 1916.	
	s.s.	tons gross.	s.s.	tons gross.
Requisitioned for Navy, Army (a), India, and Dominions	1,183	5,532,000	867	4,193,000
Requisitioned for Allies			256	883,000
Under notice	70	312,000	14	53,000
"Black Listed" for India and Dominions	50	235,000	46	189,000
"Black Listed" for Allies	278	1,091,000	325	1,183,000
carrying wheat for Allies under direction	80	290,000	39	149,000
Total war employment	1,661	7,460,000	1,547	6,650,000
Trading abroad under licence	400	1,350,000	400	1,350,000
Import Services of United Kingdom:				
Wheat, directed	98	359,000	75	282,000
Requisitioned for sugar, etc., etc.	(b) 60	240,000	(c) 132	488,000
Temporarily released	174	551,000	(d) 128	464,000
Trading under licence	1,179	5,819,000	1,254	6,345,000
Total import services and general trade	1,911	8,319,000	1,989	8,929,000
Grand total	3,572	15,779,000	3,536	15,579,000

(a) Includes ships carrying nitrate for War Office.
(b) Sugar only.
(c) Sugar, 71 s.s. of 303,000 tons; ore, timber, and flax from Mediterranean and White Sea, 61 s.s. of 185,000 tons.
(d) Ore, timber, and flax, 39 s.s. of 127,000 tons; general cargoes, 89 337,000.

Satisfactory as was this increase, the total British tonnage available for British trade was still a long way below the normal, and the apparent improvement in the tonnage position since the spring of 1916 was to a great extent discounted by the falling away in neutral entrances. During the March quarter, when requisitioning was at its height, the entrances of British ships were less by 1,100,000 tons than in 1915, but those of foreign shipping were greater by 100,000 tons. For the September quarter the decrease in British entrances amounted to 400,000 tons only; but foreign entrances, instead of showing an increase, were less than in the previous year by 350,000 tons.

Thus, the situation as regards carrying power was still grave; the more so as the last three months of the year were those in which the heaviest volume of imports normally came forward.[1] Nor was this all, for while the increasing activity of the enemy's submarines threatened further depletion of British tonnage and a probable further decrease in neutral entrances, reports had come to hand from America which indicated that a great part of the wheat supplies for the forthcoming season would have to be brought from more distant sources, entailing an additional strain on their available shipping.

Thanks to the heavy shipments during the first half of 1916, the imports of grain and flour for the cereal year ending July 31st amounted in round figures to 5,690,000 tons, or 27,000,000 quarters, a rather larger total than in either of the two previous seasons. The home crop of 1915, too, had been abnormally heavy, as the acreage under wheat had been largely increased at the expense of pasture land and barley, and the total supplies amounted to 7,400,000 tons, an increase of 12 per cent. on 1913–14. It had thus been possible, in spite of increased consumption by those enlisted in the New Armies, to accumulate the reserve stocks which the Government considered necessary to guard against a possible failure of supplies or interruption of communications. Those stocks, however, were too small to allow any considerable fall in

---

[1] Estimated seasonal distribution of import weights:

January–March	26 per cent. of the year's imports
April–June	22 per cent of the year's imports
July–September	21 per cent. of the year's imports
October–November	31 per cent. of the year's imports

imports to be viewed without apprehension, the more so as, owing mainly to the shortage of labour, the acreage sown in 1916 was much smaller than in the previous year.

Of the total imports 88 per cent. came from North America,[1] 6 per cent. from India, 3 per cent. from the Plate, and 2 per cent. from Australia.

Owing to the failure of the Australian harvest of 1914–15, there had been practically no imports from Australia in 1915, but the 1915–16 crop was in good condition, and early in 1916 it began to move. From the first, the freight and loading arrangements were under the direct control of the Australian Authorities. Exports of wheat and flour had been prohibited, except under licence,[2] since the beginning of the war, but when the 1915–16 harvest was ready to move, the Commonwealth Government made themselves responsible for the marketing of the exportable surplus. In order to encourage production, the Commonwealth and State Governments had jointly advanced to the farmers 3s. a bushel on wheat delivered at the nearest railway siding, on the understanding that the wheat would be disposed of by the Commonwealth Government, and the balance of the sale price, after deducting freight and other charges, paid over to the farmers. A special Act passed in September 1915 empowered the Government to borrow money from the Commonwealth Bank[3] for the payment of freight on Australian produce. The actual process of sale and chartering was undertaken by the Commonwealth Government, which then proceeded to fix maximum freight rates considerably below the market level, the benefit of this cheap transport going, under the arrangements, to the Australian producer.

The effect of these limitation freights, which stood in June 1916 at 110s. per ton, as compared with a market rate of 200s., was to drive tonnage out of the trade, and urgent representations were put forward by the Commonwealth Government to the Transport Department that ships should be directed to Australian ports. The great objection to this course, so long as supplies were available elsewhere, was the length of the voyage, and no ships were sent to Australia by the Carriage of Food-

[1] United States 60·5 per cent., Canada 27·5 per cent.
[2] *Commonwealth of Australia, Manual of Emergency Legislation* (January, 1916), pp. 144, 152.   [3] *Ibid.*, p. 416.

stuffs Committee; but during the first part of 1916 the Transport Department released a dozen steamers completing service in East Africa, on condition of proceeding to Australia to load wheat. This practice, however, was discontinued in June 1916, as owing to the shortage of Cuban sugar it became necessary to direct all temporarily released vessels coming free in East Africa to Javanese ports.

During the same period, January–June, 1916, the Commonwealth Government chartered, through their agents in London, some sixty steamers—Australian, British, Japanese, and neutral—for the carriage of wheat. Use was made also of requisitioned transports, and the employment of British vessels on Australian requisition for wheat cargoes to Italian and neutral ports led to protests by the Chamber of Shipping and the Transport Department.[1]

Despite the adoption of all these methods of obtaining shipping, tonnage for the Australian trade was so short that by the middle of May, 1916, only 28,000,000 bushels out of an exportable surplus of 120,000,000, had been disposed of, and the Commonwealth Government had received only £6,000,000 in purchase price, against £25,000,000 advanced to the farmers, on the balance of which interest at 5 per cent. was payable. Mr. Hughes, the Australian Premier, who was then in London, accordingly suggested to the British Government that they should purchase the unsold wheat up to 2,000,000 tons (about 37,000,000 bushels), to be delivered as tonnage became available.

To this course the Shipping Control Committee and the Transport Department strongly objected, in view of the fact that it required three or four times as much tonnage to bring wheat from Australia as would suffice to lift an equivalent amount at North American ports. On June 9th a conference was held between Mr. Hughes and representatives of the Shipping Control Committee, the Transport Department, the Treasury, the Colonial Office, and the Joint Purchasing Committee, to consider how far tonnage could be rendered available; but no definite decision was arrived at. During the same month Mr. Hughes obtained the sanction of the British Government to the transfer to the Australian Government of fifteen British ships purchased

[1] On the 18 May, 1916, there were 74 steamers registered in the United Kingdom under Australian requisition.

A WORLD SHORTAGE

by him, and to their release from their present employment, for immediate delivery.[1] These ships, however, which formed the nucleus of the Commonwealth Shipping Line, operated by the Australian Government, were not put into the wheat trade, but employed outside the war zone, chiefly in the Pacific services.

For some little time after this the negotiations relating to the purchase of the Australian crop remained in abeyance, but during August the whole question was reopened by alarming reports received as to the prospects of the North American harvest. Hitherto North America had been able, without strain, to fulfil the bulk of the Allies' requirements; but, according to the official statistics published by the United States Government, and the estimates of the Canadian crop, it appeared that the exportable surplus for 1916-17 would be less by 30,000,000 quarters than in the previous season. If these estimates should prove to be correct, the total exports from the United States and Canada would not exceed 27,000,000 quarters, and not only would it be necessary for the Allies to import large quantities from more distant sources, but there would be an actual world shortage of wheat amounting to some 12,000,000 quarters.[2]

The situation thus created was extremely serious for the Allies. The substitution of distant for near sources of supply was in itself a grave matter in view of the existing tonnage shortage and the high rate of freights; but it now appeared that difficulty might also be experienced in procuring the necessary supplies.

According to the grain trade experts North America would have shipped the greater part of its available surplus by the end of December, and in these circumstances the Advisory Committee to the Transport Department recommended, in a Memorandum dated September 12th, 1916,

[1] Of these 15 ships 9 were under requisition by the Admiralty, 4 on time-charter to the French Government, and 2 free.

[2]

	qrs.	qrs.
Total requirements of importing countries		75,000,000
North American surplus .	27,000,000	
Australian surplus (old crop) .	10,000,000	
Australian new crop (normal) .	6,000,000	
Argentine surplus (old crop) .	3,000,000	
Argentine, new crop . .	12,000,000	
Indian crop	5,000,000	
Total exportable surpluses . . .		63,000,000
World Shortage		12,000,000

that the practice of directing tramps to North American ports should be discontinued ; partly because the continuous pressure of tonnage on the North American markets must, in the circumstances, drive prices to an extravagant height, and partly because they considered that, having regard to the world shortage, the North American supplies should be used as a reserve and not quickly exhausted, leaving Great Britain wholly dependent on more distant sources. They considered that the import of North American wheat should be left mainly to the liners, which could carry the greater part of the reduced surplus, and that tramps should be freely directed to India, Argentina, and Australia. At the same time, they were apprehensive that free direction of tonnage to the Plate and Bahia Blanca might be followed by a sharp rise in prices, and that importers might hesitate to buy largely in so distant a market as Australia, fearing a fall in prices. They suggested, therefore, that it might be advisable for the Government to effect large purchases in Argentina and Australia, prior to the direction of tonnage.

At the same time, the Advisory Committee pointed out how serious was the tonnage situation arising from the replacement of so large a proportion of the North American supplies. Whereas the round voyage to North America occupied only two months, the round voyage to India occupied three and a half, to Argentina four, to Australia six. On such evidence as was available they estimated that something like 200 additional steamers would be required for the carriage of British wheat imports during 1916–17. Owing to the measures taken to restrict grain freights, little assistance could be expected from neutrals, and in the opinion of the Committee it was essential that prompt and effective measures should be taken to render additional tonnage available, by drastic restriction of non-essential imports, by reviewing the employment of ships on naval, military, and Allied service, with a view to further economies, and by the withdrawal of further ships from the inter-foreign trade.

On the same day, on September 12th, the Shipping Control Committee, after an interview with the President of the Board of Agriculture, decided that steamers should be directed, as and when possible, to proceed to Australian ports to load wheat, and on September 26th negotiations were opened, by cable, with the Commonwealth Government for the purchase of 500,000 tons of wheat f.o.b. This was at once agreed to in principle by the Commonwealth Government, but the terms of the contract were not immediately arranged, owing to the insistence of the Shipping Control Committee that all tonnage—British or neutral—employed in the carriage of wheat for the Empire or for the Allies should be controlled by a single central authority. In view of the acute shortage of tonnage, this stipulation was considered by the Shipping Control Committee as absolutely vital, and it involved, as a necessary corollary, that the Commonwealth Government should cease to operate in the c.i.f. market, their existing commitments, whether for the United Kingdom or other countries, being taken over by the central authority. Provided this condition was agreed to, the British Government were willing to go beyond their original proposal, and by a cable despatched on October 25th they intimated their willingness to purchase f.o.b. practically the whole sound Australian crop.

In the meantime, the authority referred to had come into being. On September 20th the Admiralty had recommended to the Board of Trade a scheme for joint Allied purchase of wheat, and inter-Allied chartering of ships for its carriage. This scheme was based mainly on the desirability of "limiting by Government action the high freights and consequent high prices resulting from the shortage of tonnage inevitably caused by the requisitioning of a large proportion of the mercantile marine for Government purposes," and assumed that the elimination of competition by centralised purchasing would, in effect, enable the Allies to determine the buying price. This assumption was not destined to be fully borne out, but both the Advisory Committee and the Shipping Control Committee were convinced that, from the point of view of supplies, Government purchase was now inevitable. At a conference between the Transport Department, the Trade Division, the Advisory Committee, and the Board of Trade, the proposed scheme was fully discussed, and as a result of their deliberations the Royal Commission on Wheat Supplies was established on October 11th " to inquire into the supply of wheat and flour in the United Kingdom, to purchase, sell, and control the delivery of wheat and flour on behalf of His Majesty's Government ; and generally to take such steps as may seem desirable for maintaining the supply."

The Wheat Commission was placed under the Chairmanship of the Earl of Crawford and Balcarres, President of the Board of Agriculture, and was composed mainly of grain experts, with Mr. Thomas Royden of the Shipping Control Committee to represent shipping interests. In respect both of purchase and distribution the Commission acted as far as possible through the ordinary trade channels; but the question of transport required serious consideration. The fall in freights brought about during the summer by the action of the Carriage of Foodstuffs Committee had not continued. Indian grain freights had, indeed, fallen from 270s. for the round voyage, in April, to 200s. in October; but the North Atlantic rates, which were down to 8s. in June, had risen by the autumn nearly to the April level of 12s. 6d., and the time-charter rates had advanced to 36s., as against 24s. in April. So much of the North Atlantic wheat was carried in liners that these extreme fluctuations exaggerated the average rise in the cost of transport, and the average rates were still well below those of the spring; but they were decidedly above the lowest level reached during the summer. The import values had risen in still greater proportion owing to the advance in f.o.b. prices, and by September the average price of the quartern loaf, which had stood at $8\frac{1}{4}d.$ in July, had risen to 9d., as in the previous March.

Although the freight advance was only one factor, and hitherto not the most important, in producing the increased cost of bread, it was brought into greater prominence by the probability that, for the remainder of the 1916–17 season, a large proportion of the supplies would have to be brought from more distant sources. Hitherto the enormous rise in grain freights on the longer routes had probably been borne largely by the producer or shipper, as the selling price of the wheat, including freight, had been kept down to the level of that for wheat from North America, the principal source of supply.[1] The situation was now changed. If the estimates as to the exportable surplus from North America were correct, a much larger proportion of the total import would have to be brought from distant sources, and the actual world shortage of wheat would

[1] For some discussion of this view and of the contrary opinion that the great rise in Plate freights had prevented the Argentine wheat from competing with, and possibly bringing down, the price of North American wheat, see *Second Report of the Departmental Committee on Prices* [Cd. 8483], 1917.

compel the Wheat Commission to appear as purchasers of practically all wheat on offer. It was probable, therefore, that any advance in freights, from any source, would be immediately reflected in prices, and it was quite possible that the freight on the longest route might influence to a considerable extent the general level.

On the appointment of the Wheat Commission, it was at first proposed that the Carriage of Foodstuffs Committee should direct ships to lift the grain at rates slightly more favourable to the shipowner than the Blue Book rates, in order to provide an incentive to owners to run the vessels themselves instead of throwing them on the hands of the Transport Department. The Admiralty, however, pointed out that the fixing of rates for vessels taken up under different conditions and at different ports at home and abroad, would be a very complicated business. Unless the margin between the fixed wheat freights and Blue Book rates was a wide one, many owners would prefer Blue Book rates on account of their greater certainty and regularity, and there would thus be two different systems in operation. They therefore proposed that tonnage for wheat as well as for sugar should be provided on a Blue Book basis. The question was referred to the Board of Trade and Shipping Control Committee, and it was ultimately decided that the Blue Book basis should be adopted. In truth, experience had proved that there was no logical medium between chartering in the open market, leaving freights to be determined by the law of supply and demand, and requisitioning pure and simple. Freights had been forced up by the withdrawal of tonnage from commercial employment to figures which the Government were unwilling to pay, and now that private importation had been wholly eliminated, some of the principal objections to the employment of fully requisitioned tonnage for the carriage of wheat had been removed.

A Wheat Section was accordingly formed within the Commercial Branch of the Transport Department, to provide tonnage for the purchases of the Royal Commission, and the Committee for the Carriage of Foodstuffs, having no longer any function to discharge, was dissolved. The work of the Wheat Section was complicated, however, by the necessity of providing tonnage for the Allies. While the Royal Commission was now buying for the British Government, the Joint Purchasing Committee was still operating on behalf of the Allies, and this Committee now applied to the Wheat Section for tonnage to supplement that provided by the Allies. The demands of the Allies, of France especially, were so large that it became impossible to meet them in full, simultaneously with the requirements of the United Kingdom, and the Director of Transports accordingly drew attention to the necessity of drawing up some scheme for the co-ordination of Allied wheat shipments, and working out an order of priority.

This difficulty was solved during November by the formation of an inter-Allied body known as the Wheat Executive, which exercised a general supervision over the whole of the Allied programme. The actual purchase of wheat and flour for France and Italy, as well as for the United Kingdom, was entrusted to the Royal Commission on Wheat Supplies, who took over the contracts of the Joint Purchasing Committee, and the Wheat Section of the Transport Department was instructed to provide tonnage for all three countries. The allocation of supplies, when purchased, to each country, was decided in principle by the Wheat Executive, and worked out in detail by the Royal Commission.

There remained the difficulty of providing the additional tonnage required for the transport of wheat from Australia instead of from North America. The Board of Trade did not place this quite so high as the Advisory Committee had done, but they calculated that the total number of additional ships required for the carriage of grain to Europe would come to 122 steamers of 25,000 quarters' capacity for twelve months' service, or a larger number if the time of their service was reduced.

It was clear that, in default of a great acceleration of mercantile shipbuilding, these ships could not be provided by new construction. Considerable as was the improvement in output, it was still far from keeping pace with such losses as were suffered in September. Nor was there much prospect of any large number of additional vessels being released from naval and military employment. In one direction only was there a prospect of any considerable addition to the available tonnage. On March 3rd, 1916, the anomalous position arising from the position of Portugal as an Ally of Great Britain under ancient treaties, though not a belligerent in the present conflict, had been terminated by a declaration of war by Germany, following the seizure by the Portuguese of seventy-four German and Austrian vessels lying in their ports. The gross tonnage of these ships amounted to 244,500, and it had since been arranged that Portugal, after retaining about a fifth of this tonnage for her own trade, was to hand over the rest for equal division between Great Britain, France, and Italy. Most of the ships, however, required extensive repairs, and they were only very slowly coming into service. Few of them could be reckoned upon for immediate employment.[1]

All these circumstances were reviewed by the President of the Board of Trade in a Memorandum dated October 24th, in which he went very fully into the tonnage situation. The Advisory Committee had suggested drastic limitation of imports as necessary; but the Board of Trade were still of opinion that it would be imprudent to go beyond the existing restrictions, now estimated to save from 1,500,000 to 1,800,000 tons in the course of the year. A review of the present employment of requisitioned tonnage gave no grounds for anticipating any considerable reduction, and Mr. Runciman could only suggest that the employment of shipping in the service of the Allies and Dominions, as well as of the fighting services, should be carefully watched, with a view to releasing any ships which could be spared. In three ways only could he see any possibility of increasing appreciably the available carrying power. By pressure or inducement, it might be possible to obtain additional assistance from neutral shipping; a definite understanding safeguarding the supply of material for merchant shipbuilding might enable the improvement in output to be maintained and surpassed; by increasing the facilities at the ports, the annual carrying power of the available shipping might be increased.

It was the last-named measure which offered the chief hope of immediate relief. The reports of the Port and Transit Executive Committee showed a marked improvement on the conditions existing at the beginning of the year; but the capacity of the ports had proved only just adequate to the demands of the summer traffic, and it was doubtful how far they would be able to cope with the heavier volume of trade due to arrive in the December quarter. Yet an acceleration of turn-round would do more than anything else to get more work out of the ships

[1] The agreement did not become really effective until well into 1917.

available. The Transport Workers' Battalion had already proved of inestimable service in removing congestion, and, in view of the supreme importance of avoiding delays in port at a time when every day saved was a vital matter, Mr. Runciman proposed that additional battalions should be authorised up to a total strength of 10,000 men.

On November 9th the President of the Board of Trade presented a second Memorandum, recapitulating his previous arguments, and pointing out that the problem was complicated by the continual growth of the demand for munitions. The requirements of the Ministry of Munitions, during the coming year, for iron ore alone, were placed at 2,500,000 tons over and above the 1916 import. In these circumstances the Board of Trade estimated the shortage of tonnage, in relation to all requirements, at some 400 ships, and assuming the rate of loss to be continued at the current level, they were apprehensive of a complete break-down in transport arrangements by the summer of 1917.

This view of the situation was placed before the Transport Department, who fully concurred in the proposals relating to the acceleration of shipbuilding and the Transport Workers' Battalions, but were of opinion that these measures, however beneficial, would be insufficient to avert the probability of a crisis during 1917. They accordingly urged that imports should be drastically restricted on the lines proposed by the Shipping Control Committee earlier in the year, as the only means by which an equilibrium could be restored between the supply of tonnage and the demands upon it. Meanwhile, the Commercial Branch were busily engaged in working out a programme to meet the requirements of the Royal Commission on Wheat Supplies, both for the United Kingdom and for the Allies.

CHAPTER XXIII

INCREASED LOSSES AND A NEW TONNAGE CRISIS
OCTOBER—DECEMBER 1916

So grave was the tonnage situation in the autumn of 1916 that it became necessary to scrutinise most carefully the employment of shipping in Allied as well as in British services. The Government's decision of April 25th, restricting the allocation of tonnage to France and Italy, had, on the whole, been closely adhered to during the summer months; but, even so, the assistance given to the Allies of Great Britain was a heavy strain on her depleted resources.

In one respect, indeed, this strain was now lightened: the Russian summer programme had been completed. By the middle of October the despatch of further cargoes to Archangel became imprudent, for in the conditions existing at that port there was little prospect of getting home, before the freezing of the White Sea, any further ships sent out, and the Transport Department were in no mind to risk a repetition of the disastrous experience of 1915. The Archangel Railway, though still inadequate to the requirements of the port, had now been altered to broad gauge, and thanks to the energy of Captain Bevan, the equipment of the port itself had been considerably improved, especially as regards the storage accommodation for general cargo; but the labour conditions were still very bad. Not only was the supply of labour itself insufficient, but there was a shortage of Customs officials, clerical staff, and others required for the work of supervision, which hampered the continuous day-and-night work necessary to take full advantage of the open season. Further, that season—estimated at twenty-five weeks— was cut down by the large number of public holidays, and by stoppages for rain, due to the failure to provide wet-weather clothing. By October, too, the gathering of the Russian harvest had begun, and this was followed at once by an exodus of labour from the port, which the Russian Authorities were unable or unwilling to prevent.

In such conditions the despatch of further steamers was impossible, but so energetically had the work been carried on that every commitment undertaken had already been fulfilled. A million tons of coal, and 600,000 tons of munitions and general cargo had been despatched from British ports, 300,000 tons of munitions from France, and 350,000 from the United States. Including fish and a few miscellaneous cargoes from foreign ports, the shipments of the season amounted to nearly 2,500,000 tons, about twenty-five times the normal peace time trade of the White Sea.[1]

More than 600 voyages were involved, of which some 350 were made by British steamers, which carried over 64 per cent. of the total volume of cargo, and so complete was the failure of the German submarines to interrupt this essential traffic that the losses, whether calculated on voyages or weight of cargoes, barely exceeded 3 per cent. Out of about a score of steamers lost, half were neutrals, several of them small vessels laden with fish from the United Kingdom or Scandinavia, and the only service in which the losses were at all serious, relatively to the volume of traffic, was that from the United States. On this route five ships were lost, with cargoes amounting to 30,000 tons, and one cargo fell into the enemy's hands. It was not till the end of September that the submarines succeeded in working havoc within the Arctic Ocean, but during the last few days of that month, and throughout October, the losses were numerous, and among them was the Russian *Suchan*, of 3,781 tons, bound from New York to Archangel with a cargo of ammunition, which was captured by a German submarine off the North Coast of Norway on October 7th, and successfully taken into Wilhelmshaven. Shortly after this date, however, the ability of the enemy to operate effectively in northern waters was restricted by a decree of the Norwegian Government prohibiting all belligerent submarines from entering the territorial waters of Norway.

In addition to the White Sea traffic, Russia continued to draw large supplies from the United States and Canada through Vladivostok, and a few British requisitioned

[1] These figures include the shipments made for account of the Roumanian Government.

vessels were allocated during the summer to supplement the Russian and neutral tonnage available; but the utility of this line of supply was gravely impaired by the inability of the Siberian Railway to carry the imports. So far did the removal of goods from the port lag behind the arrivals that by the end of the year the accumulations of munitions and war material were estimated at no less than 2,000,000 tons.

There was now, however, a new route which could be kept open, even during the winter months. The railway to the ice-free ports of the Murman Coast was at last approaching completion, and, though it was only a single line, badly laid, and ill equipped, it provided for the first time during the war a direct line of supply available all the year round.[1] The Russian Government accordingly requested that a winter programme of munitions and general cargo should be arranged from Great Britain, France, and the United States. The Russian estimate was that 380,000 tons of munitions and general cargo could be received at Murmansk during the winter season; but the actual capacity of the port and railway remained problematical. The necessities of Russia, however, were too urgent to permit any opportunity of supplying them to be neglected, and on October 24th the Shipping Control Committee agreed to fifteen requisitioned vessels being allocated to the service.

This was a very small allocation as compared with that required by the summer programme, and meanwhile many of the ships employed in the execution of that programme had become free for other service, or were on their way home. Those of the 1915 programme which had been frozen up during the winter months, had arrived early in the summer with the cargoes which they had loaded at Archangel, and they were soon followed by a steady stream of ships returning under requisition or on temporary release, with timber, flax, hemp, and tow for Great Britain, wheat and wood alcohol for France. Russian steamers and neutrals on time charter swelled the stream, and most of the ships which had taken out munitions from the United States brought back cargo to Great Britain on the homeward voyage. As the season advanced, it became necessary to work some steamers back in ballast, in order to

[1] The Murman Railway was officially declared open on December 8th.

avoid the risk of their being frozen in, but the number of ballast voyages was kept down to a minimum.

By the end of October the total number of British ships on requisition or black-listed for Russian service in any part of the world had fallen from 162 in September to 104. By November 30th it was down to 34, and Russia had ceased to be a serious liability so far as tonnage was concerned. The demands of France and Italy, on the other hand, were as great as or greater than ever, and occupied much of the attention of the Shipping Control Committee and the Transport Department.

The responsibilities undertaken by the British Government towards France and Italy as regards the purchase of supplies from abroad were steadily increasing. Both the French and Italian Governments had brought sugar under control, and in October arrangements were made by which they undertook to effect all purchases through the Royal Sugar Commission, and the entire Mauritius crop was handed over to France. This was followed, as we have seen, by the formation of the Wheat Executive in November. Arrangements for joint purchase did not, however, necessarily involve the provision of further tonnage, and the Shipping Control Committee still adhered to the limits previously laid down. In October, for instance, they absolutely refused a request for the allocation of further tonnage to the steel and oat service.[1] This was not all; while they had no desire to withdraw from France and Italy assistance already promised, the position had become too serious to permit acquiescence in the continued employment by those countries of more ships than they could use effectively.

It was with regard to the coal shipments to France that the main difficulty arose. The congestion of the French ports had always been a source of anxiety and during the autumn of 1916 that anxiety became acute. Although the exports of coal to France had averaged only 1,000,000 tons a month before the war, the French Government, in their urgent need of fuel, were now granting

---

[1] This service actually involved, during 1916, 233 voyages and the carriage of 210,000 tons of metal (including some copper) and 1,138,000 tons of grain. In addition, 14 voyages were undertaken for the Belgian Government. Only 3 ships were lost, one of which was salved. Distribution:
  France, 164,338 tons metal, 816,846 tons grain, 2,818 horses.
  Italy, 46,547 tons metal, 320,933 tons grain.

LICENCES FOR FRANCE REFUSED

import licences at a rate of more nearly 2,000,000, and in August 1916 over 1,600,000 tons were actually shipped, exclusive of Admiralty supplies. This figure, however, was only attained at a high cost. Discharge in France was a much slower business than loading in Great Britain. It was long before the ships returned, and in September the effect of the big coal shipments during August was felt in a grave shortage of tonnage for steel exports. By the end of September no less than 12,000 tons of shell-steel had accumulated on the quays of Newport alone, awaiting the return of tonnage held up in French ports, and the resulting congestion blocked the flow of supplies right back to the works.

On September 12th it was reported to the Shipping Control Committee that 180 steamers were awaiting discharge in French ports, and so deeply were they impressed by the waste of carrying power that they suggested the withdrawal from the French coal trade of all British vessels over 5,000 tons gross until the congestion should be cleared. On October 9th the state of the French ports again came before them, and on that date they decided to instruct the Ship Licensing Committee to refuse for the time being any further licences for ships over 2,500 tons dead-weight to French Northern or Bay ports.

Meanwhile the shipments of coal were maintained at or above the August level. In September the exports, exclusive of Admiralty shipments, amounted to 1,700,000 tons; in October to over 1,600,000. The French ports, however, were unable to receive at this rate, and the result was not to add to the effective supplies reaching the French consumer but to increase the quantity in ships awaiting discharge and used in the meantime as floating dumps. In the opinion of the Ship Licensing Committee the capacity of the French ports for the import of coal did not exceed 1,500,000 tons per month, and they strongly pressed the French Government to restrict the issue of import licences to this figure. In the meantime they consistently refused licences for the more congested ports. They took steps also to withdraw from the French coal trade the comparatively few tramps of the largest class, which were now urgently needed on the ocean routes, and to divert from Channel ports to the Bay and Mediterranean, steamers suitable for bringing back ore cargoes on the homeward voyage.

It was in the coal trade that the congestion of the French ports was felt most acutely, and few licences were refused on that account for ocean voyages. The Committee were obliged, however, during the autumn of 1916 to refuse further general licences for vessels on time-charter to French firms, feeling it undesirable, in the existing conditions, that any more tonnage should be thus removed from the possibility of effective control.

Strong as were the reasons for the attitude adopted by the Shipping Control and Ship Licensing Committees, the action taken could not but be unwelcome to France. The French Authorities did not deny the grave congestion of their ports, but they were able to point out that this congestion was due in part to the demands of the British Armies. Dunkirk, Boulogne, Calais, Dieppe, and a large proportion of the accommodation at Havre and Rouen had been handed over for the use of the British troops, thus increasing the strain imposed by the import services on other ports; 25,000 French railway wagons had been placed at the disposal of the British Armies; the services demanded by those Armies from the French railways were daily increasing.

All this was true, and it was unquestionable that France was entitled, both by her needs and her services, to the most sympathetic consideration of her demands. On the other hand, the despatch of heavily laden ships to ports already unable to deal with the volume of traffic was of no effective service to France herself, while it involved a deplorable waste of carrying power. So long as the purchases of France abroad continued to exceed the importing capacity of her ports, the authorities responsible for the control of British tonnage had no option but to restrict the sailings of British ships to the congested ports. Yet the mere refusal of licence was a crude and inequitable method of dealing with the problem. It did, indeed, preserve the carrying power of a number of ships which might otherwise have been wasted, but it was impossible for any purely British authority to discriminate accurately between essential and non-essential demands, nor could their action solve effectively the problem of port congestion, since it was always possible for the French to charter neutral tonnage in place of the ships withdrawn. On both sides of the Channel there was a growing conviction that some more scientific

THE ITALIAN COAL PROBLEM 355

solution, going to the root of the problem, must shortly be attempted.

During October the question of the Italian coal supply also came up for reconsideration. With regard to the other Italian services no great difficulty had arisen since the Pallanza Conference. The necessary supplies of grain and steel had been maintained, and the meat agreement, which expired in September, had been renewed for a further six months in a revised form. The new agreement guaranteed to the Italian Government all the meat that could be carried in Italian ships, all shipments from China by the Blue Star Line, and about 3,000 tons a month in other British ships. The total supply was expected to reach from 9,000 to 10,000 tons a month, all beef, and the necessary tonnage was arranged without much trouble. The coal supply was a more serious problem.

The 500,000 tons of coal to be supplied by the Admiralty had all been duly shipped by the end of September, but the British Government had undertaken, at the Pallanza Conference, to do their utmost to facilitate shipments at the rate of 250,000 tons additional each month for the remainder of the year, and in reliance on this promise the Italians had taken steps to reduce their imports from the United States with a view to tonnage economy.[1]

The great difficulty was, as always, the provision of shipping. It was impossible, in the existing circumstances, to allocate further British requisitioned tonnage on any considerable scale, and the number of licensed ships to which Italy was entitled had been reduced by losses. The Licensing Committee continued to operate the scheme with a margin of elasticity so far as the Italian coal trade was concerned, especially in respect of vessels returning with ore; but the bulk of the coal had to be carried by Italian and neutral shipping. Prior to 1916 Italian tonnage had performed but a small share of the work, but since the beginning of the year Italian steamers had been directed into the trade in steadily increasing numbers, and

[1] Italian imports of coal:

1916	From United Kingdom. Tons.	From United States. Tons.
September	656,000	123,000
October	656,000	77,000
November	502,000	42,000

These figures appear to include Admiralty shipments.

they were now able to carry a considerable share of the exports. Little more than half the usual amount of Greek shipping was now available, but the loss of Greek ships had been made good to some extent by neutrals chartered by Messrs. Furness, Withy & Co. The regulation compelling Scandinavian ships requiring bunkers for a ballast voyage to America, to take a coal cargo to Bay or Mediterranean ports may also have helped to drive neutral tonnage into the trade. Nevertheless, the shipping available was unequal to the carriage of 250,000 tons a month in addition to the normal average export prior to the new arrangements. Still, the shipments were largely increased and everything possible was done to induce neutrals to accept Italian coal charters.

It was necessary, however, so far as possible, to utilise for British as well as for Italian trade the tonnage thus provided. Italy had already agreed, in return for the assistance given her, to lift 25,000 tons of ore a month in Italian shipping, but the Transport Department and the Shipping Control Committee were loth to allow any steamers which might be used for ore imports to return in ballast. On the other hand, there was from the Italian point of view a valid objection to a course which considerably increased the length of the round voyage, and it became necessary, if the point was to be pressed, to find some equivalent in the coal traffic for the loss of carrying power involved. This difficulty was finally solved in November by an agreement under which the Admiralty undertook, in return for every 9 tons of ore lifted by Italian or Italian controlled tonnage [1] in excess of the agreed 25,000 tons a month, to ship to Italy an additional 4 tons of coal at Blue Book rates. The effect of this agreement was immediate, for in the month of November itself nearly 49,000 tons of ore were lifted by Italian steamers.

Apart from tonnage supplied by the Admiralty at Blue Book rates, it had been an understanding at the Pallanza Conference that the Coal Freight Limitation Scheme should be applied to the Italian trade. The undertaking given by Mr. Runciman was loyally observed. On his return to Great Britain he called the necessary meeting of coal-producers, coal-exporters, and shipowners, and a schedule of maximum freights and prices, to come into operation on

---

[1] E.g. British or neutral ships on Italian time-charter.

October 30th, was issued to govern all shipments to Italian and French Mediterranean ports.[1]

So far as British shipping was concerned, the limitation rates presented a real saving to Italy, but neutral shipping proved still less easy to control than in the Channel and Bay trades. The amount of tonnage involved was much smaller, and could more easily find alternative employment; there was no machinery so effective as that provided by the North Sea Freight Regulations, for directing tonnage into the trade. Moreover, the new Schedule came into force at the very time when the increased submarine risk threatened to drive neutrals out of the trade altogether.

The advocates of unrestricted submarine warfare were now gaining the upper hand in Germany, and as they were convinced that the greater number and extended range of the submarines now available afforded the means of making a really effective impression on the seaborne trade of the Allies, they were prepared to take the risk of friction with neutral Governments. Accordingly, the month of October was marked not only by a wide extension of the area of attack but by the especial severity with which the losses fell on neutral shipping.

From the point of view of British commerce the most serious development in the campaign was the appearance of a submarine on the American coast. The voyage of the *Deutschland* had shown that the Atlantic could be traversed in safety by vessels of this class, but no German submarine had hitherto succeeded in attacking commerce west of a line drawn some 150 miles from the Fastnet. On October 8th, however, U53 appeared off Nantucket Light Vessel, Rhode Island, and in the course of the day captured and sank five vessels, three British, one Dutch, and one Norwegian.

In European waters the submarines were ubiquitous. Ships were sunk in the Mediterranean, and in its approaches off Capes St. Vincent and Trafalgar and at the entrance to the Straits of Gibraltar, in the Bay of Biscay, off the Scillies, off the Fastnet, in the English Channel, off Tory Island, off the Orkneys, in the North Sea, the Arctic Ocean, the Skagerrak, and the Baltic. It was in the Mediterranean that the havoc was greatest. There, over forty ships of

[1] The rates from the Tyne to Marseilles, Genoa, and Naples respectively were fixed at 63s. 6d., 64s. 6d., and 62s. 6d.; British Channel rates were 5s. lower; from and to other ports in proportion.

all nationalities were destroyed, and they included two exceptionally fine vessels, the Cunarder *Franconia* of 18,150 tons on transport duty, and the *Gallia*, of 14,966 tons, belonging to the Campagnie de Navigation Sud-Atlantique. In the North Sea more than 30 neutral vessels were destroyed. As many more, British, Allied, and neutral were sunk in the English Channel, and nearly a score in the South-Western Approach. The security of trade in the Channel was further menaced on October 26th by a destroyer raid on the Straits of Dover, in which the Folkestone-Boulogne packet *The Queen* was captured; and more than a dozen vessels in various areas were blown up by mines.

Although 32 British ships, attacked by submarines, beat off their assailant, were rescued, or escaped, the total destruction of British tonnage amounted to 176,000 tons, a loss heavier by 30,000 tons than that suffered in August 1915, hitherto the blackest month of the war. The Allies lost 74,000 tons, and neutral losses amounted to 85 vessels, of 102,500 tons, exceeding by 40 vessels and 26,000 tons anything yet recorded.

These casualties to neutral shipping were very unevenly distributed. Both the Greeks and the Swedes suffered more heavily than in any previous month of the war; but it was on the Norwegians that the bulk of the losses fell. In steamers alone Norway lost over 60,000 tons gross, bringing up the total for September and October to 100,000 tons, or 5 per cent. of the whole Norwegian steam fleet at the outbreak of war.

From this heavy blow to the Norwegian mercantile marine arose a situation very threatening to the Allies. The Norwegian War Risk Insurance Association, to which all shipowners were compelled by law to belong, was organised on a mutual basis. The Association had already been heavily hit, and the effect of the October losses was to leave it with so large a deficit that there was grave danger of the scheme breaking down altogether, and of the Norwegian ships engaged in Allied trade being withdrawn and laid up. The British Government accordingly made arrangements with a syndicate of London underwriters to reinsure, for their account, the hulls of all Norwegian steamers engaged in Allied trades, at rates varying from 1·2 to 3 per cent. according to the nature of the voyage. By arrangement with the French and Italian Governments the losses and premiums under this scheme were respectively debited and credited to the country in whose interest the steamer insured was trading on each particular voyage.[1]

Even with this measure of financial relief to the Norwegian shipowner, the effect of the havoc wrought in October was inevitably severe. About half the vessels sunk in the North Sea were, as usual, small sailing vessels laden with pit-props, but they included also several steamers with cargo from Scandinavia, including five with ore from Narvik or Kirknes. For a short time there was something like a cessation of chartering at Scandinavian ports, but by the end of November there was again plenty of tonnage on offer except at Narvik, where the ore freight had risen from 15s. to 22s. a ton. The scheme of reinsurance for Norwegian vessels went a long way to steady the market, the losses in the North Sea greatly decreased during November, and the entrances from Scandinavian ports remained tolerably steady.

Much more serious was the position as regards neutral tonnage in the French and Italian coal trades. The losses in these trades were heavy. During October a dozen Norwegian steamers carrying coal to Northern French or Bay ports, or returning with pit-props, iron ore, or pyrites from the South of Spain and the Mediterranean, were sunk in the English Channel or off Ushant. Next month things were still worse. Submarines were active in the Channel, in the Bay of Biscay, off the North-West of Spain, and in the Mediterranean. The cross-Channel traffic was seriously impeded, and colliers going out to the Mediterranean or returning with ore were exposed to attack in every section of their route.

The retention of neutral shipping in the North Sea trade was facilitated by the need of the Scandinavian States for British coal, and the interest of their own producers and merchants in preserving communication with the British market. To the French and Italian coal trades these considerations did not apply, and many Scandinavian shipowners were eager to seek a safer and more remunerative employment. The North Sea Regulations had, on the whole, worked well, both in keeping up the entrances from

[1] *Government War Risk Insurance Schemes* [Cmd. 98], 1919. The agreement was not actually signed till 6 January, 1917, but the scheme took effect as from November 1916. Only 90 per cent. of the values was actually reinsured, the Norwegian Association retaining the remaining 10 per cent.

Scandinavia and in providing tonnage for France; but they were beginning to chafe. During October the obligations on ships taking the French alternative had become more onerous. Ships over 2,000 tons dead-weight had now to make an intermediate voyage to French ports south of La Rochelle and return with ore from Spain. Thus, a voyage with coal to Scandinavia had to bear the cost of a ballast voyage to the United Kingdom followed by two voyages at artificially lowered rates. Under the effects of this obligation and of the increased war risks, coal freights to Scandinavia rose rapidly, till by the end of the year they stood at £10, or even £14, as compared with 14s. 6d. before the war.

Meanwhile, the American harvests were ready to be moved, and neutral shipowners were naturally desirous of responding as usual to the seasonal demand at North American ports. It was by no means in the interests of the Allies to bunker neutral vessels for this purpose, except when the grain cargoes were to be brought to Allied ports. It was hardly possible, in all the circumstances, to refuse bunkers as a general principle, but every effort was made to retain the ships in Allied trades. This, however, was not easy. So far as Sweden was concerned, the bunker regulations had already broken down, and now even the Norwegians began to murmur.

There were, moreover, other trades outside the war zone, in which the demand for tonnage was strong. The preoccupation of British manufacturers with the supply of the Armies and the Allies, and the withdrawal of British ships from the inter-foreign trade, had created a vacuum which neutrals were eager to fill. The trade between North and South America was expanding, and so was the trade both of America and Japan with all countries of the Far and Middle East. In these trades freights were high, war risks non-existent, and bunkers obtainable at neutral ports.

Thus, while one set of factors tended to drive neutral steamers out of the dangerous trades in which they were engaged in Allied interests, another set of factors tended to draw them away by the offer of safer employment and higher remuneration. It was under these conditions that the Coal Freights Limitation Scheme was extended to Italian and French Mediterranean ports, and from the first it was clear that, so far as neutral tonnage was concerned, the extension was unworkable. Neutral vessels either left the Mediterranean trade altogether or accepted charters only for Spain, Malta, and other destinations to which the Limitation Rates did not apply.

To add to the difficulties of Italy, the friction between Greece and the Allies had been increasing all through the summer and autumn, and by the beginning of winter relations had become almost openly hostile. Thus, while the total neutral tonnage in the Italian coal trade fell away rapidly and heavily during the last two months of 1916, the Greek tonnage in that trade dwindled to nothing. For such a loss the prospect of a third share in a dozen German and Austrian steamers seized in Greek ports was but a poor compensation.

Italy was, indeed, able to earn a substantial addition to the supplies of coal shipped at Blue Book rates, by means of the coal-ore agreement; but this was not all clear gain. The total number of ships available was limited, and any addition to the requisitioned tonnage meant a decrease in the number of vessels on the freight markets.

Almost equally serious was the situation in the French coal trade. The sailings even of British steamers dropped considerably, owing to the steps taken by the Licensing Committee in October, the delays due to port congestion, and the frequent interruption of traffic by submarines in the Channel; but the falling off in neutral clearances was far heavier, and it was fast becoming evident that, if neutral vessels were to be retained in the trade, they would have to be relieved, at any rate to some extent, from the burden of Limitation Rates.

Nor was this diminution in the services of neutral shipping confined to these special trades. Everywhere neutral shipowners were escaping to safer employment, and it became obvious that something must be done to retain this essential body of tonnage in Allied service. The great difficulty was the question of insurance. With so large a proportion of their tonnage engaged in trades for which the freights had been artificially lowered, neutral shipowners were unable to pay the high premiums demanded. Shippers, too, found it difficult to cover fully on the open market cargoes shipped in neutral bottoms. Early in December it became apparent that, if the services of neutral shipping were to be retained, insurance facilities must be provided by the Government for other vessels as well as Norwegian, and for cargoes shipped in neutral bottoms. Immediate action was necessary, and an arrangement was made with the Commercial Union Insurance Company, by which the Company agreed to accept liability, on behalf of the Government, for the insurance of hulls of all neutral steamers other than Norwegian, at rates to be fixed by the Board of Trade. The company also undertook to insure such cargo on neutral steamers as could not be covered in the open market on account of the high value to be carried. As in the insurance of Norwegian steamers, an agreement was effected between the British, French, and Italian Governments for the premiums and the ultimate liability for losses to be shared between them according to the services in which the ships were employed.[1]

These arrangements were the more important inasmuch as, at the beginning of December, the principle of centralised Inter-Allied chartering of neutral tonnage had been definitely accepted as part of a very important agreement concluded between the French and British Governments.

[1] [Cmd. 98]. These arrangements did not become effectively operative until 1917.

CHAPTER XXIV

THE APPOINTMENT OF THE SHIPPING CONTROLLER
DECEMBER 1916

THERE were, in the winter of 1916, four outstanding questions of the first importance to be solved by the British and French Governments : the general situation arising from shortage of tonnage, the congestion of the French ports, the difficulties arising from the requisitioning of, or refusal of licences to, steamers chartered by France, and the provision of tonnage for the French wheat programme. The last-named of these questions was, of course, bound up with the general problem of securing the wheat supply of the Allies, which was now being considered by the Royal Wheat Commission and the Transport Department.

According to the first programme worked out by the Wheat Commission, the total requirements of the Allies for the unexpired portion of the cereal year ending August 1917 exceeded the estimated available supplies by 1,100,000 quarters (say 285,000 tons). The Commission had, accordingly, reduced the requirements of each of the Allies proportionately, in order to bring them within the capacity of the supplies. Thus reduced they amounted to 9,110,000 tons, of which 4,787,000 tons were for the United Kingdom, 2,754,000 tons for France, and 1,569,000 tons for Italy. Of this total, freight for about 1,850,000 had already been booked, leaving 7,250,000 tons still to be arranged.

In working out a programme to meet this demand, the Transport Department were able to rely on about 750,000 tons being lifted by Italian-owned vessels or British ships already on Italian service. The requirements of the French Ministry of Commerce, amounting to 1,890,000 tons, of which 1,098,000 tons remained to be freighted, would also be met by shipping chartered through the Hudson Bay Co. and freight provided by the Australian Government for c.i.f. purchases, without making further demands on

British tonnage. It remained to provide for the requirements of the United Kingdom, those of the French Ministry of War, and the balance of the Italian demand.

After allowing for liner shipments and for tramps already on service, the Transport Department estimated that a total of 174 new requisitions would be necessary during the five months December to April inclusive, of which 112 would be employed wholly in the carriage of wheat, while 62 would be required to maintain the collier service in the Mediterranean, from which a regular monthly quota of steamers was to be directed to Australia.

This was a heavy strain on the tonnage resources of the country, seeing that, on October 31st, the total number of free tramps running on commercial services for the United Kingdom, including those temporarily released, was only 328. The problem was aggravated by the fact that the greatest number of ships would be required at the time when the White Sea Service would be in full swing. Further, owing to the difficulty in collecting vessels and the length of the Australian voyage, a disproportionate amount of the wheat was timed to arrive in the later months of the cereal year, so that during the spring the stocks in all three countries were likely to run very low.

Thus the Wheat Section had hardly worked out the Australian programme when anxiety became acute as to the prospect of a grave shortage in the early months of 1917, before the bulk of the Australian shipments could be received, and steps were accordingly taken to direct a large number of tramps to North American ports during December and January in order to build up stocks. Meanwhile, the question of the French programme had been settled on a basis which relieved the Transport Department of one at least of their chief responsibilities.

On November 21st a meeting was held between Mr. Graeme Thomson, Director of Transports, Mr. J. A. Salter, Director of Requisitioning, Mr. Thomas Royden, of the Shipping Control Committee, and the representatives of the French Government, at which considerable progress was made towards a settlement of all the outstanding questions. It was agreed by both sides that the general problem of establishing an equilibrium between the French import requirements, the available tonnage, and the capacity of the French ports must be solved by France herself, through restriction of imports and improvement of port facilities. On the other hand, it was essential that a definite understanding should be arrived at with regard to the French demands on British tonnage. The French representatives were of opinion that the wheat requirements as originally estimated by the Commission Internationale de Ravitaillement were capable of reduction, and they suggested a meeting between M. Clémentel, the French Minister of Commerce, and the President of the Board of Trade, for the purpose of arriving at a working basis of co-operation. This suggestion was adopted, and on December 3rd an agreement was signed by M. Clémentel and Mr. Runciman by which the rights and obligations of the two Governments as regards shipping were fully and clearly defined.

By this agreement the French Minister of Commerce undertook, on the basis of ships already in French service, responsibility for the transport of the entire wheat supply of France, whether for the Ministry of Commerce or the Ministry of War, during the current season. It was further arranged that the whole of these supplies should, for the future, be procured from Australia, India, the Plate, and the White Sea, thus leaving the full benefit of the North American Market to the other Allies. The balance of the shipping required for this purpose, for the Archangel service, and for sugar and other miscellaneous cargoes, over and above the seventy British ships already trading under licence for the Ministry of Commerce, was to be made up with French and neutral steamers, and the whole programme was to be worked out by the Transport Department in conjunction with the Royal Commission on Wheat Supplies.

In return for this undertaking, the British Government agreed to continue the existing services carried on by requisitioned tonnage, and to permit France to charter British tonnage for ocean voyages up to the amount so employed on October 31st, 1916. They were not, however, to be under any obligation to replace ships, either requisitioned or licensed, lost in French service. They further preserved their right to reduce the tonnage now agreed upon should this be rendered necessary by further depletion of the available shipping; but in such event they agreed to consult the French Government as to the services from which ships could most easily be spared.

The same principle was applied to vessels running between the United Kingdom and France, but it was specially stipulated that time-chartered vessels in the coal trade should be used to bring back ore, pyrites, pit-props, or other essential cargoes to the United Kingdom. On their part, the French Government agreed to do everything possible to accelerate loading and discharge. It was, indeed, stipulated that " so far as continued congestion in her ports results in her having more ships than she needs to bring in the total imports which the ports can receive and expeditiously clear, France will give back vessels allotted to her." To assist in the clearing of the ports, the British Government agreed to send 10,000 railway wagons as promptly as possible, and 10,000 more with a certain number of locomotives during the early months of 1917. These wagons were to be carried by vessels in French service proceeding to France in ballast, and as deck cargoes by colliers in French service. On their arrival they were to be used to release to France an equivalent number of the French railway wagons in the service of the British Armies.

Tonnage for steel shipments from the United Kingdom was also promised so soon as the French Government should be able to name a date for the completion of discharge of steel from vessels already in French ports or on passage to Nantes, and should further be able to guarantee discharge at the rate of 500 tons per day from the date of arrival. In addition, the Board of Trade agreed to the transfer to the French flag of certain steamers constructed for French firms, and to accelerate the construction of ships ordered before the date of the agreement, on condition that when completed such ships should be employed by the French Government.

Among other questions dealt with in the agreement were the exchange of information as to the state of ports and the employment of tonnage, the adjustment of liner services so as to equalise the burden of requisitioning on the French and British lines, and the general co-ordination of shipping and import programmes. For instance, it was provided that steamers carrying horses to France should load wheat for the United Kingdom in their lower holds. Finally, it was agreed that, " All chartering of neutral steamers will be completely centralised by means of an Inter-Allied bureau in London." [1]

The effect of the Clémentel Agreement was to relieve the Transport Department of the necessity for providing tonnage for the unshipped requirements of the French Ministry of War, a saving of over 1,200,000 tons. This was a great relief, but anxiety with regard to the grain supply for 1917 was by no means at an end. A revised estimate presented by the Wheat Commission early in December showed a reduction of about 14 per cent. in the shipments contemplated, mainly accounted for by a diminution of 1,000,000 tons in the imports from North America. This reduction was due not so much to pessimism with regard to the exportable surplus as to the difficulty of arranging further credits in America. Even apart from such Government purchases as did not appear in the Board of Trade returns, the imports from the United States were now nearly five times as great as the total of exports and re-exports shipped to that country. In addition, enormous purchases of munitions and raw material had been made on behalf of the Allies, and, despite the " mobilisation of securities " by the Treasury, British and Allied credit had been strained to its utmost. It was no longer a question merely of the supplies on offer but of the extent to which further purchases could be financed. Yet, unless further credits could be arranged, the only alternative was to send out still more ships to Australia, a most uneconomical use of tonnage even if, which was very doubtful, the ships could be procured.

Meanwhile, the pressure of the demand on North America, coupled with constriction of supplies, had produced the natural effect of sending up still further the price of bread. Although the North Atlantic freights, as now fixed, worked out at only ·86d. on the wheat in the quartern loaf, as compared with 1d. in September, the import value of the wheat had risen from 7·02d. to 8d. and the price of the loaf from 9d. to 10d.

Even with the advantage of fixed freights, the necessity of procuring a large proportion of the wheat supply from Australia could hardly fail to force up prices still higher. Yet this was a smaller drawback than the loss of carrying power. Not only was the Australian voyage far longer

[1] This provision was fulfilled in January 1917 by the creation of the Inter-Allied Chartering Committee, as will be described in Vol. III.

than the North American, but the conditions on the route were very unfavourable. That portion of the Australian trade which formerly followed the Suez route, outwards or homewards, had now been diverted to the Cape, as had the whole volume of Far Eastern shipping, and the effect of these diversions had been to create grave difficulties at the South African bunker ports. The South African railways were unequal to the strain imposed on them by the demand for coal at Durban and Cape Town, and delays at those ports were frequent and lengthy. So far as possible, preference was given to British ships, but the consequent reduction in the carrying power of neutral shipping was in itself a serious matter. Nor could it be doubted that the diversion of a continual stream of wheat-ships to Australia would greatly increase the congestion.

Another direction in which the closing of the Mediterranean to through traffic was severely felt was the import of frozen meat. Apart from the addition to the length of all Australian voyages, the restrictions created very serious difficulties in the supply of meat to the Allied Armies in the Eastern Mediterranean. Not only did the homeward-bound Australian transports no longer call at Port Said, but steamers from the Plate or from the United Kingdom had to be sent out round the Cape, involving, in respect of ships from British ports, a voyage of double the former length.

The feeding of the forces in the Eastern Mediterranean was, indeed, one of the most difficult problems presented to Sir Thomas Robinson and his assistants. It was not only the ocean voyages that had to be arranged. Even greater were the difficulties involved in conveying the meat to the troops from the base in Egypt. The arrangements for distribution from Port Said had been greatly improved towards the end of 1915, but the work was still hampered both by a deficiency of facilities for unloading and storage at Port Said itself and by the liability of the small steamers employed in distribution to accident, and to submarine attack. It even became necessary on occasion to resort to the hazardous expedient of sending an ocean steamer direct to Salonika, entailing not only additional submarine risk, but very serious delays in discharging at that port, which was ill adapted to deal with ships of such a size.[1]

---

[1] Thus, on one occasion the *Murillo* took 26 days to discharge 3,000 tons of meat.

MEAT SUPPLIES MAINTAINED

Yet, despite all obstacles, the supply of the Armies was fully maintained, and there was no interruption in the distribution of rations. In all, 61,000 tons of meat were landed in the Eastern Mediterranean direct [1] and 21,000 tons were sent out from the United Kingdom, making a total of 82,000 tons in 1916, as compared with 35,000 in the previous year.[2] That the supply of meat alone for the Armies in the Eastern theatre ran into such large figures, illustrates in striking fashion the strain imposed by these distant expeditions. That the supply was adequately maintained in circumstances of such difficulty, was a real triumph for the Board of Trade organisation and the Committees which supervised the employment of insulated tonnage.

It was not only in the Mediterranean that difficulties arose. The lack of sufficient cold storage accommodation at French ports hampered both direct deliveries and the cross-Channel ferry services, and the feeding of the troops imposed a severe strain on the organisation. Apart, too, from all special difficulties of this kind, insulated steamers, in common with all others, were liable to frequent detention or diversion due to fear of submarine attack, and the total reduction in carrying power due to such delays was a serious matter. The actual insulated tonnage available was rather greater than in 1915, for the losses due to war and marine risks were more than made good by the delivery of five new vessels, the diversion of three Lamport and Holt Liners, in the spring, from the New York to the Liverpool service,[3] the release of ships by the Admiralty, and the additional insulated tonnage under the French and Italian flags; but longer voyages, port delays, and diversions so far reduced the effective carrying-power of the ships, that the total deliveries in all countries were less

---

[1] Of this total, 12,700 tons came from Australia, 35,400 tons from the Plate, and 13,000 tons from other sources.

[2] These stocks, according to the arrangements made in 1915, were held in common by the Allied Armies. The actual distribution was 53,800 tons to the British, 27,700 tons to the French, and 700 tons to the Italians. The Serbian forces were supplied in equal proportions by the British and French.

[3] These ships were not actually diverted from the New York run, but were ordered to put another "leg" on their course. By sailing Plate to New York, thence to Liverpool, and then back to New York, they were able to deliver the meat at Liverpool while maintaining, in an attenuated form, their Plate-New York service which had considerable value from the exchange standpoint.

by 2·8 per cent. than in the previous year.[1] Having regard to all the circumstances, it was a fine achievement to approach so closely the 1915 figures.

The actual amount of meat delivered was 970,000 tons.[2] Owing to the destruction of stock by the great drought of 1915, the Australian shipments dropped from 197,000 to 77,000 tons, but the New Zealand output was more than maintained, and considerably increased supplies were procured from the Plate and from various minor sources. The increased Argentine output was due in some measure to the action of the Board of Trade in acquiring, towards the end of 1915, the lease of a freezing works at Las Palmas, which had been lying idle for some years. This establishment was managed for the Board, on a profit-sharing basis, by the British Company from whom it had been leased, and gave them not only additional supplies, but a valuable insight into the conditions of the trade.

Owing to the change in the Lamport and Holt service, only 10,000 tons of the Plate product, as against 50,000 tons in the previous year, went to the United States, so that the total supply actually available for the Allies was 960,000 tons, or 13,000 tons more than in 1913. On the other hand, the demands of the Armies had so greatly increased that, despite some reduction in the British meat ration, they absorbed more than 700,000 tons,

---

[1] The total tonnage working at the end of 1915 and 1916 respectively was as follows:

	s.s.	Plate tonnage. Tons meat capacity.	s.s.	Australasian tonnage. Cubic feet insulated space.
End 1915	52	135,000	110	25,853,900
End 1916	55	148,800	113	26,618,200

These figures exclude a few ships running on minor services. The whole tonnage was regarded as more or less interchangeable, and ships were diverted from one service to another as occasion arose.

Thanks to the assistance given by the Board of Trade, the French added to their fleet during 1916, 5 steamers of 12,000 tons aggregate meat capacity, bringing up the total capacity of French shipping to 17,900 tons, and the Italians insulated 9 steamers with a total capacity of 20,000 tons.

[2] No cargoes were lost *en route*, as the ships sunk were all on outward voyages.

leaving under 260,000 tons for consumption by British civilians.[1]

Civilian requirements had, of course, been considerably reduced, owing to the increase in the number of men under arms; but even so, the amount available for civilian consumption, including home grown meat, was reduced to about 2·4 lbs. a week, per adult man, as against 2·8 lbs. in 1913. The incidence of the reduction, however, was very unequal. The rise in the price of cattle in Argentina and the increased cost of production in Australia, due to the drought, involved a considerable increase in import values. The price of home-produced meat, which now accounted for some 80 per cent. of the civilian supplies, also rose as the result of an advance in agricultural wages and the cost of feeding-stuffs and fertilisers. Thus, although the Board of Trade was

[1] Sources of meat supply, 1916:

	Beef.	Mutton.	Total.
	1,000 tons.	1,000 tons.	1,000 tons.
Plate and Patagonia	500	72	572
Australia	62	15	77
New Zealand	53	115	168
Canada	15	—	15
S. Africa	6	—	6
United States	89	—	89
Brazil	26	—	26
Venezuela and Madagascar	9	—	9
China	8	—	8
	768	202	970

Distribution of supplies, 1916:

	Beef.	Mutton.	Total.
	1,000 tons.	1,000 tons.	1,000 tons.
British Army	301	61	362
British Civilians	129	128	257
French Army	247	8	255
Italian Army	86	—	86
U.S. Civilians	5	5	10
	768	202	970

Of the British Army supplies about 65,000 tons were landed in France direct.

Of the French supplies 83 per cent., and of the Italian 62 per cent., 265,000 tons in all, were carried in British shipping.

remarkably successful, both in negotiating its contracts abroad and in regulating the distribution of supplies released for civilian consumption, the advance in meat prices during the year was very considerable, and the actual consumption of meat by various sections of the population depended mainly on the way in which their income had been affected by the war.[1]

Sugar, the third, or in order of date the first, of the three essential foodstuffs for the supply of which the Government had now assumed responsibility, had been imported during 1916 in slightly larger quantities than during the previous year; but the imports were still a long way below the normal, stocks were falling, the army consumption had increased, and it was necessary to reduce the amount released for civilian consumption. Although the Royal Commission on Sugar Supplies did their best, in releasing sugar to the wholesale trade, to distribute the shortage as evenly as possible among different classes of buyers, there were many complaints as to inequality of distribution, and some retailers were already refusing to supply sugar to customers, except on the condition of their buying a stipulated amount of other groceries at the same time. Prices also had steadily risen. The wholesale price was regulated by the Royal Commission, and a certain amount of control was also exercised over retail prices; but, in spite of this control, and though sugar had the advantage of being carried at Blue Book rates, which had not been changed since March 1915, the average retail price of white granulated sugar rose from 4d. per lb. in January 1916 to 5½d. in December. As compared with average prices in July 1914, the increase amounted to about 3½d. per lb., or 170 per cent., of which slightly more

---

[1] Top prices current at Smithfield Market for the best qualities available:

	Argentine Chilled Beef.	New Zealand Mutton.	New Zealand Lamb.
	Price per lb. d.	Price per lb. d.	Price per lb. d.
Average top price, 1913	5·50	5·15	6·15
January, 1916	9·25	7·62	7·88
June 1916	12·00	8·62	9·50
December 1916	10·62	8·38	9·50

See also *Interim Report of Departmental Committee on Prices* [Cd. 8358], 1916.

than one-third represented increased duties, and the remainder was accounted for by increased f.o.b. prices and increased cost of transport.[1]

The upward curve of prices in general had been steeply graded throughout the latter part of the year. By December the *Economist* and *Statist* Index Numbers of Wholesale Prices stood at about 90 per cent. above the level of July 1914. The Index Number of Retail prices given in the *Board of Trade Labour Gazette* had risen less sharply, but the advance was over 66 per cent. The percentage increase varied greatly as between different commodities, but it was food and clothing which were most affected, and it was the advance in food prices which caused the greatest amount of discontent.

As a result both of the continued advance in prices, and of the complaints as to inequalities in distribution, partly caused by this advance and partly accompanying it, there was a strong and widespread demand that the Government should take further steps to assure an equitable distribution of supplies, by the fixing of maximum prices, by rationing, or by both or other means. With the working of the German food regulations before their eyes, the Government were unwilling to act hastily in the matter; but the problem was in some respects easier in the United Kingdom than in Germany, owing to the large proportion of the total supply represented by imports, which could be controlled in bulk from the date of purchase, and with the enemy's experience to guide them, they could hope to avoid many of the initial mistakes which had, from the first, rendered the path of the German Food Control so thorny. Now that they had assumed responsibility for the whole wheat supply of the country, it was essential that some machinery should be devised for securing to the consumer any benefits derived from Government purchase and fixed freights, and it was highly desirable that the work of the departments already controlling essential foodstuffs should be centralised and co-ordinated.

In view, moreover, of the acute shortage of tonnage, and of the large proportion of the British mercantile marine already engaged in the carriage of essential foodstuffs, it was extremely desirable to ascertain whether, by a

[1] *Second and Third Reports of the Departmental Committee on Prices* [Cd. 8483], 1917. The freight increase represented about 1·3d. per lb. as compared with July 1914.

judicious system of rationing, the consumption could be decreased to such an extent as would appreciably relieve the strain on shipping, without injuriously affecting the national health. Accordingly the Government decided during November both that a Food Controller should be appointed, and that immediate investigation should be made as to the possibilities of rationing.

During the same month they came to other important decisions arising even more directly out of the tonnage situation. The three chief measures proposed by the President of the Board of Trade as a means of relieving the shortage were increase of the Transport Workers' Battalions, review of the tonnage in naval and military employment, and acceleration of shipbuilding. On November 28rd the Government approved the increase of the Transport Workers' Battalions to a strength of 10,000 men and instructed the War Office and Board of Trade to make the arrangements necessary for giving effect to this decision. At the same time they instructed the Shipping Control Committee to investigate in detail the employment of the ships on naval and military service, with a view to releasing as many as possible for commercial employment.

Some improvement in the cross-Channel service had already been effected as a result of the inquiry into the condition of the Northern French ports made during the summer. As a result of that inquiry Sir Eric Geddes, formerly Deputy General Manager of the North-Eastern Railway, had been sent out to investigate the whole question of military transport. His reports received additional weight from the great difficulties experienced in maintaining the supply of ammunition during the Battle of the Somme. It was ammunition which was the principal difficulty, since however careful was the stowage at the home ports, it was impossible to avoid a great deal of sorting on the other side. Ammunition, like everything else, had to be stowed with regard to the stability of the ships, but on discharge it had to be sorted and assembled before being sent to the front, and the necessity of doing this work at the ports of discharge was one of the main factors producing congestion. Colonel C. W. Paget, commanding the Railway Operating Troops at Boulogne, had for a long time been urging the formation of inland depôts to which ammunition could be forwarded, immediately on discharge, for sorting and assembly; but the railway lines were only under British control to a certain distance from the port, and he had been unable to carry out his proposal. His endeavours to improve the condition of the ports themselves had also been hampered by the general shortage of cranes and other equipment, labour, and expert supervision.

The situation was now changed. The Government had become seriously alarmed as to the position, and in October Sir Eric Geddes was sent out as Director-General of Military Railways and Inspector-General of Transportation, with a free hand to do whatever he considered necessary and to call on the Ministry of Munitions for all material required.[1] He took with him expert assistants, and it was not long before he was able to bring about a great improvement. Not only were the port facilities increased and the organisation of discharge and forwarding improved, but Colonel Paget was enabled to carry out his scheme for dealing with the ammunition difficulty. The assistance given to the French in replacing the rolling stock placed by them at the disposal of the British Armies made it possible to secure their co-operation, and large inland depôts were formed to which ammunition and other material could be forwarded for sorting and assembly without using the transit-sheds at the ports. The result was not only very greatly to facilitate the supply of the Armies, but to remove much of the pressure on the ports, thus diminishing delays and, by adding to the carrying power of the shipping employed, enabling fewer ships to do the same amount of work, or more work to be done by the same tonnage. It was not, however, till the spring of 1917 that the new arrangements were in full working order and began to produce their maximum effect.

With regard to the acceleration of shipbuilding, the third subject dealt with by the President of the Board of Trade, some progress was made during the late autumn of 1916 and a considerable number of skilled workers were brought back from the Armies for work in the marine engineering shops; but in view of the various competing claims in labour and materials, and the difficulty presented by acceleration costs, the Government inclined more and more to the conclusion that the only way out of the impasse was

[1] This was important, as the additional port equipment required was procured from the Ministry of Munitions, without depleting the equipment of British ports.

876 APPOINTMENT OF SHIPPING CONTROLLER

for them to assume direct responsibility for mercantile construction. Down to the end of November, however, they had taken no definite step in this direction.[1]

Meanwhile the question of extending the control exercised over British shipping and rendering this control more drastic and direct had come up for further consideration. The Transport Department of the Admiralty had always been anxious that the Shipping Control Committee should be provided with a statistical and administrative staff and should assume responsibility for the direct control of temporarily released and directed ships, and for the detailed allocation of tonnage to the various services. This the Committee had refused, believing that a more efficient use of tonnage would be obtained by their confining themselves to general supervision and to decisions on matters of broad general principle, leaving the actual work of administration to the departments concerned. During the course of 1916, however, the conditions had changed. The proportion of free shipping was now much smaller than at the beginning of the year; by far the greater number of tramps, in particular, were running on Admiralty requisition or under Admiralty direction. Moreover, the proportion of imports directly or indirectly for Government account had enormously increased, and the Admiralty and the Government had assumed very large responsibilities for the supply of the Allies. The Transport Department were responsible for providing tonnage for the whole of the wheat, flour, and sugar imports of the United Kingdom, nearly all the nitrate and much of the ore imported, and for the shipments of flax and timber from the White Sea; they were obliged, in addition, to find ships for the carriage of wheat, coal, steel, oats, and maize, to France, Russia, and Italy; they provided requisitioned ships or requisitioned space for innumerable consignments of munitions and other war material both for the British and Allied Governments.

[1] Output of mercantile tonnage 1916:

March quarter	80,000 tons gross
June quarter	156,000 ,, ,,
September quarter	192,000 ,, ,,
December quarter	111,000 ,, ,,
Total	539,000 ,, ,,

The total output for the year was thus about 100,000 tons less than in 1915. Including war and auxiliary vessels (1,339,000 tons) the total of new construction was 1,878,000 tons, as compared with 1,521,000 in the previous year and 2,282,000 tons in the record year, 1914.

All wheat, flour, and sugar imports were now on Government account, and the Board of Trade were responsible for the purchase, transport, and distribution of the whole meat supply of Great Britain and the Allies. Thus, over a very large proportion both of the shipping industry and of the import trade, the operation of the ordinary economic laws and the ordinary commercial incentives had ceased, and was replaced by the decisions of such authorities as the Shipping Control Committee, the Ship Licensing Committee, and the Transport Department themselves. Further, these decisions were based on Departmental demands many of which were inevitably framed in accordance with military or political considerations. There was thus a strong case for co-ordinating and tightening the machinery of Control under the supreme direction of some authority possessing sufficient knowledge of the relative importance of military, naval, Allied, and commercial requirements to enable tonnage to be allocated on a scientific basis.

As the shortage of tonnage grew more and more acute and the various demands more and more insistent, the difficulty of allocation increased, and on November 29th the Advisory Committee of the Transport Department presented to the Prime Minister and the Secretary of the Admiralty a Memorandum reviewing the whole position, and urging that the Shipping Control Committee or some other central authority should be entrusted with full powers to survey the tonnage situation as a whole and to transfer any vessel in any service to such other employment as might from time to time seem expedient in view of changing conditions.

This then was the position when, on December 4th, Mr. Asquith tendered his resignation as Prime Minister. The reported failure of the American wheat crop had rendered it necessary to look to Australia for a large proportion of the 1916-17 supplies ; the necessity of providing tonnage for the long Australian voyage threatened an acute shipping crisis in the early months of 1917. Important measures to meet this crisis had already been taken. The Clémentel Agreement relieved British tonnage of a considerable strain, disposed of the main questions at issue between Great Britain and France, and established the principle of centralised chartering of neutral tonnage ; the decision to increase the Transport Workers' Battalion to 10,000 men promised a quicker turn round in British ports ; the decision to appoint a Food Controller and to investigate the possibilities of rationing held out some prospect of reduced consumption. Shipping in naval and military service was under review; the question of State shipbuilding had been taken into consideration. Nevertheless, a serious deficiency in tonnage was still probable, and, with a view to overcoming it, the Transport Department had revived the proposals for further restriction of imports. Proposals for more direct and centralised control of merchant shipping were also before the Cabinet.

On December 7th Mr. Lloyd George took office as Prime Minister in succession to Mr. Asquith, and on the 9th he announced the appointment of Sir Joseph P. Maclay, Bart., as Shipping Controller. At the outset he was to take the Presidency of the Shipping Control Committee, but full definition of his powers was deferred until after further examination.

From the first it was decided that the Controller should have ministerial rank, but Sir Joseph Maclay was anxious to be free from attendance in Parliament, in order that he might devote his whole time to administrative work. Sir Leo Chiozza Money, M.P., was accordingly appointed Parliamentary Secretary to the Controller, for the purpose of representing him in the House of Commons. The position of the new Minister and his Parliamentary Secretary was defined and regularised by the New Ministers and Secretaries Act, which received the Royal Assent on December 22nd.[1] This Act provided also for the creation of a Ministry of Food, and on December 26th this Ministry was brought into being by the appointment of Lord Devonport as Food Controller.

With the appointment of the Shipping Controller the process of development which had been going on continuously since the end of 1915 entered on a new phase. Henceforth the work of the various bodies which had been created to meet, as they arose, the requirements of a state of war, and which had performed, individually or in cooperation, much admirable service, was to be centralised, in response to the pressure of a new emergency, in a new and more powerful authority, the Ministry of Shipping. This Ministry did not, however, spring all at once into being; it was not until the new year that the Controller was provided with an administrative staff, or

[1] 6 and 7 Geo. V, c. 68.

IMPORT RESTRICTIONS

his powers and his relations with the Transport Department of the Admiralty fully defined.

Meanwhile, the new Government was occupied with the solution of the problems which it had taken over from its predecessor. The increase of the Transport Workers' Battalions was being carried out, and the investigation of shipping in naval and military employment was proceeding under the auspices of the Shipping Control Committee. The question of shipbuilding, however, was still to be settled, and on December 15th the Government came to the definite decision that ships should be built both at home and abroad on Government account, and that any completed ships in the builders' hands abroad should immediately be purchased. By the end of December contracts had already been placed for certain ships under construction in Japan, negotiations had been opened for large purchases of tonnage building in the United States, and considerable progress had been made in the designing of standard types for construction at home.[1]

The question of import restrictions also received attention. In considering the requirements of the White Sea programme in 1917, the Shipping Control Committee had been brought up against the probability of an acute tonnage shortage during the summer months, and on December 7th, at the suggestion of the Director of Requisitioning, they requested Sir Norman Hill to make a detailed statistical examination of the position. On December 14th Sir Norman Hill presented a report in which he estimated the probable deficiency of carrying power at 500,000 tons of imports a month, and urged that steps should at once be taken to secure, by prohibition of non-essential imports, the carriage of essential supplies. This report was placed by the Shipping Controller before the Government, who were greatly impressed by its arguments, and on December 21st appointed an Inter-departmental Committee, under Sir H. Babington-Smith, to consider and report on the whole question of import restriction.[2]

There was one problem, however, which was more insistent than any other, and towards the solution of which

---
[1] The idea of concentrating on the construction of certain "standard" types of cargo vessels had been approved in principle by the late Government, but no type had yet been definitely chosen.

[2] Further discussion of this question and of the shipbuilding programme is reserved to Vol. III.

little progress had been made: the problem of the submarine. All through November and December the attacks on British, Allied, and neutral shipping continued with unabated energy. The heaviest losses were still suffered in the old areas of attack, the Mediterranean, the South-Western Approach, the English Channel,[1] and North Sea [2]; but there was a steady increase in the number of vessels sunk off the Atlantic Coast of Spain and Portugal or in the Bay of Biscay, constituting a serious threat to the French coal trade and the supplies of ore from the Mediterranean. Even more serious was the convincing proof of the increased range of action possessed by the latest types of submarine. In November two steamers, one Portuguese and one Dutch, were sunk off the Canaries; in December five vessels, British, Allied, and neutral, were sunk off the Canaries or in Funchal Roads, and Funchal, the port of Madeira, was bombarded by the enemy.

In addition several ships were sunk by mines, and the discovery of a minefield off the Isle of Man showed that at least one mine-laying submarine had penetrated into the Irish Sea. During December came the further news that a surface raider was again at work in the Atlantic. This ship, at first reported as the VINETA, was in fact the MOEWE which, again under the command of Graf zu Dohna-Schlodien, had for a second time eluded the patrols, and passing round the North of Ireland, made her way on to the trade routes.

Both in November and December the total losses of British shipping from war causes exceeded anything recorded prior to October. Indeed, the acceleration in the rate of destruction had now become truly alarming. In 1915, the average monthly loss was about 70,000, and during the first nine months of 1916, about 80,000 tons gross; but for the December quarter it rose at a bound to 176,000 tons. Nor was this all. Shipping under Allied flags was now being sunk at the rate of over 60,000 tons a month, or more than three times as fast as in 1915; but it was in respect of neutral tonnage that the curve of destruction showed the sharpest rise. In 1915 neutral losses amounted to no more than 17,500 tons

---

[1] Several of the vessels sunk in the Channel were small French sailing vessels or fishing craft.

[2] The losses in neutral shipping in the North Sea were comparatively small in November, but rose again in December.

a month. For January to September 1916, inclusive, the average rose to 80,000 tons; but for the December quarter it was no less than 100,000 tons a month. In those three months, Norway alone lost 160,000 tons of shipping.

The gravity of these losses could not be denied. If the destruction of British tonnage continued at the same rate during 1917 it was necessary to estimate for a loss of over 2,000,000 tons, an amount nearly double the total shipbuilding output of the last two years. Moreover, it was not only in the actual destruction of tonnage that the effect of the campaign was felt. Ships were continually detained in British or foreign ports on account of the proximity of submarines, and though many were undoubtedly saved by following the Admiralty instructions as to course, the necessity of deviation to avoid dangerous areas, and of zigzagging in waters where the presence of submarines was suspected, involved a serious reduction in their annual carrying power. Especially was this felt on the passage between the United Kingdom and Gibraltar, which was now exposed to attack throughout its whole length. On one voyage an Indian liner actually steamed 2,560 miles between Gibraltar and London, as against the normal 1,313. This, indeed, was an extreme instance, but there were few voyages which were not now lengthened by deviation, and though the total reduction of carrying power due to this cause was impossible to estimate, it was undoubtedly considerable and increasing.

Moreover, despite a continual development of the defensive organisation, little hope of an improvement in the situation could, at the moment, be entertained. The immunity at one time attained in the English Channel was gone, and a system of " patrolled routes " adopted in the Mediterranean had not given satisfactory results. To patrol effectively routes some hundreds of miles in length was impossible, and though special escort could be provided for transports and other vessels of military importance, the best protection of the ordinary merchantmen still lay in their own guns.

During the last three months of 1916 the total number of British steamers attacked by submarines was 206, of which 118 were defensively armed and 88 were not. Of those defensively armed 38 were sunk and 80 escaped; of the unarmed ships 60 were sunk and only 28 escaped;

55 of the armed ships attributed their escape to gunfire and 25 to other causes. Thus, while the percentage of escapes to attacks among unarmed steamers was only 32 per cent., no fewer than 47 per cent. of the defensively armed vessels attacked escaped by the effective use of their guns, and the total proportion of escapes to attacks among such vessels was 68 per cent. On the other hand, while all but 4 of the defensively armed ships sunk were torpedoed without warning, only 9 unarmed steamers suffered this fate, for the Germans still professed some regard for the conditions laid down by the United States, though they regarded them as inapplicable to defensively armed merchantmen, which they claimed the right to consider as warships. Thus, a ship armed for self-defence ran a very much greater risk of being sunk without warning than an unarmed vessel, but her chance of escape if attacked was more than twice as great. From the point of view of the preservation of tonnage there could be no question of the immense importance of defensive armament and great efforts were being made to increase the number of ships so equipped.[1]

So far as British and Allied ships were concerned the extension of defensive armament appeared to present the best hope of checking the upward curve of destruction; but neutrals could not be armed, and the effect of the submarine campaign on neutral shipping had now become a question of the utmost gravity. While the

---

[1] Analysis of Attacks, October–December, 1916:

	Attacked.	Sunk.	Escaped.	Percentage of Escapes.
Defensively armed steamers	118	38	80	67·8
Other steamers	88	60	28	31·8
Total steamers	206	98	108	52·4
Sailing vessels	22	21	1	4·5

Analysis of Escapes (steamers only):

	D.A.M.V.	Other S.s.
By gun	55	—
By speed	6	8
By weather	2	1
Rescued	—	15
Torpedo missed	13	2
Damaged but reached port	4	2
Total	80	28

One sailing vessel was rescued

entrances of British shipping during the last three months of 1916 were 11 per cent. less than during the same period of the previous year, those of foreign tonnage decreased by 20 per cent., and though the arrangements for insurance of neutral shipping might reasonably be expected to do something to counteract the tendency to withdrawal, it was clear that a serious reduction in the volume of imports brought in neutral bottoms must be anticipated during 1917.

In clearances the decrease for the three months was 15 per cent. in respect both of British and foreign tonnage, and the figures of November and December showed plainly the effect of the increased submarine activity and the shortage of tonnage. Despite the stringency of the bunker regulations, neutral clearances to France during December were less than two-thirds of what they were in October. Clearances to Italy, under the blighting effects of the Freight Limitation Scheme, coupled with increased risk, fell away far more seriously, and as both British and Italian tonnage was very short, it was evident that a renewed Italian coal crisis would mark the opening of 1917.

In view of the enormous importance to the Allied cause of maintaining the French and Italian coal supplies, this falling away in neutral clearances was as grave a matter as the decline in entrances. Moreover, any reduction in the shipments of coal to Italy and Southern France threatened a reduction in the imports of ore brought by returning colliers. Hitherto the Bunker Regulations had kept the Scandinavian entrances from Spain fairly steady, but those of Spanish shipping fell away somewhat during the last quarter of the year, and British entrances were also reduced owing to losses and shortage of tonnage. The imports of Spanish ore for the three months were only about 10 per cent. less than in the same period of the previous year; but they were 25 per cent. below the average of the two immediately preceding quarters. Moreover, the effect of the submarine campaign in the North Sea had been greatly to reduce the shipments from Narvik, and the total imports of iron ore for the December quarter fell far below the immense and increasing demands of the munitions industries.

CHAPTER XXV

THE ECONOMIC SITUATION OF THE BELLIGERENTS AT THE END OF 1916

IT was thus under somewhat depressing circumstances that the Shipping Controller took office. The problem of maintaining seaborne trade had assumed, during the course of 1916, wholly new proportions. The shortage of tonnage experienced towards the end of the previous year had arisen mainly from the requisitioning of vessels for naval and military service; its effects had been felt in rising freights rather than in shortage of supplies. Now, however, a situation had been reached in which, after effecting drastic economies in the employment of tonnage, it was admittedly impossible to obtain carrying space for essential supplies, without reducing by several million tons the importation of commodities hitherto regarded as necessaries; and this situation had been brought about mainly by the submarine attack.

Down to December 31st, 1916, the total losses of British shipping due to enemy action amounted to nearly 2,400,000 tons gross. Those of ocean-going shipping—steamers of 1,600 tons gross and upwards—were over 2,000,000 tons. Not only were these losses far in excess of the shipbuilding output in the United Kingdom; they had more than wiped out the gains due to capture or seizure of enemy vessels. Allowing on the one hand for war and marine losses, ships interned in enemy ports or locked in the Baltic, and vessels transferred or broken up; on the other hand, for new construction and tonnage acquired, the ocean-going steam shipping under the British flag was less by about 750,000 tons than at the outbreak of war.

It is true that this represented a reduction of less than 5 per cent., but as we have seen, it was the progressive ratio of loss which was the most alarming feature of the situation. During the first twelve months of war the war losses among steamers entered in the War Risks Associations amounted to 3·8 per cent. of the numbers entered. For the twelve months ended July 31st, 1916, this percentage rose to 6·06; during the last three months of 1916 it was 2·55, or at the rate of 10·2 per cent. per annum.

The Allies of Great Britain had lost through war causes over 730,000 tons of shipping of all classes (exclusive of ships interned). Down to July 1916 the losses suffered by Italy had been more than offset by the completion of vessels under construction at the date of her entry into the war and by seizures of enemy vessels in Italian ports. French tonnage too was at that date little below the 1914 total. But both in France and Italy shipbuilding was now practically at a standstill, and by December 31st, 1916, French and Italian tonnage showed a decided shrinkage. Nor was there much prospect of any further losses being replaced.

Neutral countries had lost by enemy action 840,000 tons; but in those countries shipbuilding was still proceeding, and neutral shipowners, stimulated by high freights and large profits, had placed orders freely both at home and abroad. Holland had been building largely for export, and the American shipyards were exceptionally busy. Down to June 1916 the additions had fully kept pace with the losses. The mercantile fleets of Holland and Denmark, as recorded in *Lloyd's Register Book*, were both a little larger than in 1914, and a decline of about 10 per cent. in the steam tonnage under the Swedish, Spanish, and Greek flags was more than compensated by an increase of 300,000 tons in the steam shipping of Norway. During the second half of 1916, however, the destruction of Norwegian tonnage considerably exceeded the additions. Large contracts placed by Norwegian owners were in process of execution in the American yards, but the recent acceleration in the rate of loss made it very doubtful whether losses could be made good in 1917.

America herself, and Japan, who had suffered little, were both adding rapidly to their mercantile fleets; but neither American nor Japanese shipping took any large part in the trade of the European Allies, being mainly employed for the purpose of replacing British and German tonnage in the carriage of their own expanding commerce. Moreover, while British and Allied tonnage could be directed by requisition or licence into the trades deemed most essential, the effect of bunker pressure on neutral shipping was to a great extent counteracted by the demands of the neutral States themselves, the effect of freight limitation schemes in Allied services, the attraction of high freights in distant waters from which British shipping had been withdrawn, and above all by the great and rapid development of submarine activity.

There was thus every prospect that British shipping would have to play in 1917 an even larger part than it had hitherto done in the supply both of Great Britain and her Allies, and this fact gave additional significance both to the rapid increase in the net wastage of tonnage, and to the various efforts made to economise its employment.

The tonnage on naval and military service was now less by more than one-fifth than in the spring of 1916 ; but owing to the increased requirements of the Salonika force, it was rather larger than in September. On the other hand, the proportion definitely allocated to the Allies was smaller than in that month, owing partly to the conclusion of the Russian Summer Programme, and partly to the large number of wheat-ships, whose destination was not yet finally determined. The number of " free " ships showed a considerable decrease, but including vessels temporarily released, or requisitioned for the carriage of imports, the tonnage engaged in British and general trade amounted to some 8,800,000, of which about 7,500,000 tons might be regarded as available for British imports. This was actually about the same amount as in September, and considerably above the spring total ; but the tonnage situation was much worse than these figures would suggest. In the first place, the allocation to Allied services was at its lowest during the winter months, and would inevitably show a big increase in the spring and summer of 1917, when the new Russian Programme was going forward. In the second place, the diversion of a large block of shipping to Australia would inevitably reduce the carrying power of the available shipping during the coming year. In the third place, there were urgent demands to be met which could only be fulfilled at the expense of civilian imports. The requirements of the Ministry of Munitions for 1917 were greatly in excess of those for the previous year ; in iron ore alone they showed an increase of over two million tons. The shipments of

IMPORTS DURING 1916

coal to France and Italy had fallen far below the requirements of those countries during the last few months of 1916, and a great effort would be necessary to make up the deficiency. Finally, the unchecked ravages of the submarines threatened not only a continuance of losses with which no replacements could keep pace, but a withdrawal of neutral shipping which would greatly increase the demands on British tonnage.

But if the outlook for the future was disquieting, the record for 1916 bore ample witness to the energy and resource with which the operations of British shipping had been adapted to the conditions of war, and the courage with which both British and neutral shipping had hitherto faced the greatly increased risks of trade. The German submarines had inflicted heavy losses, they had caused grievous delays through detention and deviation, they had obliged the Australian and Far Eastern trade to adopt the long passage round the Cape in lieu of the Suez route; but they had never succeeded in damming the stream of British trade; they had cut off no market or source of supply on which that trade depended. Indeed, serious as was the cumulative effect on the tonnage position of the losses sustained, the ratio of loss was very small when compared with voyages made or cargoes carried. For the first two years of war the estimated losses of cargoes carried in British ships were little over one-half of 1 per cent. of the total values, and even during the last quarter of 1916 the monthly average was less than 2 per cent.[1]

The real test of the success with which British trade was maintained must, however, be found, not in the ratio of loss, but in the volume of imports actually received. This, as shown in the Board of Trade Returns, amounted during 1916 to a little over 41,800,000 tons, but if an allowance be made for Government cargoes of fuel oil and munitions, not included in the returns, the total was probably in the neighbourhood of 46,000,000 tons, about the same as in 1915.

Effective as had been the work of the submarines, they had as yet produced no restriction of supplies comparable for a moment with the effect of the Allied blockade on the Central Powers. Anxiety with regard to the wheat supply for 1917 was indeed acute, owing to the anticipated sub-

[1] These estimates are for cargoes carried in British ships whether in the trade of the United Kingdom or not.

stitution of Australia for North America as the source of a large proportion of the supply; but the actual imports of wheat and flour for 1916 amounted to 5,715,000 tons,[1] over 9 per cent. more than in 1915, and under 4 per cent. less than the average for the five years 1909-13.

Imports of the other chief cereals were somewhat affected by the demands of France and Italy for oats and maize, which reduced the amount available for Great Britain. The Argentine maize harvest, too, showed a drop of some 16 per cent., and though decreased shipments from the Plate were compensated to some extent by increased supplies from North America, Egypt, and South Africa, the total maize import in 1916 fell short by more than 25 per cent. of the 1915 figures. The imports of oats also were further reduced, but the home production, which bore normally a large proportion to the whole consumption, had been increased during the war, and the total supplies were not below the average. Shipments of barley, on the other hand, though well below the normal, were higher than in 1915, and were still large enough to permit the diversion of a large proportion of the grain to brewing and distilling. Rice from India was imported in very large quantities, much of it for re-export, especially to Cuba and Holland, and shipments of beans from Egypt replaced the Chinese supplies with a considerable saving in carrying power.

In both meat and sugar there was, as we have already seen, a shortage of supplies at the end of 1916. In the actual shipments of meat there was little falling off, but the proportion required for the Armies necessitated reduced civilian consumption. Sugar shipments were still a long way below the normal, and in view of the demands on tonnage, it was unlikely that adequate supplies could be ensured, so long as no restriction was placed on the use of sugar for brewing and confectionery. The sources were in the main the same as in 1915, but with a view to tonnage economy the nearer sources—Cuba and the United States —were more largely drawn upon than in that year.

In respect of cereals, meat, and sugar, the main problem was the provision of tonnage. The supply of fish and dairy produce was complicated, as we have seen, by the direct competition of Germany. The redirection of Dutch and Scandinavian trade, partially checked as it was by the

[1] Reckoning 7 tons flour = 10 tons wheat.

arrangements concluded during the latter part of 1916, had serious effects. These effects, however, varied greatly as between the various commodities affected. Heavy imports of bacon from the United States and Canada more than made good the decrease in shipments from Denmark; and Holland, as a source of cheese supplies, was much less important than Canada, New Zealand, and since the outbreak of war, the States. In butter and eggs, on the other hand, the shortage was accentuated during 1916. Not only were the Scandinavian and Dutch shipments greatly diminished, but little space was available in ships homeward bound from Russia, and France was obliged to conserve her output for home consumption. Australian butter exports, too, were still affected by the drought of 1914–15. New Zealand was shipping freely; increased shipments of eggs came from Egypt, and new sources had been tapped in North America and China; but the total import of butter dwindled to about one-half, and of eggs to less than one-third of the 1913 figures. As two-thirds of the eggs and half the butter annually consumed before the war came from overseas, the reduction in the total supply was very great. The butter shortage was, however, made good to some extent by increased imports of margarine from Holland, and the development of the margarine industry at home.

For fish also the Germans were fiercely competing in Scandinavia and Holland, and of all foodstuffs the supply of fish was most exposed to the submarine attack, which threatened not only imports from abroad but the home catch. In 1915 no fewer than 192 fishing craft had been destroyed or captured by the enemy; in 1916 the number was 141. Altogether 378 fishing craft had been sunk since the beginning of the war, of which 302 were victims of the submarine. In these vessels 278 fishermen had lost their lives; mostly as the result of striking mines during the first twelve months of the war. Neither the mine nor the submarine, however, had been able to prevent the British fisherman from carrying on his trade; indeed, it was with difficulty that he was prevented from fishing in the prohibited danger areas. The real threat to the fish supply lay in the requisitioning of so large a proportion of trawlers and drifters as mine-sweepers and auxiliaries, and it was this which was mainly responsible for a reduction in the weight of fish landed on the coasts by British craft from

1,280,000 tons in 1913 to 480,000 tons in 1915 and 410,000 in 1916. Cargoes landed direct by foreign boats in the Deep Sea Fisheries were also reduced by about two-thirds. This reduction represented chiefly the proportion formerly landed by German boats; but the diversion of the Dutch and Danish catch to Germany was also a factor. Such supplies as were received from this source in 1915 and 1916 were mostly brought by Belgian fishing craft which had transferred their operations to British ports.

Imports from foreign countries, on the other hand, were well maintained. The influence of the Norwegian agreement was not fully felt till 1917, and a large proportion of the fish secured under this agreement went to Russia; but the result of the Icelandic agreement was seen in an increase of imports from 10,000 tons in 1913 and 8,500 in 1915 to 26,000 in 1916. Imports of tinned salmon, mostly from the United States and Canada, rose from 30,000 to 70,000 tons, and there was a plentiful supply of sardines from Portugal. Exports and re-exports, on the contrary, were drastically cut down, but the diminution in the home-catch was too large to be made good, and the net result was to diminish the supply of fish retained for home consumption from about 900,000 tons in 1913 to about 500,000 in 1915 and 1916.

Imports of fruit, vegetables, tea, coffee, cocoa, wines, spirits, and tobacco were, on the whole, well maintained. Imports of cocoa and coffee were indeed unusually high both in 1915 and 1916, and we have seen that this was accounted for not only by the army demands, but by re-exports some part of which found their way to the Central Powers, until checked by the action of the War Trade Department.

Taking foodstuffs as a whole, there was as yet no sign of serious deficiency. On a broad survey of the position, the actual reductions in the supply of sugar, butter, eggs, and fish were less important than the effect produced on distribution by the continual increase in the number of men under arms, and by the rise in prices. The consumption of the Armies per head, especially of bread and meat, was much above the normal, and the amount available per head for the civil population was proportionately reduced. Further, those engaged in the heavy work of the munition factories required, and were generally able to procure, an increased amount of food, while others, whose earnings or income had not risen proportionately to the increased cost of living, were obliged to reduce their consumption. It was, as we have already seen, this inequality in distribution, even more than the fear of real shortage, which had induced the Government to contemplate a policy of rationing.

For this increase in the price of food many causes were responsible : actual shortage of supplies, as in sugar, fish, and dairy produce, army consumption, Allied and neutral competition in the American markets, German competition in the markets of Scandinavia and Holland, increased costs of production, transport, and distribution, exchange and currency influences. Among these the freight factor was, of course, conspicuous. By December 1916 grain freights from the Plate stood at 145s., rice freights from Rangoon at 250s. per ton, as compared with 12s. 6d. and 23s. 9d. respectively in 1913,[1] and, though these advances were exceptional, the all-round advance was very great. Yet the freight factor was by no means the most important. Even when the percentage increase was greatest it frequently accounted for only a small proportion of the price advance, nor was the advance in prices always greater on commodities brought at high freights from the more distant markets than on those protected against freight advances by State action or long-term agreements, or produced at home under war conditions. Whatever weight may be assigned to other factors, the main cause of the universal rise in the price both of foodstuffs and materials was the pressure of an intensified demand on sources of supply which could only meet it with difficulty.

Among raw materials, particular importance attached, of course, to the imports of iron ore. In 1915, although the demand was stimulated by the rapid growth of the munitions industries, the imports were only 6,200,000 tons, 600,000 tons below the average for the three years preceding the war. By 1916 the works owned or controlled by the Ministry of Munitions were ready to absorb practically any amount that could be shipped, and we have seen that the provision of tonnage for the ore trade was a constant preoccupation of the Transport Department and of those responsible for framing the bunker regulations. Even so, the Ministry's demands could hardly be satisfied, but the total of imported ore rose to over 6,900,000 tons. In

[1] *Shipping World Year Book.*

spite of the perils of the voyage, shipments from Spain and the Mediterranean were above the normal, those from Norway were, in proportion, equally high, and even the Swedish supplies, which had fallen away to very little in 1915, fully recovered.

Closely connected with the ore trade were the imports of pyrites and pit-props. The supply of pyrites was well maintained, but the imports of pit-props were slightly below 1915 and only about two-thirds of the normal. Despite the return cargo regulations, there was a heavy fall in the French shipments, which offset an increase from Spain and Portugal. Norway, in 1915 and 1916, sent two or three times as much as before the war, in spite of the numerous losses in the North Sea, but Swedish shipments fell away somewhat in 1916, and nothing could make good the loss of the Russian supplies. The development of a new source in Newfoundland and Canada was useful, but the output was comparatively small, and it was only in the use of home-grown timber that a real solution could be found.

Imports of wood and timber other than pit-props were affected by the restrictions imposed in the spring of 1916, as well as by shortage of tonnage. The cost also had greatly increased. By the end of 1916 the average rise in import values was 140 per cent., of which about a quarter was due to increased f.o.b. prices, especially in Sweden, and the remainder to freights, though these had been somewhat checked by the influence of the North Sea Freight Scheme.[1] Wood-pulp and paper were similarly affected, and the import of stones and slates, cut down by nearly two-thirds in 1915 as a result of the German occupation of Belgium and the cessation of private building, was still further restricted.

The supplies of most other important raw materials were tolerably steady. Wool imports were somewhat affected by the Australian drought, and less also came from South America, where German agents were said to be buying up the stocks. Re-exports, however, were strictly controlled and the total supply available was sufficient for all essential needs. Cotton imports were little below the normal. The supply of flax was fully assured by the success with which the White Sea traffic was maintained, and increased shipments of hemp from India and Italy fully made good a small reduction in the imports from the Philippines. Jute

[1] *Times, Annual Financial and Commercial Review*, 19 January, 1917.

imports, on the other hand, were much below the normal owing to the reduced acreage sown in India, and it was necessary for the Government to take steps to ration the supply.

The metal group showed some reduction, chiefly due to the diminution of manufacture for export and civil consumption, but many miscellaneous materials were imported as freely as before the war. Oil-seeds, nuts, and kernels were required both for munitions purposes and for feeding-stuffs and the newly established margarine industry. Hides and leather were imported in very large quantities, especially from the United States, for army equipment. The import of fertilisers dropped, but heavy purchases for munitions raised the import of nitrate to nearly three times the normal level. Ordinary imports of petroleum were fully maintained, and to these must be added greatly increased purchases of liquid fuel for the Navy, which had now ceased to be included in the trade returns. Rubber imports, too, were well above the normal, but the direction of the trade was changed, the Brazilian product being largely replaced by that of the Malay Peninsula and Ceylon.

Imports of manufactured articles as recorded in the Board of Trade Returns showed a progressive decrease since the beginning of the war, due largely to the reservation of space on the Atlantic liners for wheat and munitions. Both the figures for manufactures and those for raw materials indicated, however, that a great deal was still being imported which could not be reckoned as essential under war conditions, and on the whole it is true to say that the German war against commerce had not yet affected British imports to an extent involving any substantial change in the habits of life of the people.

On the other hand, the problems arising from the increased cost of living were by no means confined to food-stuffs. Clothing, in particular, had risen greatly in price. By September 1916 the cost of cotton materials, underclothing, and hosiery had risen by 50 per cent., of woollen goods by 40 to 90 per cent., of boots and shoes by 60 to 75 per cent. To a great extent this rise was due to the limitation of civilian supplies by the army demand, especially for woollen and leather goods; but it reflected also a general rise in import values which affected almost all imported commodities.

The causes of this advance varied greatly. Heavy and bulky articles of low value, such as timber, were naturally specially affected by the rise in freights; but this rise, great as it was, played but a small part in producing the increased cost of high value goods such as cotton and rubber. In the main the determining factors were the demands of the war industries and the extent to which the available supplies sufficed to meet that demand and leave a surplus for civilian consumption. A few articles, such as tin, the use of which had been seriously interfered with by war conditions or restrictions, showed little or no increase in value, but the general tendency was to a sharp advance on 1915 prices.

The export trade under war conditions falls naturally into two distinct categories, the first comprising coal, including coke and manufactured fuel, and the second, all other articles. Coal in 1916 accounted for only about 10 per cent. of the total value of exports and re-exports, but in weight it was about four-fifths of the whole. By reason of its bulk it was the one branch of the export trade seriously affected by the shortage of tonnage, and it was further specially affected by the tendency to withdrawal of neutral tonnage, as before the war a little more than half the coal exported was shipped in vessels under foreign flags.[1]

Even if ample shipping had been available, the coal exports could not possibly have been maintained at their old level. The total amount raised in 1916, 256,000,000 tons, was practically the same as in 1915, but this was about 6 per cent. below the average production of the three years before the war, and the surplus available for export was further reduced by the enormous demands of the Admiralty and the munitions factories. Shortage of tonnage also played a part in restricting exports to some of the most important markets.

During the year many economies had been effected in the use of colliers on direct naval and military service, but these had been neutralised to a great extent by the increasing strain of the more distant expeditions such as those to Mesopotamia and East Africa. In other respects the situation had changed for the worse. The congestion of the French and Italian ports and the conditions of the White Sea service had always involved the use of a dis-

[1] [Cd. 9092], p. 79.

proportionately large block of tonnage in maintaining the coal supply of the Allies. To these influences had now to be added the losses, delays, and deviation due to the intensification of submarine activity in the Channel, the Bay of Biscay, and the Mediterranean. Moreover, while the difficulty of maintaining the services had increased, the proportion of coal exports shipped to Allied ports was larger than ever.

The total exports of coal, coke, and manufactured fuel, as recorded in the Board of Trade Returns, amounted to 41,150,000 tons, as against 45,770,000 in 1915; but Admiralty shipments to France, Russia, and Italy, which were mostly excluded from the returns, amounted to about 4,600,000 tons, as against 2,000,000. Of the recorded total, about 24,750,000 tons, or 60 per cent., went to France and Italy. Including Admiralty shipments, France received about 21,000,000 tons, or nearly 90 per cent. above the average of the years 1911–13. Supplies to Italy were not so well maintained, for in the Italian trade the shortage of tonnage was always acute, but well over 6,000,000 tons were shipped as commercial cargoes, and Admiralty shipments amounted to about 700,000 more, bringing up the total to over 70 per cent. of the normal. Including 1,000,000 tons shipped to the White Sea, the total exports to the chief Allies may be placed at roughly 29,000,000 tons.[1] There were also large shipments to the French possessions in Africa, for, in view of the importance of the ore mines, it was essential that Algeria and Tunis should receive at least a fair proportion of their normal supply, and the importance of Dakar as a coaling station had been increased by the diversion of shipping from the Canal to the Cape Route. Shipments to Egypt, on the other hand, diminished through the same cause.

In the allocation of the reduced surplus available for export to neutral countries, the Coal Exports Committee were guided partly by political considerations and partly by considerations of tonnage economy. These, fortunately, both pulled the same way. It was, as a rule, the nearer markets in which coal was of the most value in

---

[1] It is impossible to give the figures of coal exports with certainty, as the extent to which Admiralty shipments were included in the Board of Trade Returns cannot be ascertained. The greater part appear not to have been included.

negotiating blockade or tonnage agreements. Norway received as much as in 1913, and Denmark 75 per cent. of her 1913 supplies; Spain, the chief source of iron ore, received 80 per cent. Holland had been receiving coal from Germany in exchange for meat and agricultural produce, and British exports to the Netherlands were considerably smaller than in 1915, but they were still about two-thirds of the normal. Swedish supplies, on the other hand, were cut down to little more than one-third of the 1913 figures, and Greece received very little.

In the regulation of exports to European neutrals the dominant factors were political; it was the South American countries who suffered most by the shortage of shipping, whether through refusal of licences, or sheer inability to procure tonnage, or disinclination to pay the enormous freights now ruling.[1] The total exports to South America in 1916 amounted to 1,250,000 tons, less than half the total for 1915, and about one-sixth of the 1913 figures. The opportunity thus presented was not overlooked in the United States, and coal exports from the States to Argentina and Brazil rose from less than half a million tons before the war to about a million and a half in 1916. But whatever concern might be felt at seeing the American exporters obtaining a hold on an important market, was modified by the reflection that, but for the assistance so provided, coal urgently required for the nearer markets must otherwise have been diverted to South America, in order to maintain industries in which the Allies were interested. A big increase in American exports to Italy[2] was less desirable, as it involved an uneconomical use of tonnage, and as we have seen, great efforts were made during the latter part of 1916 to free Italy from dependence on the States.

Apart from coal there was little difficulty in finding tonnage for the export trade, and throughout 1916 the exports of British produce and manufactures continued to show an improvement on the 1915 figures in quantity as well as in value. The chief obstacles to a still further increase were the demands of the war industries on plant, labour, and material, the restrictions imposed in connec-

[1] By December 1916 coal freights to the Plate stood at 55s. per ton, as against 13s. 6d. in 1913, or 18s. 3d. in 1912.
[2] From about 300,000 tons before the war to 2,840,000 in 1915 and 1,697,000 in 1916.

tion with the blockade, and the decreased purchasing power of some foreign markets.

The iron and steel industries were, of course, strictly controlled, and the surplus available for export was greatly reduced. Although the total quantity of iron ore smelted in 1916 was within about 10 per cent. of the average of the last three years of peace, the exports diminished in bulk by nearly one-third, and of the 1916 exports no less than one-half was shipped to France. The shipments of pig-iron alone to that country amounted to 550,000 tons as against 150,000 in 1913, and in order to ensure fulfilment of the French demand, it was necessary rigorously to restrict exports to neutral countries. Many restrictions were placed also, partly for blockade purposes and partly to safeguard supplies, on the export of tinned plates and galvanised iron, and here as in other directions the way was left open to the American exporter.

In the woollen trades, as we have seen, the control was used to encourage manufacture for export at the expense of home consumption. Dyestuffs were short owing to the loss of the German supplies, and to military demands on the bases of tar colours and acids; worsted exports were heavily hit by an increase in the United States tariff; but on the whole trade was flourishing. Not only was there a strong demand from France, but shipments to the Dominions, Scandinavia, Holland, South America, and the Far East were heavy; indeed to Australia, Scandinavia, and Holland, they were well above the normal.

The greatest of the textile industries was in a less happy position, as increased shipments to minor markets in Europe, Egypt, and South America were unable to compensate for the reduction in the Indian and Chinese demand; yet, though a long way below the normal in volume, the 1916 cotton exports were better than in the previous year. The same thing is true of exports of jute manufactures, though here the diminished supply of raw material and the great Government demand prevented any return to normal conditions. Linen exports showed a more marked recovery. Busy as were the Ulster mills with work on aeroplanes and bandages, the exports of linen piece goods were considerably higher than in 1915. Exports of silk manufactures, thanks to a plentiful supply of raw material from the Far East and Italy, were well maintained.

Clothing, leather, boots and shoes, were all exported more freely in 1916 than in the previous year, and if the shipments were still a long way below the peace figures, the explanation is to be found in shortage of labour and army demands rather than in tonnage difficulties. Nor had the *entrepôt* trade as yet suffered greatly from the tonnage shortage. Whether it would be possible to continue importing over three-quarters of a million tons of goods for re-export was open to question, but the success with which this trade was maintained in 1916 played an important part both in the supply of the Allies and in the regulation of the exchanges.

Including exports and re-exports, the total value of the shipments was £604,000,000, an increase of over £120,000,000 on 1915, and very little short of the average for the three years preceding the war. Making all allowance for inflation of values, these were remarkable figures under war conditions, and the adverse balance of trade as shown by the Board of Trade Returns was £23,000,000 smaller than in the preceding year.

The financial position was, nevertheless, very serious. Whereas the excess of imports before the war had been about £130,000,000 a year, it was now about £350,000,000. Even these figures only very imperfectly reflect the position. On the one hand, they exclude Government purchases of munitions and war material; on the other hand, the invisible exports—freight, interest, commissions —had been diminished through the sale of American securities and the withdrawal of British shipping from the inter-foreign trade.

Moreover, the apparent improvement in 1916 was due almost entirely to the great increase of exports to the Allied Countries, accompanied by a slight falling off in the imports received from them. Exports to France, Italy, and Russia were valued at £166,000,000; imports from those countries at £56,000,000 only. On the other hand, against imports to the value of £400,000,000 received from the United States, Canada, and Argentina there could be set exports to one-quarter only of this amount. And it was precisely from those countries, especially from the United States, that the bulk of the unrecorded Government imports were procured, while exports on Government account went almost entirely to the Allies.

In almost every direction the influence of war demands

and of diminished exports was making itself felt. For two successive years the normal excess of exports to India, Japan, Java, Brazil, Chile, and British West Africa had been converted into an excess of imports. The value of the Chinese market had greatly diminished, and the excess of imports from New Zealand, Cuba, Spain, and Sweden had greatly increased. While the Allied exchanges had all turned heavily in favour of Great Britain, and that with the United States was artificially maintained at a discount of only 2 per cent., those with the European neutrals were all, in varying degree, unfavourable.[1]

The gravity of the position was emphasised by the increasing dependence of the Allies on the economic strength of Great Britain. Neither France nor Italy could make any pretence of paying by exports for the supplies essential to the conduct of the war. In both countries the energies of the people were absorbed almost entirely by their military effort and by those industries directly connected with the feeding, transport, and equipment of the armies. France was further handicapped by the German occupation of the districts richest in coal and iron, and in Italy the coal shortage had led to the closing of many factories in industries not directly connected with the production of war material. Yet the needs of both countries for imports had in many respects increased. Not only did they require immense quantities of munitions and material for the manufacture of munitions; they required also a much greater amount of imported food. The diversion of labour to the armies and munition factories diminished home production; the high standard of feeding in the armies led to increased consumption, especially of meat; and the military demand for fodder could only be satisfied by large imports.

In France, the total imports for domestic consumption during 1916 amounted to £606,380,000 and the exports of French produce and manufactures to £194,303,000. In 1913 the value of French imports in the special trade had been three-quarters of the value of imports; in 1916 it

[1] Exchanges on 7 December, 1916 :

	Par.	7 Dec., 1916.
Stockholm (kronor to £1)	18·159	16·40
Christiania (kroner to £1)	18·159	16·97
Copenhagen (kroner to £1)	18·159	17·60
Madrid (pesetas to £1)	25·22¼	22·22
Amsterdam (gulden to £1)	12·107	11·67

was less than one-third. Italy was in the same position. Her imports had risen from £145,500,000 to £385,600,000; her exports had increased only by some £20,000,000 to £123,500,000. Both France and Italy, moreover, were now drawing their imports from a narrower range of sources. In 1913, 13 per cent. of the French imports came from the United Kingdom and a little over 10 per cent. from the United States; in 1916 the proportions were respectively 29 and 30 per cent. Exports to the United Kingdom were less than one-fifth, to the United States little over one-tenth, of the imports received.

Thus France and Italy were becoming heavily indebted both to Great Britain and to the United States. By the end of 1916 the French exchange on New York was 11 per cent., the Italian 25 per cent. below par, and the rates on London were only slightly more favourable to Paris, and even less favourable to Rome. Russia, of course, was in a still worse position. Compelled to import coal and war material to the full capacity of the restricted routes still open, she was almost wholly unable to ship the grain which formed her staple export, and the rate on London was over 70 per cent., on New York over 40 per cent. against her.[1]

The financial strength of Paris had permitted France to take a considerable share during the earlier stages of the war in financing the other European Allies, but her position had been badly shaken by reduced production and increasing needs. More and more the economic burden of the war, supplies, transport, and finance, tended to fall on Great Britain, and it was increasingly evident that there was a serious danger of the strain becoming insupportable.

On the other hand, the internal condition of the Central Powers was such as fully to justify the peace feelers which they put forward towards the end of the year. By the autumn of 1916 the machinery of the blockade had reached a high degree of efficiency. The various rationing agreements and the agreements with neutral shipping lines were, on the whole, working well. Thanks to the number of ships calling voluntarily for examination, and to the activity of the patrols, practically the whole trade of the neutral countries contiguous to Germany came under supervision.

[1] The French exchange on London would have fallen still further but for arrangements made between the French and British Governments during the autumn, including a deposit of gold amounting to £60,000,000.

For ships sailing South-about evasion of the examination service in the Dover Straits had always been impossible, and during 1916 not more than 5 per cent. of neutral ships entering or leaving the North Sea by the North-about route succeeded in avoiding examination.[1]

What was equally important, the net-work of agreements created during 1915 and 1916, together with the development of the Allied policy towards contraband since the issue of the Retaliation Order, had removed most of the difficulties in dealing with the cargoes of ships calling or sent in, and by December 1916 practically no goods were reaching Germany from oversea sources. Such leakage as existed was mostly by way of Sweden, and during the autumn and winter the list of embargoes on goods consigned to that country increased until it covered over fifty different articles. The effect on the internal condition of Sweden was serious. The home crops had been unsatisfactory, the cost of living had risen by over 50 per cent., and there was great depression in the majority of the industries, owing to the shortage of raw materials.

Among the articles on which an embargo was laid were all kinds of margarine materials, and the effect of this measure was important, since it led to a greater consumption of butter in Sweden, with the result of cutting off the Swedish exports of butter to Germany. It was impossible, however, to interfere with the shipments of iron ore which continued to be one of the chief supports of the German munition factories. Effective direct interference was out of the question, and the hands of the British Government were tied as regards the negotiation of an agreement for diversion of the exports, by the dependence of the

[1] Neutral vessels sailing into or out of North Sea, 1916:

Called voluntarily for examination	1,878	63 per cent.
Intercepted by patrols	950	32 per cent.
Evaded patrols	155	5 per cent.
Total	2,983	100 per cent.

The lowest percentage calling voluntarily for examination was 53¼ per cent. in July; the highest, 75 per cent. in November. The percentage intercepted by the patrols varied from 26 in January to 43 in July. The greatest percentage evading the patrols was 18 in January; the lowest, 1¼ in September. It is impossible to give figures of tonnage under the three categories, but the average size of vessels evading the patrols became progressively smaller and smaller.

Allies on Sweden for certain essential munitions material, by the importance of maintaining the transit route to Russia, and by the ability of the Germans to supply Sweden with coal.

From Denmark the Germans continued to receive large supplies of meat and dairy produce, and by supplying the Danish fishermen with motor oil, they also succeeded in obtaining a certain amount of fish. They were, moreover, still obtaining fish from Norway, for the Norwegian agreement applied only to the new catch, not to the old stock. It was believed that some exporters were in fact passing off herrings caught after August 1916, as old stock, and this, with certain differences as to the interpretation of the agreement relating to copper and pyrites, led to an embargo being placed during December on exports of coal from the United Kingdom to Norway, until satisfactory guarantees were received.

Meanwhile, a large proportion of the fish, meat, and dairy produce formerly exported from Holland to Germany had been diverted to the United Kingdom, under the Dutch agreements. Owing to the difficulties which had arisen during the autumn with regard to the agricultural agreement, it was renewed during November in a revised form. The new agreement covered also other products, such as hides and skins, and had the effect of reducing materially the enemy's supplies.

The net effect of the various agreements made during 1916 was to reduce the food supplies received by Germany from contiguous neutral countries from 8·90 per cent. of the normal total consumption in the first quarter of the year to 2·18 per cent. in the last quarter, and the proportion was still further reduced by the new Dutch agreement. As to German supplies from overseas, they had been reduced, like German exports, practically to vanishing point. Efforts were still made by German agents in the United States to ship consignments destined for the enemy, but few of them got through, and the total amount of such leakage as existed at this time was very small. Nor had the *Deutschland* proved, as was widely hoped in Germany, the precursor of a regular fleet of commercial submarines, by which some appreciable degree of direct trade might be re-established. The German resources were too restricted for material to be diverted in this way from the construction of fighting submarines, and

BAD HARVEST IN GERMANY

the total cargo which such vessels could carry was too small to compensate the cost and risk. The *Deutschland* indeed made a second voyage in safety, and the total result of her two voyages was to increase the German supplies of metal by 685 tons of nickel, and 90 tons of tin, but another commercial submarine, the *Bremen*, failed to get through. Both the *Deutschland* herself and three or four similar vessels under construction were subsequently converted to naval use.

The effect on the economic position of the Central Powers, of this complete severance of their oversea communications and of the decrease in supplies from contiguous neutral countries, was very severe. As regards food supplies, the winter of 1916–17 is acknowledged by all to have been, in Germany, the worst period of the war. The harvest of 1916 was very poor, and reflected clearly the effect on the soil of the reduced supply of fertilisers, as well as of the shortage of labour and horses for agricultural work.[1] The total crops of the principal cereals showed a deficiency of over 7,500,000 tons, or 25 per cent. on the normal production, and all immediate prospect of supplies from the Balkans was destroyed by the entry of Roumania into the war. The failure of the potato-crop was even more pronounced.[2]

It has been said that, down to Easter 1916, the available food supplies, if it had been possible to enforce an equitable distribution, were sufficient to maintain the population in health, and that, even after the reduction in the meat ration

---

[1] Very large numbers of prisoners of war were put into agricultural work, but it is doubtful if their work compensated effectively for that of the additional men called to the colours.

[2] Principal crops [from Cmd. 280]:

	Average 1912–13.	1916.	Deficiency.
	1,000 tons.	1,000 tons.	1,000 tons.
Wheat	4,932	3,288	1,644
Rye	11,910	9,109	2,801
Barley	3,647	2,828	819
Oats	9,117	6,809	2,308
Total cereals	29,606	22,034	7,572
Potatoes	52,000	23,531	28,469
Raw sugar	1,892	1,546	346

at that date, there was no serious general deficiency. The normal food consumption of the German people before the war, expressed in calories, was 3,215 per head per day, or 4,020 per " average man." [1] From the medical point of view, this was excessive. The consumption per " average man " in the United Kingdom was only 3,410, and the minimum laid down by the Inter-Allied Scientific Food Commission as necessary to keep a population in health in the temperate zone was only 3,300 calories per average man, or 2,772 per head.

In the summer of 1916 the guaranteed ration per head had a value of 1,985 calories, and it was possible to supplement this with a considerable amount of unrationed food, such as fruit, vegetables, fish, and polished barley. By the autumn it had become impossible to maintain this standard, and the ration actually distributed had a calorie value of only 1,344 per head. In November it is estimated that the total supply, including unrationed food and food obtained by illicit trading, gave an average of only 1,431 calories.[2]

This was not all. Small as it was in quantity, the ration was also very deficient in quality and variety. Owing to the acute shortage of meat and dairy produce, largely due to the loss of imported fodder, the diet consisted chiefly of bread and potatoes. When the failure of the potato crop became fully manifest, potatoes were replaced by swede turnips. Thus, in addition to the net reduction in the calorie value of the ration, there was a still greater proportionate reduction in the amount of protein and fats which it contained.

As heretofore, the burden was very unevenly distributed. The producers continued to live well; the rich were able to procure additional food, though less than before, by

[1] Consumption per " average man " is average consumption per head, adjusted to the distribution of the population according to age and sex. The figures given by the Inter-Allied Food Commission for women are 2,650, and for children from one to five years, 1,650 calories. A man engaged in heavy manual labour may consume up to 4,000 or 5,000 calories per day. A man in sedentary occupation may require only 2,500, and a woman, 2,000. The minimum laid down by the Belgian Relief Commission, on the assumption that the majority of the population were largely abstaining from work during the German occupation, was 2,274 calories per head per day, or 2,842 per average man. This was stated to be the minimum on which the population could be sustained without immediate and serious physical deterioration.

[2] Most of the above figures will be found in Cmd. 280.

illicit purchases; workers in munition factories and other special occupations received supplementary rations; but the condition of the greater proportion of the 30,000,000 town dwellers, who were confined to the bare ration, was deplorable. They were kept alive only by using up the fat in their own tissues, and it is estimated that, on the average, that part of the population which was unable to procure supplementary food lost, during the "turnip winter," from 15 to 25 per cent. of their previous weight.[1]

It was, of course, the women and children who suffered most. The problem of the urban milk supply had long engaged the attention of the authorities, and supplies were confined to invalids, young children, and nursing or expectant mothers. Even this, however, it was frequently impossible to maintain, for, owing to the deterioration in the feeding of cattle, the cows were giving only about half the normal supply, and the enormous prices obtainable for butter in the illicit trade diverted from the legal recipients a considerable portion of the milk produced.

In these circumstances it is not surprising that the rate of infant mortality increased, and that rickets and other diseases due to malnutrition were widely prevalent. Even among adults there were numerous deaths due to slow starvation, and a much greater mortality due to the inability of the debilitated population to resist the ravages of tuberculosis and pneumonia. The actual increase in the civil death-rate was 14 per cent., as compared with $9\frac{1}{2}$ per cent. in 1915; but in 1917 the increase rose to 32 per cent., and a great part of this must undoubtedly be put down to the effects of this terrible winter. It is to be noted that the increase of the death-rate was higher among women than among men, since there was always a tendency for the woman to give up to her children, or to her husband, a part of the inadequate ration allotted to her.[2]

In Austria-Hungary the conditions were quite as bad, and it is little wonder that, as the winter dragged on, public attention in both countries was obsessed by the question of obtaining supplies from Roumania where the tide of war had now rolled far over the frontier. But though by December a great part of Roumania was in enemy occu-

[1] Cmd. 280, p. 5.   [2] *Ibid.*, p. 8.

pation, it had already become evident that little immediate relief was to be expected from this source. The Roumanians themselves had destroyed or damaged great quantities of the grain, and the question of transport presented insuperable difficulties.

This question was, indeed, assuming formidable proportions. On the one hand, the movement of troops and munitions imposed an enormous strain on the rolling stock of the railways. On the other hand, the substitution of inferior metals for copper and brass in the engines, the withdrawal of skilled workers, and above all the lack of lubricants, reduced the capacity of the rolling stock to stand the wear and tear of traffic. Road transport was equally affected by the requisitioning of horses and petrol for military use, and apart from its effect on the procuring of grain from Roumania, the general deterioration of the transport system added to the difficulty of distributing the internal food supplies.

Further, it hampered very seriously both the internal distribution and the export of coal. In Austria-Hungary there was a serious coal shortage by September 1916, and during the winter the position in Germany became so bad that drastic restrictions on lighting and travelling had to be imposed, and for many of the people the sufferings arising from insufficient nourishment were aggravated by cold. They were increased still further by the shortage of soap, which had now become really serious, and by the restrictions placed on purchases of clothing and footwear as a result of the exhaustion of the stocks of raw material available for civilian consumption.

It was at this heavy cost to the civil population that the German armies were fed, clothed, and equipped. Even for soldiers in garrison or behind the lines the rations were short during the winter, but for front line troops the supply was still good. Nor was there as yet any sign of an appreciable shortage in the supply of war material. On the other hand the measures taken by the Authorities to augment the existing stocks of copper, nickel, tin, brass, and bronze gave ample proof of their anxiety as to the future. The copper 1 pfennig coinage was called in to be melted down and replaced by aluminium; domestic utensils of all sorts, beer-mugs, organ-pipes, and church bells containing the coveted metals were requisitioned in large quantities, and more energetic measures than ever were taken to strip the occupied territories. Great efforts were made to increase the production of native copper and the output of the Serbian copper-mine at Bor was increased to about 7,000 tons a year.[1]

By such drastic measures the essential military supplies of metals were secured, and the occupation of Roumania afforded some prospect of replenishing the supply of lubricating oil. The Galician oil-wells were again fully at work, and now that the Roumanian wells were also available, it was hoped to obtain greatly increased supplies. It soon became evident, however, that this hope, like that of increased grain supplies, must be deferred. Under the superintendence of Lieut.-Colonel Norton Griffiths the boring plant had been destroyed and the wells blocked, with a thoroughness which extorted the reluctant admiration of the Germans, and it was months before even a fraction of the normal output could be restored.

Compared with the loss of supplies, the destruction of the export trade was a minor evil. Yet this too had its serious side. The restriction of overseas exports to a few articles allowed by the Allies to pass in consideration for neutral States, was of less importance now that so little could be bought in overseas markets; but the continued fall in the value of the mark in those contiguous countries from which some supplies could still be obtained was a serious embarrassment, adding as it did very greatly to the cost of all imports. To some extent this fall may have been attributable to decreasing belief in the ultimate victory of the Central Powers, and doubts as to the soundness of Germany's war finance, but it was also due very largely to the fact that, desirable as it was to maintain German exports to these countries, the transport difficulties hampered the movement of coal, and the demands of the armies and depletion of stocks interfered with deliveries of iron and steel and other manufactured goods. In the early part of December the German peace feelers led to a rapid recovery in the American exchange, but in other centres the effect was comparatively slight, and the year closed with the mark standing at a discount of over 80 per cent. in Holland, Switzerland, and Scandinavia. The Austrian exchanges were in still worse condition, and in

[1] The German home output was increased during the war from 30,000 to 35,000 tons.

the chief European markets the krone had now little more than half its nominal value.[1]

Thus, by the end of 1916, both groups of belligerents showed signs of approaching exhaustion. The Allies, with free access, though at high cost and with increasing risk, to the markets of the world, had hitherto been able to procure in sufficient quantities all supplies essential either for the conduct of the war or for the sustenance of their peoples. In all the Allied countries there was a certain amount of hardship and discontent arising from the shortage, and still more from the high cost of the necessaries of life—food, clothing, and fuel; but this hardship was nowhere insupportable and in Great Britain the burden was comparatively light. On the other hand, the difficulties of financing and transporting the Allied purchases abroad had enormously increased, a heavy burden of debt was piling up, and the destruction of shipping by the German submarines had passed from an inconvenience into a serious menace. In the Central Powers there was as yet no sign of a weakening of resistance, due to lack of war material, but the supply of many articles of high military value had become dangerously short.

[1] Rates on Berlin per 100 marks.

	Normal.	30 Nov., 1916.	30 Dec., 1·16.	Percentage Discount 30 Dec. 1·16.
Sweden (kronor)	88·88	59·25	57·50	35·31
Norway (kroner)	88·88	60·50	60·50	31·08
Denmark (kroner)	88·88	61·25	61·50	30·80
Holland (gulden)	59·26	40·15	41·20	30·48
Switzerland (francs)	123·45	84·70	84·87½	31·26
New York ($ and cents)	38·11	27·00	29·35	23·00

Rates on Vienna per 100 kronen:

	Normal.	30 Dec., 1916.	Percentage Discount.
Sweden (kronor)	75·61	36·00	52·39
Denmark (kroner)	75·61	38·50	49·08
Holland (gulden)	50·41	25·76	48·92
Switzerland (francs)	105·01	53·75	48·82
New York (dollars)	20·26	11·81	41·71
Germany (marks)	85·06	64·00	24·76

Above all, the blockade had imposed on great masses of the population a degree of suffering which, before the war, would have been considered as intolerable, and great, surprisingly great, as their power of endurance had been proved, it was doubtful if they could hold out until another harvest. For both sides the year 1917 was to produce a profound modification in the situation.

INDEX

Abbreviations employed: B., battleship; B.cr., battle-cruiser; L.cr., light cruiser; s/m, submarine; s.s., steamer; s.v., sailing vessel; Br., British; D., Dutch; Dan., Danish; Fr., French; Ger., German; Gr., Greek; It., Italian; Nor., Norwegian; Sp., Spanish; Sw., Swedish; U.S., American.

Abö, service to, 118
Aden, threatened attack on, 105
Admiralty, British, and flow of trade, 18, 25; conferences at, 101, 333; and inter-allied chartering, 323. *See also* "Shipping, instructions to," and "Transport Department"
Africa, East and West, campaigns in, 39, 394
—, South, bunker troubles, 368; meat from, 371 n
Aircraft, attacks on shipping, 93, 252
Alexandria, transport staff at, 210
Alexandrovsk ice-free port, 122
Alfred Hage, Nor.s.s., case of, 116, 117
Allies, increased demands for tonnage, 211, 215, 231, 246; restriction of tonnage for, 263, 264–7, 336, 349, 352; proportion of tonnage in service of, 267, 337, 386; British responsibilities to, 376–7. *See also* under countries
Aluminium, German supplies of, 161
America, South, coal exports to, 141, 396
Ancona, It.s.s., torpedoed, 207
Anderson, Anderson & Co., Messrs., 79
Anderson, Sir Kenneth S., President of the Chamber of Shipping 188
Anglia, Br. Hospital ship, blown up, 208
Antilochus, Br.s.s., attack on, 107
Antwerpen, D.s.s., sunk, 331
Appam, Br.s.s., captured, 254, 255; interned, 256
Aquitania, Br.s.s., 174

Arabic, Br.s.s., sunk, 103
Aragon, Br.s.s., 175
Archangel. port of, closed, 119; opened, 121; congestion at, 122, 316; improved conditions at, 349
Arctic Ocean, s/ms in, 315, 331, 350, 357
Ardrossan, port of, 69
Argentina, Government wheat purchases in, 78. *See also* "Plate"
Arlotta, Signor Errico, at the Pallanza Conference, 324
Armenian, Br.s.s., sunk, 96
Arndale, Br.s.s., strikes a mine, 124
Asia Minor, blockade of, 106
Asquith, Rt. Hon. H. H., 15, 56, 197; resignation of, 377
Asturias, Br. Hospital ship, attack on, 11
Atkins, Brig.-Gen. A. R. Crofton, member of the Diversion of Shipping Committee, 68 n
Australia, export of meat, 81–5, 214 n, 369 n, 370, 371 n; shortage of tonnage, 82, 204, 339; failure of the harvest, 133; negotiations for the sale of wheat, 339–43
Austria-Hungary, war with Italy, 106; trade with the United States, 151 n; shortage of foodstuffs, 165–6; case of the *Ancona*, 207; economic conditions in, 301, 400, 405, 409; war with Roumania, 308; coal shortage, 406; rate of exchange, 407
Auxiliary Patrol, 20, 39; reorganised, 97; strength, 104 n
Avonmouth, military Home Supplies Depot, 64

411

INDEX

Azov, Sea of, 31
Babington-Smith, Sir H., Chairman of Import Restrictions Committee, 379
BACCHANTE II, Br. armed yacht, 96
Bacon, British and German supplies of, 134, 309–10, 389
Ballast voyages, 245, 279, 356
Baltic, mines in, 30; German command of, 30, 113, 114, 115; effect of operations in, 118, 313; British s/ms in, 119, 159; escape of ships from, 334–5; German s/ms in, 357
BARALONG, Br. decoy-ship, 104, 109
Barley, supplies of, 133, 388
Barnes, Mr. George, 79
Barrow, port of, 69
Batavier V., D.s.s., capture of, 27, 111
Bates, Sir Percy, head of Commercial Branch, 243
Bauxite, German supplies of, 161
Beachy Head minefield, 99
Beans, supply of, 388
Beans, Soya, from Vladivostok, 121, 125
Beatty, V.-Ad. Sir David, 98
Belgian Relief Commission, 216, 404 n
Bell, Mr. H. D., head of Sugar Section, 243
Belle Isle, Nor.s.s., case of, 116, 117
Belridge, Nor.s.s., torpedoed, 12, 23, 27, 36, 110
Berlhe, M. de, 265
Bernays, Commander, in command of White Sea mine-sweeping, 124
Bevan, Capt. G. P., Principal Naval Transport Officer at Archangel, 316, 349
Biscay, Bay of, s/ms in, 109, 357, 359, 380; minefields in, 255
Bjornstjerne Bjornson, Nor.s.s., seized, 147
Black List, Ships. *See* "Bunker Control"
——, statutory, 305–6
Black Sea, s/ms in, 108. *See also* "Dardanelles"
Blockade, use of the word, 89 n
Blockade of Asia Minor, 106; in Adriatic, 106
Blockade, Ministry of, 301; Financial Section, 305
Blue Book rates, 44, 48; increased, 76
Bolton, Sir Frederic, investigations into problem of distribution, 56–7; member of the Diversion of Shipping Committee, 67, 68 n; member of the Port and Transit Committee, 196 n, 197 n
Bombs, incendiary, on ships, 34
Bo'ness, closed, 60, 64
Booth, Sir Alfred A., member of the Diversion of Shipping Committee, 68 n; Chairman of the Liverpool Co-ordination Committee, 194 n
Booth, Mr. H., member of the Diversion of Shipping Committee, 68 n
Bor, copper-mine at, 407
Bothnia, Gulf of, 116, 118, 119, 335
Brazil, export of coffee, 138; meat from, 214 n, 371 n
Bremen, Ger. commercial s/m, 403
Bristol Channel, s/ms in, 26, 91, 208
Bristol, port of, 64, 69; lack of accommodation, 66; Co-ordination Committee, 194, 200
Broadbank, Mr. J. G., member of the Congestion at Ports Committee, 70 n; member of the Port and Transit Committee, 196 n, 197 n
Brussels, Br.s.s., captured, 330
Bulgaria, declares war, 173
Bunker Control, 155–8, 233, 275–82, 296, 327–8, 356, 383, 386
Butter, shortage of, 389; in Germany, 112–13, 309–10

Calais, mines at, 100
Cameroons, conquest of the, 211
Canada, export of pit-props, 126 n, 392; of wheat, 133, 181, 339 n, 341; food supplies from, 389, 390; meat from, 371 n
Canada, Russ. ice-breaker, 119; disabled, 119; under repair, 121
Canary Is., s/ms off, 380
Cape Corso, Br.s.s., case of, 28 n
Cape Town, congested, 368
Capelle, Adm. von, German Minister of Marine, 329
Caprivi, Nor.s.s., sunk, 30
Cardiff, port of, 64
Cargoes, estimated losses of, 128, 387; insurance, 129; premiums on, 131, 332
Carile, U.S.s.s., sunk, 29
Carthage, Fr.s.s , sunk, 107
Cecil, Lord Robert, Minister of Blockade, 301
"Certificates of Origin," system of, 149, 151, 301
Chadwick, Mr. R. Burton, member of the Ship Licensing Committee, 191

INDEX

Chamberlain, Rt. Hon. A., Chairman of the Man Power Board, 195

Chandler, Mr. Alfred, member of the Congestion at Ports Committee, 70 n

Channel, English, s/ms in, 11–12, 23, 24, 26, 27, 30; immune, 34, 100; again penetrated, 208, 268, 269, 270, 331, 358, 359, 380; minefields in, 100, 109, 208, 252

Chartering, centralised, for wheat, 79, 222; for ore, 279; of neutral tonnage, 249, 264, 275; interallied, 249, 275, 322–3, 343, 366–7

Chartering Committee, Inter-Allied, 367

Cheese, supplies of, 309–10, 389

China, trade with, 135, 142, 299, 388, 389, 397; meat from, 214 n, 371 n

Christiania Coal Importers' Association, 282

City of Winchester, Br. s.s., sunk, 303 n

Clan Macfarlane, Br.s.s., torpedoed, 207

Clan Mactavish, Br.s.s., sunk, 255

Clearances, of shipping, 133, 383

Clémentel, M., French Minister of Commerce, 365

Coal, output of, 40, 141, 394; exports of, 87, 113, 115, 139–41, 178, 394–6; to France, 51, 211–12, 245, 247–8, 262, 274, 280, 319, 327, 352–4, 383, 387, 395; to Italy, 247, 262, 316–19, 355–7, 360–1, 383, 387, 395; to Russia, 212, 350, 395; freights on, 76, 319–22, 322 n, 324 n, 356, 360; French output of, 40 n; German output and exports of, 151, 406. See also " Bunker Control "

Coal Exports Committee, 139, 245, 318, 395

Coasting traffic, diminution of, 63

Cocoa, German supplies of, 137–8, 302; imports of, 390

Coffee, German supplies of, 137–8, 303; imports of, 390

Colchester, Br.s.s., capture of, 332

Colliers, naval, 176

Colsterdale Scheme. *See* " Transport Workers Battalion "

Commercial Branch. *See* " Transport Department "

Commercial Union Insurance Co., 362

Commission Internationale de Ravitaillement, 213, 246, 323

Contraband, German allegations as to, 8–9; Orders in Council as to, 13, 15–16, 306–8; German decisions as to, 27–8; Italy restricts, 106; German treatment of timber, 116–17; stoppage of, 144–5, 147–55, 165, 301–4, 400–1

Contraband Committee, 150, 304

Contraband Department, transferred to the Ministry of Blockade, 301

Copper, supplies of, 134; seizures of, 145; shortage in Germany, 145, 161–2, 313, 406–7

Corbridge, Br.s.s., capture of, 255; sunk, 255

Cotton, imports of, 134, 392; effects of war on industry, 87, 135, 299, 397; German imports of, 29, 154; as contraband, 153

Crawford and Balcarres, Earl of, Chairman of the Royal Commission on Wheat Supplies, 344

Cross-Channel transport, increase in, 169–70; delays in, 175

Cryolite, German supplies of, 161

Curzon, Lord, Chairman of the Shipping Control Committee, 229, 333

Cushing, U.S.s.s., attacked by Ger. aeroplane, 93

Dacia, U.S.s.s. (ex-German), capture of, 29

Daintree, Capt. J. D., member of the Liverpool Co-ordination Committee, 194 n

Dairy produce, Br. and Ger. supplies of, 134, 163, 309–10, 404

Dakar, guns transferred at, 206

Danish Merchants Guild, agreements with, 166, 301–2

Dardanelles campaign, economic importance of, 31–2, 126, 183; effect on tonnage, 53–4, 132, 170–3, 174–5; s/ms and, 105, 107; abandoned, 209

Dartmouth minefield, 99

Declaration of London, Allies repudiate, 306–7

Declaration of Paris, proposed repudiation of, 14

Decoy-ships, armed, 95, 256

Defensively Armed Merchantmen, 35, 205–7, 271, 330, 331, 332–3, 381–2; in action, 35, 91–2, 96, 255

De Keyser's Hotel, case of, 43

Demarara, Br.s.s., attacked by s/m, 91

Denmark, trade with, 115, 280, 309, 396; German trade with, 147, 301, 309, 402; protest against bunker regulations, 280. *See also* "Danish Merchants Guild."
Dennis, Mr. C. S., member of the Congestion at Ports Committee, 71 n
Derby, Earl of, Recruiting Scheme, 199; raises a Dockers' Battalion in Liverpool, 284
Deutschland, Ger. commercial s/m, 313, 357, 402
Deviation, lengthening of voyages by, 381
Devonport, Lord, member of the Congestion at Ports Committee, 70 n; Food Controller, 378
Dinorah, Fr.s.s., torpedoed, 23
Diplomat, Br.s.s., sunk, 303 n
Diversion of Shipping Committee, 24, 59–60, 69–73, 195, 197
Dockers' Battalion, in Liverpool, 284, 287
Dohna-Schlodien, Graf zu, in command of the MOEWE, 254, 380
Dover, port of, 64
—, Straits of, defence of, 21–2, 34, 100, 104; penetrated, 252; destroyer raid on, 358
Downs, the, 25, 26, 34; Boarding Flotilla, 148, 149
DRESDEN, Ger. L.cr., sunk, 33
Dulwich, Br.s.s., torpedoed, 11
Dumayne, Sir F. G., Secretary to the Committee on Congestion at Ports, 70, 71 n; to the Port and Transit Committee, 196 n, 197
Dumfriesshire, Br.s.v., torpedoed, 101
Dundee, port of, 64
Dunsyre, U.S.s.v., collusive capture of, 152
Durban, congestion at, 368
Dvina, River, 122; frozen, 212

Economist, Index Number, 373
Edinburgh, Br.s.v., sunk, 255
Eggs, supply of, 125, 309, 389
Egyptian State Railways, supply of coal, 40, 51, 176
Eir, Nor.s.s., collusive capture of, 152
Elbow Buoy, minefield, 99
Elizabeth IV, Nor.s.s., sunk, 331
Ellispontos, Gr.s.s., torpedoed, 30, 110
EMDEN, Ger. L.cr., 35, 135
Enemy Exports Committee, 149
Entrances, of shipping, 132, 178, 185, 225, 231, 233, 260, 271, 295, 338, 383
Esher, Lord, Chairman of the Sub-Committee on ports, 57
Essell, Lieut.-Col. F. K., member of the Liverpool Co-ordination Committee, 194
Evans, Sir Samuel, on Prize Law, 28 n
Evelyn, U.S.s.s., sunk, 29
Excess Profits Duty, 187
Exchanges, decline of British, 143, 183, 298, 399; of Allied, 400; Enemy, 152, 165, 407, 408 n
Expeditionary Force, transport of, 45, 170
Exports, volume of, 87, 135, 142, 397–8; regulation of, 88–9; effect of restrictions on, 113, 137, 161, 163, 202, 397–9; causes of decline of, 135–7, 139, 298–300; redistribution of, 142–3, 297, 398–9
Eyre, R.-Ad. F. G., member of the Mediterranean Transport Commission, 179

Falaba, Br.s.s., sunk, 36
Falsterbö, 30, 118, 335, 336
Faringdon, Lord, member of the Shipping Control Committee, 229
Fay, Sir Samuel, member of the Congestion at Ports Committee, 71 n; member of the Port and Transit Committee, 196 n, 197 n
Fernando Noronha, MOEWE off, 255
Fernie, Mr. H. F., member of the Ship Licensing Committee, 191
Fertilisers, German shortage of, 164–5, 403
Finisterre, Cape, s/ms off, 331
Finland, railway traffic with Sweden, 119
Firth of Forth, closing of the, 60
Fish, British and German supplies of, 113, 115, 310–1, 389–90
Fishing fleets, s/m attack on, 30, 98, 329, 389
Flax, supplies of, 134, 392; German shortage of, 162
Fleetwood, port of, 69
Fletcher, Sir Lionel, 41, 44
Floride, Fr.s.s., capture of, 36
Fodder, German shortage of, 164–5, 404
Folkestone-Cape Gris-nez boom, 21
Food Controller, appointment of, 374, 378

Food, Ministry of, 378
Food Supplies, British, 74, 133–4, 388–91. *See* also under separate commodities
—, Austrian, 166, 405–6
—, German, 162–5, 308–12, 401–6
Food Supplies, Cabinet Committee on, 78, 220, 293
Fourth Sea Lord's Conference on tonnage, 46, 55, 169
France, supply of coal to, 41, 51, 211-12, 241, 245, 247, 262, 274, 280, 319–21, 352–5, 359, 361, 383, 387, 395; of meat, 80–1, 213–14, 248, 371 n; of wheat, 221–3, 235, 247, 363; of steel and oats, 248, 262, 352 n; woollen exports to, 135; provision of tonnage for, 215, 246–50, 326; restriction of tonnage supplied to, 245–6, 264–6, 336, 349, 352; tonnage agreement with, 365–7; exports to, 397–8; financial condition of, 399–400
Franconia, Br.s.s., sunk, 358
Franz Fischer, detained Ger. s.s., sunk, 252
Freight Limitation Schemes, Coal, 320–2; extended to Italy, 324, 356; effects of, 327, 357, 360–1, 383
—, North Sea, 279–80, 327–8, 359
—, Ore, 278–9
—, Wheat, Australian, 339
Freights, rise in, 38, 74–7, 220; on sugar, 52, 373; on grain, 75, 182 n, 185-8, 219–20, 224, 235, 291, 339, 344, 367, 391; on coal, 76, 319–22, 322 n, 324 n, 360; on meat, 82–3, 84; on ore, 203, 278; in Baltic, 119; in North Sea, 279–80, 327, 359, 360; effect on prices, 77, 87, 186–7, 344, 372–3, 391, 392, 394; difficulty of fixing, 187–8, 234–5, 323, 345; neutral, 275
Fridland, Sw.s.s., seized, 147
Friedrich Arp, Ger.s.s., sunk, 159
Fryatt, Capt., fate of, 330
Funchal bombarded, 380
Furness, Withy & Co., Messrs., 249, 260, 264, 275, 296, 315, 316, 318, 323, 325, 326, 356

Galicia, invasion of, 146; oil-wells, 308, 407
Gallia, Fr.s.s., sunk, 358
Gallipoli Expedition. *See* "Dardanelles"
Gardiner, Mr. F. C., member of Advisory Committee, 48; mem-ber of the Carriage of Foodstuffs Committee, 190; head of the Commercial Branch, 242
Garmoyle, Br.s.s., attacked, 91
Geddes, Sir Eric, member of the Congestion at Ports Committee, 71 n; report on military transport, 374; Director-General of Military Railways, 375
Genoa, congestion at, 218; cleared off, 245
George, Rt. Hon. D. Lloyd, Prime Minister, 378
Germany, trade revives, 13–14, 29–30; trade with Holland, 112–13; friction with Sweden, 116–18; ore imports, 116, 159–60, 313, 401; British re-exports reach, 138–9, 163; supplies restricted, 144; copper output, 145; supply of mineral oils, 145–6, 164, 308, 407; expanding imports, 146–7; measures to restrict trade of, 147–51, 153–8, 163, 301–8, 310–11, 400–1; export trade stopped, 150–1, 151 n, 301, 407; coal output falls, 151 fall of exchanges, 152, 407, 408 n; methods of contraband trade, 152–3; shortage of metals, 160–2, 312–13, 406–7; of textiles, 162, 312; of food, 162–3, 308–12, 402–5; of fodder and fertilisers, 164–5; harvest fails, 309; Food Control's mistakes, 373; peace overtures, 400, 407; disease and suffering, 404-5, 409; transport conditions in, 406. *See also* "Submarine Campaign"
Gibraltar, Straits of, s/ms pass, 106-7
Gironde, s/m off, 109; minefield off, 255
Glasgow, port of, 64, 69; Co-ordination Committee, 194, 200
GLASGOW, Br. L.cr., 255
Glitra, Br.s.s., case of, 5
Glover, Sir Ernest W., member of the Advisory Committee, 48; of the Carriage of Foodstuffs Committee, 190
GOEBEN, Ger. B.cr., at Constantinople, 31
Gosling, Mr. Harry, President of the Transport Workers' Federation, 203; member of the Port and Transit Committee, 203, 287, 290
Grangemouth, port of, 60, 64
Great Britain, German allegations against, 8–10; military obliga-

416 INDEX

tions of, 45, 60–62; effect of war on economic position of, 74, 87–9, 110, 133–43, 231–2, 295–300, 387–400, 408. *See also* under "Imports," "Shipping," etc.
Greece, friction with the Allies, 361; coal to, 396
Greenbriar, U.S.s.s., sunk, 30
Greenock, port of, 69
GREIF, German raider, sunk, 254
Griffiths, Lieut.-Col. Norton, 407
Grimsby, port of, 64
Groves, Mr. James, member of the Advisory Committee, 48 n
Guadeloupe, Fr.s.s., capture of, 36
Gulflight, U.S.s.s., torpedoed, 93
Gull, minefield, 99
Gull Stream, boom across, 22, 25
Gustaf E. Falck, Nor.s.s., intercepted, 311
Guthrie, Mr. Connop, head of the General Section Commercial Branch, 243

Hain, Sir Edward, member of the Diversion of Shipping Committee, 68 n; of the Port and Transit Committee, 196 n, 197 n
Hälsingborg, services transferred to, 118
Hamilton, Brig.-Gen. A. B., member of the Mediterranean Transport Commission, 179
Hamilton, Sir Ian, lands in Gallipoli, 31
Hankey, Lieut.-Col Sir M. P. A., member of the Diversion of Shipping Committee, 68 n
Hanna, Sw.s.s., torpedoed, 27, 110
Hargreaves, Mr. W. E., suggests Bunker Control, 156
Harparanda, Swedish port, 120
Harwich, naval base, 60, 64
Hawkins, Col. T. H., Secretary of the Diversion of Shipping Committee, 67, 68 n; reports on the West Coast ports, 69, 71; on the North-Eastern ports, 72; Secretary of the Port and Transit Committee, 196 n, 197; scheme of a Transport Workers' Battalion, 284
H. C. Henry, Br.s.s., sunk, 107
Hemp, supplies of, 134
Hill, Hon. Mr. Justice Maurice, Chairman of the Ship Licensing Committee, 191
Hill, Sir Norman, member of the Diversion of Shipping Committee, 68 n; of the Port and Transit Committee, 196 n, 197 n; on the shortage of tonnage, 379
Holland, and s/m campaign, 111; trade with, 111–13, 138, 396; German trade with, 112, 147, 151 n, 163, 309, 396, 402; refusal to admit armed ships, 206; agricultural and fish agreements with, 310, 402; shipbuilding in, 385. *See also* "Netherlands Overseas Trust"
Holmden, Mr. O. G., suggests inter-Allied chartering, 323
Holt, Messrs. A. & Co., 52
Holt, Mr. R. D., member of the Advisory Committee, 48; of the Carriage of Foodstuffs Committee, 190
Home-grown Timber Committee, 237
Hood, R.-Ad. the Hon. H. L. A., in command of Dover Straits, 21
Houlder, Mr. Howard, member of the Diversion of Shipping Committee, 68 n
Hudson Bay Co., 122, 222, 263, 363
Hughes, Rt. Hon. W. M., 340
Hull, port of, 64
Humber, minefields off, 60
Hurcomb, Mr. Cyril, Commercial Branch, 242

Ireland, Agreement with, 311, 390
Immingham, naval base, 60
Imperial Defence, Sub-committees of, 57, 58
Imports, volume of, 55, 74, 133–5, 142, 231, 233, 295, 297, 387; excess of, 87–8, 297, 398; restriction of, 189, 226–8, 233, 234, 261, 262, 264, 300, 347, 379, 392
Inchcape, Lord, Chairman of the Congestion at Ports Committee, 70; of the Refrigerated Shipping Committee, 83; member of the Port and Transit Committee, 196 n, 197
India, wheat from, 78–9, 180, 183, 292, 339; reduced exports to, 135, 299, 397; balance of trade with, 142
Indianic, Sw.s.s., judgment on, 13 n
Indicator-nets, use of, 20
Industry, number of persons employed, 136 n, 299
Information Branch. *See* "Transport Department"
Insurance, marine, as blockade weapon, 156, 158
Inter-Allied Food Commission, 404

INDEX

Irish Sea, defence of, 22-3, 26, 34, 96, 104; s/ms in, 24, 26, 103; minefield in, 380
Iron and Steel, Exports of, 135, 397
Iron Ore, supplies of and tonnage for, 53, 115, 134, 177, 203-4, 260-1, 276-9, 297, 383, 391-2, 397; Official Ore Broker, 279; Coal-Ore Agreement with Italy, 356; German supplies of, 114, 116, 159-60, 313, 401
Isle of Man minefield, 380
Isodorio, Sp.s.s., sunk, 104 n
Italy, entry into war, 105-6; supply of meat to, 213, 214 n, 249, 371 n; of wheat, 221-3, 235, 247, 363; of coal, 247, 262, 316-19, 324-6, 355-7, 359, 360-1, 383, 387, 395-6, 399; of steel and oats, 248, 262. 352 n; demands for tonnage, 215, 246-50, 326; restriction of tonnage supplied to, 245, 264-6, 336, 349; Pallanza Conference, 324-5; Coal-Ore Agreement with, 356; exports to, 398; financial condition of, 399-400

Japan, trade with Russia, 120; balance of trade with, 142; captures British trade, 296, 385; ships purchased in, 379
Jason, Dan, s.v., destroyed, 103
Johnson, Mr. D. Ross, member of the Congestion at Ports Committee, 71 n
Jones, Capt. Clement, Secretary of the Shipping Control Committee, 229, 324
JUPITER, Br. B., at Archangel, 121
Jute, supplies of, 134; German shortage of, 162, 312
Jutland, Battle of, 335

Kandalaksha, lack of railways to, 122
KARLSRUHE, Ger.L.cr., 35
Karungi, Swedish port, 120
Karunki, Finnish port, 120
Katwijk, D.s.s., torpedoed, 30, 110
Kem, lack of railways to, 122
Kenmare, Br.s.s., attacked, 96
Kentish Knock, minefield, 99
Kim, Nor.s.s., seized, 147
KING EDWARD VII, Br.B., sunk, 254
Kogrund Passage, 313, 335; minefield, 336
Kola, ice-free port, 122

Königin Emma, D.s.s., sunk, 109
Kronprinsessan Victoria, Sw.s.s., judgment on, 13 n
KRONPRINZ WILHELM, Ger. raider, 36, 37; interned, 33, 252

Labour, displacement of, 136, 299
Laertes, Br.s.s., escapes from s/m, 12
Lard, seizures of, 147
La Roserina, Br.s.s., attack on, 35
Latimer, Mr. Ernest, member of the Congestion at Ports Committee, 71 n
Leather industry, 134, 398
Leelanaw, U.S.s.s., sunk, 98
Leith, port of, 64
Lewis, Mr. F. W., member of the Ship Licensing Committee, 191; of the Shipping Control Committee, 229
Libau, ships sunk on evacuation of, 119
Linen, exports of, 397
Lintrose, Russ. ice-breaker, 121
Liverpool Steam Ship Owners' Association, on the decline of wheat imports, 182; Conference with Board of Trade, 188; import restrictions proposals, 189
Liverpool, Co-ordination Committee, 193-4; members, 194 n, 200
Liverpool, Dockers' Battalion, 284
Liverpool, port of, 64, 69, 71; congestion at, 65, 193; wheat imports, 292
Living, cost of, 77, 373, 393
Lodge, Mr. Thomas, Secretary of the Ship Licensing Committee, 191
London, port of, 64, 71, 194; investigation into the, 57-8
Long, Brig.-Gen. S. S., member of the Diversion of Shipping Committee, 68 n
Louisiania, Dan.s.s., judgment on, 13 n.
Lulea, German trade with, 313
Lusitania, Br.s.s., sunk, 92-4

Maclay, Sir Joseph P., Shipping Controller, 378
McLean, Col. W. R. J., in command of the Transport Workers' Battalion, 285, 289
Macrosty, Mr. H. W., 79
Madagascar, meat from, 214 n, 371 n
Madeira, s/ms off, 380

418 INDEX

Maize, supplies of, 133, 388
MAJESTIC, Br.B., sunk, 106
Malmland, Sw.s.s., sunk, 103
Malmö, services transferred to, 118
Maloja, Br.s.s., blown up, 251
Man Power Board, 195
Manchester, port of, 64, 69, 71
Margarine, supplies of, 134, 163, 389; materials, 113, 138–9, 393, 401
Maria, D.s.s., case of, 5
Marie Glaeser, Ger.s.s., case of, 28 n
Marmora, Sea of, Br. s/ms in, 106
Maroni, Fr.s.s., capture of, 256
Martens, Messrs. R. & Co., 121, 316
Maryport, 69
Mathwins, Messrs., 44, 238, 240
Mauretania, Br.s.s., use of, 174
Meat, British and Allied supplies of, 79–85, 133, 213–14, 248–9, 368–72, 388; sources and distribution, 214 n, 371 n; freights and prices, 82–3, 82 n, 84, 372 n; shortage in Germany, 309–10, 404
—, products, contraband trade in, 147, 303–4
Medea, D.s.s., sunk, 27, 111
Mediterranean, situation in, 31–2, 105–6; s/ms in, 106–8, 207, 208, 251, 257–8, 268–9, 271, 330–1, 357–8, 380; difficulty of trade defence in, 108; transport conditions in, 170–5, 209–10; defensively armed ships in, 205–7, 332–3; shipping diverted from, 257–8
Mediterranean, Transport Commission, 179, 209–10
Mercantile Marine Association, 101
Mesopotamian Expedition, 39, 211, 394
METEOR, Ger. raider, blown up, 103; sinks the *Verdandi*, 117; lays mines in the White Sea, 124
Milk shortage in Germany, 405
Millar, Mr. H. R., member of the Diversion of Shipping Committee, 68 n
Minefields, British, 21, 99, 111
—, German, 21, 29, 30, 31, 111; laid by s/ms, 98–9, 100, 109, 208, 251–2, 268, 380; by METEOR, 103, 124, 316; by MOEWE, 254–5
—, Swedish, 336
—, Casualties from, 29, 30, 33, 36, 99, 103, 109, 124, 208, 251, 254–5, 268, 358
Miners, enlistment of, 40, 141
Minesweepers, work of the, 29, 99, 109, 124, 252, 316

Minnetonka, Br.s.s., 175
MOEWE, Ger. raider, sinks ships, 254–7; lays mines, 255; second cruise, 380
Molybdenum, purchase of, 160
Money, Sir Leo Chiozza, Parliamentary Secretary to the Shipping Controller, 378
Moore, Mr. H. T., member of the Congestion at Ports Committee, 70 n
Moray Firth, minefield, 103
Mudros, base at, 108, 171; congestion at, 172–3
Munitions, Ministry of, 136; recruits transport workers, 201; requirements, 260, 348, 386, 391
Murillo, Br.s.s., 368 n
Murman Coast, 122; railway to, 123, 351

Navigation, restrictions on, 24–6, 60, 99–100
Narvik, ore exports, 159, 327, 383
Nava, Signor G., at the Pallanza Conference, 324
"Navicert System," 304
Nebraskan, U.S.s.s., torpedoed, 93
Netherlands Overseas Trust, 147, 149 n, 155, 166; rationing agreement, 302, 303
Neumond, Karl, 153
Neutral colours, British use of, 9, 10, 111
New Zealand, export of meat, 81–5, 214 n, 370, 371 n; shortage of tonnage, 82
Newcastle, port of, 64
Newfoundland, export of pit-props, 126, 392
Newhaven, port of, 64
Niandarma, broad gauge line from Vologda, 123
Nickel, German supplies of, 160–2, 313, 403
Nicosian, Br.s.s., attacked, 104
Nieueport minefield, 21
Nitrate as contraband, 165
Noble, Mr. W. J., member of the Congestion at Ports Committee, 71 n
Nordkyn, Nor.s.s., blown up, 30
Norrköping, sailings suspended, 118
North-about Route, s/m attacks on, 97–8, 103, 109, 124, 357
North Atlantic, grain trade, 182–4, 188–9, 220–1, 235, 291–3, 296
North Channel, net barriers across, 22, 104
North-Eastern ports, report on, 72

INDEX 419

North Sea, s/ms in, 27, 30, 98, 103, 109, 111, 268-9, 329-32, 357, 359, 380; minefields in, 21, 29, 99, 111, 268; conditions of trade in, 110-15, 279-80, 327-8, 359-60
Norway, trade with, 115, 126, 396; German trade with, 147, 159, 302, 402; "rationing" agreements with, 302, 303; fish agreement with, 310-11, 390; enforces neutrality, 315

Oats, supplies of, 133, 388
Odessa, Ger.s.v., case of, 28 n
Oil seeds, British and German supplies of, 113, 138, 393
Oils, mineral, German supply of, 145-6, 164, 308, 407
Oils, vegetable, German supply of, 163
ORAMA, Br.A.M.C., 306 n
Orduna, Br.s.s., attacked by s/m, 96
Orlov, Cape, minefield, 124
Ostend, submarines based on, 111, 208
Oversea Prize Disposal Committee, 38
Owen, Mr. T. Woodward, Official Ore-broker, 278

Paget, Col. C. W., in command of Railway Operating Troops at Boulogne, 374
Palembang, D.s.s., torpedoed, 268
Pallanza, Conference at, 324, 355
Paper and materials, imports restricted, 234, 392
Paris, Allied Conference at, 322
Patagonia, Br. s.s., torpedoed, 108
"Penalty Rents," 69, 286, 290
Pentland Firth, minefield, 254
Perim Harbour, shelling of, 105
Perm, Russian river port, 122
Persia, Br.s.s., torpedoed, 207
Petroleum, supplies of, 393. *See also* "Oils, Mineral"
Petrozavodsk, railway to, 123
Phillips, Sir Owen, 85 n
Phosphate, German supplies of, 165
Pilotage regulations, 24-5
Ping Suey, Br.s.s., attacked, 91
Pit-props, supply of, 117, 125-6, 276, 278, 392; as contraband, 116-17
Plate, River, meat from, 83-4, 213, 214, 214 n, 369, 370, 371 n; wheat from, 180, 235, 292, 339

Port and Transit Committee, 191, 197; members, 197 n; work of, 198-204, 225, 277, 283-92, 347; on restriction of imports, 226
Port Said, guns transferred at, 206, meat ships at, 368
Ports, pre-war enquiries into, 56-60; closing of, 60, 64; army and navy demands on, 61-4, 72; Board of Trade Committee on Congestion at, 70-1; Joint Committee on Congestion of, 196; labour supply at, 69-70, 199, 201, 283-4, 287; congestion of British, 38, 55, 65-6, 73, 174, 195-6, 276, 290-2, 347, 353; of French, 56, 175, 245, 293-4, 353, 354; of American, 261; of South African, 368. *See also* "Transport Workers Battalions," "Railway Wagons," "Penalty Rents," "Transit Sheds."
Portugal, export of pit-props, 126 n; seizes German ships, 347
Presidente Mitre, Argentine s.s., capture of, 306 n
Prices, effect of war on, 77, 87, 186-7, 372-3, 391-4. *See also* "Freights"
Pringle, Mr. P. J., member of the Congestion at Ports Committee, 71 n
PRINZ EITEL FRIEDRICH, Ger. raider, 37; interned, 33, 252
Prizes and interned ships, use of, 38-9, 77
Prize Courts, decisions of, British, 13 n, 16 n, 28 n; French, 29; German, 5-6, 27-8, 116-17
Puget Sound ports, 75, 120
Pungo. "*See* MOEWE"
Purdie, Mr. T. P., member of the Ship Licensing Committee, 191
Pyrites, imports of, 134, 177, 203, 392

Queen, Br.s.s., capture of, 358

Raiders, surface, s/ms compared with, 2, 34-5, 135; news of, 253, 380
Railway Trucks, pooling of, 67, 69, 201, 237, 277, 285-6
Railways, capacity of, 58-60; pressure on, 61; Russian, 120, 122-3, 349, 351; Siberian, 351; South African, 368; German, 406
Ramazan, Br.ss., sunk, 107

420 INDEX

Rathlin Island, 22
Rationing agreements, 166, 301-2
Raumo, services to, 118, 119
Reichsanzeiger, warning to neutrals in, 8
Requisitioning, of shipping, right of, 43-4; inequalities in, 48-9; "proportionate," 49-50; of insulated space, 82-6 of liner space, 241. *See also* "Blue Book Rates," "Shipping," "Transport Department"
Requisitioning Branch. *See* "Transport Department"
Requisitioning (Carriage of Foodstuffs) Committee, 190-1, 204; members, 190; work of, 220-4, 234-5, 246-7, 291, 293, 344; on restriction of imports, 227; effect on neutrals, 296; dissolved, 345
Retaliation Order, 15-16, 144, 148, 195
Return Cargo Regulations. *See* "Bunker Control"
Rhode I., s/m off, 357
Rice, large imports of, 388
Riga, Gulf of, attack on, 119
Rijn, D.s.s., judgment on, 13 n
Rijndam, D.s.s., sunk, 251
Ritson, Mr. A., member of the Diversion of Shipping Committee, 68 n
Robeck, Adm. de, 171, 209
Robertson, Sir H. R., member of the Congestion at Ports Committee, 70 n; of the Liverpool Co-ordination Committee, 194 n
Robinson, Mr. F. P., Joint Secretary of the Carriage of Foodstuffs Committee, 190
Robinson, Sir Thomas B., directs meat purchases, 79, 80, 213, 214, 248, 368
Rodd, Sir Rennell, at the Pallanza Conference, 324
Roper, Mr. Garnham, 79
Roumania, exports to Germany, 146, 308; declares war, 308; supplies to, 314; destruction of grain, 405-6; of oil-wells, 407
Royal Edward, Br.s.s., sunk, 107, 171
Royal Mail Steam Packet Co., 120
Royden, Sir Thomas, advises on transport, 41; member of the Advisory Committee, 48; of the Transport Commission, 179; of the Shipping Control Committee, 229, 364; investigation into the condition of French ports, 293; member of the Royal Commission on Wheat Supplies, 344
Royden-Fletcher Report, 42
Rubber, supplies of, 393; German supplies of, 144, 312-13; agreement with U.S. exporters, 155
Runciman, Rt. Hon. Walter, President of the Board of Trade, memorandum of Jan. 11th, 1915, 46; Chairman of the Committee on the Diversion of Shipping, 59; memorandum from Shipowners, 67; on restriction of imports, 228, 234; Conference at Pallanza, 324; Conference at the Admiralty, 333; proposed remedies for the shortage of tonnage, 347-8
Russia, grain stocks in, 31; importance of Dardanelles to, 32, 126; transit route to, 118, 119-20; credits granted to, 119; trade of, and supplies to, 120-3 125-6, 212, 263-4, 314-16, 349-52
Russian Bank for Foreign Trade v. *Excess Insurance Company* case, 43 n

Sailing vessels, demand for, 75, 114; attacks on and protection of, 100-2, 114; under State Insurance Scheme, 129
St. George's Channel, defence of, 23, 96, 104
Salonika Expedition, effects on tonnage, 173, 209, 210, 264, 336
Salter, Mr. J. A., Joint Secretary of the Carriage of Foodstuffs Committee, 190; Director of Requisitioning, 239, 240, 364
Sanderson, Capt. Harold A., member of the Diversion of Shipping Committee, 68 n; of the Ship Licensing Committee, 191
Saunders, Mr. G. W., 239
Saxon Prince, Br.s.s., capture of, 256
Scheer, Admiral, 270
Scholefield, Mr. Arthur, member of the Ship Licensing Committee, 191
Seely, Col. J. B., 57, 58
Shields, Mr. D., member of the Congestion at Ports Committee, 71 n
Ship Licensing Committee, 191-2, 265, 318, 377; members, 191; work of, 217-220, 295; report of, 224, 226, 227, 231; extension of powers, 244-6; and Allies, 265-6, 353-4

INDEX

Shipbuilding, decline in, 37, 168-9, 226, 232, 346; efforts to accelerate, 236, 269, 333, 375; State programme, 379; output, 169 n, 232 n, 333-4, 376 n; abroad, 295, 379, 385
Shipowners, proposals for relieving congestion, 67, 69; on the decline of wheat imports, 182-23; profits of, 187; conference with, 188
Shipping, Mercantile, British, instructions to, 18-20, 24, 95, 101-2, 253, 256, 258, 381; confidence displayed by, 18, 26; requisitioning of, 38-40, 45-6, 51-4, 77-9, 83-4, 122, 169, 173, 176-7, 181, 202-3, 204, 225, 232, 234, 242, 277-8, 317, 342; requisitioned, status of, 47, 52; economies in use of requisitioned, 174-5, 176, 264, 336, 374; chartered to Allies, 177, 215; profits of, 187; proposed control of, 235; in inter-foreign trade, 267-8, 295-6; losses of, 34, 35, 37, 102, 109, 127-8, 169 n, 208, 252, 257, 268, 269, 271, 331, 332, 334, 358, 380, 381, 384-5. *See* also "Clearances," "Defensively Armed Merchantmen," "Entrances," "Freights," "Requisitioning," "Tonnage"
—, Allied, in British trade, 271, losses of, 36, 209, 271, 330-1, 358, 380, 385; activity of Japanese, 120, 385; employment of Italian, 215, 222, 355-6
—, Canadian, requisitioning of, 181
—, Enemy, seized by Italy, 106, 215 n; by Portugal, 347; in Greek ports, 361; losses of, 106, 160; activity of, 159-60
—, Neutral, threatened by s/ms, 5-6, 8-9, 27-8; defies s/ms, 26-7, 28-9, 111, 178; activity in British trade, 132; agreements with, 147, 148, 153, 155; withdrawal of Greek, 178; supply of, 233, 272-3, 274, 295-6, 327, 356; allocated to Allies, 296, 326; insurance of, 358-9, 361-2; withdrawal of, 359-61, 383; losses of, 36, 209, 268, 331, 332, 358, 381, 385. *See* also "Bunker Control"
Shipping, Chamber of, 182, 188
Shipping Control Committee, 229-30; work of, 233, 236, 237-8, 267, 269, 293, 314, 377; and wheat, 340, 342-3; restriction of tonnage for Allies, 261-5, 352, 353; protest against an Inter-Allied Committee, 322
Shipping Controller, appointment of, 378
Shipping, Ministry of, 378
Siberian Railway, 351
Silk, supplies of, 134, 397
Silloth, port of, 69
Skagerrak, s/ms in, 357
Slade, Vice-Adm. Sir Edmond J. W., 42; Chairman of the Oversea Prize Disposal Committee, 38; of the Diversion of Shipping Committee, 67, 68 n, 71
Sloop Squadron, 104
Smalls, the, net defences, 96, 103
Smith, Sir E. Wyldbore, at the Pallanza Conference, 324
Smythe, Messrs. Ross T., Government Chartering Agents, 222, 243, 247 n, 267, 292
Société Suisse de Surveillance Économique, 166, 302
Somme, Battle of the, 374
Soroka, lack of railways to, 122
South Goodwin, minefield, 99
South-Western Approach, defined, 26 n; s/ms in, 30, 34, 90-1, 91-3, 96, 103, 104, 127, 208, 268, 269, 358, 380
Southampton, port of, 64
Southland, Br.s.s., torpedoed, 107
Spain, ore trade, 53, 276, 383; export of pit-props, 126 n; coal supply, 396
Spee, Adm. von, destruction of his squadron, 120
Stampalia, It.s.s., sunk, 331
State Insurance Scheme, effects of, 18, 26, 68, 128, 131; working of, 69, 128-31; increase in insured values, 130; premiums raised, 332
Statist, Index Number, 77, 186, 373
Statutory Black List, 305
Stewart, Mr. W. A., Head of Ore Section, Transport Department, 203
Stigstad, Nor.s.s., case of, 16 n
Stileman, Admiral H. H., member of the Liverpool Co-ordination Committee, 194 n
Stockholm, sailings suspended, 118
Stones, imports restricted, 234
Stuart-Wortley, Brig.-Gen. Hon. A. R. M., member of Port and Transit Committee, 197 n
Submarine Campaign, inception and character of, 1-11; American protests against, 11, 93, 207

270, 329; consequences to Germany, 12–17, 94, 144; checked, 34; compared with surface raiders, 34–5, 135; new methods, 96–7; shifts to Mediterranean, 105, 107–9; extended radius, 269, 357, 380; restricted, 270; intensified, 329, 357, 380; effects of, 387; attacks on shipping, 11–12, 23–4, 26–7, 30, 34–6, 90–3, 96, 97–8, 101–3, 107, 109, 111, 114, 123–4, 207–9, 251–2, 257, 268–71, 315, 329–32, 350, 357–9, 380–2; measures against, 18–23, 24–6, 35, 91, 94–6, 97–9, 100–2, 104, 205–7, 332–3

Submarines, British, in Sea of Marmora, 106; in Baltic, 119, 159–60
Suchan, Russ.s.s., capture of, 350
Suez Canal, attack on, 32; measures against mine-laying, 33
Sugar, carriage of, 52, 78; imports, 64–5, 142, 241; shortage, 372, 388; price, 372
Sussex, Fr.s.s., sunk, 270, 329
Svein Jarl, Nor.s.s., torpedoed, 111
Svyatoi Nos, delays to shipping off, 124
Sweden, trade with 115–18, 396; German trade with, 116, 147, 159–60, 302, 309, 401; transit route to Russia, 118–20; friction with, 281, 302, 335–6; rationing agreements with, 302; embargo on shipments to, 402
Swept Channel, traffic in and attacks on, 98–100, 104, 114
Switzerland. See " Société de Surveillance Économique "
Sydland, Sw.s.s., judgment on, 13 n

Tea, German supplies of, 137–8, 303
Teiresias, Br.s.s., strikes a mine, 33
" Temporary Release," 46, 52–3, 177, 241–2, 267, 277
TENBY CASTLE, Br. armed trawler, sinks *Friedrich Arp*, 159
Tenth Cruiser Squadron, 148, 159
Thames, River, restriction of navigation in, 60
Thompson, Mr. J. Hannay, member of the Congestion at Ports Committee, 71 n
Thomson, Mr. Graeme, Director of Transports, 41, 364; member of the Port and Transit Committee, 197 n
Thordis, Br.s.s., attack on, 35

Tirpitz, Admiral von, 329; *My Memoirs*, 2 n
Timber, supply of, 125, 134, 234, 392; as contraband, 116–7; home-grown, 126, 237
Tin, supplies of, 134; German supplies of, 161, 313, 403
Tinplate, restrictions on export of, 137, 397
Tod Head minefield, 99
Todd, Mr. Stanley, member of the Diversion of Shipping Committee, 68 n
Tokomaru, Br.s.s., sunk, 214 n
Tonnage, shortage of, 37–8, 74, 174, 177–9, 211, 215, 218–19, 225–6, 230–3, 261–3, 266–7, 300, 317, 336–8, 346–7, 364, 373, 377, 379, 386; for meat, 82; for coal, ore, and timber, 178; for wheat, 181–5, 339, 340, 342, 346, 364; for ore, 276–7, 279; for coal, 317, 327, 357, 360–1, 383; agreement with France as to, 364–7
—, Insulated, *see* " Meat "
Tornea, railway to Karunki, 120
Tory Island, 357; minefield, 31
Trade, adverse balance of, 142, 297, 398
Trade, Board of, on transport, 41; on port congestion, 67, 195; on meat supplies, 79–80; on wheat supplies, 182, 188, 190, 222, 345; on tonnage shortage, 188; on ship licensing, 191, 244; on import restrictions, 228, 264, 347; charter neutral ships, 249, 264; responsibilities of, 377; Index Number, 186, 373
Trade, Board of, Committee, on Congestion at Ports, 70, 71, 197
Trade, Seaborne. *See* " Clearances," " Entrances," " Exports," " Imports," and " Shipping," and under countries
Trading with the Enemy Act, 305; Committee, 88
Trafalgar, Cape, 357
Transit-sheds, importance of, 65–6, 67, 175–6
Transport Department, work and organisation of, 41–2, 44–6, 65, 170–1, 173–5, 178, 181–2, 237–44, 376–7; Advisory Committee, 48–50, 78–9, 178, 181, 202, 224, 228, 242, 341–2, 377; Card Index of Shipping, 240–1; Collier Section, 238; Commercial Branch, 241–3; Requisitioning Branch, 239–40; Wheat Section, 345

INDEX 423

Transport Workers' Battalions, 284–90, 348; increase, 374, 377, 379
Transport Workers' Federation, 287, 288, 290
Trawlers, as escorts, 94
Tregoning, Mr. W. H., member of the Ship Licensing Committee, 191 n
TRIUMPH, Br.B., sunk, 106
Tubantia, D.s.s., torpedoed, 268
Tungsten, German supplies of, 160
Tuskar, the, net defences, 96, 103

U 27, Ger. s/m, sunk, 104
U 28, Ger. s/m, sinks ships, 26, 27
U 32, Ger. s/m, caught in the nets, 34
U 41, Ger. s/m, sunk, 109
U 53, Ger. s/m, sinks vessels, 357
UC 5, Ger. s/m, lays mines, 109
Ulk, Ger. comic paper, quoted, 312
Underwood, Lieut.-Com., 293
United States, protests against s/m campaign, 11, 93, 207, 270, 329; against British use of neutral flags, 11; trade with Germany, 13, 29–30, 146–7, 151, 151 n, 158 n, 301 n; War Risks Bureau, 30; agreements with exporters in, 145, 153, 155, 303, 304; British exchanges in, 143, 183, 399; refuses to admit armed ships, 206; munitions from, 260–1; captures British trade, 296, 396, 397, sale of securities in, 297–8; protests against Black List, 305–6; bad harvest in, 341, 377; British credit strained in, 367; shipbuilding in, 385; tariff, 397; British and Allied indebtedness to, 398, 400; meat from, 214 n, 371 n; proportion of wheat imports from, 339 n. *See also* " North Atlantic Grain Trade "

Venezuela, meat from, 81, 214 n, 371 n
Verdandi, Sw.s.s., sunk, 117
Vienna, Br.s.s., 103 n
Ville de Lille, Fr.s.s., sunk, 12
VINETA. *See* " MOEWE "
Vladivostok, trade of, 120, 125; congestion at, 350–1
Vologda, 122; broad gauge line to Niandarma, 123

Waimana, Br.s.s., 206
Walker, Sir Herbert A., member of the Congestion at Ports Committee, 71 n
War Risks, on neutrals, 26; American, 30; Swedish, 115, 116–17; on Roumanian s.s., 315; British undertake neutral, 358–9, 361–2. *See* also " State Insurance Scheme "
War Risks Associations' instructions communicated through, 258 *See* also " State Insurance Scheme "
War Trade Department, 88, 140
War Trade Intelligence Department, 89, 304
War Trade Statistical Department, 89, 304
Warner, Mr. L. A. P., Secretary of the Liverpool Co-ordination Committee, 194 n; visit to French ports, 293
Warrack, Mr. J. H., member of the Diversion of Shipping Committee, 68 n
Webb, Capt. Richard, member of the Diversion of Shipping Committee, 68 n
Wemyss, R.-Ad. Rosslyn E., 209
West Coast ports, 64; report on, 69, 71; strain on the, 292
Westburn, Br.s.s., brings news of MOEWE, 254; capture of, 255; sunk, 256
Wheat, Government purchases of, 78–9, 183, 222; imports of, 133, 180, 220–1, 224, 235, 291–3, 297, 338–9, 388; problem of decline in, 180–5; from Australia, 204, 339–41; world shortage of, 341; purchase of Australian crop, 342–3; programme for, 1916–17, 363–4, 367; freights and prices, 75, 182 n, 185–8, 219–20, 223 n, 224, 235, 291, 339, 344, 367, 391
Wheat Executive, 346, 352
Wheat Supplies, Royal Commission on, 343–6, 348, 363, 367
White List, Ships'. *See* " Bunker Control "
White Sea, icebreakers in, 119; 1915 trade, 122–3, 212; minefield, 124, 316; ships frozen in, 212–13; 1916 programme, 263–4, 314–16, 349–52; winter programme, 351; 1917 programme, 379, 386
Whitley, Rt. Hon. J. H., Chairman of the Carriage of Foodstuffs Committee, 190

Wilhelmina, U.S.s.s., intercepted, 13
William Dawson, Br.s.s., blown up, 104 n
Williams, Mr. Robert, 290
Wilson, Major-General Sir A., in command of the Suez Canal defences, 32
Wireless telegraphy, restrictions, 95
Wood. *See* "Timber"
Wool, imports of, 134, 392

Woollen industry, effect of war on, 87, 134, 135, 299, 397

Yacht Squadron, 95, 97

Zaanstroom, D.s.s., capture of, 27, 111
Zamora, Sw.s.s., case of, 16 n
Zeebrugge, s/m base at, 111, 208
Zeppelin raids, 100, 206
Zevenbergen, D.s.s., attacked by a Ger. aeroplane, 93

www.ingramcontent.com/pod-product-compliance
Lightning Source LLC
Chambersburg PA
CBHW032011300426
44117CB00008B/984